AF828919

APPLYING CARE ETHICS TO BUSINESS

Issues in Business Ethics

VOLUME 34

Series Editors:

Wim Dubbink, *CMO, Centre for Corporate Social Responsibility, Tilburg University, The Netherlands*
Mollie Painter-Morland, *Department of Philosophy, DePaul University, USA*

Consulting Editor:

Pat Werhane, *Director, Institute for Business and Professional Ethics, DePaul University, USA*

Former Series Editors:

Brian Harvey, Henk van Luijk†, Pat Werhane

Editorial Board:

Georges Enderle, *University of Notre Dame, USA*
William C. Frederick, *University of Pittsburg, USA*
Campbell Jones, *University of Leicester, United Kingdom*
Daryl Koehn, *University of St. Thomas, USA*
Andreas Scherer, *University of Zurich, Switzerland*
Horst Steinmann, *University of Erlangen-Nürnberg, Germany*
Hiro Umezu, *Keio University, Japan*
Lu Xiaohe, *Shanghai Academy of Social Sciences, P.R. China*

For further volumes:
http://www.springer.com/series/6077

Applying Care Ethics to Business

Edited by

MAURICE HAMINGTON

Metropolitan State College of Denver, Denver, CO, USA

MAUREEN SANDER-STAUDT

Arizona State University, Glendale, AZ, USA

Springer

Editors
Maurice Hamington
Adobe Place 1645
Highlands Ranch
Colorado 80126
USA
mhamingt@mscd.edu

Maureen Sander-Staudt
W. Columbine Dr. 12502
El Mirage
Arizona 85335
USA
maureen.sander-staudt@asu.edu

ISSN 0925-6733
ISBN 978-90-481-9306-6 e-ISBN 978-90-481-9307-3
DOI 10.1007/978-90-481-9307-3
Springer Dordrecht Heidelberg London New York

Library of Congress Control Number: 2011932918

© Springer Science+Business Media B.V. 2011
No part of this work may be reproduced, stored in a retrieval system, or transmitted in any form or by any means, electronic, mechanical, photocopying, microfilming, recording or otherwise, without written permission from the Publisher, with the exception of any material supplied specifically for the purpose of being entered and executed on a computer system, for exclusive use by the purchaser of the work.

Printed on acid-free paper

Springer is part of Springer Science+Business Media (www.springer.com)

Acknowledgements

My thanks go foremost to my family, friends, and colleagues, who put the "care" in my "care ethics", especially my partner, David. This volume grew from many revisions of an original paper, which, as a manuscript, received patient and thoughtful commentary from my colleagues at Arizona State University, Dr. Jackie Gately, Dr. Bertha Manninen, and Dr. Shari Collins-Chobanian. I am also tremendously grateful to my co-editor, Dr. Maurice Hamington, for his mentorship and buoyant cultivation of this project, as well as for the thoughtful commentary from the staff and reviewers at *Springer*. Thank you to my research assistants, David Delgadillo and Tanya Moushi, who lent their computer and organizational skills. Finally, this work was informed by many business experiences and relations, so thanks also to those countless individuals and institutions who influenced my thinking on the application of care ethics to business.

Maureen Sander-Staudt

A scholarly volume of original chapters involves the good will and hard work of many people. Most of all, thanks go to the participating authors who take a leap of faith to join a project like this—at first without a certain publishing contract, and ultimately with no remuneration. For *Applying Care Ethics to Business,* the contributors represent an array of accomplished scholars who have many demands on their time but they thought that the further development and application of care ethics was a significant enough endeavor to add to their research agenda. In addition to the contributors, there are so many individuals who are involved in the shaping, editing, and production of a book such as this. I would like to thank the anonymous reviewers of the book as well as Springer commentators, Dr. Wim Dubbink and Dr. Mollie Painter-Morland, for their feedback on the manuscript. Much appreciation also goes to Philosophy of Law and Ethics Editor, Neil Olivier, and his assistant, Diana Nijenhuijzen, for shepherding this project through revision and production. Finally, I would like to thank my co-editor, Maureen Sander-Staudt who is a delight to work with and who brought so much insight and character to this book. As always, I appreciate the love and support of my partner, Stephanie, which makes my scholarly pursuits possible.

Maurice Hamington

Acknowledgements

Introduction: Care Ethics and Business Ethics

Maureen Sander-Staudt and Maurice Hamington

Corporations are places in which both individual human beings and human communities engage in caring activities that are aimed at mutual support and unparalleled human achievement.
—R. Edward Freeman and Jeanne Liedtke (1991)

Background

The end of the second millennium saw a number of changes in the realm of business, among them, acknowledged economic triumph of Capitalism over Communism, a proliferation of unregulated global market ventures, the failing of several world banks, and profound decreases of confidence and stability in global financial systems. As markets struggle for recovery, business ethicists seek to illuminate how values can be conceptualized and operative in business for greater human flourishing in the upcoming years, with care ethicists specifically calling for a more central reformative and informative place to be made for the value of care. Virginia Held, for example, uses a care perspective to call for limits on markets, and surmises that: "If we see care as an important value and framework of interpretation for government and civil society, as well as for the sphere of the personal, we will approach many of the issues involved in the expansion of the market differently from those for whom the protection of rights or the maximization of preference satisfaction are the only public concerns" (Held 2006).

The emergence of care ethics as a distinct moral theory is attributable to the work of psychologist Carol Gilligan and philosopher Nel Noddings in the mid-1980s. Both charged traditional moral frameworks with male bias and declared a "care perspective" to be a legitimate if not superior alternative to the "justice perspectives" offered by Utilitarianism and Kantianism. Often understood as a species of feminist ethics, but also pursued in more gender-neutral contexts, care ethics has been applied fruitfully to a variety of disciplines, including business studies. Although there have been significant in-roads made toward applying care ethics to business by authors such as R. Edward Freeman, Warren French, Daryl Koehn, Jeanne Lietdka, Alexander Weiss, and others, this volume marks one of the first attempts to make this collaboration more explicit and detailed.

Care ethics is a comparatively young moral framework with many components yet to be worked out, but the authors included in this volume agree that a morality rooted in care fruitfully departs from traditional justice approaches to business, and yields new insights into ethical business conduct that can improve markets for the better. In this they confer with Mona Harrington, who argues that we ought to "add care to the pantheon of national social values," and that a most important key to changing a country's care system is the workplace (Harrington 2000). Although many essays in this volume are critical of "business as usual," the purpose of this collection is not to pursue the more radical, but possibly legitimate reasons given by some care ethicists to reject Capitalism wholesale (Tronto 1994; Sevenhuijsen 1998). Rather, it opens the possibilities for various economic systems to be rendered more compatible with the goals of care without slipping into naivety or utopian pursuits. Certainly, care ethics recommends different approaches to business, positing corporate responsibilities that seem enlarged by traditional standards, but most authors agree that care it is not entirely incompatible with the goal of profit, and that no one, including a business person, is required to feel or express care for everyone and everything, or in a way that causes severe self-deprivation.

Defining and Delineating Care

As evident by the diverse utilizations of the concept of care in this volume, "care" is difficult to define because of its vast connotations. Care ethicists define care variously as a set of dispositional attitudes (Noddings 1984), a practice (Tronto 1994), a labor that is inherently relational (Ruddick 1989), and a motivational virtue (Slote 2001). Many care ethicists define care most fundamentally as a face-to-face practice to underscore that care is work that must be done on a direct level, and that involves energy expenditure and personal investment on the part of its practitioners. In order to narrow the scope of care and highlight its dimensions of social power, Diemut Bubeck further distinguishes "care" from "personal service," the former which involves meeting the needs of those who are unable to meet such needs themselves, the latter which involves meeting needs for others who could meet such needs themselves (Bubeck 1995).

For similar reasons, Held inclines toward defining care as a practice, but broadly, so as to avoid the presumption that care is paradigmatic only of mothering, or of caring for children, the sick, or elderly (Held 2006, 31). She notes that care refers also to the work of extended families, hospital and domestic workers, teachers, and many others. Building on the distinction between the feeling of "caring about" something, and the activity of taking care of, or "caring for" someone, Held observes that "caring for" someone is distinct from "caring for" a certain kind of music. Although doubtful that warm feelings must always accompany the labor of care, she speculates that humans tend to care for others best when both senses of "caring for" are operative. Held concludes that care must be able to refer concurrently to work, motive, value, and more. The ambiguity in care ethics thus resists a precise or fixed central meaning of "care," but provides care ethics with the advantage of flexible adaptability.

Following Held's cue, "care" in *Applying Care Ethics to Business* is understood alternatively as an epistemology, goal, motive, emotion, skill, virtue, practice, orientation, and often some combination of these. However defined, care ethicists minimally share a worldview that highlights human vulnerability and the embodied, frail, mortality of life, in which inter-dependencies are basic if sometimes obscure, and caring practices of some minimal sort are requisite. As a moral epistemology, care ethics is skeptical of abstract and universal principles, especially rational procedural mechanisms like the Principle of Utility and the Kantian Categorical Imperative, that presume people to be interchangeable, and moral judgments to be derivable like deductive math problems. Rather, care ethics relies upon contextualized knowledge and wisdom, informed by principles, but honed by practical experiences and empathetic appreciation of and response to others.

As a moral goal and virtue, care ethics seeks to maintain relationship by promoting the well-being of care-givers and care-receivers in networks of social relations. Care involves maintaining the world and meeting the varied needs of self and others, needs that greatly originate with the body. An ethic of care builds on the motivation to care for those who are dependent and vulnerable, including oneself, and is inspired by memories of being cared for, and one's ideal self. Following in the sentimentalist tradition of moral theory, care ethics also affirms the appropriate use of emotion to gather and act upon moral wisdom. Practitioners who care well exercise the skills and sub-virtues of care, identified by various authors as attention, respect, response, and completion (Noddings 1984; Tronto 1994; Held 2006; Engster 2007). In a nutshell, these virtues direct a caring agent to take note of a situation that requires response, to respectfully dialogue with others to ascertain their full perspective and foster their agency in articulating and meeting the needs identified, and to competently respond by manifestly and completely meeting the needs of others according to their own legitimate assessment. Several essays in this volume explore how caring skills, virtues and ways of knowing may be employed in business contexts to enhance economic relations, while others explore questions of economic distribution, and contest traditional assumptions underlying contemporary business theories and practices.

Care ethics emphasizes dimensions of morality evolved from feminist theory that today enjoy robust intellectual exploration. Bolstered by sometimes critical feminist writings on care throughout the 1980s and 1990s, feminist scholars and non-feminist scholars are increasingly taking care ethics seriously, applying it to social and political issues, including questions about business ethics, and providing fresh and timely insight into ideal business values and commitments. Many of these questions have to do with the ways in which business has traditionally been considered a male domain, and care a practice associated with women in the home. Such traditions cast long shadows, in that although more women than men now attend college and vocational schools in the U.S., women continue to be underrepresented as CEOs, perform the most care work without pay, dominate lower paid caring professions, and suffer from a wage gap in all professions. This wage gap is especially pronounced for women who are mothers or provide care for adults in some capacity. Increasingly, these workers depend upon other relatively disadvantaged women to meet their care responsibilities. Even as more women around the world enter diverse corporate domains, and more men share the work of care, care ethics helps to highlight how care continues to be marginalized in business and economic markets in ways that are biased and unjust for those who continue to do this work, or who are associated with caring traits.

However, despite the strong association between care ethics and feminist ethics, these fields are not synonymous (Borgerson 2007). Moreover, recent theoretical work on care ethics has moved beyond explicit gender associations—care ethics may have required reassessment of moral theory from the perspective of women's experience, but that should not imply that care is not or should not be practiced or engaged by men. This volume includes authors who sometimes develop explicitly feminist care ethics, and others who do not. Although the relevance of sex, gender, and other social differences to care is uncontested, the theoretical scope of care ethics is distinct and broad enough that the essays in this book at times leave off and outstrip the foci of feminism, even as the authors remain vitally concerned about meeting the needs of women, children, and others (Engster 2007). Taken together, these essays reveal that although care ethics can and should be applied to business in ways that promote justice for women as they are currently situated in relation to caring virtues and practices, they also reflect that care ethics is a comprehensive moral approach that broadly attends to the need for care in all humans, and even many non-human life forms.

The Unique Applications of Care Ethics to Business—Interdependent Relations, Sustainability and Globalization

A care ethical approach to business is unique because it conceptualizes mutual interdependency and cooperative relationship as ontologically basic. It thus challenges the assumption that an individualistic, competitive, or aggressive marketplace is inevitable, without dismissing the strategic value of these traits in certain situations. It also challenges the idea that individuals are predominantly rationally self-interested and autonomous, and that an overriding motive for profit in business is sound if constrained by human rights, equal opportunity, and fair acquisition, without consideration to how this motive may or may not meet caring needs. Care has historically been a relational value reserved for the private sphere and has seldom been applied to business endeavors. In many ways, care ethics' emphasis upon connection and cooperation as well as the growth and well-being of the other make it appear to be the antithesis of the corporate character. Nevertheless, many contemporary care ethicists question if moral approaches based on autonomous agents are adequate to address a shrinking and interconnected world—particularly one marked by increased global interdependency, awareness of embodied needs for basic goods such as food, housing, and medical care, and enhanced technological capacities to meet such needs. The authors included in *Applying Care Ethics to Business* offer a distinct perspective from which to reconsider how we go about thinking about corporate responsibility and business ethics. They defend the goals of care as potentially compatible with goals of business, but reject the notion that ideals of care are only appropriate in business when conducive to profit making.

A care ethical approach to business also offers unique ways for addressing contemporary challenges and evolutions in business relations, including issues of sustainability and globalization. Sustainability, understood as lifestyle patterns that leave fair and ample resources to future generations is a challenge for business in terms of making work spaces and practices more sustainable, and also in terms of providing products that can help individuals and societies live in more sustainable ways. Whereas other moral theories such as Utilitarianism and Kantian deontology struggle to take future generations into account because as not-yet-existing persons their moral status is compromised (as they lack key factors for moral status in such theories, such as sentience, rationality, or established interests), care ethics readily posits inter-generational and environmental relations as among relations that should also be responsibly maintained. That is, care ethics is concerned about sustainability because much of care is focused on maintaining life and this includes being responsible for the well-being of future generations. This and other caring activities are dependent upon healthy environments, and so care ethics has an interest in promoting sustainable business practices, and "caring about the environment" is upheld in care ethics as both a virtue and motive of ideal businesses, which needs to be balanced against other business goals.

A care ethic is also much less likely to struggle conceptually with the problem of having moral obligations to future people and beings. Much may be made of the impossibility of knowing exactly the needs of persons and beings not yet born, and the way that the very uncertainty whether such beings will in fact be born undermines moral obligation, but care ethics sidesteps these problems with its ontology. The practice of caring involves caring for future generations, some already existing and others that have projected existence. In maintaining relations, care ethics promotes practices that are more likely to project the existence of future generations, and in so doing, dependency relations are established that bring with them normative obligations. Care ethics highlights that business owners, workers, and customers are typically responsible for (and depend upon) multiple generations of progeny, and that these responsibilities, although private and specific in some ways, serve as a general experiences that can motivate enhanced care for environmental health in the paid workplace. In focusing on embodiment as well as rationality, care ethics posits the likelihood that future generations for some period of time will have embodied needs and interests similar to our own, such that they will benefit from access to clean water and air, nutritional and humanely produced food, and sustainable forms of transportation and fuel sources. Like the Native American principle of "seven generations"—making decisions based on how a proposed action will affect seven generations to come, care ethics applied to business recommends a forward looking decision making model that takes into account our obligation to several future generations.

In a similar manner, care ethics provides an innovative guide for business in a global age. Nel Noddings originally restricted the global extent of caring obligations based on geographical proximity because of the psychological limits to the extent of one's empathy and the pragmatic ability to care effectively over broad distances. However, later care ethicists challenged Noddings view, developing global theories of care from which the global implications of business care relations can be extrapolated. For instance, Fiona Robinson develops a critical ethics of care that attends to the relations of dependency and vulnerability that exist on a global scale (Robinson 1999). She posits that unlike deontological or utilitarian theories, a global ethic of care is responsive and attentive to the difference of others without a presumption of universal homogeneity. With a distinct political focus, Held and Eva Feder Kittay examine how global caring relations continue to be marked by relations of gender and other social stratifications that lead to unequal benefits between and within nations around the world. Held notes cultural constructs of masculinity in state behaviors, and calls for cooperative values to replace hierarchy and domination based on gender, class, race and ethnicity (Held 2006). Kittay describes how care itself has become a globalized industry, resulting in a "global heart transplant" whereby individuals, most often poor women of color, leave their own families to care for the families of the wealthy of other countries (Kittay 2008). Such international relations of care give rise to questions of caring distributions that cross national boundaries, questions that apply to business in that economic relations permeate and determine global dynamics of care and dependency.

When applied to business, a globalized ethic of care underscores the potential and pitfalls of conducting international business in ways conducive to the provision of care. Because it is averse to generalized principles, a care ethic recommends few fixed requirements for conducting business on a global scale, but it does affirm the importance of care relations and the need to maintain the ability to care as business becomes more cosmopolitan. A care ethic is therefore suspect of the tendency of individuals in higher management to be aloof from the private struggles of those lower than them, and of being able to purchase caring services in ways that render them oblivious to the caring needs of others. It is wary of the ability of businesses to import labor that leaves workers, families, and local communities unable to meet their own caring needs. It cautions against the temptation to conduct business abroad more irresponsibly than one would in one's own proximate space. Although it is unlikely to demand fixed or universal international labor standards, it generally resists global business practices that lead to unacceptable inabilities to care. It is sensitive to how global economic imperialism makes it more difficult for local businesses to compete, and coercively impels labor migration that divides families and creates "care deserts." A care ethic reveals the particularity of business personnel who are distant, whether geographically, culturally, or both. On the side of positive recommendations, it encourages business practices that achieve parity in global care relations, and are innovative in improving care delivery and the meeting of dependency needs. Finally, care ethics calls for cooperative values to replace hierarchy and domination based on gender, class, race and ethnicity that currently characterize most global business relations.

Although international business is fraught with dangerous threats to the ability to care, it also provides some of the channels necessary to overcome the limits that concerned Noddings. Even if one cannot care for others directly and in person, one can "care-about" others living far away, and this motive can initiate international channels for achieving "caring-for"—channels which traverse business relations and global economic webs. For better and worse, in business relations, individuals can have a more pronounced efficacy to care or not, and the obligation of international businesses are thereby enlarged. Whereas it is not always evident how we are dependent on individuals living far away from us, international business relations preeminently reveals global interdependencies.

By illuminating how humans around the world rely upon one another for daily goods needed to maintain life (although not equally so), care ethics illuminates the global dimensions of caring markets and the influence of business on international systems of care delivery. For example, a globalized care ethic traces how the food of one country is produced in another, how political oppression and unrest affects distant markets, how the ability to be "independent" is achieved largely through unequal access to purchased services—and how all of these dynamics construct differing means and methods for the maintenance of relational life (or not). In all of these ways, a political and global care ethic holds international business relations responsible for care provision, but also looks to them as possible channels for achieving adequate and equitable care delivery on a global level. Care ethics thus provides a novel approach to business relations, but its idealism and demandingness may lead some to be skeptical of its appropriateness as a business ethic

Commonly Perceived Flaws of Care Ethics

Although we believe that care ethics has much to offer as a business ethic, the project of applying care ethics to business is not without problems. Ethics in business is considered to be a general anathema, but a business ethic based on care is vulnerable to even more than the usual skepticism because it esteems traits that are perceived as liabilities in business—compassion, empathy, and concern for others. One of the earliest objections of this sort was that care ethics is a kind of "slave morality" valorizing the oppression of women and other socially disempowered groups (Puka 1990; Card 1990; Davion 1993) (although Puka, at least, reconsiders this critique in his essay in Chapter 10). The concept of "slave morality" is associated with the philosopher Frederick Nietzsche, who held that oppressed peoples tend to develop moral theories that reaffirm subservient traits as virtues. Following this tradition, the charge that care ethics is a slave morality interprets the different voice of care as emerging from patriarchal traditions characterized by rigid sexual hierarchies and divisions of labor. As a more "feminine" value, care seems out of place in the "masculine" world of business. Accordingly, achieving care in business sounds good, but realistically may be overly naïve and idealistic in the context of business relations, construed as they are as inherently aggressive, self-promotional, brutal, and profit driven.

This objection further implies that the voice of care may not be an authentic or empowering expression, but a product of false consciousness that equates moral maturity with self-sacrifice and self-effacement. As such, care is a liability for any business person, but perhaps especially for women and other disempowered individuals, because it appears to encourage passivity and weakness. This critique issues caution against uncritically promoting caring practices and inclinations because those who predominantly perform the work of care, or exhibit caring traits, often do so to their own economic disadvantage. To the extent that care ethics encourages care without further inquiring as to why one cares, and whether one always should care, it fails to be an ethic suitable for business. Leaving gender implications aside, an ethic of care may also be seen as a poor guide for business because caring is inherently incompatible with some of the main goal of business—efficiency, muscling out competitors, and generating profit.

Following from the ambiguity of the concept of care, and the prevalence of a care ethic to eschew general principles, a third problem that arises in the context of business is that care ethics offers only ambiguous and haphazard guidelines for business decisions. Even if it is accepted that business agents ought to care about others to some extent, it is not clear for whom or what they should care, and how caring measures ought to be balanced when there are conflicts of interest. Should business persons care about their competitors as much as their own clients and employees? When there is a conflict between a client and an employee, should a manager stand up for the employee, or insist that "the customer is always right?" If a co-worker discovers evidence that another worker is engaged in a nefarious practice that harms the company, is it more caring to expose their wrong doing to higher management, or to confront the co-worker in private? Advocates of care ethics view this ambiguity as an advantage that provides space for flexible and nuanced reasoning, and allows for the application of practical reasoning, but this seems a less than satisfactory way of answering the question of what one should do when moral dilemmas arise.

A fourth and final problem is that a care ethic may be too narrowly focused to serve as a comprehensive moral theory in business. Although care is an important value, it is not exhaustive, and does not seem to address a great number of other moral ideals that are equally, if not more, important in business. The values of honesty, integrity, acuteness in caution and risk, work ethic, and many other ideals also feature in business, but do not seem to fall squarely under the ideal of care. A business person, especially one who manages other people, needs to be more than caring to be ethical, and perhaps this trait is of secondary importance to being organized, communicative, fair, responsible, or trust-worthy. Of course, advocates of care ethics will be quick to point out that many of these ideals and traits can and do fall under the spectrum of caring, or at least are not incompatible with it.

What is to be made of this series of objections? First, the contributors to this volume challenge the stereotypical characterizations of care and business that thread through many of these critiques. They resist the view of care as inherently "soft" or "feminine," and business as inherently "hard," or "masculine," and show how care can be a strategic asset to the goals of business by fostering relations, improving productivity and morale, and strengthening communities. Although care may involve taking a posture of certain responsibility towards others, it is compatible with decisiveness, shrewdness, and difficult decision making. A company that is caring need not be one that is weak in the face of competition, or unable to terminate workers when warranted. Neither is it accurate to view heartlessness, aggression, or self-absorption as inherently desirable qualities in business. Whereas companies may adopt these traits within free market capitalism, this is not the only business dynamic available, and arguably not the best.

There are similar flaws with the objections that care is unable to provide any clear guidelines for decision making in business, and is too narrowly focused to serve as an adequately comprehensive business ethic. This is because although care ethics promotes caution in relying dogmatically or exclusively on abstract principles as guides, it need not promote aversion to principles altogether. The admonition to maintain relationships, and to be cognizant and responsive to the needs of others, are two general principles central to an ethic of care. But more than providing such principles, an ethics of care recommends itself as a method and way of orientating oneself towards the world. And when we consider how wide the network of interdependent relations runs, and how much care as a practice, motive, ideal, virtue, and method permeates and intertwines with economic dealings, the potential focus of an ethic of care becomes markedly enlarged. We do not suggest that everything in business is of care ethical significance, in that ethics itself has a limited function in business. Rather, questions of moral significance in business are relevant to care ethics at the very least in the form of needed motivation—the fundamental question of "why should I care?" What this means is that determining what is morally correct action in business is only half the battle, one need also muster the concern enough to act (or to refrain from acting). Moreover, because the normative dimensions of business involve acts, decisions, and policies that effect individuals embedded in relations, "care" understood as a practice, virtue, ideal, and method, are all widely implicated in business as well.

However, while these three conceptual objections may be answerable, the more pragmatic concern that a caring moral orientation can be a liability for individual workers and companies is harder to dismiss. It is not difficult to find examples of individuals and companies whose propensity to care prove their demise in business (one need only watch an episode of *The Apprentice* to see this dynamic instantiated). Numerous studies have shown that individuals (especially women) who appear overly sentimental, concerned with the well-being of others, or responsible for caring for others, are routinely discriminated against in hiring and promotional decisions. Whistle blowers are typically fired, not rewarded. Companies caring too much can be vulnerable to hostile takeovers and competitive failures. Thus, it is hard to deny that care can be a dangerous ethic to espouse, especially for women, who face the multiple burdens of having to prove themselves to be equally capable as men of being "tough" (but not "bitchy"), while at the same time being socialized and expected to be caring. Of course, it was the degradation of care that Gilligan argued against in the first place, insisting that a care ethic can be a "different" moral orientation without being "inferior," and that we might do better to espouse a pantheon of moral theories. We can only hope that in compiling this volume, and illuminating some of the affinities between an ethics of care and business, that these ongoing negative and discriminatory trends can be alleviated.

Chapter Organization

The essays included in *Applying Care Ethics to Business* are divided into four parts. Part I is devoted to the theme of care ethics' relevance to justice, distribution, and economic theory. Part II includes essays detailing how care ethics might inform corporate decision making. Part III provides analyses of case studies that illuminate how care ethics may be applied to concrete business, and Part IV examines the enhancement of corporate cultures through the inclusion of caring values in the workplace.

Perhaps because of the original antagonism between care ethics and the "justice perspectives" of deontology and utilitarianism, attention has only recently turned to how care ethics might generate normative accounts of just distributions of market resources, or inform economic theory more generally. Care ethicists agree that economic markets should meet the needs for care in ways that are just, but there is less agreement about what type of economic theories and practices are best suited to doing so. Authors such as Held posit that care ethics gives reason to limit the scope of markets to make room for values other than profit, especially in areas where care is central, such as education, health, and social services (Held, 2006). This approach implies that care ethics is inherently critical of free market capitalism, and is inherently inclined toward socialist and Marxist theories of economics, a view espoused by Bubeck (1985), Deborah Stone (2000), Kittay (1998), and others. But other care ethicists such as Engster call for more neutrality, looking instead to how different economic systems might variously and creatively meet the basic needs for care. After clarifying that care ethical critiques of "justice perspectives" do not entail a lack of concern or appreciation for justice altogether, care ethicists are poised to speculate how distributive justice might be differently understood in care ethics, and how these understandings turn economic theory in new directions.

Part I of this anthology explores these intersections, and generates basic frameworks for understanding how care ethics might apply to business more precisely. In his essay, Thomas Hawk (Chapter 1) explains why we ought to care in organizational settings, surmising that doing so may allow us to avoid the classist, hierarchical elitism and the ongoing marginalization of persons fostered by dominant moral and organizational theories. Providing a comprehensive historical outline of the development of care ethics and its primary conceptual features, Hawk traces the neglect of care ethics in management research and organizational literature applied to a variety of domains, and describes how care might be more accurately measured in the Gross Domestic Product. Picking up where Hawk leaves off, Julie Nelson, in Chapter 2 explains why care ethics is more relevant and operative within commerce than supposed. Attacking cultural patterns of conceptual dichotomies such as justice and care, masculinity and femininity, reason and emotion, etc., Nelson acknowledges both positive and negative dimensions of masculinity and femininity, as well as competition and cooperation. She construes care and justice as mutually informative, and challenges the ideas that individuals are best understood as "economic men," that businesses reduce to mechanical profit-maximizers, or that markets must be hyper competitive. Nelson further resists the choice of having to endorse the current structure and functioning of corporations as they are, or of having to replace current economic structures with something completely different, opting instead for a "commitment to ethical reflection and action in economic life, right here and right now."

In Chapter 3, Andrew Terjesen exudes optimism about the compatibility of care ethics and economics, based on the contention that Adam Smith, considered by many to be the father of capitalism, himself intertwined moral and economic theory in a way reflective of modern day care ethics. Noting both the affinities and non-affinities of Smith's philosophies with an ethics of care, Terjesen argues that care ethics makes a good candidate for reshaping economics closer to Smith's original vision—"a form of capitalism that does not vex our moral sensibilities." Dimitria Gatzia likewise explores the possible harmony between care ethics and markets in Chapter 4, but exhibits less optimism that caring markets can be developed within current dominant economic frameworks. Gatzia diagnoses the incompatibility of care ethics with dominant socioeconomic paradigms of industrialized countries as a conflict emerging from neo-liberalism, which she rejects as a morally inadequate economic theory and practice. Because it makes care irrelevant to economic policy, Gatzia charges that neo-liberalism has created a host of social problems, including poverty, hunger, and homelessness. In her estimation, reformulating neo-liberal based markets into caring economies means moving away from values of competition, preference satisfaction, and unbridled accumulation, toward markets that "aim to meet human needs" and that are built on the idea that the "need for housing, nutrition, education, and health are prior to the desire for luxuries." But Gatzia speculates that transforming markets in this way also requires transforming other key institutions away from wage labor and privatized ownership of the means of production, in favor of corporate economic democracies.

Part II of *Applying Care Ethics to Business* considers more closely how care ethics might inform corporate decision making. The first two essays address specific insights yielded by care ethics for stakeholder theory. Stakeholder theory has become a prevalent thread in business ethics developed foremost by R. Edward Freeman, in response to Milton Friedman's argument that the moral obligations of businesses are to grow profits for stockholders and to avoid illegal and deceptive activities (Freeman 1984; Friedman 1970). Contrary to Friedman's view, Freeman argued that businesses have moral obligations to all of those who have a stake in or are affected by their corporate policies. In Chapter 5, Daniel Engster postulates that care ethics benefits stakeholder theory by providing a normative foundation for it, and by clarifying some of its finer points, including answering who counts as a stake holder and how conflicting interests of stakeholders ought to be adjudicated. As a normative foundation care ethics explains why business should care about stakeholders as well as stockholders, namely, because business and care activities share a common internal goal—to foster the survival and functioning of humans according to the principles of proximity, relationship, and urgency. Although Engster does not recommend completely subordinating economic activities to caring goals, he gives care primacy because "productive work may be said to exist at root for the sake of supporting our ability to care" such that "when business practices controvert care, they undermine their own social and moral justification."

Similarly, in Chapter 6, Daniel Palmer and Mary Lyn Stoll use care ethics to redress what they see as a lacuna of moral phenomenology in stakeholder theory—the missing analysis of inner psychological and affective states exhibited in moral agency and response to stakeholders near and distant. Apart from other care ethicists who speculate that incorporating values of care into business can be conducive to economic goals like productivity, efficiency, and profit generation, they strike a distinction between instrumental and normative approaches to stakeholder theory, arguing that care ought to be a moral priority in business, even when it cannot be empirically demonstrated that prioritizing care furthers the instrumental goals of business. Drawing upon the relational and motivational aspects of care ethics, they consider the case of sweatshop labor in order to demonstrate how care ethics improves upon a liability account of global justice in assessing and responding to the harms of sweatshops.

The next two essays in this part scrutinize how care ethics can play a role in making better business decisions, and for dealing with aftermath of good intended decisions gone foul. In Chapter 7, Sheldene Simola contemplates the implications and benefits of care ethics for J.R. Rest's framework for moral problem solving. Although Rest's framework has four components: (1) recognition of a moral problem, (2) judgment for right action, (3) intention formation for response, and (4) implementation of ethical action, traditional interpretations of his model have found significance for moral philosophical analysis only in the second aspect, assessing the course for right action. Refuting this assumption, Simola explains how an ethic of care enhances all four stages identified by Rest due to its emphasis on emotion, empathy, and attentiveness, as well as its proclivity for proactive encouragement of healthy relations and creative non-zero-sum resolutions.

Looking more to the unpredictable side of business, Daryl Koehn's (Chapter 8) essay demonstrates how care ethics has advantages for anticipating and responding to the sometimes unforeseen consequences of business decisions. Citing the unfortunate outcomes of decisions relating to bottled water programs for digging wells in Africa, labor law revision in China, and corporate legislation against fuel waste, oil spill indemnity, and disability discrimination in the U.S., Koehn illustrates the precarious nature of even good intentions in business. She explains why care ethics, with its stress on interdependence and the cultivation of relational emotions such as empathy, sympathy, and trust, render it superior for dealing with unintended consequences in business over the ethics of utilitarianism and deontology.

Part III of *Applying Care Ethics to Business* engages several specific applications of care ethics. Business ethics is an applied discipline so no matter how attractive care ethics is on a theoretical level, confronting the complexity and entanglements of commerce provides the ultimate test of the efficacy of care theory. The authors in this part take a wide variety of approaches to reflection on applications and potential applications of care resulting in varying assessments. In a very timely analysis Chapter 9, Jill Hernandez argues that current political narratives that justify aggressive enforcement of immigration policy at workplaces are morally flawed. As an alternative, Hernandez suggests that a care framework would better serve the interests of the relevant stakeholders including the enforcement agencies, businesses, and the employees. To bolster her claims, Hernandez engages in three case studies of workplace immigration policy enforcement at Marshalltown, Iowa; New Bedford, Massachusetts; and, Postville, Iowa. Drawing from these experiences, Hernandez contends that a care framework has the potential to bind the interests of stakeholders rather than viewing them as at odds with one another. Hernandez explains, "Grounding the bottom line for immigration policy enforcement as well as for the economy in the mutual care of communities and employees ensures the business interests and the needs of the employees are inextricably related." Accordingly, care is perceived as collaborative structure that counters traditional competitive models.

Wrapping significant ethical analysis in a whimsical yet straightforward manner, Bill Puka addresses the application of care in corporate America in Chapter 10. Employing an accessible and frank approach to care, Puka offers a memo to "Upper, Middle-level Mgt and rank and file." Directly taking on business misconceptions of care ethics, Puka describes care as not requiring "sacrificing one's interest" and providing "an invisible-handish argument, in a sense, that approaching people without ulterior motives better serves such motives, and other of one's interest as well." Puka's message is exceedingly practical as he offers the "Nuts and Bolts" of how businesses can be more caring. As part of this practical approach, Puka offers a series of case vignettes to demonstrate how care might be applied in work situations. In the informal and engaging style of this chapter, Puka reinforces many of the themes from the previous chapters of this collection. Ultimately, Puka declares, "How does one apply Care in business, one's own business situation? Watch, look, listen, try out, test, and practice. We already Care to as significant extent, as research shows. . . . The task then is to build on what we already do."

In Chapter 11, Mathew Brophy uses the unseemly yet growing phenomenon of "bumfights"—paying the homeless to engage in demeaning activity—as a jumping off point to analyze the limitation of traditional justice approaches to morality in commerce. In this sense, "bumfights" are both an actual case study and a metaphor for transactions where human care is deficient. For example, ethical systems of justice typically assume the autonomy of individuals to engage in commercial exchanges. Brophy points out that "homeless persons tend not to be equally autonomous in comparison to the average person." Brophy finds connective themes between "bumfights" and a variety of cases of ethical breakdowns in business. For Brophy, "the justice view fails to recognize reciprocal duties of care beyond mere contractual obligations." Supporting a theme that runs throughout *Applying Care*

Ethics to Business, Brophy does not view care ethics as incompatible with profitability, yet concludes that profits devoid of caring and human respect are morally hollow.

Finally, how corporate culture could become more imbued with the values of care is the focus of Part IV. At no time has the lack of caring culture been more notoriously exemplified than in the Enron scandal of 2002. The ethical lessons of the Enron scandal are many. The documentary film, *Enron: The Smartest Guys in the Room* (2005), based on the best-selling book of the same name (2003), graphically demonstrated how the cutthroat corporate culture at Enron fueled and sustained an atmosphere that made unethical and illegal activity possible. Organizational culture represents an intangible yet ever present factor in business ethics. As Armstrong, Williams, and Barrett describe, "it is the impact of many small organizational factors that contribute to the overall health and morality of an organization. It seems too simplistic to conclude that Enron and WorldCom problems are based wholly on greed and not the integration of organizational factors" (2004). Systems of moral adjudication are excellent at assessing specific actions, such as rule or rights violations, but the accountability of organizational culture—shared symbols, meaning, and values—in the activity of business is much more difficult to pin down. Nevertheless, culture can be such a potent force in corporate existence that it occupies an important focal point in the burgeoning field of organizational behavior. Certainly, one adjective not commonly associated with corporate culture is "caring." Enron's culture can be described as the antithesis of caring with its extreme emphasis on self- interest and individual advancement.

The company's compensation structure contributed to an unethical work culture, too—by promoting self-interest above any other interest. As a consequence, the team approach once used by Enron associates deteriorated. Performance reviews were public events and poor performance was ridiculed (or employees were fired through a "rank and yank" process) (Sims and Brinkman 2003). Keep in mind that Enron was a celebrated Wall Street darling prior to its collapse and there would likely be little negative attention given to its culture if it were not for the company's collapse and illegal activity. Can a corporate culture be caring? Would such an atmosphere significantly alter the ethical behavior of the organization? In Part IV, authors explore the relationship between care ethics and corporate culture.

Although the notion of care as a virtue is a relatively new concept, the idea that loyalty is a virtue has a very long tradition. Corporate culture has historically entailed a certain degree of loyalty. However, corporate loyalty has a morally ambiguous standing. On the one hand, a sense of commitment and pride that comes with loyalty can contribute to an *espirt de corps*. On the other hand, disproportionate loyalty can also lead to overlooking or concealing unethical behavior. In a thoroughgoing examination of loyalty, Julinna Oxley and D.E. Wittkower contend that the source and framing of loyalty is crucial to appraising its moral standing. In Chapter 12, Oxley and Wittkower find a significant difference between loyalty as a workplace obligation versus loyalty that arises organically out of care and felt mutuality. They claim, "By approaching loyalty as an expression of care, we are able to make sense of the intuition that the natural development of loyalty is praiseworthy and rightly contained within out conception of the ideal employee, but at the same time is neither a duty nor a virtue, and not always an unambiguous good." In the process of their examination of loyalty, Oxley and Wittkower explore the significantly related concepts of whether one can be loyal to a corporation and how a corporation can be said to "deserve" loyalty. Given the ever-increasing fluid nature of employee relations to organizations reflection on the nature, scope, and basis of loyalty as offered here is particularly timely.

Part of the reluctance of those in the business community to embrace care as an archetype of corporate culture is that the term evokes feelings and emotional ties not commonly associated with business. Successful businesses are associated with rationality, innovation, opportunism, and hard work. By contrast, care might be an important concept to market to customers, but it does not seem to fit in the equation of a successful business. In Chapter 13, Maurice Hamington engages an ignored aspect of care ethics: its epistemic quality. Caring entails processes of knowledge. Real learning occurs when one cares and one cannot care without knowledge. Hamington explores business trends in knowledge management as well as the movement advocating the creation of learning organizations in regard to the contribution of care. In this manner, caring is framed as a form of inquiry: "An ethic of care conceptualized as a form of interpersonal inquiry can foment a learning organization within a culture of care and trust. A caring culture is a moral environment that is sensitive and responsive to a broad range of stakeholders. Caring does not preclude self-interest or the profit motive but it does establish a commitment to knowing and acting on behalf of others." According to Hamington, a corporate culture of care is one that embraces growing and learning.

In the last essay, Chapter 14, Maureen Sander-Staudt not only explores the notion of whether corporations can be caring but also the efficacy of using a virtue framework toward this end. Virtue theory is as old as the Western tradition in philosophy, but its application has historically been in regard to individual morality. Sander-Staudt describes a corporate virtue as a "habitual individual and collective property of excellence that refers to both disposition and practice." Because care ethics has both a performative and dispositional dimension, such a definition of corporate virtue is particularly applicable. Furthermore, Sander-Staudt situates corporate caring virtues in a framework of care sub-virtues including attention, responsibility, and respect. Integrating numerous theorists who have developed the idea of social and political approaches to care, the chapter offers applications of care ethics in business that are not in opposition to profitability and in fact support financial performance. In this manner, Sander-Staudt contends that care is a "supreme public good, and that corporations have unique and presiding functions in its delivery."

Together the chapters in this volume express the belief that because business is ultimately relational, an ethics of care provides an innovative and needed moral framework for guiding business. Far from being an inappropriate ethic when applied to business, an ethic of care is shown to recommend styles of comportment, principles for decision making, and attention to practical dynamics that are sorely needed in an age of expanding, and often impersonal, economic dealings. In the emerging age of global business, interdependencies become more visible, and the intersections between economic trade and care relations become pronounced. Rather than being removed from themes of care, the world of business possesses unique responsibilities, and offers much potential for achieving just and compassionate care relations in the broadest sense.

References

Armstrong, R.W., R.J. Williams, and J.D. Barrett. 2004. The impact of banality, risky shift and escalating commitment on ethical decision making. *Journal of Business Ethics* 53: 365–370.

Borgerson, Janet L. 2007. On the harmony of feminist ethics and business ethics. *Business and Society Review* 112 (4): 477–509.

Bubeck, Dietmut. 1985. *Care, justice and gender*. Oxford: Clarendon Press.

Card, Claudia. 1990. Caring and evil. *Hypatia* 5 (1): 101–108.

Davion, Victoria. 1993. Autonomy, integrity, and care. *Social Theory and Practice* 19 (2): 161–182.

Engster, Daniel. 2007. *The heart of justice*. Oxford: Oxford University Press.

Freeman, R. Edward. 1984. *Strategic management: A stakeholder approach*. Boston: Pitman.

Friedman, Milton. 1970. The social responsibility of business is to increase its profits. *The New York Times Magazine*, September 13, 1970.

Gibney, A. (director). 2005. Enron: The smartest guys in the room (film). Magnolia Pictures.

Gilligan, Carol. 1982. *In a different voice*. Cambridge, MA: Harvard University Press.

Harrington, Mona. 2000. *Care and equality: Inventing a new family politics*. New York, NY: Routledge.

Held, Virginia. 2002. Care and the extension of markets. *Hypatia* 17 (2) (Spring): 19–33.

Held, Virginia. 2006. *The ethics of care: Personal, political and global*. New York, NY: Oxford

Kittay, Eva Feder. 1998. *Love's labor: Essays on women, equality, and dependency*. New York, NY: Routledge.

Kittay, Eva Feder. 2008. The global heart transplant and caring across national boundaries. *The Southern Journal of Philosophy* XLVI: 138–165.

Mclean, B. and Elkind, P. 2003. *The smartest guys in the room: The amazing rise and scandalous fall of Enron*. New York, NY: Portfolio.

Noddings, Nel. 1984. *Caring: A feminine approach to ethics and moral education*. Berkeley, CA: University of CA Press.

Puka, Bill. 1990. The liberation of caring: A different voice for Gilligan's 'different voice'. *Hypatia* 55 (1): 58–82.

Robinson, Fiona. 1999. *Globalizing care*. Boulder, CO: Westview Press.

Ruddick, Sara. 1989. *Maternal thinking: Toward a politics of peace*. New York, NY: Ballentine Books.

Sevenhuijsen, Selma. 1998. *Citizenship and the ethics of care*. New York, NY: Routledge,.

Sims, R.R., and J. Brinkmann. 2003. Enron ethics (or: culture matters more than codes). *Journal of Business Ethics* 45: 243–256.

Slote, M. 2007. *The ethics of care and empathy*. New York, NY: Routledge.

Stone, Deborah. 2000. Why we need a care movement. *The Nation* February 25: 1–5.

Tronto, Joan. 1994. *Moral boundaries: A political argument for an ethic of care*. New York, NY: Routledge.

Contents

Contributors

Matthew Brophy High Point University, High Point, NC, USA, mbrophy@highpoint.edu

Daniel Engster Department of Political Science, University of Texas, San Antonio, TX, USA, Daniel.Engster@utsa.edu

Dimitria Electra Gatzia Department of Philosophy, The University of Akron Wayne College, Orrville, OH, USA, dg29@uakron.edu

Maurice Hamington Institute for Women's Studies and Services, Metropolitan State College of Denver, Denver, CO, USA, mhamingt@mscd.edu

Thomas F. Hawk Department of Management, Emeritus, Frostburg State University, Frostburg, MD, USA, thawk@frostburg.edu

Jill Hernandez Department of Philosophy, University of Texas, San Antonio, TX, USA, jill.hernandez@utsa.edu

Daryl Koehn Department of Ethics and Business Law, University of St. Thomas, Minneapolis, MN, USA, koehnd@stthomas.edu

Julie A. Nelson University of Massachusetts Boston, Boston, MA, USA, julie.nelson@umb.edu

Julinna Oxley Coastal Carolina University, Conway, SC, USA, joxley@coastal.edu

Daniel E. Palmer Department of Philosophy, Kent State University, Kent, OH, USA, dpaler1@kent.edu

Bill Puka Department of Philosophy and Psychology, Rensselaer Polytechnic Institute, Troy, NY, USA, billpuka@gmail.com

Maureen Sander-Staudt Arizona State University, Phoenix, AZ, USA, maureen.sander-staudt@asu.edu

Sheldene Simola Department of Business Administration, Trent University, Peterborough, ON, Canada, ssimola@trentu.ca

Mary Lyn Stoll Department of Philosophy, University of Southern Indiana, Evansville, IN, USA, mlstoll@usi.edu

Andrew Terjesen Department of Philosophy, Rhodes College, Memphis, TN, USA, ajterjesen@gmail.com

D.E. Wittkower Department of Philosophy and Religious Studies, Old Dominion University, Norfolk, VA, USA, d.e.wittkower@gmail.com

Part I
Justice, Distribution, and Economics

Chapter 1
An Ethic of Care: A Relational Ethic for the Relational Characteristics of Organizations

Thomas F. Hawk

Introduction

The emergence of an ethic of care as a comprehensive ethical framework is a recent phenomenon in the long history of philosophical ethics that includes virtue ethics, utilitarian ethics, deontological ethics, and justice ethics as its primary traditions. And while the philosophical, cognitive psychology, and educational literatures have given reasonable consideration to an ethic of care, the only sector in the domain of organizational and business management and policy where there has been more than a rare appearance of articles on an ethic of care over the last 30 years is in the specialized journals of business ethics, journals not usually read by mainstream organizational and management researchers. Furthermore, business ethics and corporate social responsibility texts, for the most part, ignore an ethic of care or offer only a proforma mention of it.

Although recent corporate ethical scandals such as Enron, Worldcom, the mortgage junk bond crisis of 2008, and the exorbitant salaries and bonuses paid to many financial executives are not new to the corporate world, they have again brought the issue of ethical behavior in both the corporate and the governmental sectors into front page news. Questions arise that focus on such issues as what ethical frameworks, if any, are used by those whose decisions resulted in these scandals, what is the adequacy of the ethical frameworks in use, what alternative ethical frameworks could yield a higher level of ethicality, and who shoulders the responsibility for the ethical development of the individuals who lead in the corporate and governmental sectors.

Many care ethicists would like to offer an ethic of care as the appropriate ethical framework for the organizational world. So what is an ethic of care, how has it evolved since Carol Gilligan (1977, 1982) introduced the term "ethic of care" in her critique of Kohlberg's (1969, 1981) model of moral development, and how does an ethic of care compare and contrast with the more traditional ethical frameworks found in Aristotle's virtue ethics (Irwin 1985; MacIntyre 1981, 1988),

T.F. Hawk (✉)
Department of Management, Emeritus, Frostburg State University, Frostburg, MD, USA
e-mail: thawk@frostburg.edu

M. Hamington, M. Sander-Staudt (eds.), *Applying Care Ethics to Business*,
Issues in Business Ethics 34, DOI 10.1007/978-90-481-9307-3_1,
© Springer Science+Business Media B.V. 2011

Kant's deontological ethics (Ellington 1983; Bowie 1999), Mill's utilitarian ethics (1969), and Rawls' justice ethics (1971, 2001)? That is the subject of the first half of this chapter. What coverage has there been of an ethic of care in the business ethics literature in particular and the organizational management and leadership literatures in general to allow organizational management educators, scholars, and practitioners to even be aware of and consider the use of an ethic of care in organizations? And finally, what reasons justify the use of an ethic of care in organizations and what possible controversies surround its use in organizational management? These are the issues I want to cover in the second half of the chapter.

Caring and an Ethic of Care

An ethic of care starts from the fundamental position of the relationality of all humans with each other and the environment, and the interweaving of multiple relationships as the basic human condition throughout life. Care—the ongoing concern for the well-being and the constructive development of the one caring, the one or ones cared for, and the relationship—is the core value. An ethic of care recognizes that all situations, particularly those where action must be taken, have ethical characteristics and that no two ethical or moral situations are identical or nearly identical. The clear and explicit implication is that we must become conversant with the concrete uniqueness of each ethical situation, including those who are impacted by the actions that emerge out of the ethical dilemma. In order to do so, we must draw on our full repertoire of capabilities, including cognitive, affective, intuitive, physiological, and imaginative. An ethic of care also sees the private and public domains, not as dichotomous, but as interwoven and where the moral and the political are always present. An ethic of care is value, practice, and process across the full scope of human activities.

Although there are numerous valuable philosophical contributions to the development and evolution of an ethic of care as a comprehensive moral framework emerging from the feminist literature (see for instance Ruddick 1980, 1990; Jaggar 1983; Ferguson 1984; Kittay and Meyers 1987; MacKinnon 1989; Friedman 1993; Held 1993; Walker 2007), an ethic of care begins with Gilligan (1977, 1982) and Ruddick (1980) and progresses through the central and fundamental contributions of Noddings (1984, 2002), Tronto (1993), Held (1995a, 2006) and Slote (2007), with Held (2006) and Slote (2007) providing the most comprehensive review of and case for an ethic of care to date.

Gilligan (1977, 1982) was not the first to provide an insightful exploration of the phenomenon of caring. Both Mayeroff (1965, 1971) and Gaylin (1976) offer careful and sensitive conversations on caring. Gilligan, however, is the first to use the term "ethic of care" and develop it more fully in the context of relationality and feminist moral development. Her focus on the moral reasoning of women was embedded in the larger emerging feminist concerns about false universalization of male-based models, undefined or inadequately defined terms, and circular reasoning

(Minnich 1990) as well as the marginalization of women, the oppression of groups not in power, and feminist views on knowing and reality. Noddings provides the first in-depth elaboration of an ethic of care. Tronto expands the consideration of an ethic of care to the public and political domains. And Slote and Held make cogent cases for an ethic of care as a comprehensive ethical framework that is at least the equivalent of, if not in many ways superior to and more realistic than, the dominant ethical frameworks of Aristotle (virtue ethics), Kant (deontological ethics), Mill (utilitarian ethics), and Rawls (justice ethics).

On Caring

Mayeroff (1971, 1–2) describes caring as "helping another grow and actualize himself, a process, a way of relating to someone that involves development, in the same way that friendship can only emerge in time through mutual trust and a deepening and qualitative transformation of the relationship." For Mayeroff, the process is more fundamental than the product, with the product—the development of the other—resulting from being in the present for the other and the self and not imposing on the other what the self would will the other to do. The one-caring experiences the other, the one cared-for, as separate from but also linked with herself, or what Mayeroff (1965, 463) calls "identity-in-difference" for the one-caring. Being in the present necessarily involves drawing on the past with its many interpretations and meanings for the one cared for. The one caring experiences the worth of the one cared for and responds to her as she is.

Caring is a continuous process but has its ebbs and flows, its more intense and its more relaxed moments. The one caring must demonstrate and cultivate the characteristics of devotion, constancy, patience, trust, humility, and courage in himself as well as in the other. Devotion involves the whole person. Constancy requires the continuous involvement with the one cared for although not necessarily in the physical presence of the other. The one caring must also have patience with the one cared for by giving that person the time for realization, insight and communication. Trust (Baier 1994; Govier 1997, 1999) emerges as the relationship deepens but also is found in encouraging the other to discover what it is that contributes to the further development of the one cared for. Humility is present in the on-going process of learning about the other and one's self in the context of the caring relationship. Finally, it takes courage and patience to stay with the relationship and the one cared for when there are setbacks, failed efforts, and flawed actions.

At times, Mayeroff clearly views caring as a relational phenomenon between the one caring and the one cared for. At other times, he seems to regard caring as a personal attribute or virtue, when he describes the caring individual as patient, humble, courageous. However, his exploration of the phenomenon of caring, his recurring focus on relationality and on caring as a process, and his emphasis on the development of the one cared for in his/her own terms, clearly set the ground for the fuller development that follows in Gilligan, Noddings and others.

Gaylin (1976) takes a naturalistic position that caring is biologically embedded in the human species as a mechanism for its survival, continuation, and on-going development. Although Gaylin's focal context is the critical caring nature of the parent-child relationship, he clearly presents caring as integral to relationships throughout the entire life span. "Caring, of course, is not just a function of the mother-child relationship. Caring—that is, the protective, parental, tender aspects of loving—is a part of relationship among peers, child to parent, friend to friend, lover to lover, person to animal, and multiple other patterns" (p. 63). He continually returns to the theme of caring as the necessary condition for constructive development as a creative individual capable of loving and caring in return.

Meyeroff and Gaylin offer a sound basis on which to build an ethic of care but do not use the term "ethic of care" nor do they connect their explorations of the phenomenon of caring with feminist views on knowing and reality. There are, however, numerous points of commonality between their work and what emerges as a generalized ethic of care with Gilligan and beyond.

Women's Voice and an Ethic of Care

Gilligan's (1977, 1982) focus on an ethic of care emerged when she began to investigate the reasons that women did not score as well on the moral development scale developed by Lawrence Kohlberg (1969, 1981). Her research led her to understand that women were much more likely to value the maintenance of relationships and the well-being of those involved in the relationship in their moral reasoning. This contrasted with the ultimate valuing of individual autonomy and formal rights in moral rationality found in the highest scale of the Kohlberg model of moral development. Kohlberg's model had been built on data taken from Harvard University male students only and then universalized to apply to all humans, leading Gilligan to claim that Kohlberg's results were incomplete and that his model of moral development was biased and falsely universalized. Gilligan also criticized Kohlberg's use of hypothetical moral dilemmas as the correct way to understand people's moral experiences and views because of the absence of rich and thick description of the situation. Rather, her ethic of care is grounded in the every day lives and experiences and moral dilemmas of ordinary people in the context of a full range of responsibilities and relationships rather than rights and rules. (Note: Those interested in further exploring the Gilligan-Kohlberg differences and critiques of Kohlberg's model should read Flanagan 1982a, b; Kohlberg 1982; Flanagan and Jackson 1987; Blum 1988; Waterman 1988; Puka 1982, 1990; Kroger-Mappes 1994; Reiter 1996; Heyes 1997; Henry 2001; Kreb and Denton 2005; and Maxwell 2010.)

Gilligan gave this moral development perspective of women the explicit name of *an ethic of care*. Gilligan described an ethic of care as follows:

> After caring for self and a sense of responsibility to the other, the third perspective focuses on the dynamics of relationship and dissipates the tension between selfishness and responsibility through a new understanding of the interconnection between other and self. Care

> becomes the self-chosen principle of a judgment that remains psychological in its concern with relationships and response but becomes universal in its condemnation of exploitation and hurt. (Gilligan 1982, 74)

Thus a progressively more adequate understanding of the psychology of human relationships—an increasing differentiation of self and other and a growing comprehension of the dynamics of social interaction—informs the development of an ethic of care. This ethic, which reflects a cumulative knowledge of human relationships, revolves around a central insight, that self and other are interdependent.

Gilligan's development of an ethic of care focused on two fundamental concerns: one that addresses developing an articulation of an ethic of care, the other addressing the issue of women's voice in the construction of moral models and moral reasoning. Gilligan saw the development of an ethic of care as progressing through three general stages: the caring for one's self, the sense of responsibility for another at the expense of one's self, and the reconciliation of the two with a focus on the caring for the other as well as oneself in a dynamic, interconnected, healthy relationship. This emphasis on relationships emerged out of the early parent-child relationship and the societal structuring of the roles of women to caring, nurturing roles. Out of Gilligan's interviews with the women in her study, she concluded that "we know ourselves as separate only insofar as we live in connection with others, and that we experience relationship only insofar as we differentiate other from self" (1982, 63). Caring and the concern for relationships lead to the rejection of exploitation, oppression, and hurt and a primary attention to constructive human development for a healthy society.

Gilligan also had much to say about the issue of women's voices in moral reasoning. Here her concern was the virtual absence of their perspectives in the development of moral models. She was quite clear in her critique of the extension of data from male subjects for a model of moral reasoning to a model that was assumed to apply to all humans. This issue anticipated Elizabeth Minnich's (1990) exploration of "false universalization," "undefined terms," and "circular reasoning" as a part of feminist epistemology. It also anticipates the issues of political context and boundaries put forward by Joan Tronto (1993). But I shall address this latter issue later in this review of an ethic of care.

The significance of Gilligan, then, is for her seminal use of the term "ethic of care," the clear relational characteristic of an ethic of care, an attempt to describe an ethic of care, her focus on the voice of women in the development of moral models, and her exposure of the false universalization of Kohlberg's model of moral development and the use of hypothetical scenarios for assessing moral development.

An Ethic of Care Articulated

Noddings (1984), in the first comprehensive development of an ethic of care, saw an ethic of care as an on-going relational process. A caring relationship is not an ethic of abstract principles, universals, or rules leading to the ideal of individual autonomy through cognitive rationality, but rather as one concerned with the primacy of building healthy relationships set in the concreteness of each moral situation and using all of one's capabilities to arrive at actions that enhance the one or ones cared for, the one or ones caring, and the relationship. The one caring "apprehends the other's reality, feeling what he feels as nearly as possible" (1984, 16). This means preserving "the uniqueness of human encounters since so much depends on the subjective experience of those involved in ethical encounters and conditions (that) are rarely sufficiently similar" (1984, 5) to warrant ignoring context and using abstract universals.

For Noddings, all ethically caring relationships involve engrossment, displacement of motivation, commitment, and confirmation. Engrossment means meeting the other or others as one-caring, as totally as possible for the entire time during which the caring encounter takes place. Displacement of motivation means stepping out of one's personal frame of reference and into the other's. Although there may be legal or formal constraints placed on the relationship, such as the teacher-student relationship or the nurse-patient relationship, they do not displace or weaken the caring relationship. Commitment requires steadfastness to the relationship, even in difficult times, by both the one caring and the one cared for. And confirmation asks the one caring to see the one cared for as he or she sees himself or herself in the most positive light, what potentially might be. The caring relationship defines both individuals but it does not sacrifice either individual. Rather, caring is serving the well-being and constructive development of the other and one's self at the same time.

Noddings (1984) saw circles of caring relationships that move out from the center, or the one caring. They are: an inner circle of loved ones, primarily family; a second circle of those with whom we interact on a regular basis, such as friends and colleagues and, for faculty, their students; and a third circle that is comprised of the rest of the world. For the inner circle, the caring relationship is the most intense and sustained. For the second circle, one moves in and out of the caring relationship, depending on the contexts and the number of individuals to whom the caring is directed. The final circle is so vast that only general and sporadic caring behaviors can take place. However, individuals may find specific charitable and/or volunteer activities in the third circle that offer the individual an opportunity to engage more deeply in caring activities. Noddings (1984) does not effectively develop her ethic of care outside the first two circles. However, her later work (2002) does expand her view of an ethic of care to show how, with sufficient ethic of care development in the home, one can actualize an ethic of care in the wider societal and global context.

Noddings is also deliberate in her differentiation of caring about and caring for. She is careful to say that caring about is insufficient to constitute an ethic of care unless it is accompanied by the concrete, specific, and responsible action of caring for that result in enhancing the well-being of the other. Both are integral to an ethic of care. In so doing, Noddings anticipates, or perhaps sets the stage for, Tronto's (1993) position that an ethic of care is both disposition and practice and Held's (2006) statement that an ethic of care is both value and practice.

Expanding Caring's Domain

Tronto's (1993) major contribution lies in her clear expansion of an ethic of care to the political domain while, at the same time, dissolving the private/public dichotomy that is characteristic of deontological, utilitarian, and justice ethics. She notes that artificially built boundaries (see also Wilber 2001) and false dichotomies between the moral and the political and the private and the public arenas for morals have worked to the disadvantage of women and an ethic of care when caring is relegated to the moral and the private, largely done by women, to the exclusion of the public and the political, primarily the historic domain of men. She makes the fundamental point that all moral arguments are made in a political context. And her vision of the moral life is one that provides "us with a way to respect and deal justly with others. In order to do so, we must honor what most people spend their lives doing: caring for themselves, for others, and for the world" (1993, x).

Tronto's conceptualization of an ethic of care is that it is "a species activity that includes everything that we do to maintain, continue, and repair our world so that we can live in it as well as possible. That world includes our bodies, ourselves, and our environment, all of which we seek to interweave in a complex, life-sustaining web" (1993, 103). She constructs caring as defined culturally, continuous, and a disposition and a practice.

Caring for Tronto, like Noddings, is an ongoing process that consists of four interconnected and often overlapping phases (1993, 106): caring about, taking care of, care-giving, and care-receiving. Caring about means recognizing that a need exists and assessing that the need should be met in some way. Taking care of involves taking on some responsibility for that need and constructing some action to respond to it. Care-giving is the actual act of meeting the need for care. And care-receiving finds the one cared for responding to the care he/she receives. In addition to these four phases of caring, Tronto says that there are four ethical elements of care: attentiveness, responsibility, competence, and responsiveness. Attentiveness includes attentiveness to one's needs as well as the needs of the other or others. Responsibility generates the felt desire to fill the unmet need, whether one's own or that of another. Competence means that, short of resource inadequacies, one has the knowledge, skills, and ability to assess the situation and carry out the chosen act(s) to fill the care needs. And responsiveness involves considering the other as that individual sees and interprets herself.

There are many similarities of Tronto's conception of an ethic of care to that of Noddings. The latter's engrossment, displacement of motivation, and commitment are, in my view, equivalent to Tronto's attentiveness, responsiveness, and responsibility. Both caring conceptions are relational, contextual, and processual in character. But Tronto extends Noddings (1984) by dissolving the artificially created dichotomies of private/public and the moral/political. By inference, if not by overt intention, then, Tronto places morality at the center of political activity which she describes as historically having to do with public policy and resource allocation. This is particularly true for issues surrounding whose needs and which needs should be met and how. For Tronto, caring, in its full range of the continuum from the private through the public contexts, "requires a deep and thoughtful knowledge of the situation, and all of the actors' situations, needs, and competencies. Those who engage in a care process must make judgments: judgments about conflicting needs, strategies for achieving ends, the responsiveness of care-givers, and so forth" (1993, 136). Caring is a process that requires ongoing communication and conversation among all those impacted by the moral judgments in the full spectrum from personal relationships to societal relationships at the level of the nation.

Finally, Tronto discusses the distance between care givers and care receivers. She is concerned about the struggle that care givers have to separate their own needs from those of the care receivers and how to resolve them. This includes the perspective and interpretive separations as well as the struggle to find acceptable courses of action to meet both their own needs and those of the one(s) cared for.

Even though Tronto is the first to clearly dissolve the private/public dichotomy and integrate the moral and political, she stops short of offering any extensive and concrete proposals for what a caring organization or society might look like. Others will follow to take up this task.

Empathy and Caring

Michael Slote (2007) has offered a highly integrative and holistic argument for an ethic of care as a comprehensive ethical framework. The core idea on which he builds his arguments is that of empathic caring, particularly "mediated associative empathy" (Hoffman 2000) as opposed to "projective empathy" which is how Slote characterizes the empathy found in Noddings (1984). Slote, however, indicates that Noddings' engrossment is essentially the same as mediated associative empathy. For Slote, this empathy involves the "feelings of another (involuntarily) aroused in ourselves, as when we see another person in pain. It is as if the pain invades us" (2007, 13). This empathy contrasts with sympathy where we might have supportive feelings for the other person even if we do not actually or imaginatively feel his/her pain or act to alleviate it.

Slote addresses three fundamental issues found in the ethic of care literature through the lens of empathy. The first has to do with the scope of caring beyond those who are temporally and/or spatially proximate and those who are temporally and/or spatially distant. It offers a way to bridge the artificial private/public and moral/political boundaries discussed by Tronto and the most distant circle of care described by Noddings (1984). The second addresses the concern for autonomy that is so central to the ethical frameworks of Aristotle's virtue ethics (Irwin 1985; MacIntyre 1981, 1988), Kant's deontological ethics (Ellington 1983; Bowie 1999), Mill's utilitarian ethics (1969), and Rawls' justice ethics (1971, 2001). The third focuses on the issue of rationality, also central to the ethics of Kant, Mill, and Rawls.

Care ethicists have had almost no difficulty in morally justifying an ethic of care for those in our circle of extended family, particularly with regard to maternal care (Ruddick 1980, 1990), and close friends (Friedman 1993). Even Noddings' second circle of those with whom we have regular contact outside the inner circle has, by and large, been accommodated within an ethic of care. This has been particularly so for the educational context (Hult 1980; Noddings 1988, 1992; Marshall et al. 1996; Goldstein 1999; Katz, Noddings, and Strike 1999; Dalmiya 2002; Holmes 2004; Johnston 2006) and the nursing and health care domain (Fry 1989; Curzer 1993; Pierce 1997; Gremmen 1999; Bowden 2000; St. Clair 2001; Cardol, DeJong, and Ward 2002; Cronqvist et al. 2004; Tarlier 2004). However, it is those who are distant, both in time and space, who have presented challenges for the care ethicist. Slote uses the term "humanitarian caring" to encompass those who are temporally and spatially distant. He proposes that a mature and developed empathic caring, encouraged and stimulated along the way through childhood and adolescence (see also Noddings 2002), can lead to humanitarian caring. Slote points out the key role that imagination (Mills 1959; Greene 1995; Byrne 2005) in general and moral imagination, in particular, (Johnson 1993; Werhane 1999; Fesmire 2003; Kekes 1991, 2006) play in developing humanitarian caring. This development of moral imagination through empathy is not just for the here and now but also through imagining what action(s) to take and how the person might feel if the action(s) takes place as expected. Johnson (1993), Werhane (1999), Fesmire (2003), and Kekes (2006) in particular, emphasize the critical role of moral imagination in identifying with the "others" who have a stake in a given situation requiring moral judgment and in creating morally sound actions to address the situation. Kekes' (2006) model of corrective imagination for examining the past, exploratory imagination for creatively exploring future possibilities, and disciplined imagination for integrating the two is particularly well-suited for empathic caring from the very personal to the humanitarian.

The issue of autonomy of the other, or non-interference with the other's right to act, has also been a significant issue of controversy for care ethics. Care ethicists have had a challenge in addressing the concerns of rights and justice ethicists who claim a ground from a perspective of justice and rights so prevalent in Kantian and Rawlsian ethics (Ellington 1983; Rawls 1971, 2001; Bowie 1999). This disagreement has centered on the central assumptions that underlie Kantian, Millsian, and Rawlsian ethical frameworks as compared to those that underlie an ethic of care. For the former, those assumptions are that there are universal moral principles or rules, that the process for arriving at a moral choice is rational in the cognitive sense only, and that the highest moral developmental plane to which an individual can aspire is for individual autonomy.

Even Aristotelian virtue ethics, which shares the general positions of situational contextuality and holistic human capabilities with an ethic of care, has the universalistic and autonomy assumptions of Kant, Mill, and Rawls. In Kantian, Millsian, and Rawlsian ethics, relationship is not considered at all, except in the freely chosen and contractarian sense, and, for Aristotle, it is done so only in the context of the public Greek polis where only free male citizens count. For the latter, an ethic of care, the core assumptions center around the primacy of relationships throughout our lives, the critical role of understanding context, especially since the belief is that there are no two ethical situations requiring moral perception, moral imagination, judgment, and action that are identical, and the process of arriving at moral choices involves the whole person since no one can have a valid claim to be rational in the limited cognitive sense. (For extensive discussions of these assumptions, see Friedman 1993; Johnson 1993; Baier 1994; Held 1995a, 2006. Also, Udovicki 1993; Kroeger-Mappes 1994; Held 1995b; Deveaux 1995; Clement 1996; Rumsey 1997; Katz, Noddings, and Strike 1999; Dienhart 2000; and French and Weis 2000 address specifically the issue of justice, rights, and care.) Slote addresses the issue of autonomy by contrasting the atomistic view of self/persons of the justice and rights ethical frameworks with the relational characteristic of an ethic of care from an empathy perspective. He defines autonomy as "the developed and exercised capacity to think and act for oneself" (2007, 62). His argument is that a mature and developed empathic caring in a person will necessarily respect the other as an individual to think and act for oneself, but is also not hesitant to recognize and address one's own needs. He also indicates that when one is treated well as a child "in relationship" with parent, then one is more likely to treat others with empathic caring and respect later, with an emphasis on respecting the other's capacity to think and act as the one cared for.

For the rationality issue, Slote makes clear his distinction between theoretical/epistemic rationality and practical rationality. He describes the former as cognitive only and as the rationality embedded in the ethics of Kant, Mills, and Rawls. The rationality of an ethic of care is practical rationality and practical reasoning (Rorty 1988), or one where the individual uses all of his/her capabilities, including affective, intuitional, and imaginative, to arrive at a reasonably defensible assessment of the uniqueness of the context and a reasonable action to care in collaboration with those who are part of the relationship (see also Rooney 1994, for a discussion on the value of reasoning and the abuses of reason). MacIntyre (1981, 1988) provides another extensive discussion of the differences in rationality and particularly practical rationality with respect to virtue ethics and Kantian ethics.

The justice and rights issue, however, is one that remains controversial for an ethic of care. Some care ethicists, such as Gilligan, Noddings, and Held, see care and justice as complementary, with one of the two taking a more dominant role, depending on the context. Others, however, such as Slote, see care and justice as incompatible and suggest that an ethic of care needs to extend its developmental process through conversations that address care's ability as a comprehensive moral framework in the political and legal domains. In so doing, an ethic of care can potentially reveal the inadequacy of justice ethics to effectively address moral issues in those public domains as it already has been shown to be essentially woefully inadequate for what has been in the past called the private domain.

I want to raise one more fundamental issue about the care/justice controversy. That issue focuses on the definition or meaning of the word justice. Sterba (1986) describes four conceptions of justice: a libertarian concept, a welfare liberal concept, a socialist concept, and a perfectionist concept. Holtman (2003) takes essentially a Kantian/Rawlsian approach to theorizing about justice but finds three strategies for doing so: abstraction, idealization, and appeal to utopia. Each of these different approaches to the meaning of justice carry with it different answers to the questions (1) what rights do people deserve, (2) what is the minimum for each of those rights, (3) who deserves the rights and when, and (4) how to resolve conflicts among rights. None of the conceptions or definitions of justice adequately addresses the four questions, a conclusion also echoed in MacIntyre (1988). So the differing and inconsistent meanings of the term justice and the absence of agreement suggests that perhaps Slote is right to focus an ethic of care on its own path to embrace the political and legal domains without attending to the calls of the justice advocates to meet their own conception of justice. However, while it appears that justice advocates are not united in their views on justice, it remains that care ethicists are likewise not of the same mind when it comes the relationship between an ethic of care and an ethic of justice, however it is defined.

An Integrated Ethic of Care

Finally, Held (2006) offers the most comprehensive examination of an ethic of care to date. She describes an ethic of care as both practice and value. She defines caring as (p. 35) "a relation in which carer and cared-for share an interest in their mutual well-being." She goes on to say (p. 36):

> Care is a practice involving the work of care-giving and the standards by which the practices of care can be evaluated. Care must concern itself with the effectiveness of its efforts to meet needs, but also with the motives with which care is provided. It seeks good caring relations.

For actual practices of care we need care as a value to pick out the appropriate cluster of moral considerations, such as sensitivity, trust, and mutual concerns, with which to evaluate such practices.

Held presents an in-depth exploration of the care/justice controversy (see citations on the same issue in the discussion of Slote 2007). She builds the case for the position that care is a wider, more fundamental ethical concept than justice (fairness, equity) and that while there can be care without justice, there cannot be justice without care. She recommends that we examine every situation from both care and justice perspectives across all moral contexts, giving the appropriate weight to each depending on the ethical context.

Summarizing an Ethic of Care

While the preceding discussion provides a reasonable summary of the ethic of care literature in relation to the purposes of this chapter, a comprehensive exploration of an ethic of care is obviously beyond the scope of this chapter. However, those interested in delving further into the literature should read Held (2006) along with Slote (2007). What I would like to do here is to summarize what I have covered to this point before I examine where an ethic of care has emerged in the organizational leadership and management literature.

First, an ethic of care begins with the recognition that we are all embedded in a web of relationships throughout our respective lives. Those relationships help constitute who we are and are becoming, where the development process is on-going. Thus, an ethic of care assumes the primacy of relationship instead of assuming the ultimate ideal of independent and separated autonomy while ignoring relationship.

Second, an ethic of care assumes that there are no two situations requiring moral judgment that are identical or nearly identical. Thus, the focus of an ethic of care is on understanding the concrete context and particulars of a situation, including who has a stake in the resolution and a rich description of factual and interpretative information surrounding the situation. The focus is not on determining what abstract, universal principle(s) might apply to the situation. Rather, it is crafting a set of ethical responses that address the well-being of all those in the relationship and affected by the actions. Indeed, an ethic of care takes the needs of the relationship and those who participate in the relationship as the starting point for ethical responsibility and responsiveness as opposed to depending upon generalized, external, overarching universal principals or rules.

Third, an ethic of care supports human development and well-being—that of the one or ones cared for, the one caring, and the relationship. There is a reciprocity of mutual well-being in that the relationship works to the development and well-being of both and as well as for the relationship.

Fourth, an ethic of care relies on the whole person for the processes of being attentive, responsive, competent, and responsible (Tronto 1993), engrossment, displacement of motivation, commitment, and confirmation (Noddings 1984), and empathy (Hoffman 2000; Snow 2000; Slote 2007). Cognitive, affective, intuitive (Haidt 2001, 2003), and imaginative (Mills 1959; Johnson 1993; Werhane 1999; Fesmire 2003; Byrne 2005; Kekes 1991, 2006) capabilities are brought to bear on the situation rather than being limited to explicit cognitive rationality. The capabilities include such competencies as listening, articulating and framing, observation, questioning and inquiry, empathy, imagination, responsiveness, and responsibility. This leads to practical rationality and practical reasoning as opposed to the strictly cognitive rationality of the other ethical frameworks.

Fifth, an ethic of care always leads to some concrete, empathically constructive act or actions. Ethical assessments and judgments about what to do carry with them both the obligation to care and consequences for both the one(s) cared for and the one caring. There must be some effective, constructive result from an ethic of care act and it should be constructively developmental in character.

Sixth, an ethic of care, in its development over the last 30 years, has become, for many care ethicists, a comprehensive ethical framework that can encompass the full range of moral issues experienced by humans across the private/public continuum. Morality is just as fundamental to the public and public policy domain as it is to the private aspects of our lives. The two are not separate but interwoven. An ethic of care can include a caring for the non-human environment and all non-human life forms as well.

And finally, an ethic of care has moved beyond an ethical framework that is characteristic of just women. Men have the same potential to take an ethic of care perspective as women, although the socialization process into male stereotypes may make it more problematic for them.

One dark side of caring is the risk of focusing too strongly on the one cared for and sacrificing the well-being needs of the one caring. Another is its purely instrumental use by organizational leaders to maintain the power status quo. And two areas of continuing controversy are the care/justice debate and the issue of care ethic's genesis within privileged, educated, white females and how introducing women of color and uneducated women in poverty might alter the conversations on and nature of an ethic of care.

Now that I have completed a brief review of the emergence and on-going evolution of an ethic of care, I would like to examine the coverage of an ethic of care in the organizational management literatures and present some reasons that justify an ethic of care as the preferred ethical framework for the organizational context.

The Relational Character of Organizations

An ethic of care has emerged only within the last 30 years as a comprehensive ethical framework from the early feminist literature. It is an ethical framework that has challenged the fundamental assumptions that underlie the dominant ethical models of virtue ethics, deontological ethics, utilitarian ethics, and justice ethics and sought a major place in the conversations on ethical issues. Where have feminist views on knowing, reality, and morality appeared in the organizational world? What is the pattern of consideration of an ethic of care in business and organizational ethics in particular? What empirical research has emerged on care in general and an ethic of care specifically in the management and leadership domains? And what arguments support an advocacy of an ethic of care for the organizational and societal contexts? These are central questions that are the focus of the last half of this chapter.

Care and Feminist Views in the Organizational World

The organizational world, from the smallest one person business through all sizes of companies and corporations to governments and societies, is replete with relationships. Within an organization that has two or more employees, there are on-going and dynamic relationships vertically and/or horizontally. Every employee brings a network of personal relationships that are not generated by the employment context but nonetheless impact on that context. The reverse is also true. And any organization that produces a product or service has reciprocal relationships with suppliers, buyers, competitors, and customers as well as a multitude of other stakeholders who have a vested interest in the short and long term impact of the activities in which the organization engages. Whether we like it or not or want it to be otherwise, we inhabit a world of multiple, dynamic, and interwoven relationships that demand attention to well-being and, hopefully, constructive cultivation.

Where have feminist voices in general and the ethic of care voices in particular appeared in the world of organizations? Clearly, they have appeared in the philosophical world as indicated by the ethic of care review in the first half of this chapter. And in almost a companion relationship, the educational domain is an organizational context in which caring and care ethics are recurring themes of discussion (e.g., Darwall 1977; Hult 1980; Noddings 1988, 1992; Diller 1993, 1996; Boyd 1993; Applebaum 1996; Marshall et al. 1996; Goldstein 1999; Katz, Noddings, and Strike 1999; Dalmiya 2002; Holmes 2004; Buttner 2004; Burton and Dunn 2005; Johnston 2006; Hawk and Lyons 2008; Gabriel 2009).

Yet there are other organizational and institutional contexts in which feminist concerns and an ethic of care are appearing. Perhaps the most understandable is the field of nurse-patient and doctor-patient relationships in the healing and therapy delivery domain (e.g., Fry 1989; Curzer 1993; Pierce 1997; Gremmen 1999; Bowden 2000; St. Clair 2001; Cardol, DeJong, and Ward 2002; Tarlier 2004; Haegert 2004; Cronqvist et al. 2004). These articles have in common several themes, two of which focus on the desire to be effective care givers yet take care of their own needs and the frequent demands of their organizations for efficiency and profitability.

More surprisingly, an ethic of care has also appeared in the domains of social policy, political theory, and law. In the social policy and political theory domains, authors have argued convincingly of the need for care-oriented policies to address the critical role that care plays in the well-being of all in a society and the ways in which care is marginalized in society and its organizations (Ferguson,1984; MacKinnon 1989; Held 1993; Deveaux 1995; Sevenhuijsen 1998, 2003; Robinson 1999; Folbre 2001; Kittay 2001; Noddings 2002; Hankivsky 2004; Hamington and Miller 2006; Engster 2007; Eisler 2007; and Smith 2008). In the area of law and the legal context in which organizations operate, Bartlett (1990), Rhode (1990, 1993), Gavison (1992), Gutman (1993), and Higgins (1997) critique the strong rights and justice orientation of the law from the feminist and care perspectives.

Then there is the corporate domain, where the areas of stakeholder theory, knowledge and creativity management, accounting, and, most recently, leadership offer opportunities to connect to the relationality of an ethic of care and an inherent concern for the ethical. Stakeholder theory (e.g., Freeman 1984, 1994, 1999, 2010; Wicks, Gilbert, and Freeman 1994; Burton and Dunn 1996; Rowley 1997; Hendry 2001; Phillips 2003; Friedman and Miles 2006; Jones, Felps, and Bigley 2007; Freeman, Harrison, and Wicks 2007; Simola 2007) and its strong focus on firm-stakeholder relations is the only strategy and corporate social responsibility model (Mele 2008) that has built a connection to feminist ethics and the relationality of an ethic of care (Wicks, Gilbert, and Freeman 1994; Burton and Dunn 1996). In the area of knowledge management and creativity, Von Krogh (1998) and Von Krogh, Ichijo, and Nonaka (2000) devote significant space to the critical role that caring plays in cultivating effective creativity and knowledge innovation. For the field of accounting, Reiter (1996, 1997) makes an excellent case for at least a partnership of an ethic of care and an ethic of justice in the auditing process. And relational leadership (Uhl-Bien 2006; Binns 2008; Cunliffe 2009) has recently emerged as an alternative to the heroic and largely individualistic and male-oriented model of leadership that has dominated the field. Leadership has a decidedly relational character as a process and an on-going conversation, whether it involves generating a vision of the organization's future, facilitating the collaboration to interpret and define the current situation, facilitating the generation of concrete ideas for action and a choice among those ideas, facilitating the execution and follow-through on the action chosen, particularly in teams, or developing or mentoring the people in the organization. Unfortunately, only Binns (2008) makes the connection to an ethic of care. Finally, Caputo (2002), Machold, Ahmed, and Farquhar (2008), and Delios (2010) directly suggest that an ethic of care is an ethical posture compatible with corporate interests.

In the business ethics literature, there are those who argue for the congruence of feminist ethics and business ethics, such as Wicks, Gilbert, and Freeman (1994), Dienhart (2000), French and Weiss (2000), Liedtka (1996, 1998), and Borgerson (2007). Others, however, decry the near exclusion of an ethic of care and caring in business ethics literature (DeMoss and McCann 1997). Both positions are supportable, but from differing bases of evidence. Although an ethic of care has been an occasional topic in the two primary business ethics journals, *Journal of Business Ethics* and *Business Ethics Quarterly*, more than three quarters of business ethics and corporate social responsibility texts offer no consideration of an ethic of care, while the remaining texts do so in a token or proforma manner. Current business ethics and corporate social responsibility handbooks (e.g., Crane et al., 2008; Brenkert and Beauchamp 2010), special journal issues (e.g., *Academy of Management Executive*, May 2004; *Journal of Management Education*, February 2006; *Academy of Management Learning and Education*, September 2006), journal article reviews of business ethics (e.g., Kahn 1990; Trevino, Weaver, and Reynolds 2006), and journal dialogue responses (e.g., Audi 2009; Jacobs 2009, to Locke 2006) provide virtually no consideration of an ethic of care. The same can be said for reviews in the leadership area (e.g., Gini 1997; Bass and Steidlmeister 1999; Avolio 2005; Brown and Trevino 2006; Rhode 2006). So if faculty and students do not see texts and articles that describe and discuss an ethic of care, then they cannot be aware of the vocabulary of an ethic of care and consider an ethic of care as ethical framework. The same situation applies in the empirical research on an ethic of care in the management literature in general.

Empirical Research on an Ethic of Care in Organizations

The empirical research on an ethic of care or care in general in the management of organizations is very limited, with Victor and Cullen (1988), Kahn (1993), and McAllister and Bigley (2002) offering some initial insight but very little use of an ethic of care.

Victor and Cullen (1988) surveyed employees across four companies and found different ethical climates both across the organizations and within each of the organizations. They empirically derived five different ethical climates, one of which they labeled as caring. Gilligan (1982) is the only ethic of care citation they make, offering no effective description or discussion of an ethic of care.

Kahn's (1993) research focuses on the impact of relational care-giving within social services organizations that have a mission to deliver care-giving services to clients. He was interested in what constitutes care-giving among the members of an organization and how the patterns of care-giving among the organizational members impact the care-giving to the clients. By using extensive observation and interviews, he found five patterns of organizational care-giving: flow, with care-giving flowing downward hierarchically; reverse-flow, with care-giving flowing upward hierarchically; fragmented, with care-giving flowing in both directions hierarchically and across peers; self-contained, where there is not care-giving flowing upward or downward, only within the peer group; and barren, where there is no organizational care-giving. He found that flow, reverse-flow, and fragmented care-giving had positive impacts on client care-giving and relationships. Kahn did not examine the impact of care-giving flows from outside the organization to organizational members.

McAllister and Bigley (2002) surveyed managers and professionals across a number of organizations and industries to investigate the impact of organizational care on employee organizational-based self-esteem. They hypothesized that organizational care would positively impact organizational-based self-esteem through organizational fairness and job autonomy, thereby increasing organizational effectiveness. They defined organizational care as (p. 895) "a deep structure of values and organizing practices centered on fulfilling employees' needs, promoting employees' best interests, and valuing employees' contributions." Their survey results showed that organizational care was significantly associated with organizational-based self-esteem and organizational care was significantly associated with both perceived fairness and perceived job autonomy.

What is also noteworthy in the empirical research on organizations is the near total absence of rich description of the actual ethical posture or character of different organizations longitudinally, particularly corporate organizations. Bowie (1999) describes what a Kantian corporate organization might look like and provides isolated examples of specific situations where a corporation took a Kantian posture. But he provides no examples of corporations that consistently reflect a Kantian ethic throughout an organization on a longitudinal basis. It also appears that there is no empirical research that provides richly described examples of corporations that reflect a consistently virtue, utilitarian or justice ethical postures.

Empirical Research on an Ethic of Care in the Educational Context

There is not much more in the management pedagogical literature. They focus on the relationship between teacher power and the flexibility to create a caring learning environment (Noblit 1993), the caring posture of assistant principles in primary, middle, and secondary schools (Marshall et al. 1996), the characteristics of caring advising relationships in higher education (Holmes 2004), the facilitation of case discussions on social issues management from an ethic of care perspective in higher education (Burton and Dunn 2005), and the phenomenon of university faculty giving up or not giving up on students' learning (Hawk and Lyons 2008).

Noblit (1993) did an ethnographic study of the impact of teacher power on providing a caring environment in which the teacher's student could learn. The study revealed that a teacher exercising his or her power over classroom learning processes and structure could be used effectively to cultivate a caring culture in the class and caring relationships between the teacher and the students.

Marshall et al. (1996) present a qualitative study of award winning primary, middle, and secondary school assistant principles who had intentionally chosen an ethic of care orientation as the core characteristic of the way they engaged their relationships with students, faculty, and staff. Many of them acknowledged that they had turned down promotions for a position as principle because they wanted to continue reflecting an ethic of care in the performance of their responsibilities and did not believe the command and control bureaucratic structure of the school system would allow them to do so as principals.

Holmes (2004) investigated the character of the caring advisor-advisee relationship at a major state university where the advising model is a full-time staff of professionally trained advisors for all undergraduate students in a particular college of the university rather than an advising model that was faculty-based or peer-based. Advisees had the same advisor for the full time of their undergraduate experience. Holmes described the developmental advisor as mentor, Mom, teacher, guide, advocate, expert, cheerleader, and role model. His inductive research led to six characteristics of the caring advising relationship.

- Caring advisors create and maintain a comfortable, welcoming environment for caring advising encounters.
- Caring advisors are prepared for the encounter and are fully present once the caring encounter is underway.
- Caring advisors are sincere, compassionate, trustworthy, and willing to go the extra mile.
- Advisor accuracy and knowledge are essential components of caring advising.
- Caring cannot be achieved by formula; caring advising is enacted in unique, personal ways.
- Caring can be inconsistently present in advising practice.

For Holmes, the critical role was of building and cultivating trust.

Burton and Dunn (2005) contrast the facilitation of a case discussion from a traditional ethical principles and rules perspective with a case discussion from an ethic of care perspective. Drawing on their own experiences of facilitating both types of case discussions, they conclude that an ethic of care perspective is significantly more congruent with the relational complexity of actual management contexts than one from an ethical principles/rules perspective. They also point out the value in providing case evidence that allows students to understand the contextual richness of the many different relationships that organizations have with stakeholders both within and outside of the organization.

Hawk and Lyons (2008) surveyed graduate students' beliefs about whether or not faculty had given up on them and their learning in undergraduate and graduate courses. The authors found that 44% of their students indicated that they believed that at least one faculty member had given up on them and their learning during their higher education experience. The authors asked the students to describe the behaviors that they believed sent the signal that the faculty member had given up on them, what they as students did about the situation, and what behaviors a faculty member could engage in that would signal they had not given up on the student's learning. Hawk and Lyons found that the faculty giving up behaviors could be described as either lacking in recognition respect for the student as an individual or lacking in appraisal respect for the student as a learner (Darwall 1977; Hult 1980; Diller 1993, 1996; Boyd 1993; Applebaum 1996), ranging from mild severity to strong severity. They also found that students see "a caring relationship" with the instructor as including such behaviors and classroom management techniques as establishing a safe and encouraging environment, recognizing learning style differences, providing developmental feedback, and being available to students.

Although not empirical, Thayer-Bacon (1993, 2000) offers an extensive re-examination of traditional critical thinking models and processes to integrate the relationality of an ethic of care into what she describes as constructive thinking where respect for whole person experiential learning and knowing, for differing perspectives, and for attentive or authentic listening (Fiumara 1990) are fundamental to the constructive thinking processes. More recently, Thayer-Bacon (2003) discusses the importance of an ethic of care in relational learning and relational epistemologies (see also Goldstein 1999).

Summary of Empirical Research on an Ethic of Care

The empirical research in both the organizational and the instructional contexts is not sufficient to draw any prescriptive conclusions. However, an ethic of care would not be congruent with the emergence of rules or principles to apply. Rather, an ethic of care focuses on competencies such as inquiry, listening, observing, attentiveness, responsiveness, and responsibility and would ask those situated in an ethical dilemma to engage authentically, respectfully, and ethically in conversation (Ayim 1997) with those who would be impacted by the actions generated out of the dilemma. That would include participation in defining the situation, generating the actions considered, choosing the actions, and implementing the actions. Ayim (1997) describes ethical conversations as caring, honest, collaborative, and democratic.

Why Should We Care with an Ethic of Care in Organizations?

Up to this point and within the constraints of a chapter format, I have offered what I hope has been an effective review of an ethic of care, its evolution over the last 30 years, and the fundamental position that relationality has in its character. I have also reviewed an extensive set of conceptual and empirical literature in the organizational and management fields in general and the business ethics area in particular to show how fundamentally relational the organizational world appears to be.

I also want to make my position clear about my overall view of the activities of working in and managing organizations because that view directly impacts how I interpret the key relevance of an ethic of care to the organizational context as a process and practice. My many years of experience in organizations and organizational activities has led me to view them as highly contextual and dynamic. They are a complex combination of different people and multiple resources that change from issue to issue and even within the artificially designated time frame for a given issue. We as individuals are continually learning and changing so that what an individual brings to an organizational conversation at a given point in time will change for the next conversation as a result of the experiences from the previous conversations. I believe this is so physiologically, cognitively, affectively, intuitively, and imaginatively. This is a very dynamic, process, social constructionist, and interpretivist view of the organizational world that I bring to my caring about an ethic of care. That dynamic, continuity-oriented process, and the subsequent rich contextual uniqueness of each moral situation are highly congruent with my views on an ethic of care.

So why should we who work in an organizational world of unique human beings embrace an ethic of care as our primary ethical standard? Because we are all in an inter-connected web of overlapping organizational and personal relationships throughout our lives, relationships that define who we are and are becoming and that to one degree or another matter to us and those with whom we are in relationship. In a more narrow sense, we are organizational researchers who care as knowers (Dalmiya 2002), we are faculty with students who expect to learn from and with us (Noddings 1988, 1992; Goldstein 1999; Johnston 2006), and we are, in almost any capacity, engaged in organizational activities. As organizational researchers, we should care for the issues we research and our fields of knowing, the integrity with which we carry out the research and develop our knowing, and the people with whom we engage in doing that research.

As faculty, we not only have the opportunity to engage in relationships of care with our students as emerging learners and our colleagues but also to enhance the awareness of ethical characteristics of most, if not all, decision making that goes on in organizations. As members of organizations and consultants to organizations, we also have multiple relationships within those organizations that deserve a strong caring character for the mutual benefit of all concerned with what is done in the organization.

I would now like to address four issues that, in my mind, have been, to one degree or another, effectively addressed within an ethic of care as a comprehensive ethical framework for the organizational context. They are: (1) the issue of autonomy within relationality; (2) the relationship between rationality and whole person reasoning; (3) the scope of an ethic of care across the unjustifiably dichotomized private and public domains; and (4) the issue of care, markets, and bureaucracy.

An Ethic of Care, Autonomy, and Relationality

There are many ethicists who are concerned about the issue of individual autonomy within an ethic of care. This is especially an issue for those who subscribe to one of the dominant ethical frameworks of virtue ethics (Aristotle and MacIntyre), deontological ethics (Kant), utilitarian ethics (Mill), or justice ethics (Rawls) and those who support a Kohlbergian model of moral development where the highest level of moral development is the autonomous, rational individual.

The concern, in my mind, turns on two issues. The first is how one conceptualizes an ethic of care and the second is how one conceptualizes autonomy (Deveaux 1995; Keller 1997). In addressing the first, my review of the evolution of an ethic of care over the last 30 years has shown that, as currently developed, an ethic of care emphasizes not only care for the cared for but also care for the one caring and for the relationship between them. The one caring must be care-full for herself or himself on a relatively equal footing with those others for whom the care is directed. The caring relationship is one that is mutually beneficial and developmental for both the one caring and the one cared for. Both are on-going processes as long as the relationship lasts. The one caring is separate and distinct from the one cared for and the one caring must continue to monitor his or her own well-being, growth, and competencies in order to competently and successfully engage in the caring relationship. Most care ethicists have been clear about not suborning the needs and the development of the one caring to the one cared for.

The second issue focuses on how one conceptualizes autonomy. Keller describes the way in which autonomy is conceptualized in the dominant ethical frameworks:

> A model of autonomy that conceives the self as free and independent, bound only by those rules one has given oneself, obligated only by those relationships one has freely entered into, is abstract, empty, and unrealizable. Impartiality, following rules, and the use of reason to the exclusion of affect are all inappropriate for making moral decisions in the sphere of interpersonal relationships. (1997, 154)

Keller goes on to reconceptualize autonomy so that the concept is reconcilable with an ethic of care. Her reconceptualization describes "autonomy in relation" as a set of competencies that includes cognitive, imaginative, affective, and intuitive carried out with integrity. The communicative competencies of speaking, questioning, listening, and reasoning are integral to autonomy in relation. She also makes it clear that all of these competencies are learned in relationship with others who stand in as models and teachers and learning facilitators. And all those competencies are brought to bear on caring for not only the other but also oneself.

A further definitional issue that arises is whether or not autonomy is a goal or an on-going and emerging process. Is there really an end-state that one reaches and in which one can be called autonomous? Care ethicists would insist that both justice autonomy and relational autonomy are life-long and never ending processes.

There are two epistemological issues that emerge for me here and that will emerge again in some of the remaining issues to cover. They are how one defines or uses a term (Minnich 1990) and the use of false dichotomies. In this case, there needs to be careful attention given to how ethicists supporting different ethical models define or use a term that, on the surface, appears to be the same. The second is falsely dichotomizing autonomy and relationality—one cannot exist if the other exists. But again, it hinges on one's definition of the terms that are dichotomized and whether or not they are self-serving to one's position.

It is clear to me that an ethic of care has successfully addressed the issue of a redefined autonomy within an ethic of care. It cannot be said, however, that the dominant ethical frameworks have successfully addressed the issue of relationality and autonomy. Quite the contrary, those frameworks ignore relationality to focus only on a rule based and rational autonomy in the public domain. The wider embrace of an ethic of care would suggest a preferable ethical position.

Care, Rationality, and Reason

A second issue that supports the choice of an ethic of care focuses on another definitional controversy, the concept of rationality that is characteristic of the dominant ethical frameworks. For the ethical models offered by Kant, Mills, and Rawls, it is clear that their use of the term rational is a cognitive rationality, one unencumbered and unaffected by emotion, intuition, and imagination. All three consider impartiality to be a key characteristic of the autonomous individual who achieves high levels of moral development. The issue is not so clear for virtue ethics, and MacIntyre (1988) goes into great depth to differentiate between cognitive rationality and practical reasoning where the lines between pure rationality and reasoning affected by anything other than logic are less well-defined.

An ethic of care, on the other hand, readily acknowledges and welcomes all of the perceptual, interpretive, decisional, and implementing capabilities of individuals in situations requiring moral action. The whole person capabilities of cognitive reasoning, emotion, intuition, and imagination are inextricably woven together to act on the value that is care. Care ethicists ask the question, Where is there a truly rational individual? Their answer is that not only are there none but also that a life without affect, emotion, imagination, and intuition would not be worth living. Rooney (1994) supports the use of reasoning but, from a feminist perspective, challenges the agenda-driven abuse and distortion of reason that emerges from those wishing to play down feminist arguments and perspectives. Johnson (1993) makes a convincing case not only for the ever present imaginative use of metaphor in the languages of all societies but also for the fundamental role of imagination in projecting the likely impact of actions that are being considered and the concerns of those not present to represent themselves. Werhane (1999) reinforces these positions in the context of organizational management. Greene (1995) articulates the critical role of the arts in developing the imagination and creativity. And Kekes (2006) presents a three part model of moral imagination where analytical imagination examines our experiential history for lessons, the creative imagination directs our projection into the future, and the integrative imagination brings the first two together in a coherent and holistic set of actions.

The whole person capabilities position of the care ethicists is supported by the research on the brain that has emerged over the last 20 years. Damasio (1994), LeDoux (1996, 2002), Schwartz and Begley (2002), and Zull (2002) have reported on the research that has resulted from the use of three dimensional and longitudinal brain imaging technology to study how the brain responds to injuries, how it changes during learning and over time, and what parts of the brain are involved in differing mental activities. The clear picture is that the emotional centers of the brain are continually involved in all mental activities. Interest, curiosity (Kashdan 2009), commitment, intentionality, choice, satisfaction, pride, disappointment, and attachment are all significantly influenced by the emotional centers of the brain. Even before the emergence of brain imaging technology, Solomon (1988) makes the case for the integral relationship between emotions and judgments.

There is also research that examines the relationship between brain functioning and the ethical posture of the individual. Gazzaniga, a pre-eminent neuroscientist, arrives at a position that is highly congruent with an ethic of care:

> I believe that we should look not for a universal ethics comprising hard and fast truths, but for the universal ethics that arises from being human, which is clearly contextual, emotion-influenced, and designed to increase our survival. That is why it is hard to arrive at absolute rules to live by that we can all agree on. But knowing that morals are contextual and social, and based on neural mechanisms, can help us determine certain ways to deal with ethical issues. (Gazzaniga 2005)

Gazzaniga's views also provide an opening for the consideration of a more intuition-based model of ethical behavior such as offered by Haidt's (2001, 2003) social intuitionist model.

The research reported in LeDoux (1996, 2002) and Schwartz and Begley (2002) show that the brain is continually changing over our life span, although the rate of change is slower as we get older. Even more interesting is the research that shows that the intentional efforts of the mind can rewire the brain. The ethical implications for the values we hold and the abilities to successfully cope with the contextual complexity of ethical situations is significant. Again, an ethic of care, with its emphasis on using all of the human capabilities, not just cognitive rationality, reflects a sounder basis for making ethical judgments than the limited cognitive rationality of the dominant ethical frameworks.

Care in the Private and Public Domains

The dominant ethical models of Kant, Mills, and Rawls have effectively dichotomized the private and public domains. While ignoring what they label as the private world of an individual's home, they instead focus on the public arena of governmental policy and contractarian relationships among so called intentional, autonomous equals. That is not to say that one cannot bring ethical considerations from Kant, Mills, and Rawls into one's private life. Rather, it wasn't important to them to do so.

Aristotle's virtue ethics were set primarily in the context of the public Greek polis where only free male citizens could participate. Aristotle did discuss the key importance of the virtues in the context of friendship with other free male citizens and the responsibility of the free male citizen to inculcate the virtues into his offspring. Otherwise the private context of family was largely absent from his virtue ethics.

Care ethicists, on the other hand, began with care and relationality as the central human condition in both the family and among friends. From the start, care ethicists also saw the centrality of caring relations in teaching and learning, in the context of physical and emotional well-being and therapy delivery, in the community, and in care for the environment. And it wasn't long before the evolution of care ethics saw Tronto (1993) expand the domain of an ethic of care into the public domain at the level of society and the nation. Since then, authors such as Sevenhuijsen (1998, 2003), Robinson, (1999), Folbre (2001), Kittay (2001), Noddings (2002), Hankivsky (2004), Engster (2007), and Eisler (2007) have argued convincingly for a care perspective at the societal level. Engster, in particular, has elaborated not only a comprehensive definition of care and well-being but also an extensive and detailed list of ways in which a nation and corporate organizations can and should reflect a strong care orientation as well as a justice orientation. Engster suggests that caring, with its necessary virtues of attentiveness, responsiveness, and respect, represents a basic morality for the minimal decent treatment of others that we should all follow. Caring, at a minimum, involves meeting the basic needs of individuals, developing their capabilities, and helping them to survive and function. Vital biological needs include access to adequate food, sanitary water, appropriate clothing and shelter, sufficient rest, a clean environment, basic medical care, and protection from harm, as well as the need, at least among infants and children, for physical contact and holding, with adjustments to the provision of these goods to the particular needs of different individuals. Helping individuals to develop or sustain their basic capabilities includes sensation, movement, emotion, imagination, reason, speech, affiliation, and, in most societies, literacy and numeracy. The goal here is to enable individuals to develop and maintain as much as possible the innate capabilities that are necessary for social functioning, where social functioning means being able to work and obtain the resources necessary for survival, being able to care for oneself and others, and having the opportunity to pursue some conception of the good life. Caring also helps individuals to avoid harm and relieve unnecessary or unwanted suffering and pain so that they can carry on with their lives as well as possible.

The artificial dichotomizing of the private and the public for ethical purposes is a false dichotomy. Rather, care ethicists see a continuum from the private to the public that is highly interwoven and where it is very difficult to separate one from the other. We bring our private lives into our public lives and the public domain constantly intrudes on our private lives. The two overlap to a considerable degree. More importantly, the issue of ethical behavior is just as relevant to the public domain as to the private domain. And for this issue of domain coverage, an ethic of care claims the broader field of relevance than do the dominant ethical frameworks.

Care, the Market, and Bureaucracy

Riane Eisler (2007), in her book *The Real Wealth of Nations*, makes a cogent argument for an economy that is centered on the concept of care. Among the numerous issues she discusses, she examines the profound centrality of care and the degree to which it is not measured and under-measured as part of what we generally call gross domestic product. All of the unmeasured caring activities—raising children, taking care of family members and friends at times of illness and in old age, volunteer work in the community and around the globe to serve those in need and to repair the environment—do not count as part of the measured output of gross domestic product. And then there are those activities where the market wage for the activity is less than its value to society. Furthermore, Eisler argues, there are numerous activities that are measured and counted as part of the gross domestic product that should be given a negative sign because of their destructive contribution to the constructive development of the human species and the planet. These include, to one degree or another, the war and arms industries and the industries that pollute the environment and produce unsafe products.

I would like to raise some additional issues that circle around the idea of care and the market. The first is the degree to which market price reflects actual cost. There are many government subsidies to companies and industries in the form of tax breaks and direct subsidies that distort market pricing and the market. One example is the government subsidies given to the nuclear power industry in the nuclear fuel cycle and limiting the insurance indemnification for nuclear power accidents. Without the legislated cap on insurance liability, insurance for nuclear power plants would be prohibitive. There are also externalized costs not included in the market price, such as: (1) the significant environmental costs associated with mountain top removal to get to coal or the drilling and production for oil, especially offshore, and the air, water, and ground pollution that is generated by extraction and production processes that dump untreated or only partially treated wastes; (2) the workplace health and safety costs that have been shifted to the employee or not addressed at all; (3) product health and safety costs not reflected in the cost of the product; and (4) the long term environmental costs of waste disposal of both products and packaging and decommissioning of obsolete or abandoned production plants.

A second issue is the degree to which market price reflects value. This is an issue raised by care ethicists, particularly Held (2002, 2006). While Eisler advocates an honest recognition of not only the value of caring activities as well as the appropriate signs to the larger measured set of overall activities, Held raises the issue of whether the market with its sole economic measure is the appropriate place for a range of caring activities, such as child care, education, health care, citizenship development, encouraging cultural activities, and protecting the environment and asks if the market encompasses the most desirable transactions between and among people. Her position is that market norms are driven only by contractarian rights and economic value and, even if there is such a thing as fair competition and fair markets, cannot promote values that reflect an ethic of care and the values associated with it such as sensitivity, attentiveness, empathy, responsiveness, and taking responsibility. She also raises fundamental questions about whether or not there really is fair competition and whether or not all exchanges are voluntary.

Even beyond these issues are those of how one defines the market, what are the rules of the market, and who effectively gets to participate in making the rules of the market. These issues bring in the importance of the institutional context (Peng et al. 2009) of the market. For those who believe in the free market and would prefer to address the issues of care, education, and health care in the market, there are numerous companies and industries that work actively out of the general public view to create the distortions that make the market considerably less than free and perfect. Held makes her position clear:

> Areas such as health care, child care, education, the informing of citizens, and the production of culture could all be thought of as domains in which values other than economic gain should be accorded priority. (2006, 116)

and again:

> The danger is that when we import the language and the concepts of the marketplace and, for instance, evaluate schools in terms of productivity, efficiency, competition, and lower costs, we also import the foundations and goals of the marketplace, which sees these as means to economic gain. (2006, 120)

For Held, the markets are unable to reflect and actively advance values beyond the economic, such as mutually shared care and concern.

Care ethicists are not advocating the dismantling of the market. Held is clear on that point. However, care ethicists are raising the question of the appropriate context for cultivating values that are not market-oriented and the key role that an ethic of care can take there.

Perhaps an even more fundamental issue centers on the declared significance of justice in the public domain that, organizationally, is characterized by bureaucracy as well as hierarchy and competition. If justice as a moral principal is suppose to prevail in the public domain, then why is injustice so widespread in both the governmental and corporate sectors across all societies? Ferguson (1984) examines bureaucracy and hierarchy from a feminist perspective, concluding that bureaucracy and hierarchy are authoritarian tools for control and predictability by the elites. The result is depersonalized organizations, the isolation of individuals, and a society of domination. She then asserts that the relationality and contextuality of feminist ethics offers a significant alternative for a non-bureaucratic and relational approach to organizing that is more congruent with human life as it is actually lived as well as more humane and caring. Thayer (1981) takes a parallel path to examine hierarchy and competition, arriving at a position that is very similar to Fergruson's. Thayer describes the alternative as consensually democratic in process and non-hierarchical in organization. Both Ferguson and Thayer construct arguments that are supportive of Slote's (2007) position for the incompatibility of justice and care and that ask us to question the institutional contexts in which the issue of the choice of a moral framework is made.

Summary

The four issues I have discussed in this section are all integral to the choice of an ethical framework and the organizational context in which it is made. They cannot be avoided. My analysis has been supportive of the overall claim that an ethic of care is more congruent with the realities that we encounter in our daily private and public lives and the fundamental reality that we are all in an interlocking web of constantly changing relationships. An ethic of care, with its emphasis on active and informed engagement in democratic processes and its preference for non-hierarchical and non-bureaucratic organizing, offers a comprehensive moral framework that more accurately reflects human reality, a value of constructive human development, and a practice through which all can benefit developmentally.

Conclusion

Those in the organizational context looking for a rule or universal principle-based ethical framework that holds rational autonomy and justice as the highest form of development will not find it in an ethic of care. Rather, they will find an ethical framework that acknowledges the fundamental relationality and interconnectedness of all humans and one that urges us to move in the direction of bettering the well-being of all, human and non-human. They will find an ethical framework that values all of the sensing and communicative capabilities of the human. They are the cognitive, the affective, the intuitive, and the imaginative, all of which need to be brought to bear in each situation requiring moral judgment as each moral situation is characterized by a unique set of characters, a unique context, and a unique place in the continuity of time. Those capabilities are manifested in such individual competencies as questioning and inquiry, listening, observation, self-reflection, articulation, conversational engagement, practical reasoning, attentiveness, responsiveness, responsibility, and empathy. They will find an ethical framework that acknowledges the highly blurred and amorphous boundary, if one exists at all, between the private and the public domains for morality. And they will find an ethical framework that not only values care-in-relation but also the effective practice of care-in-relation.

Then again, isn't that very congruent with what we expect to find in the organizational context and in the people who work there? Time and again, I hear employees describe their organizational environment as one of dynamic complexity and changing relationships just as we as individuals are continually changing. Do not those for whom we work and with whom we work ask us to understand the rich complexity of what is going on within the organizational setting and in the larger society? Do we not need to bring to bear on that rich and dynamic complexity all of our capabilities and skills as well as an effective ethical stance?

Unless the fundamental agenda of bureaucracy, hierarchy, managerialism, and token nods to the ethicality of organizational activities is to support and sustain the economic, political, and social control by a classist, hierarchical elite, and the ongoing marginalization of numerous groups of peoples, then why not embrace an ethic of care and strive for the well-being of all?

References

Applebaum, B. 1996. But that is not what I mean: Criticizing with care and respect. In *Philosophy of education 1996*, ed. Frank Margonis,77–86. Urbana, IL: Philosophy of Education Society.

Audi, R. 2009. Objectivity without egoism: Toward balance in business ethics. *Academy of Management Learning and Education* 9 (2): 263–274.

Avolio, B.J., and W.L. Gardner 2005. Authentic leadership development: Getting to the root of positive forms of leadership. *Leadership Quarterly* 16 (3): 315–338.

Ayim, M.N. 1997. *The moral parameters of good talk: A feminist analysis*. Waterloo, ON: Wilfred Laurier University Press.

Baier, A.C. 1994. *Moral prejudices: Essays on ethics*. Cambridge, MA: Harvard University Press.

Bartlett, K.T. 1990. Feminist legal methods. *Harvard Law Review* 103 (4): 829–888.

Bass, B.M., and P. Steidlmeier. 1999. Ethics, character, and authentic transformational leadership behavior. *Leadership Quarterly* 10 (2): 181–217.

Binns, J. 2008. The ethics of relational leading: Gender matters. *Gender, Work, and Organization* 15 (6): 600–620.

Blum, L.A. 1988. Gilligan and Kohlberg: Implications for moral theory. *Ethics* 98 (3): 472–491.

Borgerson, J.L. 2007. On the harmony of feminist ethics and business ethics. *Business and Society Review* 112 (4): 477–509.

Bowden, P. 2000. An "ethic of care" in clinical settings: Encompassing "feminine" and "feminist" perspectives. *Nursing Philosophy* 1 (1): 36–49.

Bowie, N.E. 1999. *Business ethics: A Kantian perspective*. Malden, MA: Blackwell.

Boyd, D. 1993. Criticizing with care: Response to Diller. In *Philosophy of Education 1993*, ed. Audrey Thompson, 246–249. Urbana, IL: Philosophy of Education Society.

Brenkert, G.G., and T.L. Beauchamp. eds. 2010. *The Oxford handbook of business ethics*. New York, NY: Oxford University Press.

Brown, M.E., and L.K. Trevino. 2006. Ethical leadership: A review and future directions. *Leadership Quarterly* 17 (6): 595–616.

Burton, B.K., and C.P. Dunn. 1996. Feminist ethics as moral grounding for stakeholder theory. *Business Ethics Quarterly* 6 (2): 133–147.

Burton, B.K., and C.P. Dunn. 2005. The caring approach and social issues in management education. *Journal of Management Education* 29 (3): 453–474.

Buttner, E.H. 2004. How do we "dis" students?: A model of (dis)respectful business instructor behavior. *Journal of Management Education* 28 (3): 647–673.

Byrne, R.M.J. 2005. *The rational imagination: How people create alternatives to reality*. Cambridge, MA: MIT Press.

Caputo, R.K. 2002. Social justice, the ethics of care, and market economies. *Families in Society: The Journal of Contemporary Human Services* 83 (4): 355–364.

Cardol, M., B.A. DeJong, and C.D. Ward. 2002. On autonomy and participation in rehabilitation. *Disability and Rehabilitation* 24 (18): 970–974.

Clement, G. 1996. *Care, autonomy, and justice: Feminism and an ethic of care*. Boulder, CO: Westview Press.

Crane, A., A. McWilliams, D. Matten, J. Moon, and D.S. Siegel. (eds.). 2008. *The Oxford handbook of corporate social responsibility*. New York, NY: Oxford University Press.

Cronqvist, A., T. Theorell, T. Burns, and K. Lutzen. 2004. Caring about—caring for: Moral obligations and work responsibilities in intensive care nursing. *Nursing Ethics* 11 (1): 63–76.

Cunliffe, A.L. 2009. The philosopher leader: On relationalism, ethics and reflexivity—A critical perspective to teaching leadership. *Management Learning* 40 (1): 87–101.
Curzer, H.J. 1993. Fry's concept of care in nursing ethics. *Hypatia* 8 (3): 174–183.
Dalmiya, V. 2002. Why should a knower care? *Hypatia* 17 (1): 34–52.
Damasio, A. 1994. *Descartes' error: Emotion, reason, and the human brain*. New York, NY: Penguin Books.
Darwall, S.L. 1977. Two kinds of respect. *Ethics* 88 (1): 36–49.
Delios, A. 2010. How can organizations be competitive but dare to care? *Academy of Management Perspective* 24 (3): 25–36.
DeMoss, M.A., and G.K. McCann. 1997. Without a care in the world: The business ethics course and its exclusion of a care perspective. *Journal of Business Ethics* 16 (4): 435–443.
Deveaux, M. 1995. Shifting paradigms: Theorizing care and justice in political theory. *Hypatia* 10 (2): 115–119.
Dienhart, J.W. 2000. Just caring, caring justice. *Business and Society Review* 105 (2): 247–267.
Diller, A. 1993. Can we reach a rapprochement between educational criticism and nurturance? In *Philosophy of Education 1993*, ed. Audrey Thompson, 238–245. Urbana, IL: Philosophy of Education Society.
Diller, A. 1996. Criticizing with care and respect for what we are all up against. In *Philosophy of Education 1996*, ed. Frank Margonis, 86–89. Urbana, IL: Philosophy of Education Society.
Eisler, R. 2007. *The real wealth of nations: Creating a caring economics*. San Francisco, CA: Berrett-Koehler Publishers.
Ellington, J.W. 1983. *Ethical philosophy (Kant)* (trans). Indianapolis, IN: Hacket Publishing Company.
Engster, D. 2007. *The heart of justice: Care ethics and political theory*. New York, NY: Oxford University Press.
Ferguson, K.E. 1984. *The feminist case against bureaucracy*. Philadelphia, PA: Temple University Press.
Fesmire, S. 2003. *John Dewey and moral imagination*. Bloomington, IN: Indiana University Press.
Fiumara, G.C. 1990. *The other side of language: A philosophy of listening*. London: Routledge.
Flanagan, O.J. 1982a. Virtue, sex, and gender: Some philosophical reflections on the moral psychology debate. *Ethics* 92 (3): 499–512.
Flanagan, O.J. 1982b. A reply to Lawrence Kohlberg. *Ethics* 92 (3): 529–532.
Flanagan, D., and K. Jackson 1987. Justice, care, and gender: The Kohlberg-Gilligan debate revisited. *Ethics* 97: 622–637.
Folbre, N. 2001. *The invisible heart: Economics and family values*. New York, NY: New Press.
Freeman, R.E. 1984. *Strategic management: A stakeholder approach*. Boston, MA: Pitman.
Freeman, R.E. 1994. The politics of stakeholder theory: Some future directions. *Business Ethics Quarterly* 4 (4): 409–421.
Freeman, R.E. 1999. Divergent stakeholder theory. *Academy of Management Review* 24 (2): 233–236.
Freeman, R.E. 2010. *Stakeholder theory: The state of the art*. New York, NY: Cambridge University Press.
Freeman, R.E., J.S. Harrison, and A.C. Wicks 2007. *Managing for stakeholders: Survival, reputation, success*. New Haven, CT: Yale University Press.
French, W., and A. Weis. 2000. An ethics of care or an ethics of justice. *Journal of Business Ethics* 27 (1/2): 125–136.
Friedman, M. 1993. *What are friends for? Feminist perspectives on personal relationships and moral theory*. Ithaca, NY: Cornell University Press.
Friedman, A., and S. Miles 2006. *Stakeholders: Theory and practice*. New York, NY: Oxford University Press.
Fry, S.T. 1989. The role of caring in a theory of nursing ethics. *Hypatia* 4 (2): 88–103.
Gabriel, Y. 2009. Reconciling an ethic of care with critical management pedagogy. *Management Learning* 40 (4): 379–385.

Gavison, R. 1992. Feminism and the public/private distinction. *Stanford Law Review* 45 (1): 1–45.
Gaylin, W. 1976. *Caring*. New York, NY: Alfred A. Knopf.
Gazzaniga, M.S. 2005. *The ethical brain*. New York, NY: Dana Press.
Gilligan, C. 1977. In a different voice: Women's conceptions of self and of morality. *Harvard Educational Review* 17 (1): 481–517.
Gilligan, C. 1982. *In a different voice*. Cambridge, MA: Harvard University Press.
Gini, A. 1997. Moral leadership: An overview. *Journal of Business Ethics* 16 (3): 323–330.
Goldstein, L.S. 1999. The relational zone: The role of caring relationships in the co-construction of mind. *American Education Research Journal* 36 (3): 647–673.
Govier, T. 1997. *Social trust and human communities*. Montreal, QC: McGill Queens University Press.
Govier, T. 1999. *Dilemmas of trust*. Montreal, QC: McGill Queens University Press.
Greene, M. 1995. *Releasing the imagination*. San Francisco, CA: Jossey-Bass Publishing.
Gremmen, I. 1999. Visiting nurses' situated ethics: Beyond "care versus justice". *Nursing Ethics* 6 (6): 515–527.
Gutman, A. 1993. Can virtue be taught to lawyers? *Stanford Law Review* 45 (6): 1759–1771.
Haegert, S. 2004. The ethics of self. *Nursing Ethics* 11 (5): 434–443.
Haidt, J. 2001. The emotional dog and its rational tail: A social intuitionist approach to moral judgement. *Psychological Review* 108 (4): 814–834.
Haidt, J. 2003. The emotional dog does learn new tricks: A reply to Pizzaro and Bloom (2003). *Psychological Review* 110 (1): 197–198.
Hamington, M., and D.C. Miller. (eds.). 2006. *Socializing care: Feminist ethics and public issues*. Lanham, MD: Rowan and Littlefield Publishers.
Hankivsky, O. 2004. *Social policy and the ethic of care*. Vancouver, BC: University of British Columbia Press.
Hawk, T.F., and P.R. Lyons 2008. Please don't give up on me: When faculty fail to care. *Journal of Management Education* 32 (3): 316–338.
Held, V. 1993. *Feminist morality: Transforming culture, society, and politics*. Chicago, IL: University of Chicago Press.
Held, V. (ed.). 1995a. *Justice and care: Readings in feminist ethics*. Boulder, CO: Westview Press.
Held, V. 1995b. The meshing of care and justice. *Hypatia* 10 (2): 128–132.
Held, V. 2002. Care and the extension of markets. *Hypatia* 17 (2): 19–33.
Held, V. 2006. *Ethics of care: Personal, political, and global*. London: Oxford University Press.
Hendry, J. 2001. Economic contracts versus social relationships as a foundation for normative stakeholder theory. *Business Ethics: A European Review* 10 (3): 223–232.
Henry, S.E. 2001. What happens when we use Kohlberg? His troubling functionalism and the potential of pragmatism in moral education. *Educational Theory* 51 (1): 259–276.
Heyes, C.J. 1997. Anti-essentialism in practice: Carol Gilligan and feminist philosophy. *Hypatia* 12 (3): 142–163.
Higgins, T.E. 1997. Democracy and feminism. *Harvard Law Review* 110 (8): 1657–1703.
Hoffman, M.L. 2000. *Empathy and moral development*. New York, NY: Cambridge University Press.
Holmes, C.E. 2004. *Handle with care: The significance of caring in academic advising*. Unpublished doctoral dissertation, University of Texas, Austin, TX.
Holtman, S.W. 2003. Three strategies for theorizing about justice. *American Philosophical Quarterly* 40 (2): 77–90.
Hult, R.E. 1980. On pedagogical caring. *Educational Theory* 29 (3): 237–243.
Irwin, T. 1985. *Nichomachean ethics (Aristotle)* (trans). Indianapolis, IN: Hacket Publishing Company.
Jacobs, D.C. 2009. Dialogue on Locke's business ethics. *Academy of Management Learning and Education* 8 (2): 259–262.
Jaggar, A.M. 1983. *Feminist politics and human nature*. Lanham, MD: Rowan and Littlefield.

Johnson, M. 1993. *Moral imagination: Implications of cognitive science for ethics*. Chicago, IL: University of Chicago Press.
Johnston, D.K. 2006. *Educating for a caring society: Classroom relationships and moral action*. New York, NY: Teachers College Press.
Jones, T., W. Felps, and G.A. Bigley 2007. Ethical theory and stakeholder-related decisions: The role of stakeholder culture. *Academy of Management Review* 32 (1): 137–155.
Kahn, W.A. 1990. Toward an agenda for business ethics research. *Academy of Management Review* 15 (2): 311–328.
Kahn, W.A. 1993. Caring for the caregivers: Patterns of organizational caregiving. *Administrative Science Quarterly* 38 (4): 539–563.
Kashdan, T. 2009. *Curious?* New York, NY: William Morrow.
Katz, M., N. Noddings, and K.A. Strike. 1999. *Justice and caring: The search for common ground in education*. New York, NY: Teachers College Press.
Kekes, J. 1991. Moral imagination, freedom, and the humanities. *American Philosophical Quarterly* 28 (2): 101–111.
Kekes, J. 2006. *The enlargement of life: Moral imagination at work*. Ithaca, NY: Cornell University Press.
Keller, J. 1997. Autonomy, relationality, and feminist ethics. *Hypatia* 12 (2): 152–164.
Kittay, E.F. 2001. A feminist public ethic of care meets the new communitarian family policy. *Ethics* 111 (3): 523–547.
Kittay, E.F., and D.T. Meyers. (eds.). 1987. *Women and moral theory*. Lanham, MD: Rowan and Littlefield.
Kohlberg, L. 1969. Stage and sequence: The cognitive-development approach to socialization. In *Handbook of socialization theory*, ed. D.A. Goslin, 347–480. Chicago, IL: Rand McNally.
Kohlberg, L. 1981. *Essays on Moral Development. Vol.1, The Philosophy of Moral Development*. New York, NY: Harper and Row.
Kohlberg, L. 1982. A reply to Owen Flanagan and some comments on the Puka-Goodpaster exchange. *Ethics* 92 (3): 513–528.
Krebs, D.L., and K. Denton. 2005. Toward a more pragmatic approach to morality: A critical evaluation of Kohlberg's model. *Psychological Review* 112 (3): 629–649.
Kroeger-Mappes, J. 1994. The ethic of care vis-à-vis the ethics of rights: A problem for contemporary moral theory. *Hypatia* 9 (3): 108–131.
LeDoux, J. 1996. *The emotional brain*. New York, NY: Simon and Schuster.
LeDoux, J. 2002. *The synaptic self*. New York, NY: Penguin Books.
Liedtka, J.M. 1996. Feminist morality and competitive reality: A role for an ethic of care. *Business Ethics Quarterly* 6 (2): 179–200.
Liedtka, J.M. 1998. Constructing an ethic for business practice: Competing effectively and doing good. *Business and Society* 37 (3): 254–280.
Locke, E. 2006. Business ethics: A way out of the morass. *Academy of Management Learning and Education* 5 (3): 324–332.
Machold, S., P.K. Ahmad, and S.S. Farquhar 2008. Corporate governance and ethics: A feminist perspective. *Journal of Business Ethics* 81 (3): 665–678.
MacIntyre, A. 1981/2007. *After virtue*. Notre Dame, IN: University of Notre Dame Press.
MacIntyre, A. 1988. *Whose justice? Which rationality?* Notre Dame, IN: University of Notre Dame Press.
MacKinnon, C.A. 1989. *Toward a feminist theory of the state*. Cambridge, MA: Harvard University Press.
Marshall, C., J.A. Patterson, D.L. Rogers, and J.R. Steele 1996. Caring as career: An alternative perspective for educational administration. *Educational Administration Quarterly* 32 (2): 271–294.
Maxwell, B. 2010. Does ethical theory have a place in post-Kohlbergian moral psychology? *Education Theory* 60 (2): 167–188.
Mayeroff, M. 1965. On caring. *The International Philosophical Quarterly* September: 462–474.

Mayeroff, M. 1971. *On caring*. New York, NY: Harper and Row.
McAllister, D.J., and G.A. Bigley 2002. Work context and the definition of self: How organizational care influences organization-based self-esteem. *Academy of Management Journal* 45 (5): 894–904.
Mele, D. 2008. Corporate social theories. In *The Oxford handbook of corporate social responsibility*, ed. A. Crane, A. McWilliams, D. Matten, J. Moon, and D. Siegel., 47–82. New York, NY: Oxford University Press.
Mill, J.S. 1969. *Utilitarianism*. Toronto, ON: University of Toronto Press.
Mills, C.W. 1959. *The sociological imagination*. London: Oxford University Press.
Minnich, E.K. 1990. *Transforming knowledge*. Philadelphia, PA: Temple University Press.
Noblit, G.W. 1993. Power and caring. *American Educational Research Journal* 30 (1): 23–38.
Noddings, N. 1984. *Caring: A feminine approach to ethics and moral education*. Berkeley, CA: University of California Press.
Noddings, N. 1988. An ethic of caring and its implications for instructional arrangements. *American Journal of Education* 96 (2): 215–230.
Noddings, N. 1992. *The challenge to care in schools: An alternative approach to education*. New York, NY: Teachers College Press.
Noddings, N. 2002. *Starting at home: Caring and social policy*. Berkeley, CA: University of California Press.
Peng, M.W., S.L. Sun, B. Pinkham, and H. Chen 2009. The institution-based view as a third leg for a strategy tripod. *Academy of Management Perspectives* 23 (3): 63–81.
Phillips, R. 2003. *Stakeholder theory and organizational ethics*. San Francisco, CA: Berrett-Koehler.
Pierce, S.F. 1997. A model for conceptualizing the moral dynamic in health care. *Nursing Ethics* 4 (6): 483–495.
Puka, B. 1982. An interdisciplinary treatment of Kohlberg. *Ethics* 92 (3): 468–490.
Puka, B. 1990. The liberation of caring; A different voice for Gilligan's "Different Voice". *Hypatia* 5 (1): 58–82.
Rawls, J. 1971. *A theory of justice*. Cambridge, MA: Harvard University Press.
Rawls, J. 2001. *Justice as fairness*. Cambridge, MA: Belknap Harvard.
Reiter, S.A. 1996. The Kohlberg-Gilligan controversy: Lessons for accounting ethics education. *Critical Perspectives on Accounting* 7 (1): 33–54.
Reiter, S. 1997. The ethics of care and new paradigms for accounting practice. *Accounting, Auditing, and Accountability Journal* 10 (3): 299–324.
Rhode, D.L. 1990. Feminist critical theories. *Stanford Law Review* 42 (3): 617–638.
Rhode, D.L. 1993. Missing questions: Feminist perspectives on legal education. *Stanford Law Review* 45 (6): 1547–1569.
Rhode, D.L. (ed.). 2006. *Moral leadership: The theory and practice of power, judgment, and policy*. San Francisco, CA: Jossey-Bass.
Robinson, F. 1999. *Globalizing care: Ethics, feminist theory, and international relations*. Boulder, CO: Westview Press.
Rooney, P. 1994. Recent work in feminist discussions of reason. *American Philosophical Quarterly* 31 (1): 1–21.
Rorty, A. 1988. *Mind in action: Essays in the philosophy of mind*. Boston, MA: Beacon Press.
Rowley, T.J. 1997. Moving beyond dyadic ties: A network theory of stakeholder influence. *Academy of Management Review* 22 (4): 887–910.
Ruddick, S. 1980. Maternal thinking. *Feminist Studies* 6: 342–367.
Ruddick, S. 1990. *Maternal thinking: Toward a politics of peace*. New York, NY: Balantine Books.
Rumsey, J.P. 1997. Justice, care, and questionable dichotomies. *Hypatia* 12 (1): 99–113.
Schwartz, J.M., and S. Begley 2002. *The mind and the brain: Neuroplasticity and the power of mental force*. New York, NY: Harper Perennial.
Sevenhuijsen, S. 2003. The place of care: The relevance of the feminist ethic of care fro social policy. *Feminist Theory* 4 (2): 179–197.

Sevenhuijsen, S. 1998. *Citizenship and the ethic of care: Feminist considerations on justive, morality and politics*. New York, NY: Routledge.
Simola, S. 2007. The pragmatics of care in sustainable global enterprise. *Journal of Business Ethics* 74 (2): 131–147.
Slote, M. 2007. *The ethics of care and empathy*. New York, NY: Routledge.
Smith, A.M. 2008. Neoliberalism, welfare policy, and feminist theories of social justice. *Feminist Theory* 9 (2): 131–144.
Snow, N.E. 2000. Empathy. *American Philosophical Quarterly* 37 (1): 65–78.
Solomon, R.C. 1988. On emotion as judgments. *American Philosophical Quarterly* 25 (2): 183–191.
St. Clair, V. 2001. Caring: The moral motivation for good occupational therapy practice. *Australian Occupational Therapy Journal* 48 (4): 187–199.
Sterba, J.P. 1986. Recent work on alternative conceptions of justice. *American Philosophical Quarterly* 23 (1): 1–22.
Tarlier, D.S. 2004. Beyond caring: The moral and ethical bases of responsive nurse-patient relationships. *Nursing Philosophy* 5 (3): 230–241.
Thayer, F.C. 1981. *An end to hierarchy and competition: Administration in the post-affluent world*. New York, NY: Franklin Watts.
Thayer-Bacon, B.J. 1993. Caring and its relationship to critical thinking. *Educational Theory* 43 (3): 323–340.
Thayer-Bacon, B.J. 2000. *Transforming critical thinking: Constructive thinking*. New York, NY: Teachers College Press.
Thayer-Bacon, B.J. 2003. *Relational epistemologies*. New York, NY: Peter Lang.
Trevino, L.K., G.R. Weaver, and S.J. Reynolds 2006. Behavioral ethics in organizations: A review. *Journal of Management* 32 (6): 951–990.
Tronto, J. 1993. *Moral boundaries: A political argument for an ethic of care*. New York, NY: Routledge, Chapman, and Hall.
Udovicki, J. 1993. Justice and care in close relationships. *Hypatia* 8 (3): 48–60.
Uhl-Bien, M. 2006. Relational leadership theory: Exploring the social processes of leadership and organizing. *Leadership Quarterly* 17 (6): 654–676.
Victor, B., and J.B. Cullen 1988. The organizational bases of ethical work climates. *Administrative Science Quarterly* 33 (1): 101–125.
Von Krogh, G. 1998. Caring in knowledge creation. *California Management Review* 40 (3): 133–153.
Von Krogh, G., K. Ichijo, and I. Nonaka 2000. *Enabling knowledge creation*. New York, NY: Oxford University Press.
Walker, M.U. 2007. *Moral understandings: A feminist study in ethics*. New York, NY: Oxford University Press.
Waterman, A.S. 1988. On the uses of psychological theory and research in the process of ethical inquiry. *Psychological Bulletin* 103 (3): 283–298.
Werhane, P.H. 1999. *Moral imagination and management decision making*. New York, NY: Oxford University Press.
Wicks, A.C., D.R. Gilbert, and R.E. Freeman 1994. A feminist reinterpretation of the stakeholder concept. *Business Ethics Quarterly* 4 (4): 475–497.
Wilber, K. 2001. *No boundary: Eastern and western approaches to personal growth*. Boston, MA: Shambhala Publications.
Zull, J.E. 2002. *The art of changing the brain: Enriching teaching by exploring the biology of learning*. Sterling, VA: Stylus.

Chapter 2
Care Ethics and Markets: A View from Feminist Economics

Julie A. Nelson

Introduction

Addressing the question of how, or whether, care ethics is relevant to the world of commerce is full of potential pitfalls—pitfalls that arise from our common dualistic patterns of thought. One such trap, as discussed in the Introduction to this volume, is the belief women do care ethics, while men do justice ethics. This bowdlerized and incomplete version of the story has, unfortunately, become much popularized.[1] If we think that Gilligan discovered a *new* type of moral understanding or *women*'s type of moral understanding, I believe we miss the most important insight of her work. Gilligan's (1982) work is remarkable because it brought to light a modality that was *already in widespread use*, but whose existence had been made invisible by existing traditions of philosophical thought. Her recognition and articulation of care ethics began to make discussion of it intellectually respectable.

A second problematic pattern is our tendency to think that social life and economic life happen in distinct spheres. While we may grant that interpersonal, family, and civic life are laden with meaning, ethical depth, and opportunities for care, we may believe that, in contrast, modern capitalist, market-oriented, competitive economic life obeys its own impersonal and mechanical rules. Many people dismiss the notion of "business ethics" entirely—as an oxymoron—because they believe that firms, being inherently driven to maximize profits, simply do not have any ethical decision-making space. Among those who admit a role for ethics, many see a role for certain impersonal rational ethical principles, but find the (presumed) insertion of "touchy-feely" care concerns too far-fetched. And then there are those who put more

[1] As I write, the Wikipedia entry on "care ethics" is disseminating this view, and it has even infiltrated at least one textbook on business ethics (see citation in Borgerson 2007). Care ethics is sometimes even referred to as "the feminist" approach. In fact, the question of what is—and is not—feminist about care ethics is a topic of lively debate (Borgerson 2007; Tong and Williams 2009).

J.A. Nelson (✉)
University of Massachusetts Boston, Boston, MA, USA
e-mail: julie.nelson@umb.edu

M. Hamington, M. Sander-Staudt (eds.), *Applying Care Ethics to Business*, Issues in Business Ethics 34, DOI 10.1007/978-90-481-9307-3_2,
© Springer Science+Business Media B.V. 2011

priority on ethics, and less on preservation of current systems, and conclude that if we want a more humane economy we must first destroy the impersonal capitalist machine. That is, they believe we must completely turn our backs on large-scale, corporate, global, privately-owned, and/or profit-making enterprises and competition, and build a new economy based on small scale, noncorporate, local, worker- or community-owned, nonprofit enterprises and cooperation. Note that whether they are defending capitalism from care ethics, or care ethics from capitalism, all of these commentators agree that capitalism and care ethics are intrinsically incompatible.

Insights from the field of feminist economics can help us explore care ethics and its relevance for contemporary business, and aid in achieving rich and nuanced analysis, because it challenges these dualistic conventional understandings of both gender and economic behavior at deep levels. The image of "economic man"—the character who is said to populate the (presumed) free market automaton—is recognized, within feminist economics, as being both heavily gendered and entirely mythical. If individuals, businesses, and markets really were so impersonal and mechanical, then care ethics would, indeed, be inapplicable. But what if this image is wildly misleading, as a guide to actual economic life?

This essay argues that neither abandoning economies to care-free functioning, nor trying to invent a completely new economic system, are intellectually defensible or practically implementable answers to the very severe contemporary economic problems we face. Parallel to the case of Gilligan and moral development, I make the case that what we need to do, instead, is bring existing modalities of economic behavior to light, and argue for granting them intellectual respectability. We can "discover" and articulate the importance of care issues that have been there all along. Only after we have accomplished this, can we think pragmatically about what it would mean to have a more humane economy—and perhaps help create the space for actions directed to making it come about.

Beyond Economic Man

The field of feminist economics, in its contemporary incarnation, began to bloom with the 1993 publication of *Beyond Economic Man: Feminist Theory and Economics* (Ferber and Nelson 1993). While feminists had earlier noted that women and women's traditional experiences were much neglected in the mainstream economics discipline, by the late 1980s a number of us had also noticed that the very definition, core assumptions, central models, and preferred methods of mainstream economics were distinctly gender biased.

Dualistic Thinking—Insights from Philosophy

As a number of writers on the history and philosophy of science (e.g., Easlea 1980; Keller 1985; Harding 1986) had pointed out during the 1980s, dualisms such as those shown in Table 2.1 have underlain much of Western philosophy and culture. Rationality, autonomy, and math, for example, all have masculine cultural

Table 2.1 Splitting the world: Western philosophy

Higher order	Lower order
mind	body
rationality	emotion
autonomy	dependence
self-interest	other-interest
quantitative	qualitative
general	particular
masculine	feminine

associations, while emotion, dependence, and qualitative analysis have all been commonly seen as more feminine. What is more, the dualism is hierarchical, with the masculine-associated side generally considered to be of higher value. This was institutionalized into notions of science during its Enlightenment-era origins, when, for example, the scientific enterprise was described as an attempt to "raise a masculine Philosophy . . . whereby the Mind of Man may be ennobled with the knowledge of Solid Truths" (Henry Oldenburg, an early Secretary of the British Royal Society, quoted in Keller 1985, 52).

It is critically important to note here that the point being made is about *how we think*, not about differences between men and women. Feminists often make a distinction between "sex" and "gender," wherein "sex" is used to refer to biological differences between males and females, while "gender" refers to cultural beliefs constructed on the base of (preponderant) sexual dimorphism.[2] So the issue is not whether men, for example, have more mind or less body than women: They manifestly do not. Rather, the point is that there is a deep *cultural pattern* of defining male as being dichotomously different from, and superior to, female, and defining minds as being radically disconnected from, and superior to, nature, matter, and emotion.

Dualistic Thinking—Insights from Psychology

Although currently immensely popular, questions of whether male or female brains are wired differently, with differing tendencies towards one sort of behavior or another, are rather irrelevant to this point about cultural patterns. While findings of differences are made much of, empirical studies actually tend to show large overlaps in the distributions of the vast majority of male and female capacities and behaviors (Jaffee and Hyde 2000; Hyde 2005). (Those who strongly associate women with care, for example, would do well to remember Margaret Thatcher—as well as involved fathers.)

[2]Recent feminist literature has become more complicated as scholars deal with intersexuality, transsexuality, and the like. But the sex/gender distinction provides a rough typology that is useful when examining cultural stereotypes.

But while contemporary psychology does not support the existence of hard-and-fast, categorical differences in behavior between the sexes, it does confirm that we *love to think* in terms of hard-and-fast, categorical differences! Psychologists have found that our brains tend to perceive the world through cognitive routines that save on mental effort by lumping wide ranges of qualities and objects together into simple categorizations and associations, among which masculinity/femininity is a noticeable case (Bem 1981; Knutson et al. 2007; Nosek et al. 2007). Laboratory studies show that people tend to recognize and process information more quickly when it fits into pre-existing *gender schema* (such as Table 2.1) than when it conflicts.[3] While such mental shortcuts often harmlessly speed up our thinking, they can also severely limit and bias our thinking. Being able to respond to stimuli in ways *contrary* to an existing schema is often interpreted as a sign of mental agility, in the psychological research.

A Brief History of "Economic Man"

So how do these philosophical insights and psychological research relate to the image of "economic man"? Mainstream economic theories are built on the assumption that humans function as individual, autonomous, rational, self-interested actors—all masculine-stereotyped terms. Let us take a brief look at the historical development of this notion.

In part, it goes back to the eighteenth century work of Adam Smith (Smith 1776 [2001]). Although Smith was a much more complex thinker than his modern legacy would suggest, one part of his thought has had a profound impact on how we think about economics: Smith suggested that economies could be seen as functioning like giant machines, in which the "invisible hand" of markets magically channels the energy of individual self-interest into service of the social good. At the time that Smith wrote, of course, machinery was radically changing people's lives, and Newtonian physics—which explained many mechanical phenomena—seemed the epitome of science. So it was understandable that he applied such a mechanical metaphor to economic life. Smith laid the groundwork for thinking about economies in mechanical, a-social, self-interest-oriented terms.

But the full-fledged notion of "economic man" did not really get developed until the nineteenth century, when John Stuart Mill (1836) attempted to lay the groundwork for a discipline of economics that would be both fully scientific and carefully demarcated from other endeavors. Mill explicitly peeled off many dimensions of human experience: human bodies were considered to be the topic of the natural

[3]It is also possible to enter this topic of biased or schematic thinking through linguistics and philosophy, by examining the role of metaphor in shaping how we think (Lakoff and Johnson 1980). See Nelson (1992) and for applications to up-down thinking about gender, Nelson (2006) for an application to the "economy is a machine" metaphor, and Hamington (2009) for an application to the "business is a game" metaphor.

sciences; conscience and duty were consigned by Mill to the realm of ethics; life in society was given its own discipline. What was left for economics to deal with was "man [sic] . . . solely as a being who desires to possess wealth, and who is capable of judging of the comparative efficacy of means for obtaining that end" (38). This added an assumption of rationality to the idea of "economic man" as a-social and self-interested.

Why did Mill believe that he had to separate out a very thin slice of human life for analysis by each of the various fields? He believed that this was required by the nature of *science*. Significantly, his model for science was geometry, and its methodology of reasoning from abstract principles. Mill, to his credit, argued that no economist would ever be "so absurd as to suppose that mankind" is really described by only the parts of human nature selected for study in economics (38). Unfortunately, however, what remained and flourished in later economic thought was not Mill's modesty concerning the ad hoc premises and limited applicability of the geometry-like discipline he proposed, but rather his idea that economics must base itself on an image of autonomous, rational, self-interested beings in order to be "scientific." This approach received a big boost in the late nineteenth century when "neoclassical" economists found that they could mathematically formalize Mill's idea of desiring the greatest wealth.

The inventors of neoclassical economics assumed that individual consumers or workers are rational, self-interested, autonomous agents who maximize a mathematical function that represents their levels of satisfaction or utility. By analogy, firms were seen as rational, autonomous actors who maximize a mathematical function that represents their profits, that is, excess of revenues over costs. These assumptions continue to form the core of mainstream economic analysis today.

What is Left Out

Note, then, that the notion of "economic man" is doubly gendered. First, in leaving out all aspects of human life having to do with bodies, emotion, dependence, or other-interest, it highlights only culturally masculine-associated notions of humanity, while blocking out consideration of feminine-associated ones. Not only are the occupations of feeding, cleaning, and nursing bodies (traditionally assigned to women) made invisible, but *everyone*'s experiences of social life in general and of dependency in childhood, illness, and old age in particular, are denied. "Economic man," in contrast to real humans, neither ever needs care nor has any responsibility or desire to give it. Secondly, the origin of, and continued allegiance to, "economic man" reflects the impact of a gender-biased view of scientific endeavor, which prioritizes mathematical and abstract thinking, and denigrates qualitative analysis or delving into particulars. In attempting to achieve "scientific" status, the discipline of economics has, ironically, instead fallen into dogma. A certain biased methodological view has led to a dogged allegiance to the assumption of self-interested agents and mechanical markets, when a more impartial and empirical examination of economic life (see below) leads to quite different conclusions. Feminist economics criticizes standard, neoclassical approaches not because (with all their math) they are too objective, but because (with all their dogma) they are not objective enough. The discipline has been to use a card came analogy, playing with only half a deck.

And the problem is not just with academic economics. Neoclassical notions of profit maximization and competition have saturated the popular image of economic life. The rigid, gender-schematic thinking that shaped the roots of economic thought from Enlightenment times has since then become a fully-bloomed thicket that traps our thought.

An Alternative to Dichotomous Thinking

As a tool for developing a more flexible—less biased, and less arbitrarily hierarchical—sort of thinking, a "gender-value compass" (Nelson 1992; 1996) may be useful. Instead of thinking of masculine-superior and feminine-inferior polarities, as shown in Table 2.1, what happens if gender and value are instead considered as marking out distinct dimensions, as shown in Fig. 2.1?

That is, what both masculine- and feminine-associated characteristics and behaviors are acknowledged as having both positive and negative dimensions?

For example, take the stereotype that men are more individuated and autonomous than women, while women are more embedded in relationships. In actuality, of course, men could not survive without having been raised in families and permeated by the values and customs of their societies and women have identities and wills of their own. We are all, in fact, *both* individuated and connected in relationships, as illustrated in the top half of Fig. 2.2. The positive complementarity between the top two cells indicates that both our individuality and our interrelatedness can be celebrated. But what if we try to have one without the other? The myth of the "separative" self pretends that complete isolation is possible; the myth of the "soluble" self pretends that individual boundaries can be made to totally disappear (Nelson 1992; England 2003). For example, the cultural idea that a man, Mr. John Jones, can be "self-made," while a woman becomes Mrs. John Jones when she marries, illustrates the negative complementarity between the bottom two cells.

"Economic man" is a perfect example of a mythical separative self. This myth needs to be challenged, but not by an opposing emphasis on equally mythical, stereotypically feminine-associated ideals of boundlessness and harmonious

Masculine, Positive	Feminine, Positive
Masculine, Negative	Feminine, Negative

Fig. 2.1 The Gender-Value Compass

Fig. 2.2 Individuality and Relation in the Gender-Value Compass

M+ individual	F+ related
M– separative	F– soluble

solubility. Rather, we need to get more sophisticated in our thinking, realizing the possibilities of both/and, rather than a dualistic either/or.

Discussions of ethics, and discussions of markets, are often marked by exactly such traps of either/or thinking. With some practice, these too can be overcome.

Implications for Ethics

Discussions of care ethics and justice ethics often tend to fall into an either/or dichotomy: either one applies universal rational principles (justice) *or* one emphasizes the arising of particular sentiments and personal relations of responsibility (care). But can these really be separated?

Care Within Justice

Consider, as a first example, the "Heinz dilemma," one of the stories used in Gilligan's path breaking work. A subject is asked to consider the situation of a man named Heinz, whose wife is deathly ill. He cannot afford a drug which might save her life. Should Heinz steal the drug? This story had been used by psychologist Lawrence Kohlberg as a way to assess a subject's progress towards ethical reasoning using principles of justice: The ethically mature subject should (presumably) weigh the principle of protecting life against the principle of protecting property, and conclude that since life is more important, Heinz should steal the drug. Gilligan found her subjects, instead, often worried about who would care for the wife if Heinz went to jail, how the theft might affect the druggist's family, whether some kind of agreement could be worked out between Heinz and the druggist, and so on—efforts to try to maintain relationships while also meeting needs. If we think dichotomously, we tend to see the Kohlberg-Gilligan debate as a matter of an ethic of justice *versus* an ethic of care. Gilligan appears to have raised an *alternative* orientation to that of reasoning about individual rights and principles.

But consider some variations on the Heinz dilemma. What if, instead of asking, "Should Heinz steal the drug to save his wife's life?" subjects were asked "Should Heinz steal to save his neighbor's life?" or "Should Heinz steal to save a stranger's life?" Presumably, if the principle of life versus property were all that was involved, the answer "Heinz should steal" should remain the same. But few people, I think, believe that ethics demand that we have infinite responsibility. If we ask ourselves to "Should I be willing to risk everything to save a stranger's life—and do I actually do this?" the answer is clearly "no." So *within the very question* that is supposedly (by the Kohlbergian view) about universal principles, is an *implicit* base of assumptions about interpersonal relations, particular responsibilities, and care. While mere "principle" should not count a wife as more valuable than a stranger; actual relationships and practice show us that, as humans, we do not act simply on mere principle. Questions of appropriate relationships, appropriate conduct within relationships, and the degree of merited *self*-care all—of necessity—arise and demand to be balanced. This example illustrates how Gilligan did not discover some new sort of ethical approach, but rather uncovered and articulated a dimension that was already there.

Care, Perhaps, Before Justice

Another example of how justice and care are complementary or intertwined comes from contemporary research on the roles of reason and emotion in individuals' ethical judgments and action. In studies using brain imaging, observation of people with specific brain damage, and other techniques, psychologists have found that moral judgment is—initially at least, and often entirely—more a matter of affective moral response than of moral reasoning (Greene et al. 2001; Haidt 2001; Greene and Haidt 2002). Moral reasoning, rather than being part of the process of coming to a judgment, is more often involved in possible *post hoc* justifications of a judgment already arrived at intuitively. That is, we sense the "rightness" or "wrongness" of something, and then may work to come up with reasons and principles that justify what we feel. This is not to say that moral reasoning plays *no* role—people may in some circumstances consciously reflect on their intuitive judgments, and then change their mind. But research suggests, that this occurs be relatively rarely.

For questions of positive moral *action*—as opposed to moral judgment—emotional responses such as empathy, sadness, and shame seem to be particularly important, while the role of moral reasoning is particularly weak. One can be an expert on the many ways of formulating principles of justice, but if one does not *care* about acting justly, all the principles in the world will have no effect on behavior.[4]

These current trends in research also emphasize the social and cultural aspects of moral judgments. Individuals do not develop their moral capabilities in a vacuum. While overt structures of legal and social rewards and sanctions obviously have substantial effects on the behavior of individuals and organizations, more covertly, the

[4]In the words of feminist philosopher Karen Warren, "The ability to care (and emotional intelligence generally) is necessary (psychologically, physically, and causally) for moral reasoning ... So ... One should care because one cannot reason morally, be motivated to act morally, choose to act morally, or value certain practices as moral ... *unless one cares*" (2000, 112, emphasis in original).

very structure of ethical valuation is shaped by myriad cultural practices. Customs, rituals, and repetitive bodily movements, for example, inform moral intuitions from an early age. Ethical approaches can be seen as based in cultural knowledge, which is "a complex web of explicit and implicit, sensory and propositional, affective, cognitive, and motoric knowledge" (Haidt 2001). Similar to Gilligan's work, this research strongly questions the idea that we are rational, autonomous principle-followers, and brings back in emotions, social connections, and the body.[5]

Justice and Care

All of this analysis suggests that, far from being opposed to each other, justice and care are as two legs, or two sides of coin. The two orientations may be analytically distinguishable (according to a categorization that we ourselves create—just like we create gender), but they are united in practice. Putting them into a gender-value compass, we can think of them having a positive complementarity, as illustrated in the top two cells of Fig. 2.3. The bottom two cells indicate, again, what happens if we try to have one without the other. The illusion that justice can exist without care leads to coldness. On the other hand, an overly sentimental emphasis on care, to the exclusion of justice, leads to unjustifiable favoritism. One can also think of another problem with purely rational justice being a lack of motivation to act, while unreflective impulsiveness can be a problem with an empathy-only approach.

For example, consider a picture that appeared in national newspapers many years ago. The photo showed a Latin American family sitting around an aged and lonely immigrant man whom they had taken into their circle of friendship, care, and

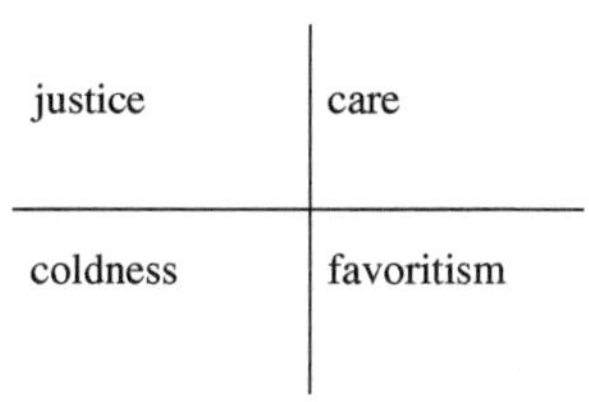

Fig. 2.3 Justice and Care in the Gender-Value Compass

[5]From a feminist perspective, however, it is shocking to see the lack of credit given to feminist theorists who have pointed out the gender biases in traditional Western liberal philosophy (as in Table 2.1 above), and to Gilligan. While psychologist Jonathan Haidt's much-cited article on an interpersonal and social approach to moral judgments (Haidt 2001) critiques Kohlberg and others for their overly rationalist, individualist, and disembodied approach, he neglects Gilligan and the Kohlberg-Gilligan controversy entirely, citing male authors as the originators of the social and interpersonal approach. While there may be issues internal to the psychology profession that explain the omission of any mention of Gilligan, this looks distressing like yet another case of a point being noticed only when a man makes it.

protection. Very nice. The old man, however, was Dr. Josef Mengele, the notorious Nazi war criminal. I use this to remind myself that one should not one-sidedly elevate considerations of care over considerations of justice.

Implications for Economies

Neoclassical economics teaches that markets and businesses are mechanical mechanisms populated by self-interested, autonomous "economic man." Individual consumers or workers are seen as discrete, separative agents who maximize mathematical utility functions, while firms are portrayed as discrete, separative economic actors that maximize mathematical profit functions. If these teachings were true, only the thinnest sort of rationalist and individualist ethics might be applicable. In fact, the only ethical judgment admitted by many mainstream economists is to hold sacrosanct the value of free individual choice.

Is Ethics Unnecessary/Impossible?

Conservative, free-market economists furthermore argue that ethical considerations beyond this are *unnecessary*, because the "invisible hand" of markets automatically assures that self-interested actions serve the social good. In contrast, critics from the political left say that incorporating rich ethical considerations in market-oriented systems is *impossible*, because the juggernaut of global corporate capitalism obeys only its own inhuman rules. Because firms are profit maximizers, these critics reason, the capitalist system simply institutionalizes greed and self-interested competition. Ethical action therefore, it is reasoned, requires supplanting this system with something else—something more altruistic and cooperative. If one assumes that businesses are intrinsically mechanical and anti-social, then the idea of "business ethics," much less "care ethics" in business, seems impossible. But is it?

But what if the economy is not a machine and people in their economic lives are not "economic man"? The feminist analysis described above notes that these beliefs are based, not on empirical study of actual behavior, but on a physics-envy methodological bias and the macho image of the separative self.[6] There is, in fact, plentiful evidence that these beliefs are wildly off the mark. The biased nature of these beliefs can be examined at three organizational levels: the level of human individuals, the level of businesses, and the level of markets.

[6] See (Nelson 2003) for a discussion of the role of images of "separative" and "soluble" firms in contemporary economic thought.

Individuals Are Not "Economic Man"

Starting with the simplest organizational unit—the human individual—there is, in fact, considerable empirical evidence that people do not leave their feelings, values, ethics, sociality, and search for meaning behind when they enter commercial life. The vast business literature on the psychology of employee motivation, for example, shows that people are complex social animals, even when at work (Herzberg 1987). Research on motivation finds that people are generally motivated by a mix of intrinsic rewards (such as enjoyment or a feeling of contributing to something worthwhile) and extrinsic rewards (such as money or status) (Ryan and Deci 2000). Phenomena of care, including caring about one's coworkers or customers, caring about the quality of the product or service one provides, or caring about the impact of one's business on the world, are endemic to well-run businesses—as well as often missing in poorly-run ones (Kusnet 2008). Feminist economists have been especially interested in this topic, since so many women have traditionally been employed in "caring work" such as nursing or teaching (Folbre and Nelson 2000). Of course, other human motivations besides money and caring—including a desire for dominance or revenge, or a desire to maintain rigid hierarchies of race, class, or gender—show up in the workplace as well. The unemotional, a-social employee who gets only disutility from expending effort at work, and utility from pay, is a fiction invented by economists.

Academics may be more likely to acknowledge our own nonpecuniary interests in our work, than the possibility of nonpecuniary interests on the part of business leaders. While we generally feel that we do our work at least partly for the love of knowledge or learning, or for the social good, we may assume that a business person qua businessperson must be interested only in money. But consider how some leaders talk about what they do. For example, David Packard (of Hewlett-Packard) once said, "Profit ... is not the proper end and aim of management – it is what makes all of the proper ends and aims possible," with the proper aim being to "make a contribution to society" (Collins and Porras 1994). Others talk about feeling good about providing jobs, needed services in a community, quality bread, path breaking books, interesting innovations, environmental improvements, or express pride in carrying on a legacy or tradition. Don't most people want to do something worthwhile? Surveys of business leaders suggest that shareholders are often only one of many constituencies considered in decision making (along with workers, communities, suppliers, creditors and so on).[7]

Some executives, of course, have bought into pure "bottom line," money-oriented, short-term thinking, and blare on loudly about it in the press and in business publishing. And some leaders, it may be objected, may voice interests in jobs or the environment purely as a public relations move. But—speaking here entirely on the level of individual motivations—isn't there something quite

[7] Jay W. Lorsch and Elizabeth Maciver, Pawns or Potentates (1989) as cited in D. Gordon Smith (Smith 1998, 291). See also the discussion in Sen (1983).

dehumanizing about taking the stereotype of the greedy, single-minded Chief Executive Officer and applying it, untested, to all business leaders, simply because they seem to be different from "us"? (And isn't this even a bit *unethical*?)

Now a further objection, of course, can be raised. One may grant that an *individual* businessperson may be very moral and care a great deal about the social good, but then go on to argue that the *structure* of businesses will either extinguish that impulse (perhaps by causing that person to be fired for poor profit-making performance) or make it ineffective (through procedural or groupthink factors)—because, of course, firms *must* maximize profits.

Businesses

The belief that firms are mechanical profit-maximizers can be hard to overcome. Many believe, for example, that profit maximization is mandated by law. But an actual examination of the relevant legal codes and case law shows that this is not so. The codes say that the purpose of a business is to run a business—profit is generally not even mentioned.[8] Many state legal codes explicitly state that the interests of stakeholder groups such as employees and customers, long-term interests, and the interests of the larger community, can all be legitimately be taken into account in business decisions (Adams and Matheson 2000). And the belief that directors or executives will be hauled into court if they act on any goals other than profit maximization is quite exaggerated. It is actually quite difficult to remove an officer through legal action (Smith 1998; Nelson forthcoming).

The idea that executives will automatically be sacked if they do not profit-maximize gets far more credence than it deserves. The current business news is, for example, full of cases of financial industry CEOs who are being kept on—and even getting multi-million dollar bonuses—after leading their organizations into ruin. Now, it may not be clear why this is an argument *against* the "profit maximization" dogma, since in many people's minds the phrases "profit maximization" and "greedy CEOs" seem to point to the same phenomenon. In actuality, though, there is a critically important difference.

Firms are complexly structured social organizations. The owners of a firm, which in the case of a corporation are its shareholders, are in principle the recipients of the firm's profits. Profits are what is left over after all revenues are gathered in, and all necessary expenses are paid, and the shareholders are supposed to receive them through payments of dividends or through increases in the value of their shares. A corporation has a Board of Directors which is supposed to oversee the management of the firm, and the board in turn hires (and approves the compensation packages for) the top executives who handle the firm's day-to-day operations. So "profit maximization" or "creating value for the shareholders" should mean *not* paying any more than is strictly necessary to get managerial talent—that is, should

[8] See discussions in Nelson (2006, forthcoming)

require keeping a lid on CEO salaries and bonuses. Shareholders are among the people most outraged by the skyrocketing executive compensation packages of recent decades, as articles in magazines such as *Fortune* attest (Kirkland 2006).

Ironically, the CEO compensation fiasco has developed, in good part, as a direct result of theories based on "economic man." Not being able to believe that anyone would have sufficient incentive to run a business in the interest of shareholders (and/or employees, customers, the community, society, etc.) for a mere fair and reasonable salary, neoclassical economists suggested giving CEOs stock options and bonuses based on performance. This means that CEO compensation goes up when the price of company shares go up or certain other goals are achieved. In theory, then, their pecuniary interests and the shareholders' pecuniary interests would become aligned. But if people are opportunistic enough to care only about their own compensation and not about their company, they are also opportunistic enough to figure out how to game this system. And a number have, aiming to maintain a short-term illusion of profitability just long enough to cash in their options, or sitting as directors on each other's boards and voting each other big bonuses based on meeting routine goals. Others—less opportunistic—have resisted the call.

There are many reasons to believe, right now, that many businesses are ethically broken, and that substantial changes are needed in firm structure, governance (e.g. the composition and duties of the Boards), and regulation to get businesses back on track. But the reason firms are ethically broken is not *because* they automatically "profit maximize." They don't. Instead, the belief in "economic man" and narrow goals has itself served, over time, to corrupt earlier notions of business responsibility, in a sort of self-fulfilling prophecy.

A firm is not made up of one individual, with one goal. Rather, it is made up of executives, managers, and workers engaged in a joint activity, embedded in relations with suppliers, customers, shareholders, creditors, communities, governments, the natural environment, and so on. The fields of business management, organizational behavior, and economic sociology would have far less work to do, of course, if businesses were as simple as conventional economics assumes them to be. Business ethicists have plenty of work cut out for them in investigating how businesses can best be structured to carry out their social and environmental responsibilities (Paine 2002). Neoclassical economic dogmas, however, should not be allowed to stand in the way.

Of course, it may be granted that individual *people* and individual *firms* may be essentially human and social, but then argued that *the market* is the ultimate impersonal mechanism.

Markets

Don't the forces of market competition demand that firms squeeze out every last penny of profit, or they will go out of business? Doesn't market competition, in itself, reinforce dog-eat-dog competition, values of greed and self-interest, and a race to the bottom on social and environmental protections? There are two flaws in this argument.

First, markets are not, in fact, nearly as competitive as portrayed in the abstract, mechanical model. Wal-Mart, ExxonMobil, IBM, Verizon, Microsoft, and the like are hardly the sort of anonymous, powerless companies that populate the neoclassical theory of perfect competition. The economic conditions they face do not dictate their decisions to them: They normally operate with some "slack"—that is, some excess of revenues over strictly necessary expenses. This slack gives them some room for discretion. They may, as discussed above, pay outlandish salaries to their CEOs—or build sumptuous headquarters, or go on acquisitions binges, or pour money into political campaigns. Or they may raise the wages of their lowest-paid workers, "green" their company, start a company day care center, or invest in impoverished communities. Some of these positive sorts of actions may also, of course, be profitable, but the point here is that with some "slack," they can also be accomplished even if they are only profit-neutral or somewhat costly. Since many businesses are not on a razor's edge of competition, their decisions can be made with some discretion. This opens the possibility of realizing that business practices are complex and laden with ethical possibilities and ramifications.

Second, the idea that markets are somehow mechanical also assumes that "the market" somehow exists "it itself," separable from society and government, and separable from more cooperative social values such as trust and cooperation. Considered from a different point of view, market interactions can be seen to be *entirely dependent* on values of trust and cooperation, systems of social mores, and government laws and regulations. Neoclassical economists imagine that perfectly competitive markets can run well "on their own" because of subsidiary (and often well-hidden) assumptions that actors are perfectly rational, perfectly informed, have perfect foresight about the future, and trade all goods that are relevant for well being. In the real world, in contrast, there are in fact symbiotic relationships between social values and market values, and between governmental activity and market activity.

In order for a trade to take place, for example, the trading partners have to trust each other—that is, trust that the items being exchanged have the value that is claimed for them. Because actors in real life do *not* possess "perfect information," this requires ethical norms of honesty, backed up by social institutions such as business reputations, ratings bureaus, government regulations concerning disclosure or product quality, and the courts. Market exchange also requires a physical environment that is not unduly polluted or depleted, again requiring coordinated social and political action. The more honest and considerate trading partners are—the more they see their exchange as a cooperate endeavor to benefit both parties and society, rather than a selfish grab—the more smoothly markets can run. Were people to generally display no concern for social cohesion, ethics, or responsibility, and display pure opportunism at every turn, then every economic transaction would need to be tightly policed... and then someone would have to police those doing this policing, and so on ad infinitum.

This applies even on a global scale. Yes, one can certainly point to cases of racing-to-the-bottom, as some corporations seek to locate production in nations with ever-lower wage levels, looser labor and environmental regulations, and lower taxes. But there are limits to such opportunism. Countries and corporations that take this low road are likely to eventually run into problems of degraded levels of worker health and education, polluted environments, poor public infrastructure, corruption, and/or civil unrest—the very opposite of a healthy "business climate."

Take away a concern for ethics, and leave markets to "self-regulate," and the result is a train wreck—as we have learned from the 2008 (and ongoing) financial crisis. Everyone from mortgage brokers to lending institutions to rating agencies followed the neoclassical advice to pursue self-interest, and the result was not market bliss, but market disaster. And while neoclassical economics says that agents are autonomous and rational in their decision-making, the financial crisis has yielded plenty of evidence to the contrary. Asset markets, including markets for housing and financial instruments, are very sensitive to *social beliefs* about the value of the asset involved.[9] People will often buy an asset based not on some rational calculation of its fundamental worth, but because they have confidence that *other people believe* that the asset is valuable. As the field of behavioral finance investigates, such herd behavior, along with emotional responses such as excitement and overweening optimism, are key elements in the formation of speculative bubbles such as the one we witnessed in the housing market.

Market behavior, then, is not something separate from the social behavior of emotional, embodied, interconnected human beings, but simply another variant of it. Ethical approaches, and coordinated community or governmental forms of management relevant for other aspects of social life are equally relevant to economic life.

Competition and Cooperation

In order to keep this in mind, it may be helpful to deconstruct dichotomous thinking about competition versus cooperation. Competition refers to trying to do as well as or better at something than someone else, while cooperation refers to coordinating activities with someone else in a joint effort. The usual view is that one precludes the other, and that market-oriented capitalism is all about competition. Instead, thinking about them as complementary phenomena that each have both positive and negative aspects, may be more helpful, as illustrated in Fig. 2.4.

competition	cooperation
race-to-the-bottom	collusion

Fig. 2.4 Competition and Cooperation in the Gender-Value Compass

[9]This is true also about an asset often thought to be cold and impartial: *money*. For discussion, see Nelson (2006)

Competition can have positive aspects because—as economists are right to point out—it can give people incentives to be creative, hard-working, and look for ways to produce things more cheaply. Of course, the form of the competition makes a big difference. Innovation in the form of creating a new cure for disease can increase human welfare, while innovation in the form of new opaque and deceptive financial instruments decreases it. Cutting costs through increased energy efficiency is generally a good thing, while cutting costs by cutting the wages of the poorest workers in a race to the bottom is not. But what this leads back to is exactly the point that ethics—ethics of honesty, and ethics of caring about the wellbeing of flesh-and-blood human beings—cannot be avoided in economic life. Competition is not "structurally," by its nature, good or bad: It is as good or bad as we make it.

While cooperation tends to carry positive connotations of harmony and helpfulness in working for the social good, it is important to note that cooperation can also have bad consequences. In economic life, it can take the form of collusion and exclusive deals among companies, which are the very things that undermine the healthy aspects of market competition. Too-close cooperation between businesses and government gives us the military-industrial complex, as well as Congressional actions that exclusively serve Wall Street constituencies. As in life in general, when "the social good" is defined over too narrow a social group, cooperation means the solidarity of "insider" groups who may serve themselves at the expense of "outsider" groups. Feminist and civil rights activists had to struggle for decades, for example, to crack the highly cooperative white-male-solidarity behaviors that prevailed among employers and union leaders, in order to allow women and minorities the chance to compete for jobs.

The positive complementarity between competition and cooperation arises because, as pointed out above, a spirit of cooperation between buyers and sellers, and between businesses and governments, is just as necessary as competition for successful market functioning. But neither competition nor cooperation on its own, or any naïve mix of the two, is "structurally" good. The devil is in the details, and only specific, applied ethical evaluation can help us judge economic phenomena as more or less worthy of approbation.

Too Easy on Corporations?

Does the fact that I have not roundly condemned global corporate capitalism mean that I think believe that things are good as they are? Of course not. Inequalities within and between nations are at levels that are totally morally unjustifiable and socially insupportable. Problems of climate change and other environmental consequences of our current fossil-fuel-based economics of production have driven many species to extinction and threaten our human future. Lucrative international trade in arms and drugs threatens stability everywhere. Concentrations of wealth and concomitant political power turn democracy into a sham.

One should, however, be leery of touting the benefits of businesses simply being local, non-profit, or small, as "structural" ways of assuring good behavior.

"Local" can mean community-responsive, but it can also simply mean parochial and narrow-minded. Non-profit versus for-profit status may be more a matter of legal charters and tax filings, than of actual motivations or behaviors of complex organizations. (Witness, for example, the recently skyrocketing, corporate-CEO-mimicking, salaries of presidents of nonprofit colleges.) "Small" can be good when it means breaking up excessive concentrations of power, but it may also mean "too small" to do much good, or to create a beneficial countervailing, competitive counterweight to other more powerful interests. We can also be reminded by feminist scholarship that small, local, organizations dedicated to goals other than profit are not necessarily well-behaved: While, for example, "the family" is often idealized as a small scale organization based on love and connection, feminists are only too aware of the women and children crowding domestic violence shelters.

What my analysis claims is that we do not have to resign ourselves to our contemporary serious economic problems because "that's the way the system works," nor seek to jump from our present economic structures to something completely different before we can begin to address them. The myth that economies are machines essentially gives business leaders, workers, consumers, and investors operating within current system an ethical "free pass"—one can always fall back on the excuse that "the system made me do it." A better understanding of the role of justice and care in economic life instead demands commitment to ethical reflection and action in economic life, right here and right now.

Conclusion

The title of this volume, *Applying Care Ethics to Business*, might seem to imply that care ethics arises from somewhere outside of business, and must be brought in from the outside in order to be applied. This essay has argued, in contrast, that the image of businesses as immune to ethical concerns and operating outside of normal social relations is a fiction invented by a particular lineage of economic theorists. The fact that this fiction has been accepted by so many is supported by culture-wide rigid and gender-biased patterns of thought.

Business and economic life are part of social and ethical life. Justice and care are orientations that can be used by both men and women to address the dilemmas we face in our lives together on this planet. Can we be agile enough in our thinking to get over old dichotomies, and put our capacities to good use?

References

Adams, Edward S., and John. H. Matheson. 2000. A statutory model for corporate constituency concerns. *Emory Law Journal* 49: 1085–1135.

Bem, Sandra Lipsitz. 1981. Gender schema theory: A cognitive account of sex typing. *Psychological Review* 88 (4): 354–364.

Borgerson, Janet. L. 2007. On the harmony of feminist ethics and business ethics. *Business and Society Review* 112 (4): 477–509.

Collins, James C., and Jerry I. Porras. 1994. *Built to last*. New York, NY: Harper Business.
Easlea, Brian. 1980. *Witch hunting, magic and the new philosophy: An introduction to debates of the scientific revolution, 1450–1750*. Atlantic Highlands, NJ: Humanities Press.
England, Paula. 2003. Separative and soluble selves: dichotomous thinking in economics. In *Feminist economics today: Beyond economic man*, ed. M.A. Ferber, and J.A. Nelson, 33–59. Chicago, IL: University of Chicago Press.
Ferber, Marianne A., and Julie A. Nelson (Eds.). 1993. *Beyond economic man: Feminist theory and economics*. Chicago, IL: University of Chicago Press.
Folbre, Nancy, and Julie A. Nelson. 2000. For love or money – or both? *Journal of Economic Perspectives* 14 (4): 123–140.
Gilligan, Carol. 1982. *In a difference voice: Psychological theory and women's development*. Cambridge, MA: Harvard University Press.
Greene, Joshua D., R. Brian Sommerville et al. 2001. An fMRI investigation of emotional engagement in moral judgment. *Science* 293 (September 14): 2105–2108.
Greene, Joshua D., and J. Haidt. 2002. How (and where) does moral judgment work? *Trends in Cognitive Sciences* 6 (12): 517–523.
Haidt, Jonathan 2001. The emotional dog and its rational tail: A social intuitionist approach to moral judgment. *Psychological Review* 108 (4): 814–834.
Hamington, Maurice 2009. Business is not a game: The metaphoric fallacy. *Journal of Business Ethics* 86: 473–484.
Harding, Sandra 1986. *The science question in feminism*. Ithaca, NY: Cornell University Press.
Herzberg, Frederick. 1987. One more time: How do you motivate employees? *Harvard Business Review* (September–October): 109–120.
Hyde, Janet Shibley. 2005. The gender similarities hypothesis. *American Psychologist* 60 (6): 581–592.
Jaffee, Sara, and Janet Shibley Hyde. 2000. Gender differences in moral orientation: A meta-analysis. *Psychological Bulletin* 126 (5): 703–726.
Keller, Evelyn Fox. 1985. *Reflections on gender and science*. New Haven, CT: Yale University Press.
Kirkland, Rik. 2006. The real CEO pay problem. *Fortune*.
Knutson, Kristine M., L. Mah et al. 2007. Neural correlates of automatic beliefs about gender and race. *Human Brain Mapping* 28: 915–930.
Kusnet, David 2008. *Love the work, hate the job: Why America's best workers are more unhappy than ever*. Hoboken, NJ: Wiley.
Lakoff, George, and Mark Johnson. 1980. *Metaphors we live by*. Chicago, IL: University of Chicago Press.
Mill, John Stuart. 1836. On the definition of political economy; and on the method of philosophical investigation in that science. *London and Westminster Review* : 1–29.
Nelson, Julie A 1992. Gender, metaphor, and the definition of economics. *Economics and Philosophy* 8: 103–125.
Nelson, Julie A. 1996. *Feminism, objectivity and economics*. London: Routledge.
Nelson, Julie A. 2003. Separative and soluble Firms: Androcentric bias in business ethics. In *Feminist economics today: Beyond economic man*, ed. M.A. Ferber, and J.A. Nelson. Chicago, IL: University of Chicago Press.
Nelson, Julie A. 2006. Can we talk? feminist economists in dialogue with social theorists. *Signs: Journal of Women in Culture and Society* 31 (4): 1052–1074.
Nelson, Julie A. 2006. *Economics for humans*. Chicago, IL: University of Chicago Press.
Nelson, Julie A. Forthcoming. Does profit-seeking rule out love? Evidence (or not) from economics and law. *Washington University Journal of Law & Policy* 35.
Nosek, Brian, Mahzarin Banaji et al. 2007. Gender-science IAT. https://implicit.harvard.edu/implicit/.
Paine, Lynn Sharp. 2002. *Value Shift*. New York, NY: McGraw-Hill.
Ryan, R.M., and E.L. Deci. 2000. Intrinsic and extrinsic motivations: Classic definitions and new directions. *Contemporary Educational Psychology* 25: 54–67.

Sen, Amartya. 1983. The profit motive. *Lloyds Bank Review* (147): 1–20.
Smith, Adam. 1776[2001]. *An inquiry into the nature and causes of the wealth of nations*. New York, NY: P.F. Collier & Son.
Smith, D. Gordon. 1998. The shareholder primacy norm. *The Journal of Corporate Law* 23: 277–323.
Tong, Rosemarie, and Nancy Williams. 2009. Feminist ethics. In *Stanford Encyclopedia of Philosophy* (Fall 2009 Edition), ed. Edward N. Zalta. http://plato.stanford.edu/archives/fall2009/entries/feminism-ethics/
Warren, Karen J. 2000. *Ecofeminist Philosophy: A western perspective on what it is and why it matters*. Lanham, MD: Rowman & Littlefield.

Chapter 3
Adam Smith Cared, So Why Can't Modern Economics?: The Foundations for Care Ethics in Early Economic Theory

Andrew Terjesen

Introduction

In his lifetime, Adam Smith was much more well-known for his work *The Theory of Moral Sentiments*, which went through six editions before his death, than for his *Wealth of Nations*. Today the situation is reversed and many people are unaware that the "Father of Capitalism" was a Professor of Moral Philosophy at the University of Glasgow (at least until he resigned his commission to become a private tutor, but at the end of his life he returned to the University in an honorary position). Smith saw his work in moral philosophy and economics as part of a larger whole that was to be completed when he had finished a book on jurisprudence.[1] The aim of this chapter is to show the extent to which Smith's moral and economic works are interrelated as part of a single ethical vision of capitalism. Despite the prevailing tendency to view economics as a value-neutral science, ethics should play a role in our discussion of economic issues, as well as the more theoretical aspects of the discipline. Moreover, the kind of ethical theory that is at the center of these discussions should be structurally similar to the one Smith propounded in *Theory of Moral Sentiments* (TMS).

As part of the argument, it will be shown how modern care ethics shares an affinity with key aspects of Smith's moral theory (and in fact that care ethics might be the contemporary ethical theory that bears the strongest similarity to Smith's, but I will not argue for that stronger claim here). Since Smith's moral theory was integral to shaping his economic theory and modern economic theory has its roots in Smith's work, it should follow that care ethics could have an equivalent role in modern discussions of economic issues.

[1] Unfortunately, Smith died before the book on law was completed and he instructed his executors to destroy it along with all of his other papers and correspondence. All that survives are some lecture notes by his students in his Jurisprudence class at the University of Glasgow published as his *Lectures on Jurisprudence* (Smith 2009).

A. Terjesen (✉)
Department of Philosophy, Rhodes College, Memphis, TN, USA
e-mail: ajterjesen@gmail.com

M. Hamington, M. Sander-Staudt (eds.), *Applying Care Ethics to Business*, Issues in Business Ethics 34, DOI 10.1007/978-90-481-9307-3_3,
© Springer Science+Business Media B.V. 2011

It is also the intent of this chapter to make economists aware of the need to consider the ways in which economics relies on morality to curb some of the excesses of capitalism and that this might interest them in exploring moral theory alongside more general economic questions. Given the proposed similarities between Smith's moral theory and care ethics, this would suggest that care ethics might be a good place for those interested in business ethics to start (even though it has not been one of the moral theories traditionally inserted into business ethics discussions).

At this point one might ask why it should matter what Adam Smith thought about the relationship between ethics and economics. In the almost two and a half centuries since Smith first published his *Wealth of Nations* economic theory has developed and in some ways is very different from what Smith had envisioned. To begin with, Smith endorsed a labor theory of value which is no longer compatible with modern economics.[2] In addition, modern economics includes equations and concepts that were developed in response to the industrialization and globalization of business. Smith's ideal of capitalism is very much rooted in the smaller scale practices of his time. He could not have envisioned companies that are larger and more powerful than many countries. So, even if Smith's vision of economics was in part a moral vision, we can't just extrapolate that modern economics should also be guided by a moral vision.

This is a fair point, but it also highlights another challenge posed by the chapter (and this volume in general). Modern economics might no longer resemble what Smith envisioned precisely because Smith was concerned about the dangers of scale and completely anonymous and impersonal business relationships. If we look back at Smith's theory, we might find a sketch of the kind of changes that need to be made in our vision of economics in order to better cope with the kind of ethical dilemmas that have arisen in the last few years. It would also be a challenge to consider that economic agents need to be held morally responsible for the outcomes of the system (even if there was no active intent to put millions of people out of work by outsourcing, it might still be something that businesses need to look at through a moral lens). A caring approach to economics will undoubtedly yield a different form of capitalism than the one advocated by certain politicians that treats the unregulated market as the solution to all social problems. Interestingly, some authors who have explored the kind of capitalism that a caring perspective would produce are also quick to recognize what many proponents of a laissez faire approach ignore: that Smith's vision of economics was a moral one.[3] One reason why we should look

---

[2]Gavin Kennedy calls into question the idea that Smith really held a labor theory of value. If Kennedy is right, then Smith would be closer to modern economic theory. However, Kennedy admits that Smith's presentation of his ideas in the *Wealth of Nations* is muddled, so there is as much reason to think that Smith held to a labor theory of value and was ambivalent about it as there is to think he didn't hold one at all. For more on Kennedy's interpretation of Smith see his *Adam Smith's Lost Legacy* (Kennedy 2005).

[3]Two works that deal with a caring approach to economics (and reference the connections Smith has to Care Ethics) are Nancy Folbre, *The Invisible Heart: Economics and Family Values* (Folbre 2001) and Riana Eisler, *The Real Wealth of Nations: Creating a Caring Economics* (Eisler 2007).

back at Smith is that it reminds us that capitalism is not as narrowly-defined as some politicians would have you believe, and so a deviation from their particular model of capitalism is not automatically socialism. Before taking a deeper look at how Smith's moral vision shapes his economics, we need to spell out the content of his moral vision.

The Elements of Care in Smith's Moral Theory

Unlike other ethical theories like Kantianism or Consequentialism, care ethics does not have a clearly defined principle. This makes it very difficult to look back historically and determine whether some thinker was a proto-care ethicist. Smith, along with his friend David Hume, has been claimed by care ethicists as an early practitioner, but it is not clear that he truly fits that category. Even if we don't have a principle of Care that we can measure Smith against, we can consider the common elements of care ethics and see if they are contained within Smith's theory.

As Virginia Held defines it, "the central focus of the ethics of care is on the compelling moral salience of attending to and meeting the needs of the particular others for whom we take responsibility" (p. 10).[4] At the very beginning of his *Theory of Moral Sentiments*, Smith expresses a view that he shares with Hume and other eighteenth century philosophers like Francis Hutcheson and Joseph Butler that seems very close to what Held describes. Smith states that a concern for the welfare of others is an undeniable part of human experience. Like Hume, Smith acknowledges that this other concern is not the only motivation human's have. We can also be self-interested. Those who speak of "Das Adam Smith Problem" (a name derived from a nineteenth century German debate over how Adam Smith could be the author of both a book on moral sentiments and on self-interested capitalism) sometimes ignore the fact that Smith ascribed to the view that we are possessed of two motivational structures that can come into conflict, but often can work together.

A second feature that Held identifies in care ethics is that "in the epistemological process of trying to understand what morality would recommend and what it would be morally best for us to do and to, the ethics of care values emotion rather than rejects it ... such emotions as sympathy, empathy, sensitivity and responsiveness are seen as the kind of moral emotions that need to be cultivated" (p. 10) Given that Smith's book was a theory of *moral sentiments*, he would seem a perfect embodiment of this aspect of care ethics. And the fact that the moral sentiment that he seems to pay the most attention to is what he calls "sympathy" would appear to be the clincher.

Smith describes the process by which we come to understand what others are feeling (and then become moved by their emotions) in the following way:

> As we have no immediate experience of what other men feel, we can form no idea of the manner in which they are affected, but by conceiving what we ourselves should feel

[4]Held (2006).

> in the like situation .... By imagination we place ourselves in his situation, we conceive ourselves enduring all the same torments, we enter as it were into his body, and become in some measure the same person with him. (TMS I.i.1.2)[5]

What Smith is describing sounds very much like what people today would call projective or imaginative empathy.[6] And the result of this empathy seems to be exactly what care ethicists desire. By imagining ourselves in the situation of someone on the rack, we not only come to understand what they feel, but we also create in ourselves a reflection of their emotion. And that mirrored emotion (while not as strong as the person suffering) is strong enough to move us to take action. At least, it will so long as no competing self-interested desire overwhelms our emotional reaction to the suffering.

In Smith's work, the word "sympathy" is used in many different ways. This is not too surprising since even today "sympathy" is a real linguistic workhorse. However, Smith is also using "sympathy" to cover concepts that contemporary thinkers have associated with "empathy." So sympathy includes pity, benevolent concern, emotional contagion and projective imagining. What is sometimes ignored, even by people who are familiar with Smith's moral philosophy, is that he also uses "sympathy" in a way unique to his philosophy.[7] In trying to distinguish his use of "sympathy" from the ordinary usages of his time (such as "pity"—a confusion which led many psychologists to embrace "empathy" as an alternative), he makes the following remark: "Pity and compassion are words appropriated to signify our fellow-feeling with the sorrow of others. Sympathy, though its meaning was, perhaps, originally the same, may now, however, without much impropriety, be made use of to denote our fellow-feeling with any passion whatever" (TMS I.i.1.5). Sympathy in this instance is defined as the pleasurable feeling of connection with someone else's mental state. People often use sympathy to describe the feeling being sympathized with, for example, when speaking of feeling sympathy for someone who has just fallen down someone might be referring to the pain they imagine the person who fell is feeling. They would not be referring to the way it feels to share a mental state with someone. The use of sympathy to mean "fellow-feeling" is very much in line with a care ethics approach as it both emphasizes using emotion to discover moral truth and places a great deal of value on connectedness and relatedness.

---

[5] Smith (2009b).

[6] Although both "sympathy" and "empathy" are words with Greek roots, neither of them was very common in the ancient world. *Sympatheia* was mainly used to describe the mysterious causal relationship between the body and soul in NeoPlatonic thought. In fact, the first usage of "sympathy" the OED records is in the context of discussing Plato's notion of the soul. Consequently, "sympathy" has often been a placeholder for causal relationships that we don't quite understand. "Empathy" enters the lexicon in the twentieth century as a translation of a word coined by Theodore Lipps to describe how we can project ourselves into a visual illusion. The crossover between the two terms and varied ways in which they are defined in relation to each other makes this author wary of committing to a particular usage as the "correct" one for either term.

[7] This particular facet of Smith's usage of sympathy was brought to light for me in Robert Sugden's "Beyond empathy and sympathy: Adam Smith's concept of fellow-feeling." *Economics and Philosophy* (2002).

It's especially interesting that when Smith uses the word "sympathy" that way, it is his first usage of the term in his *Theory of Moral Sentiments.*

This usage of sympathy to mean a kind of connectedness indicates another way in which Smith's moral theory resonates with care ethics. As Samuel Fleischacker notes in his *On Adam Smith*'s Wealth of Nations: *A Philosophical Companion*, "Smith has a far more deeply social conception of the self than did his predecessors. ... for Smith all of our feelings, self-interested and benevolent, are *constituted* by a process of socialization" (p. 47).[8] Fleischacker is contrasting Smith with other moral sentimentalists such as David Hume. Hume is the philosopher that care ethicist are more likely to invoke (presumably due to his more prominent place in the history of philosophy), but it is possible that Smith is a better fit for care ethicists as he embraces a more explicitly social conception of the self. Part of the reason that care ethicists put a great emphasis on relationships, as opposed to duties or rights, is because they conceive of the self as a fundamentally relational entity. For a care ethicist what makes someone who they are includes the social roles they fulfill (as parent, child, co-worker, member of a neighborhood, and so on). This is an explicit rejection of the individualistic picture of the self often used in economic models. Care ethicists deny that we can truly conceive of ourselves as self-interested and detached agents who are solely concerned with our own good. Smith's recognition that our identity and values are shaped by our social interactions is a starting point for the care ethicist's rejection of the *homo economicus.*[9]

I do not intend to claim that Smith's use by care ethicists is without its problems. In her defense of an Ethic of Care, Joan Tronto has raised important concerns about embracing these eighteenth century moral sentimentalists as part of the care ethics tradition.[10] To begin with, as Tronto notes, Smith seems to fall prey to the eighteenth century tendency to associate the sentiments within the sphere of women's lives. In the *Theory of Moral Sentiments*, Smith states:

> Generosity is different from humanity. Those two qualities, which at first sight seem so nearly allied, do not always belong to the same person. Humanity is the virtue of a woman, generosity of a man. The fair-sex, who have commonly much more tenderness than ours, have seldom so much generosity. That women rarely make considerable donations, is an observation of the civil law. Humanity consists merely in the exquisite fellow-feeling which the spectator entertains with the sentiments of the persons principally concerned, so as to

---

[8]Fleischacker (2004).

[9]Admittedly while Smith's theory seems more open to the influence of society on us, many of his comments about character and virtue lean towards a standard Hobbesian view of human nature as being fundamentally atomistic which would not be as compatible with the notion of a relational self deployed by many Care Ethicists. Nonetheless, I will argue that Smith's view of the self is not as starkly individualistic as it has been stereotypically portrayed in the narrative of eighteenth century thought. The fact that Smith's economic theory depends on a somewhat connected notion of self opens up the possibility that a more connected and relational notion of self could provide a moral foundation for a form of capitalism.

[10]I must thank an anonymous reviewer for Springer Press for encouraging me to be more explicit in addressing these concerns, especially Tronto's critique which is found in *Moral Boundaries: A Political Argument for an Ethic of Care* (Tronto 1993).

> grieve for their sufferings, to resent their injuries, and to rejoice at their good fortune. The most humane actions require no self-denial, no self-command, no great exertion of the sense of propriety. They consist only in doing what this exquisite sympathy would of its own accord prompt us to do. But it is otherwise with generosity. We never are generous except when in some respect we prefer some other person to ourselves, and sacrifice some great and important interest of our own to an equal interest of a friend or of a superior. (TMS IV.i. 21)

Self-command as described by Smith is a virtue that enables us to "under the heaviest and most unexpected misfortunes, continues to behave with fortitude and firmness" (TMS III, i, 86). As presented by Smith, self-command is the means by which we control our passions so that our self-interest does not cause us to abandon our principles or modify our judgments to suit our own needs. One problem with self-command for a care ethicist is that Smith describes it in such a way that it becomes associated with maleness. He refers to self-command as being an expression of manhood or a manly quality several times in his discussion of the virtue. For care ethicists who see care ethics either as a rejection of a male-dominated conception of morality or as an attempt to articulate a notion of morality that is rooted in female experience, the identification of a central virtue with a masculine perspective would be a barrier to common ground with Smith.[11] Before coming to that conclusion, it is worth noting Smith's remark that "Our sensibility to the feelings of others, so far from being inconsistent with the manhood of self-command, is the very principle upon which that manhood is founded" (TMS III, i, 76). The care ethicist could build upon the fact that Smith's description of masculinity does not draw a sharp distinction between acting "manly" and being sensitive and receptive to the feelings of others.

Tronto introduces eighteenth century moral sentimentalism in *Moral Boundaries* to illustrate a major change in ethical thinking that she argues occurred during that century. According to Tronto, the moral sentiments and the contextual morality that arose out those sentiments were increasingly displaced by an emphasis on universal reason (p. 30). In her narrative, Smith represents a departure from a pure theory of moral sentiments as he relies upon self-command (arising from reason) to regulate our sentiments (p. 47). As moral sentimentalists ended up on the "losing side" of ethical debates in the eighteenth century, the moral sentiments were increasingly associated only with women in such a way that lessened their importance and contained women in a way that limited their participation in the public sphere (p. 54). The above quote from Smith is certainly guilty of the marginalization of women's perspectives that feminist ethics has called to our attention. I will address Tronto's concern about creeping universalism in Smith's ethics in the next section.

[11] The quote also exhibits a very problematic bit of reasoning, based upon social practice, that seems to essentialize a lack of charity in women. Regardless of whether Smith himself was an essentialist about masculinity it should be possible to re-contextualize his ideas about self-command and humanity without being committed to theses that might be viewed as problematic from a feminist perspective. (Much as has been done with Kant's unenlightened views about gender.)

The problematic aspects of Smith's views are a reminder that the parallels to care ethics have their limits. However, the intent of this chapter is not to make the case that care ethicists interested in business ethics should adopt Smith's moral theory. The point is that in important ways, care ethics resembles Smith's moral theory and those resemblances involve elements of Smith's philosophy (notably, a concern for the welfare of others, a reliance upon sentiment in our moral judgments, and a socially dependent sense of self) that forms a bridge between ethics and economics. Care ethicists should be able to use the relevant elements of care ethics to engage ethically with economics in the same way that Smith did.

Can the Impartial Spectator Care?

Tronto's concern about Smith is related to another common feature of care ethics. Held states that "the ethics of care rejects the view of the dominant moral theories that the more abstract the reasoning about a moral problem the better because the more likely to avoid bias and arbitrariness, the more nearly to achieve impartiality" (p. 11). Care ethics rejects the language of abstract and impartial moral theory because it seems to undermine the concrete relationships that seem essential to a caring perspective. The virtue of self-command is representative of an important divergence between Smith's moral theory and care ethics. What remains to be seen is whether this is an aspect of Smith's theory that is integral to his bridging of economics and ethics.

According to Smith, children lack self-command, but as they get older they learn how to exercise discipline over their feelings (TMS III, i, 64). It seems then that despite all of the emphasis on moral sentiment in Smith's theory, our emotions are still subject to higher principles. As Smith explains it:

> The man who acts according to the rules of perfect prudence, of strict justice, and of proper benevolence, may be said to be perfectly virtuous. But the most perfect knowledge of those rules will not alone enable him to act in this manner: his own passions are very apt to mislead him; sometimes to drive him and sometimes to seduce him to violate all the rules which he himself, in all his sober and cool hours, approves of. The most perfect knowledge, if it is not supported by the most perfect self-command, will not always enable him to do his duty. (TMS VI, iii, 1)

Admittedly, Smith distances self-command from the rules of justice, so that does suggest that the virtue is not an example of the justice-orientation that care ethicists are trying to distinguish themselves from. However, the above quoted passage implies that what self-command does is guarantee that our passions are in conformity with the rules of prudence, strict justice and proper benevolence. It is hard to see how a virtue could enable us to be in conformity with such abstract rules (and rules that are also supposed to be drained of "improper" emotion) without being itself the embodiment of a set of abstract rules.

While the virtue of self-command would seem good evidence that Smith's moral theory falls somewhat outside of care ethics, it does not mean that a care ethicist could not find a way to re-appropriate Smith as a part of care ethics. To begin with,

Smith acknowledges that self-command is a context-sensitive moral virtue. As he puts it, "the point of propriety, the degree of any passion which the impartial spectator approves of, is differently situated in different passions" (TMS VII, iii, 14). A care ethicist could build upon this to produce a version of Smith's moral theory that is more amenable to the care ethics approach. Just because the textual evidence is very strong against a relativistic reading of Smith's mature moral theory that does not preclude a NeoSmithian care ethics from being developed. Smith's particular concerns about relativism in moral theory are not shared by all care ethicists and that issue is not inextricably linked to his overall moral theory. The aspects of Smith's theory that conflict with care ethics could be extracted or at least muted without undermining the value of the rest of his theory or its connection to economics. So, it appears then that Smith offers a way in which care ethics can be introduced to economics and have a significant role.

Smith does appear to make great use of the impartial perspective in his moral theory. Self-command is part of the solution that Smith developed in response to the problem that one's sympathetic motivations could be trumped by self-interested motivations. The virtue of self-command was inculcated by imagining an external judge of our actions, which Smith called the "impartial spectator." By imagining ourselves as an impartial spectator who has no ties to anyone involved in the situation before us, we can better approximate the appropriate sentiment without the interference of our personal interests. In addition, the idea that we were being judged by an impartial spectator strengthened our resolve to comply with the demands of morality. Since his moral theory relies so heavily on this particular device, it would seem a stretch to consider Smith's theory as relevant to care ethics.

It is a matter for Smith scholarship as to whether Smith really intended the impartial spectator to be an abstract, impersonal and theoretical device. Tronto herself notes that Smith did not give the impartial spectator a significant role in the first edition of the *Theory of Moral Sentiments*, nor did he discuss the virtue of self-command (p. 47). At least one tradition of interpretation favors seeing the impartial spectator as a generalization of actual consensus in society (in which case it would not necessarily violate the concreteness requirement that Held identifies) and does so by relying more on earlier editions of TMS.[12] It is beyond the scope of this chapter to settle the interpretive debate and it is not necessary to do so anyway. Regardless of whether Smith himself was a proto-care ethicist, what matters for our purposes is whether his moral theory could be adapted into a care ethics. If that is possible and if (as will be argued in the second half of this chapter) Smith's ethical theory is intertwined with his economic theory, then it follows that care ethics can be intertwined with some form of capitalism. In that case, care ethics would be an important part of properly functioning business and of great importance to Business Ethics.

[12]For one influential relativistic (although empirically based) interpretation of Smith, see Campbell (1971). The author's inclination is to regard Campbell's work as an interesting extension of Smith, but not as an accurate interpretation of the text given Smith's expressed goals for a moral theory. However, just because it is not what Smith intended does not mean it could not form the basis of a NeoSmithian theory.

There seem to be two main ways in which a care ethicist could embrace Smith's moral theory without accepting the impartial spectator (at least as described in Smith's work). The first way would be to simply reject the need for an impartial corrective. Basically, it would be Smith's theory of moral sentiments without the impartial spectator. A relativistic approach to the moral sentiments may be consistent with the early views of Smith. If one goes through *The Theory of Moral Sentiments*, one finds the impartial spectator referred to in various ways such as "every impartial spectator," "the real or supposed spectator," "the spectator, from whom we can expect the least sympathy and indulgence," and "the most impartial spectator.[13]" Such phrases suggest that there is not a single fixed ideal of the impartial spectator that everyone shares. Since the impartial spectator would not then embody the elements of moral theory that seem inconsistent with care ethics, it would seem then that based on the elements that resonate with care ethics one could adopt Smith's moral theory as a form of care ethics. As some commentators have argued, it is entirely possible that the early Smith held views that are consistent with all the notable aspects of care ethics. But, it is also very clear that as Smith revised later editions of his *Theory of Moral Sentiments* he removed some of the more egregious instances where his theory was leaning towards relativism and even included a passage that clearly identified his moral theory with objective moral values. So, while someone might appropriate elements of Smith's moral theory (other than the impartial spectator) to create a care ethics, it is not likely to be a theory that Smith himself adopted.[14]

Another option for bringing Smith's moral theory more into line with care ethics is to preserve the spirit of the impartial spectator as a device that guarantees moral truth but to create a device that does so using the resources of care ethics. Nel Noddings seems to provide a possible device with her notion of the "ethical ideal." Noddings describes the "ethical ideal" as follows:

> When I reflect on the way I am in genuine caring relationships and caring situations – the natural quality of my engrossment, the shift of my energies toward the other and his projects – I form a picture of myself. This picture is incomplete so long as I see myself only as the one-caring. But as I reflect also on the way I am as cared-for, I see clearly my own longing to be received, understood, and accepted. There are cases in which I am not received, and many in which I fail to receive the other, but a picture of goodness begins to form. I see that when I am as I need the other to be toward me, I am the way I want to be – that is, I am closest to the goodness when I accept and affirm the internal "I must". (p. 49)[15]

Instead of some impartial spectator that is the idealization of our judgmental capacities, we can have a notion of some idealized caring relationship that can serve as a check on our egotistical desires. The ethical ideal is not impartial or abstract in the way that most proponents of care ethics would find objectionable. Yet it could serve the function of correcting our empathic responses so as to produce proper

[13]TMS II, i, 2, 2; TMS III, iii, 21; TMS III, iii, 38; TMS III, iv, 4.

[14]It is also not a strategy I would recommend for care ethics as it seems to simply ignore one of criticism of care ethics—that a theory based on individual sentiment will lead to a form of relativism that is counterproductive to moral discourse.

[15]Noddings (1984).

moral sentiments. And in case there is any concern that this ethical ideal is another relativistic standard, one can appeal to the similarity in human nature and the caring experience in order to ensure that people's ethical ideals are more or less the same. Much like Hume and Smith do in their own work, Noddings makes optimistic statements about human nature that are meant to support her moral theory. At one point she asserts, "All but the most deprived (and, perhaps, depraved) of human beings feel the pain and joy of others, and each of us has access through memory to our own caring and being cared-for" (p. 104).

As I have strived to make clear, it is not appropriate to say that Smith was himself a care ethicist. All the evidence available indicates that Smith clung to certain metaethical principles that are regarded as inconsistent with care ethics. Nonetheless, his moral theory does contain the seeds of a care ethic that a contemporary care ethicist can nurture in a fairly simple manner. The only major obstacle to counting Smith's moral theory as a form of care ethic seems to be his commitment to an abstract and universal moral perspective in the form of the impartial spectator. It could be argued that this arises from a desire to make sure that his moral theory cannot be accused of relativism. Nowadays, the charge of relativism is not fatal to a moral theory and there are several ways in which moral truth has been identified (some of which would be sufficient to avoid Smith's concerns and still be acceptable to a care ethicist). Although relativism need not be a reason for rejecting care ethics, proponents of the theory should address concerns that a lack of universal principles can lead to relativism or an inability to condemn actions that people usually disapprove of. The impartial spectator was Smith's way of addressing this concern, but Noddings' ethical ideal is another possibility. Care ethicists are also strongly advised to consider some corrective solution along the lines of an ethical ideal or "impartial" spectator (where this is not an abstract, impersonal construction), because it can be a response to some other criticisms leveled against care ethics. For example, Tronto (among others) has identified parochialism as a danger for care as a political ideal (pp. 170–172). By relying on our actual sentiments they naturally privilege the needs of those close by over distant others. Interestingly, Tronto recognizes that Smith's move towards more universalistic language is a response to the increasing social distance caused by the increasingly globalized world of the eighteenth century (and beyond) (pp. 46–47). A decision procedure resembling the ethical ideal or an impartial spectator would also be a helpful tool in dealing with the concern articulated by James Rachels that the context-sensitivity of care ethics creates too much ambiguity about our moral responsibilities.[16]

Smith describes self-command as the virtue that makes it possible for us to empathize with any person no matter how far removed we might be from them socially or how much we might be inclined to demonize them as a member of different ethnic group (TMS I, i, 42). Also, self-command is supposed to give us power over the "most ungovernable passions of human nature" (TMS I, i, 45). What Smith seems to have in mind are the retributive emotions as well as the desire

[16]Rachels (1999).

for self-preservation which often lead people to act against what they know to be morally correct. Pride and the priority people place on self-gratification are two great impediments to moral judgment according to Smith. What Smith recognizes is that we cannot rely on mere sentiment (or our relationships with other people) to always give us a sense of the right thing to do. We need to be able to distinguish moral sentiments from non-moral sentiments and that is what Smith uses the impartial spectator to do; and we need to have a mechanism by which we are moved by moral sentiments over the more powerful non-moral sentiments and that is the purpose of self-command. As has already been discussed, there is some evidence that some care ethicists and moral sentimentalists have tried to find ways of addressing this problem without committing themselves to abstract principles like Smith does.

The universalistic tendencies in Smith's theory (especially his final version of it in the sixth edition of TMS) are only a real cause for concern if they are intimately connected to the features that enable Smith to bridge the divide between ethics and economics. Even then, the real issue is whether those features are necessary to bridge that gap. We have already seen that Smith's moral and economic theories display some of the prejudices of his cultural milieu concerning women and the domestic sphere. Later economists in the nineteenth and twentieth centuries developed economic theory in ways that only further marginalized women by increasing the separation of the domestic sphere from economic theorizing. However, capitalism is not a single monolithic theory. Smith's brand of capitalism is not identical to either the Austrian or Chicago Schools of Economics (despite what each of them claims). Care ethics would undoubtedly produce another variation on capitalism. My point is that care ethics can make use of its similarities with Smith's moral theory to insert itself more centrally into a critique of current economic theory. And it can do so in a way that does not require an outright rejection of capitalism in all its forms. As I will demonstrate in the remaining sections, the elements of Smith's moral theory that share similarities with care ethics are important to his economic theory. The main point of difference is not as important and so it might be dispensed with without sacrificing the idea that what economics needs might be found in care ethics. As I have tried to show in this section, Smith's impartial perspective was an evolving response to certain metaethical concerns he had. If one did not share those concerns, the impartial perspective would not be needed. Even if one did share those concerns, we have seen an example from Noddings as to how to address those concerns without evoking an abstract and impersonal perspective.

A Place for Care in Smith's Economic Theory

One famous quote from Smith's *Wealth of Nations* (WN) is the following line from the second chapter of the work: "It is not from the benevolence of the butcher, the brewer, or the baker, that we expect our dinner, but from their regard to their own interest" (WN I, ii, 2).[17] To many people this seems to be a clear indication that economics views human beings as purely self-interested (the so-called *homo economicus*). However, this reading of the passage is too narrowly focused. If one looks to the larger passage in which the line appears, one finds a much more complex picture of humanity within the economic sphere.

Smith continues the passage with the observation that, "man has almost constant occasion for the help of his brethren, and it is in vain for him to expect it from their benevolence only. He will be more likely to prevail if he can interest their self-love in his favour, and show them that it is for their own advantage to do for him what he requires of them" (WN I, ii, 2). While this seems to be a further endorsement of the *homo economicus*, Smith qualifies his observation in an interesting way. He says that someone who appeals to self-interest is "more likely to prevail," this suggests that an appeal to benevolence could work (and might even work on a fairly regular basis). The problem here seems to be with the fact that we are constantly in need of help and so it is not surprising that Smith recognizes that there would quickly be benevolence fatigue if we made use of it too often. I might ask someone to do me a favor and drop a letter off on their way out of the building so that I could wait at my desk for a phone call. But if I was constantly asking someone to run errands for me without any recompense the demands I placed upon them would become too much. Besides, it is one thing to ask someone to drop a letter off for me if I'm stuck at my desk, it's quite another to ask them to do so because I don't feel like walking downstairs.

The clincher of Smith's discussion of the appeal to benevolence (and what is crucial for showing that there is a place for care in economic theory) is Smith's remark about beggars:

> Nobody but a beggar chuses to depend chiefly upon the benevolence of his fellow-citizens. Even a beggar does not depend upon it entirely. The charity of well-disposed people, indeed, supplies him with the whole fund of his subsistence. But though this principle ultimately provides him with all the necessaries of life which he has occasion for, it neither does nor can provide him with them as he has occasion for them. (WN I, ii, 2)

Smith takes for granted that a person in true need, that is someone who does not have enough to eat, will be able to procure food from someone that he meets. All the "necessaries of life" will be provided by well-intentioned people. This is not to say that the beggar would live a life that we might consider desirable. Even if they have enough to eat so that they don't die of starvation right at that moment, they might not get proper nourishment or a healthy and safe environment to live in. Nonetheless, Smith presumes in this passage that no society would be devoid of members who would respond to appeals to benevolence even when there was no particular benefit to the individual and in all likelihood there would be some cost to the individual (although it might be no more than the cost of sandwich).

That Smith would make this presumption is not surprising if one has read his *Theory of Moral Sentiments*. The very first line of that book is: "How selfish soever

[17] Smith (2009a).

man may be supposed, there are evidently some principles in his nature, which interest him in the fortune of others, and render their happiness necessary to him, though he derives nothing from it except the pleasure of seeing it" (TMS I, i, 1). If one reads Smith, it becomes clear that his economic agents are infused with the kind of concerns and sentiments that Smith associates with a moral agent. For example, in discussing how masters of a factory or business should treat their workers he states, "If masters would always listen to the dictates of reason and humanity, they have frequently occasion rather to moderate, than to animate the application of many of their workmen" (WN I, viii, 43). Smith thinks that any reasonable person would recognize that they ought not to work their employees too hard in the pursuit of profit. Smith does not deny that the maximization of productivity is something that makes sense from an economic perspective. Instead he claims that no business owner should want to do that and he seems hopeful that most business owners will be the sorts of people who listen to the dictates of humanity. In fact, as I'll argue shortly, this concern for others is integral to Smith's defense of his theory against criticism.

Someone might object to this reading of Smith as placing too much emphasis on select passages and ignoring the overall theme of the work. After all, in the famous invisible hand passage, Smith remarks that "By pursuing his own interest he frequently promotes that of the society more effectually than when he really intends to promote it. I have never known much good done by those who affected to trade for the public good" (WN IV, ii, 9). This seems to be a clear statement that, at least in the *Wealth of Nations*, Smith is promoting an exclusively self-interested approach and casting aspersions on any attempts to view economics through a moral lens. The problem with such a strong reading is that it takes the passage out of context (the debate over whether there should be laws protecting and encouraging domestic industry over foreign investment). Smith's point seems to be more about an informational problem than a problem of what motivations we pursue. Smith thinks it is fairly obvious that there are a number of advantages to investing in domestic industry and so in most cases it is not necessary to require people to do so. In cases where domestic investment is not desirable, there are probably reasons (such as the cost of production) that are good reasons not to require domestic investment as it would only makes the economy more inefficient and raise the cost of goods for everyone. People who try to make laws governing foreign and domestic trade do so with very little understanding of the complex system they are dealing with and so, in most cases, they will do more harm than good. The investor should still be attendant to moral concerns when making choices about their investment; they just shouldn't try and work towards some global solution that will address the moral problems throughout society.

It would seem that this localized approach to morality would be something that care ethicists would be very receptive to. Smith's argument for less government regulation is based upon a belief that attempts to abstract from the particular details of the situation yield inefficient (and sometimes even harmful) judgments. Thus we can see that a central aspect of care ethics (context-sensitivity) is not only an important part of Smith's moral theory, but also at the heart of his argument for reducing government regulations of commerce. The invisible hand has been criticized for making overly optimistic assumptions about how markets function and being blind to the effects of power and status differentials. As I have tried to show in the discussion of this famous passage, Smith's argument against government regulation should not be thought of as an appeal to some natural order or providence that ensures that self-interest will always yield the public good. Instead, one should see Smith's argument as expressing a deep skepticism about the ability of a central government to regulate the market. As Tronto notes (p. 47), Smith's moral philosophy exhibited a similar skepticism towards the attempts to instill civic virtue through government institutions. The invisible hand argument is really rooted in the belief that it is usually better to err on the side of less regulation.

On this interpretation, Smith cannot be criticized for being naïve about the market, but one can still question the idea that less regulation will usually work out better. A further defense of Smith's position depends on another connection with care ethics—the idea that our sentiments will guide our actions, specifically the sympathy which interests us in the fortunes of other. Smith's discussion of foreign tariffs is an example of Smith's assumption that people's behavior in the market should be governed by those moral sentiments. Smith was a staunch opponent of all tariffs on foreign goods that were not connected to the costs of importing those goods. Even if a country's trading partners were unwilling to lift tariffs on the country's exports, Smith still thought it was advisable to get rid of tariffs on imports. However, there are a few instances in which he recommends a gradual or moderate approach to get rid of foreign tariffs. One of them is if a particular domestic industry is an important part of the economic life of the country (because it employed a great many people) and it would be dramatically affected by foreign competition (think of the textile industry in the South or the auto industry in the Midwest). In those cases, Smith recommends a gradual change in tariffs so as to allow time for the workers in those industries to find a new livelihood. According to Smith:

> Humanity may in this case require that the freedom of trade should be restored only by slow gradations, and with a good deal of reserve and circumspection. Were those high duties and prohibitions taken away all at once, cheaper foreign goods of the same kind might be poured so fast into the home-market as to deprive all at once many thousands of our people of their ordinary employment and means of subsistence. The disorder which this would occasion might no doubt be very considerable. (WN IV, ii, 40)

Smith appeals to humanity (not economic benefit or self-interest) as the reason why a country should take a careful approach when removing trade regulations on some industries. The presumption here is that humanity (in other words sympathy) should be a reason that affects economic policies. And, I would argue, Smith needs to make this appeal to humanity in order to justify his rather strong skepticism towards regulation. In the nineteenth century, economics severed the connection to sympathy and it has left neoclassical economics without a sufficient defense of some of its basic assumptions.[18] Capitalism needs Smith's theory or something like it (for example, care ethics) to fulfill that justificatory role. Undoubtedly the moral theory chosen would influence the exact regulations that would be permitted and prohibited, but that is not to be worked out in this chapter.

The Intertwining of Ethics and Economics in Smith (and Beyond)

So far I have defended the idea that care ethics could play a role in economic theory inasmuch as economic transactions involve people whose natural sentiments will incline them to create moral relationships with the people they transact with. This idea is not a radical addition to economics. The free-market advocate Milton Friedman is famous for saying that the social responsibility of business is to maximize profits. His defense of this view contains an important caveat. He says a CEO "has direct responsibility to his employers . . . to conduct the business in accordance with their desires, which generally will be to make as much money as possible while conforming to the basic rules of the society, both those embodied in law and those embodied in ethical custom."[19] Even the proponent of the laissez-faire Chicago School (which has been accused of underwriting an entirely amoral approach to economics) recognizes that business will usually be constrained by some basic ethical norms that the participants in the system recognize. Unlike Smith, however, Friedman is not committed to any particular ethical system as being the one that should govern all human beings and he is open to the possibility that a business might choose to skirt ethical norms if the investors were to agree to it explicitly. Friedman is generalizing about most people; he is not making a normative judgment about them as Smith does.

The ways in which Smith's ethics intertwine with his economics go deeper than just an observation about human desire. Several times in the *Wealth of Nations* Smith makes appeal to ethical notions in order to make suggestions about the proper workings of the economy. For example, in a discussion of taxes Smith states that those who own luxury carriages should bear a greater portion of the tax burden for the maintenance of roads. This burden would even exceed the amount that might be accounted for by the extra stress on the road those carriages produce. Smith's general principle about taxation is that "subjects of every state ought to contribute towards the support of the government, as nearly as possible, in proportion to their respective abilities; that is, in proportion to the revenue which they respectively

[18] An excellent analysis of the shift away from sympathy in nineteenth century economics can be found in Peart and Levy (2005). Peart and Levy argue that the loss of sympathy is one of the causes of the growing inequalities in economic markets in the industrial age and an unfortunate departure from Smith's original vision.

[19] Friedman (1970).

enjoy under the protection of the state" (WN V, ii, 25). But in the case of luxury carriages he puts the extra burden on the rich because in his words:

> When the toll upon carriages of luxury, upon coaches, post-chaises, &c. is made somewhat higher in proportion to their weight, than upon carriages of necessary use, such as carts, waggons, &c. the indolence and vanity of the rich is made to contribute in a very easy manner to the relief of the poor, by rendering cheaper the transportation of heavy goods to all the different parts of the country. (WN, V, i, 75)

Smith justifies the tax or toll imbalance based upon qualities that are usually deemed immoral and certainly are presented as deserving our disapprobation. We can see then that for Smith, moral judgments have a role to play in setting economic policy. Much like with tariffs, Smith thinks that the excesses of an unregulated market can be curbed by an appeal to our moral sentiments.

Arguing that the rich should bear a greater tax burden because it is the right thing to do for the sake of the overall society (as well as a punishment for immoral behavior) is just one example of Smith appealing to moral concerns in his discussions of the economic structure of society. Smith states that the government has a responsibility to fund public works projects whenever they are "to the highest degree advantageous to a great society" but are such that the cost of undertaking them would never recoup the cost of the investment (WN V, i, 69). One might be tempted to read "advantageous" in a self-interested way. However, the fact that it appeals to a common good (the advantage of society) would count against that reading. Moreover, while some of the examples he gives (like justice) could be described as systems that it is to our advantage to participate in, not all of the examples of public works are things that would benefit us indirectly. A notable example of this can be found in his remarks on education in the *Wealth of Nations.*

Smith has a number of negative things to say about public education, but he also recognizes that there are some things that can only be taught in a public education system. To wit, those subjects which are deemed impractical or useless such as philosophy or the classics. Smith thinks it is important that the youth receive a basic education in the classics because he feared that the growing division of labor was eroding people's moral sensibilities and sense of civic responsibility. And Smith is clear that he thinks it a real moral failing of society if it fails to develop its citizens moral capacities. As far as he is concerned, "A man without the proper use of the intellectual faculties of a man, is, if possible, more contemptible than even a coward, and seems to be mutilated and deformed in a still more essential part of the character of human nature" (WN V.1.189). Smith even goes so far as to state that even if there was no benefit to society to educate the general populace, the state should still turn its attention to the issue of public education. Once again, Smith is basing public policy on moral concerns.[20] Concerns which his moral theory says would be shared by anyone who was able to adopt the perspective of the impartial spectator and set aside their own concerns.

[20] And again, his appeal to morality serves to mitigate another aspect of capitalism that is often criticized. In this case, it is the division of labor that many see as dehumanizing.

Conclusion

Although only a few examples have been offered, it should be clear at this point that there is a strong case to be made for the interrelationship between ethics and economics in Smith. Some commentators have suggested that the *Wealth of Nations* is consistent with Smith's moral theory, but that within the text itself actual moral and sympathetic concerns are muted.[21] Fleischacker has marshaled several passages (beyond those cited here) to illustrate that the *Wealth of Nations* is rife with moral concepts, such as equity and justice, and they play a role in many of Smith's economic assessments and prescriptions.[22] In light of his arguments and the evidence presented in this chapter, the reader should be persuaded to at least take very seriously the notion that economics can and should be guided by a moral vision.[23]

It has been a further contention of this chapter that Smith's moral theory (or a moral theory that contains its core features of context-sensitivity and a reliance upon moral sentiments, especially sympathy) is particularly well-suited to serving as the moral guidelines for economic theory and practice. His moral theory is based on many of the same assumptions about human nature as his economic theory and is designed in such a way that it often can correct for the excesses that an overly narrow focus on profit maximization can produce. Business leaders who only look at the numbers are losing sight of the people affected by their decisions. Smith's moral theory encourages us to connect with people and see things from their point of view, and so it can serve as a great counterbalance to this phenomenon. Care ethics shares many of the features of Smith's moral theory (and in the areas in which they diverge care ethics could make use of other moral notions to do the same work as Smith's impartial point of view). As a result, care ethics is a very good candidate for a moral theory that could help to reshape economics in a way that is closer to Smith's original vision—a form of capitalism that does not vex our moral sensibilities.

References

Brown, V. 1994. *Adam Smith's discourse: Canonicity Commerce and Conscience*. London: Routledge.

Campbell, T.D. 1971. *Adam Smith's science of morals*. London: Allen & Unwin, Ltd.

Eisler, R. 2007. *The real wealth of nations: Creating a caring economics*. San Francisco, CA: Berrett-Koehler.

Fleischacker, S. 2004. *On Adam Smith's "Wealth of Nations": A philosophical companion*. Princeton, NJ: Princeton University Press.

Folbre, N. 2001. *The invisible heart: Economics and family values*. New York, NY: New Press.

[21] For a defense of this particular interpretation see Brown (1994).

[22] Especially pages 48–55. Among the goals of that section is to refute Brown's take on Smith's approach to the *Wealth of Nations*.

[23] Space does not permit me to make the full argument, but I hope to have sown the seeds for the idea that an adequate defense of capitalism relies upon a moral theory like Smith's. The theory would be untenable without these moral presuppositions.

Friedman, M. 1970. The social responsibility of business is to increase its profits. *New York Times Magazine* September 13.

Held, V. 2006. *The ethics of care: Personal, political and global*. Oxford: Oxford University Press.

Kennedy, G. 2005. *Adam Smith's lost legacy*. Basingstoke: Palgrave Macmillan.

Noddings, N. 1984. *Caring: A feminine approach to ethics & moral education*. Berkeley, CA: University of California Press.

Peart, S., and D. Levy. 2005. *The "Vanity of the philosopher": From equality to hierarchy in post-classical economics*. Ann Arbor, MI: University of Michigan Press.

Rachels, J. 1999. *The elements of moral philosophy*. New York, NY: McGraw Hill.

Smith, A. 2009a. *Inquiry into the nature and causes of the wealth of nations*, 2 volumes. Indianapolis, IN: Liberty Fund.

Smith, A. 2009b. *The theory of moral sentiments*. Indianapolis, IN: Liberty Fund.

Sugden, R. 2002. Beyond empathy and sympathy: Adam Smith's concept of fellow-feeling. *Economics and Philosophy* 18: 63–87.

Tronto, J. 1993. *Moral boundaries: A political argument for an ethic of care*. London: Routledge.

Chapter 4
Towards a Caring Economy

Dimitria Electra Gatzia

Introduction

Neo-liberalism is the predominant economic paradigm in most of the industrialized world. Its key institutions are markets, private or state ownership of the means of production, and wage-labor (Schweickart 1980). The main role of traditional business ethics is to provide guidelines for moral conduct within the neo-liberal paradigm—it is for this reason the term "business ethics" is often used interchangeably with "corporate ethics."[1] Traditional business ethics involves two distinct areas of interest. Firstly, it aims to explain moral conduct pertaining to relations between employers and workers within a corporation. As such it addresses issues arising from the organization of a corporation such as wages, labor unions, working conditions, job discrimination, workers rights, etc. Secondly, it aims to explain moral conduct pertaining to relations among corporations, consumers, and the environment. As such it addresses issues arising from the activities of corporations such as responsibilities to customers and, lately, the environment. Since traditional business ethics operates within the confines of the neo-liberal paradigm, it plays a limited, if any, role in evaluating the paradigm itself. The recent financial crisis, however, has reignited the discussion on the role of business ethics propelling the topic to the forefront of philosophical discourse.

The aim of this paper is to show that a business ethic based on the ethics of care is superior to traditional business ethics. It shall be argued that neo-liberalism is inconsistent with the ethics of care since it either excludes caring institutions or treats them as preferences to be satisfied as the "free" market sees fit. Unlike traditional business ethics, a business ethic based on the ethics of care can play an important role in challenging the neo-liberal paradigm. Many business issues that

[1]The terms "corporate" or "corporations" are intended to have a wide scope as to include any private or state owned company.

D.E. Gatzia (✉)
Department of Philosophy, The University of Akron Wayne College, Orrville, OH, USA
e-mail: dg29@uakron.edu

M. Hamington, M. Sander-Staudt (eds.), *Applying Care Ethics to Business*, Issues in Business Ethics 34, DOI 10.1007/978-90-481-9307-3_4,

© Springer Science+Business Media B.V. 2011

are treated as peripheral by traditional business ethics can thus take central stage in a business ethic based on the ethics of care.

The Ethics of Care

The ethics of care is a normative ethical theory. It differs from deontology and consequentialism in two important respects.[2] Firstly, it acknowledges the important role certain emotions play in moral reasoning. Traditional moral theories, by contrast, view emotions as irrational and thus antagonistic to the reasoning process. As Rousseau aptly observed, however, moral reasoning is best when "guided ... by reason and modified by empathy."[3] Rousseau recognized that reason, in the absence of moral emotions, could pervert moral judgment. Adam Smith, the father of "free market" economics, also believed sympathy and proper moral sentiments to be of crucial importance for the proper functioning of society. Contemporary moral psychology seems to support Rousseau's and Smith's claims. Pizarro (2000), for example, argues that moral emotions play an integral role in the process of moral judgment. The ethics of care is consistent with such assessments. It views "sympathy, empathy, sensitivity, and responsiveness as the kind of moral emotions that need to be cultivated not only to help in the implementation of the dictates of reason but to better ascertain what morality recommends" (Held 2006, 11). It further recommends that ruthlessness, insensitivity, and inability to build intimate relationships, which are staples of neo-liberalism, should be replaced by moral emotions (Fraser and Gordon 2006).

Secondly, the ethics of care "respects rather than removes itself from the claims of particular others with whom we share actual relationships ... [and] calls into question the universalistic and abstract rules of the dominant theories" (Held 2006, 11). It views the interests of individuals "as importantly intertwined rather than as simply competing" (Held 2006, 15). It "focuses on attentiveness, trust, responsiveness to need, narrative nuance, and cultivating caring relations" because it recognizes that protecting and promoting the actual specific interests of those involved requires attending to the contextual details of a situation (ibid.). Those particularly vulnerable to society's choices and their outcomes are given additional consideration, which is measured according to the level of their vulnerability and affectedness. Traditional theories, by contrast, seek fair solutions between competing individual interests and rights and "give primacy to such values as autonomy, independence, noninterference, fairness, and rights" (Held 2006, 129). While the ethics of care aims to safeguard individuality, it recognizes that "noninterference ... even between equals can be isolating and alienating" (Baier 1994, 24). It thus

[2] Slote (1998) views the ethics of care as an agent-based virtue ethics of caring. Held (2006) argues that Slote "misses the centrality of caring relations for an ethics of care" (p. 51). A caring person, according to her, not only needs to have the intention to care and the disposition to care effectively but must also participate in caring relations. Although I agree with Held, whether the ethics of care is an independent moral theory or a version of virtue ethics is not pertinent to my argument.

[3] See Rousseau (1986).

aims to remove isolating and alienating barriers among individuals and maintains that traditional theories "miss out on essential and ineliminable aspects of human life" such as social, communal, and emotional (Groenhoul 2004, 55). Their view of dependency as a character defect, for example, tends to stigmatize those who are unable to care for themselves (Fraser and Gordon 2006). The ethics of care reclaims dependency as an inescapable feature of the human condition and aims to dispel the myth that independence is inextricably tied to individuality. It thus encourages society to treat those who cannot care for themselves with dignity and respect. In viewing interdependence as a necessary condition for achieving individual interests, the ethics of care offers an alternative way of assessing moral conduct in the context of business. It can pave the way for adopting a business ethic that challenges the neo-liberal paradigm.

The Aim of Economics

The preferred term for economics until late nineteenth century was "political economy." Political economy originated from moral philosophy and it was developed as a study of the economy of a state. The moral, political, and economic spheres, at that time, were treated as hybrids. In the quest for objectivity and universality, neo-liberal economists began treating economics as a "hard" science inadvertently isolating it from its primary aim, i.e., to improve people's lives. This realization has prompted some to argue that economics is best understood as a "policy science" rather than a "hard" science (Varian 2000). Varian, for example, notes that "Keynes was only half joking when he said that economists should be more like dentists. Dentists claim that they can make peoples' lives better; so do economists" (2000, 353). Viewing economics as a policy science, i.e., as a science of prescribing deliberate plans of action to improve people's lives, provides a basis for evaluating neo-liberalism. For, it allows us to ask: What sort of deliberate plan is prescribed by neo-liberalism? How does such a plan purport to improve people's lives? Does neo-liberalism succeed in improving people's lives?

Answering these questions requires an understanding of the main tenets of neo-liberalism. Neo-liberalism reduces prices of all products and services to the supply and demand behavior of individuals, which is then reduced to wants and productive abilities of individuals (Wolff and Resnick 1987, 45). No distinction is made between desires and needs. The desire for golden toilet seats, for example, is no different from, nor prior to, the need for potable water (Baruchello 2008). It is assumed that the pursuit of rational self-interest, when led by the forces of the unregulated market or, to borrow Adam Smith's term, "the invisible hand", tends to benefit society as a whole by maximizing its wealth. Thus, its key aim is continual maximization of profit. Adam Smith articulates these ideas in the following passage:

> Every individual ... generally, indeed, neither intends to promote the public interest, nor knows how much he is promoting it. By preferring the support of domestic to that of foreign industry he intends only his own security; and by directing that industry in such a manner as its produce may be of the greatest value, he intends only his own gain, and he is in this,

> as in many other cases, led by an invisible hand to promote an end which was no part of his intention. (*The Wealth of Nations*, Book IV Chapter II)[4]

Neo-liberalism equates the wealth of a nation, and hence its wellbeing, with its economic growth, which is measured in terms of the total amount of goods and services produced either by all nationals of a country (i.e., gross national product or GNP) or within a country (i.e., gross domestic product or GDP). Empirical studies, however, show that increases in per capita GDP are not identical to the economic wellbeing of the people. Although the annual GDP of the United States reached 14 billion in 2008 and 2009, the nation's official poverty rate increased from 12.5% in 2007 to 13.5% in 2008 (U.S. Census Bureau). Out of the 37.3 million people in poverty in 2007, 13.3 million were children under 18. The numbers increased to 39.8 and 14.1 million respectively in 2008. Despite the high rates in per capita GDP, the poverty rate in the United States is colossal. Inequality in the United States has risen considerably in the past 30 years, with the top 1% capturing 10% of all income in 1979 and over 23% in 2007 (Schmitt 2009). Meanwhile, the GDP per capita increased from 1,038 billion in 1970 to 14,259 billion in 2009 (U.S. Census Bureau). This shows that the wealth of nations, measured in terms of their GDP, is consistent with the poverty of their people. Similarly, increases in per capita GNP are "not identical with improvement in the economic well-being of real human beings" (Cobb 2007, 365). This is more noticeable when GNP per capita is compared to the Index of Sustainable Economic Welfare (ISEW) for the United States. Unlike the GNP measure, the ISEW measure assumes that "the well-being of society as a whole is affected by the condition of the poorest" (Cobb 2007, 365):

> Computation of the ISEW begins with the personal consumption but then adjusts this in relation to income distribution ... The index then adds for household services, chiefly the contribution of housewives. It subtracts for "defensive costs," that is, costs that result from economic growth and the social changes ... [and] for the reduction of natural capital, and adds or subtracts for change in the net international position. (Cobb 2007, 365)

A comparison of economic growth as measured by per capital GNP with economic wellbeing as measured by per capital ISEW shows that from 1951–1990 the former more than doubled (it went from $3,741 to $7,756) the latter rose less than 15% (from $2,793 to $3,253). From 1971-1990, the former rose by 43% while the latter fell by 5%. Since the GDP and the GNP per capita are an average of output divided by the number of people, they cannot provide accurate information about the distribution of national income between the wealthy and the poor. The ISEW is a better indicator of wellbeing since it takes into consideration a number of factors that contribute to the poverty of the people.

Empirical studies show that poverty "has mental health consequences that are negative, widespread and sometimes severe" (Fryer 2006). Research in neuroscience, for example, suggests that the brains of children who grow up in poverty

[4]Smith's claim is not a metaphor but a metaphysical assumption, specifically a Providential conception of human affairs. See Denis (2005) and Nicholls (1992).

tend to have higher levels of stress hormones than children of more affluent families.[5] Excessive levels of stress hormones cause irreparable harm to children's brains since they "disrupt the formation of synaptic connections between cells in the developing brain" and affect the blood supply.[6] Stress hormone levels also affect neural development associated with language disabilities and memory impairment. When such mental disabilities are coupled with external conditions including inadequate nutrition and exposure to environmental toxins, the effects of poverty are even greater. People in poorer countries are more likely to be affected by environmental toxins due to industrialization. The alarming increase in cancer rates in industrialized countries, however, suggests that neo-liberal policies have serious adverse effects on wealthier countries.[7] It follows that the deliberate plan prescribed by neo-liberalism fails to eradicate poverty and maximize wellbeing.

Rational Self-Interest and Irrational Societal Outcomes

Despite overwhelming evidence to the contrary, neo-liberalism continues to be the dominant economic theory. Neo-liberalism assumes that individuals act independently and have perfect information allowing them to pursue their rational self-interest (Wilber 1998, 94). Under these conditions, rational self-interest is indeed expected to promote rational social outcomes. However, as Wilber notes, "the more realistic assumption is that one person's behavior affects another's and that each has less than perfect knowledge of the other's likely behavior" (1998, 94). The recent financial crisis exemplifies how the pursuit of rational self-interest can lead to irrational societal outcomes. Although each company aimed to maximize its profit, their collective actions brought about the near collapse of the global economy.

Global warming is another example of how rational self-interest can lead to irrational societal outcomes. We are now on the precipice of environmental destruction (McMurtry 1999). Yet, neo-liberalists continue to advocate consumerism. Instead of viewing the economy as "a subsystem of a finite biosphere that supports it", neo-liberalism treats it as existing "in a void", thereby encouraging unsustainable growth (Daly 2005, 100):

> When the economy's expansion encroaches too much on its surrounding ecosystem, we will begin to sacrifice natural capital (such as fish, minerals and fossil fuels) that is worth more than the man-made capital (such as roads, factories and appliances) added by the growth. We will then have what I call uneconomic growth, producing "bads" faster than goods - making us poorer, not richer. Once we pass the optimal scale, growth becomes stupid in the

[5] The results were presented at the American Association for the Advancement of Science meeting in Boston.

[6] See Cookson (2008).

[7] The International Agency for Research on Cancer (IARC) reports that global cancer rates are expected to increase by 50% to 15 million in the year 2020. (Press Release No 145 in April 3, 2003.)

> short run and impossible to maintain in the long run. Evidence suggests that the U.S. may already have entered the uneconomic growth phase. (Ibid.)

The conflict between economic growth and environmental protection has stimulated discussion about sustainable growth. However, as Daly and Townsend note, "[e]ven 'green growth' is not sustainable ... To delude ourselves into believing that growth is still possible and desirable if only we label it 'sustainable' or color it 'green' will just delay the inevitable transition and make it more painful" (1993, 268). Recognizing that "under conditions of interdependence and imperfect information, rational self-interest frequently leads to socially irrational results" can provide the impetus to reject neo-liberalism (Wilber 1998, 94).

The Neo-Liberal Dogma

Despite the devastating effects of neo-liberal policies, the mainstream view in American society and most of the industrialized world is that there is no viable alternative. Alternatives are mentioned in mainstream media only to be promptly dismissed as quixotic. At the same time, defenders of neo-liberalism never acknowledge that irrational market outcomes are systemic. They instead attribute them to either internal or external inefficiencies of the market—external inefficiencies are attributed to government regulations while internal inefficiencies are attributed to gluttony, or some other flaw, of economic actors in the market. The collapse of Enron exemplified the tendency to treat economic failures as a problem of a few greedy individuals who had lost their moral compass or, as the mainstream media reported, "a few bad apples."

The financial crisis is a more recent example of the failure of neo-liberalists to acknowledge that irrational market outcomes are systemic. Defenders of neo-liberalism attribute the financial crisis on the "secrecy" among economic actors, which "goes against the basic requirement of an efficient market transaction" (Duska 2006, 219). Financial firms, Duska asserts, had "forgotten what they are about" and focused exclusively on the maximization of profit[8] (2006, 219). This is indeed a curious remark given that neo-liberalism encourages economic actors to remain unconcerned with society at large and focus exclusively on maximizing their profit. Financial firms, pace Duska, seem to have acted in accordance with the neo-liberal paradigm. Such behavior, however, far from increasing the nation's wealth brought the global financial market to its knees. The global economy would have collapsed in the absence of governmental intervention.[9]

The unwavering faith in unregulated markets has given rise to the claim that markets are the new religion. Loy (1997), for example, acknowledges that it is difficult to define religion but argues that if

[8]The Financial Crisis Inquiry Commission Report published in January 2011 paints a similar story.

[9]This explanation is nevertheless incorrect since it ignores that the financial sector was aware that the were selling "bundles" of and selling insolvent loans. For a comprehensive analysis see Baruchello (2011).

> we adopt a functionalist view and understand religion as what grounds us by teaching us what the world *is,* and what our *role* in the world is, then it becomes obvious that traditional religions are fulfilling this role less and less, because that function is being supplanted—or overwhelmed—by other belief-systems and value-systems. Today the most powerful alternative explanation of the world is science, and the most attractive value-system has become consumerism. (275)

Neo-liberalism, Loy maintains, should be understood as a religion because it fulfills a similar role. For, "the discipline of economics is less a science than the theology of that religion, and its god, the Market, has become a vicious circle of ever-increasing production and consumption by pretending to offer a secular salvation" (Loy 1997, 275). History shows that unquestionable faith in religious doctrine can lead to tragic outcomes. The same can be said about unquestionable faith in economic doctrine. Economic systems that produce adverse social outcomes are flawed from the point of view of the ethics of care but can find justification in traditional moral theories.

Justice, Rights and the Ethics of Care

Traditional moral theories are consistent with neo-liberalism and have been used throughout history to justify it. Nozick (1974) and Rawls (1971), for example, use deontology[10] to defend two distinct theories of justice consistent with the neo-liberal paradigm. Although such theorists might value care, they do not view it as a moral constrain but rather as an "optional extra" (Baier 1994, 25). However, as Baier aptly notes, giving primacy to rights has traditionally led to "the oppression of those on whom the primary right-holders depended on to do the sort of work they themselves preferred not to do" (1994, 25). The "domestic work was left to women and slaves, and the liberal morality for rights-holders was surreptitiously supplemented by a different set of demands made on domestic workers" (Baier 1994, 25). The same can be said about business relations between employers and workers.

The exploitation of workers by employers "is sugar-coated by the paternalistic show of concern for them" (Baier 1994, 131). Employers have the right to deprive workers of their retirement by filling for bankruptcy but workers have no right to additional compensation even when rises in productivity result in increased profits. Recently, the Supreme Court further extended the rights of employers, thereby contributing to the oppression of the workers. It ruled that workers cannot sue their employer over wage discrimination unless they have filed a formal complaint with a federal agency within the first 6 months of the occurrence. No exceptions were made for cases in which workers were unaware of being subjected to discrimination during the first 6 months despite that they might continue to be discriminated to the present day (*Ledbetter v. Goodyear*). This decision ignores workplace realities since workers are often required to sign confidentiality agreements that prevent them from discussing their salaries with coworkers. It also affects female workers more

[10]Natural Law Theory provides justification for the former while Kantian Ethics provides justification for the latter.

than it affects their male counterparts since the former are more likely to encounter pay discrimination. Such cases suggest that the liberal morality of the employer is surreptitiously supplemented by a different set of demands made on the workers. Although employers and workers are equal in the eyes of the law, in reality the former are afforded rights to dominate, oppress, and exploit the latter. Just as the legal equality between women and men has not yet manifested in equal pay, the legal equality between employers and workers has not yet manifested in equal political power. The recent push for austerity measures in the United States and Europe is another example of the tendency to expect workers to absorb the costs of neo-liberal policies; in this case the cost of the deregulation of the financial market.

The ethics of care recognizes that "unless a human society incorporates, encourages, and supports the development of caring practices in its citizens, the society cannot sustain itself" (Groenhoul 2004, 12). Since humans exist "in the context of affectionate relationships with other humans ... social, communal, and emotional aspects of human life are critical to any surviving society" (Groenhoul 2004, 24). Neo-liberalism, however, views communities as "instrumental mechanisms for the satisfaction of individual preferences" and treats these aspects of human life as irrelevant (Held 2006, 131). Consequently, this is the first time in the history of civilization that enormous food surpluses and famine exist simultaneously. Nozick's entitlement theory can provide justification for such adverse outcomes: so long as the original acquisition and the subsequent transfers of the holdings were just, such states of affairs are justifiable. No such justification, however, can be provided from the point of view of the ethics of care since it

> clearly implies that society must recognize its responsibilities to its children and others who are dependent, enabling the best possible bringing up and educating of its future generations, appropriate responses to its members in need of health care, and assistance with the care of dependents. It clearly implies that the members of wealthy societies must recognize their responsibilities to alleviate the hunger and gross deprivations in care afflicting so many members of poor ones. (Held 2006, 159)

The priority the ethics of care assigns to care is "not meant to displace justice and judgments made on the basis of justice" or rights since it "does not require that we surrender a commitment to universal principles" but "simply that we recognize that as they have been thus far constructed, they do not cover all possible conditions in the world" (Held 2006, 149). The ethics of care can incorporate considerations about justice and rights.[11] It can maintain that any economic system that assigns priority to the maximization of profit while failing to distinguish between frivolous desires and real needs cannot be just.[12] Rights that promote domination, oppression, and exploitation cannot be justified from the point of view of the ethics of

[11]Held (1993) believes that the ethics of care is only applicable to the private realm and proposes to combine it with the ethics of justice, which she views as applicable to the public realm. Gelfand (2004), on the other hand, argues that justice can be conceived as a part of caring. Slote (1998) makes a similar argument.

[12]McMurtry's value theory offers a compelling criterion to determine real needs. See McMurtry (2005).

care. The ethics of care "calls for the transformation of the different segments of society, with caring values and cooperation replacing the hierarchies and dominations of gender, class, race, and ethnicity" and recommends that economies focus "on actually meeting needs rather than enriching the powerful" (Held 2006, 161). Considerations about care can steer society in the right direction. For, as we shall see in the next section, once we define "care as the serious and complex set of practices that it is," we can "immediately recognize that care is not private, not banal, and not indiscriminately charitable" (Tronto 1996, 151).

Care as a Personal, Political, and Economic Concept

The emphasis an ethic of care places on personal relations has contributed to the narrow understanding of care as a personal concept. Feminist theorists, however, have recently challenged the idea that care should be confined to the private sphere. Mary Daly, for example, identifies care as an inherently social activity and argues that "making provisions for care . . . affects a whole series of societal settlements" (2002, 251). As societies "respond to the needs associated with care, they are altering the division of labour, cost and responsibility among and within the state, market, voluntary/non-profit sector and family" (2002, 261). In most welfare states, for example, childcare is treated as paid labor, often in the form of paid leave afforded to the parents. In neo-liberal states, however, it is treated as domestic and thus unpaid labor since it is not a transaction occurring *in* or *through* markets (Wolff and Resnick 1987). It is only treated as paid labor when it enters the market where it is viewed as a service available to parents for a fee. In the absence of a profit incentive, neo-liberalism makes no provisions for childcare or any other social needs. The ethics of care, by contrast, views childcare, among other things, as a social responsibility.

Joan Tronto argues that the idea of care can be extended to the political sphere. Care can be understood as a political concept because it can serve "in both of the usual senses in which we use the language of politics: care is both a goal . . . and a strategy" (1996, 143). As a goal, it can be viewed as a collective ideal. Societies that place priority on personal gain over the common good produce individuals who become self-centered and insensitive towards others. Such societies ultimately perish. Instead of viewing society as an aggregate of consumers aiming to independently satisfy their own desires, the ethics of care invites us to view society as an association of citizens who find fulfillment in the service to their fellow humans. As a strategy, it can be used to affect outcomes in the political process. Viewing the current health care debate from this perspective, for example, can provide the basis for rejecting the current paradigm of health care as a commodity and adopting a new paradigm of health care as a social service. This, in turn, can provide the grounds for instituting a universal health care system.

Smith (2005) argues that even though many social idealists and feminist ethicists distance themselves from market relations, care should be understood as an economic concept. Indeed, Held maintains that caring institutions should be positioned *outside* the market:

> In practices such as those involved in education, child care, health care, culture, and protecting the environment, market norms limited only by rights should not prevail, even if the market is fair and efficient, because markets are unable to express and promote many values important to these practices, such as mutually shared caring concern. (2006, 120)

Smith agrees with Held (2006) that markets as prescribed by neo-liberalism cannot provide for the caring institutions society needs, but argues that markets need not be inconsistent with the notion of care since it might be possible to extract caring qualities from markets (2005, 11). The recognition that, pace neo-liberalism, markets require sustained intervention can provide the impetus to alter them in order to better contribute to human aims:

> To this end, rather than writing and worrying about what "the" market is, and how "it" works, we might think about the politics of a complex web of institutions of production, consumption and exchange in the same way Elizabeth Grosz has encouraged us to think about the body ... [She] argues that the body should be assessed in terms of "what it can do, the things it can perform, the linkage it establishes, the transformations it undergoes". (Smith 2005, 17)

Markets, Smith argues, can be viewed as an alternative "route to post-capitalism: one which reclaims the markets for society by making them different" (2005, 14). This can allow society to move from "the competitive 'welfare place' of neo-liberal states towards the care-full space of a reformatted economy" (Smith 2005, 16).

As it will be shown in the next section, markets need not be inconsistent with alternative economic systems and can be transformed to better contribute to human aims. Such transformations, however, cannot occur within neo-liberalism, which is inconsistent with the ethics of care. More generally, any economic theory that is inconsistent with the ethics of care cannot support such market transformations. This realization can provide the impetus to view business ethics apart from the neo-liberal paradigm.

Towards a Caring Economy

Schweickart defends an economic system, which he calls "Economic Democracy," that retains some version of the market but allows society to reclaim the means of production and eliminate wage labor (1980, 1992, 1996).[13] Its three basic features are:

> 1) each productive enterprise is managed democratically by its workers; 2) the day-to-day economy is a market economy: raw materials and consumer goods are bought and sold at prices determined by the forces of supply and demand; 3) new investment is socially

[13] For other alternatives to capitalism see Nürnberger 1998; for limits of market organizations see Nelson 2005; for an exposition on various economic systems see Gary and Joyce Pickersgill 1974.

> controlled: the investment fund is generated by taxation and dispensed according to a democratic, market-conforming plan. (1992, 19)

Economic Democracy allows society to reclaim the means of production. Workers manage the means of production, but they do not own them. These are "the collective property of the society. Societal ownership manifests itself in" a legally binding agreement according to which "value of the capital stock of a firm be kept intact" through the use of a Depreciation Fund (Schweickart 1992, 8). Workers can sell off their capital stocks only by replacing them with others of equal value. This encourages them to view the health of their company as an extension of their own wellbeing. The social control of new investment is designed to "alleviate the "anarchy" of capitalism"—that is, to discourage overproduction of goods that cannot be sold for profit (Schweickart 1992, 9). The investment fund, which is funded by capital taxes, eliminates usury. A society that does not offer personal loans in order to collect interest is not only more equitable, but it also fosters caring relations among its members. People are encouraged to view others as ends in themselves rather than as means to maximize profit. When the dynamics between people change so does their outlook. When people learn to view others as a means to maximize profit, they do not hesitate to oppress and exploit them. But when they learn to give and receive care, they no longer view others as mere means to their own ends.

Economic Democracy also eliminates wage-labor. It thus replaces the hierarchy between employers and workers with a democratic system—one person, one vote—which allows workers to fully participate in the decision process. This "aims at breaking the commodity character of labor-power and the attendant alienation" by giving each worker a vote and a specific share of the net revenue (Schweickart 1992, 8). Rather than viewing other workers, from a competitive viewpoint, as obstacles to one's success, one is encouraged to adopt a collaborative viewpoint and to bond with others. The elimination of wage-labor discourages society from thinking of human beings as a mere resource (Tronto 1996). Terms like "human resources" are inherently demeaning since they encourage viewing workers as mere commodities to be bought and sold in the market. Eliminating wage-labor fosters caring relationships among citizens not only within a particular society but also across the globe. Viewing other countries as mere human or material resources necessary to our economic growth encourages imperialism, exploitation, and oppression.

Under neo-liberalism, the market has a dual function. It "allocates goods and resources" but also "determines the course and rate of future development" (Schweickart 1992, 9). Economic Democracy eliminates the latter function of the market. It does not view the market "as an absolute good, the paradigm of free human interaction" but rather "as a useful instrument for accomplishing certain societal goals" (1992, 21). It rejects the neo-liberal view of markets as domains in which social interactions are reduced to exchanges between individuals who share no social ties (Held 2006, 112). This is consistent with the ethics of care, which recognizes that market relations involve "personal exchanges between persons who have social connections with each other and exchanges that incorporate various of the values other than market ones of the items or services being traded" (Held 2006,

112).[14] The ethics of care encourages building caring relations not only with those with whom we share our planet but also with future generations from whom we are borrowing it. It views the destruction of the planet as taxation without representation since costs incurred by us are passed on to future generations.

Replacing these neo-liberal institutions with caring institutions that encourage cooperation can eliminate hierarchies and domination of class, gender, and race. Neo-liberalism's presupposition that humans are self-interested by nature has transformative effects on people's attitudes. Empirical studies show that exposure to microeconomics had a significant effect on generosity for Arts and Sciences majors but little effect on generosity for Economics majors (Bauman and Rose 2009). Moreover, economic students tend to free ride far more than other students:

> except for students of economics who score far lower, 40–60 percent of the subjects studied did not try to free ride but engaged instead in cooperative behavior to produce a social good. (Held 2006, 113)

The results are hardly surprising given that neo-liberalism neither incorporates nor encourages the development of caring practices, but is concerned primarily with rational self-interest. Free riders, in this view, are indeed acting as rational self-interested players since they benefit by shifting the costs to other players. The neo-liberal view of humans as mere calculative, self-interested, independent players concerned exclusively with the fulfillment of their own desires seems to be a self-fulfilling prophecy.

Just as exposure to neo-liberal ideology can have negative effects on human attitudes, exposure to the value of care can have positive effects. If the people behind Rawl's veil of ignorance, for example, were exposed to "Ruddicks's "maternal thinking" . . . they might have reasoned to different conclusions than Rawls's two principles of justice about liberty and the distribution of goods by the difference principle" (Tronto 1996, 144). Similarly, if people were exposed to the ethics of care, they might have found Nozick's theory of justice deplorable; Nozick treats any voluntary transactions as being just but allows that "voluntary" need not imply choice (Schweickart 1980, 31).

The Business of Caring

Traditional business ethics functions as a corporate ethic. It aims to explain moral behavior pertaining to the relations either between employers and workers or among corporations, consumers, and the environment. Since it operates within the confines of neo-liberalism, it is not in a position to challenge neo-liberal institutions or practices. To illustrate this let us compare the approach of traditional business ethics to that based on the ethics of care towards two dominant institutions of neo-liberalism: the corporation and wage-labor.

---

[14]Held argues that neo-liberalism ignores these relations.

A corporation is an institution whose purpose is imbued by law. According to Milton Friedman, the corporation has "one and only one social responsibility ... to use its resources and engage in activities designed to increase its profits so long as it stays within the rules of the game, which is to say, engages in open and free competition without deception or fraud"[15] (1982, 133). Friedman maintains that no corporation should spend its money "for purposes it regards as socially responsible but which it cannot connect to its bottom line" (Bakan 2004). Social responsible actions are thus encouraged only insofar as they do not encroach upon the maximization of profits. When conflicts arise between corporate and social benefits, the former always take priority over the latter. A corporation "compels executives to prioritize the interests of their companies and shareholders above all others and forbids them from being socially responsible—at least genuinely so" (Bakan 2004, 37). Therefore, attempts to blame executives for social irresponsibility fail to properly distinguish between an institution and an individual. Executives might be caring individuals but they are bound to be unethical if the institution they participate in is designed to be unethical. Similarly, slave owners might care about their slaves but they are nevertheless monstrous individuals because the institution of slavery in which they participate in is monstrous.[16] Since executives are obligated to prioritize the interests of their companies and shareholders above all others, it behooves us to ask whether the corporation is a moral person, especially since legal personhood was conferred on it by law.

Applying the Psychopathy Checklist (PCL) to the corporation shows that it exemplifies all of the typical characteristics of a psychopath (Bakan 2004). These include callous unconcern for the feeling of others, incapacity to maintain enduring relationships, reckless disregard for the safety of others, deceitfulness, incapacity to experience guilt and failure conform to social norms (ibid.). As Dr. Hare, a leading researcher in psychopathy, notes, a "*lack of empathy* and *asocial tendencies* are ... key characteristics of the corporation" (Bakan 2004, 57). When corporations get caught breaking the law, for example, "they pay big fines and ... continue doing what they did before. And in many cases the fines and the penalties paid by the organization are trivial compared to the profit that they rake in" (ibid.). Such fines are thus viewed as the cost of doing business. Like psychopaths, corporations "refuse to take *responsibility* for their own actions", they "are *unable to feel remorse*" and attempt to "*manipulate* everything, including public opinion" (ibid.). Their aim is to project an image that resonates with the public even though it may not correspond to reality. "Human psychopaths are notorious for their ability to use

[15]Decisions made by individuals who interact with one another *through* or *in* markets often have negative effects on individuals *outside* the market. Economists use the term "externalities" to refer to such costs. Air or water pollution is an example of an externality (Wolff and Resnick 1987). It is worth noting that corporations can pass such costs to others without violating Friedman's provisions since externalities need not arise from either deception or fraud.

[16]Noam Chomsky provides this analogy in the documentary "The Corporation", which is based on the book by Joel Bakan (2004).

charms as a mask to hide their dangerously self-obsessed personalities. For corporations, social responsibility may play the same role" (ibid.). The failure of BP, for example, to comply with maintenance and safety regulations is contrary to the socially responsible image it tries to project. Recently, BP changed its name from "British Petroleum" to "Beyond Petroleum" in an effort to appear environmentally conscious. In reality, increasing the demand for petrochemicals continues to be its primary goal (ibid.).

A traditional business ethics approach to corporate conduct involves explaining which actions are unethical and determining what constitutes a just fine or penalty for the given violation. The corporation as an institution is not challenged since it is presupposed that its rights are as important as anyone else's rights. A business ethic based on the ethics of care, by contrast, can challenge the existence of such institutions on the basis that they are legal persons who are psychopathic by design. It follows that there can be no ethical grounds for their existence in a society that embraces caring practices. The ethics of care aims to replace corporations with institutions that are designed to promote rather than hinder the common good.

Neo-liberalism views humans as commodities to be sold and bought in the unregulated market and identifies "work" with "wage labor." The role of traditional business ethics is thus to determine what constitutes a fair wage. "From the moral point of view, prices, like wages, should be just or fair", proclaims a contemporary business ethics textbook.[17] Since a portion of the profits must be allocated to wages, employers and workers have an inherently antagonistic relationship. Employers want to pay workers as little as possible while workers want to get paid as much as possible. Since employers occupy positions of power over the workers, they are more likely to benefit when a compromise is reached.[18] For, as Adam Smith aptly noted, a "manufacturer [or] a merchant, though they did not employ a single workman, could generally live a year or two upon the stocks which they have already acquired. Many workmen could not subsist a week, few could subsist a month, and scarce any a year without employment" (*The Wealth of Nations*, Book I Chapter VIII).

The antagonistic relations existing between employers and workers cannot be resolved on the basis of rights alone. States can, and frequently do, limit collective bargaining rights. This was as true in Adam Smith's days—who notes that the "masters, being fewer in number, can combine much more easily; and the law, besides, authorizes, or at least does not prohibit their combinations, while it prohibits those of the workmen" (ibid.)—as it is today. The fact that the minimum wage continues to be below the living wage in the United States, one of the most affluent countries on the planet, is further evidence that employers continue to control the political process. Despite laws aimed to protect workers, decreases in the profit margin frequently translate to layoffs while increases in productivity rarely translate to benefits

[17] See Shaw 2011: 230.

[18] Since executives virtually determine their own pay by appointing the board of trustees, they are not on a par with an average worker.

for the workers. From the traditional business ethics point of view, the former constitutes an ethical economic transaction so long as it is based on fair contractual agreements while the latter constitutes a supererogatory act.

Identifying "work" with "wage labor" has consequences on class and gender hierarchies. Women's reproductive functions tend to either limit their work to the home or create a "second shift" problem of unpaid housework or childcare and waged labor. Feminists have long argued that the term "work" must be redefined to include non-wage-earning labor (Fraser and Gordon 2006; Held 2006). Although this is a good start, it cannot be the end goal since redefining the term "work" would have no effect on the antagonistic relations between employers and workers. Giving priority to care can reshape our view of the relation between public and private life and transform economic policy. The way we view leisure, time, work, dependence, independence, and care are inextricably connected to our socioeconomic life. As Fraser and Gordon (2006) remind us, the current stigmatized view of welfare dependency historically emerged along with neo-liberal practices. The ethics of care can justify the elimination of wage labor on the basis of its adverse effects on individuals and society. Although individuality and self-determination are consistent with the ownership of the means of production by workers, wage labor is not.

Concluding Remarks

The above discussion illustrates that business ethics based on an ethic of care is superior to traditional business ethics. The ethics of care can be used to show that economic systems that exclude caring institutions, or treat them as preferences to be satisfied as the "free" market sees fit, are inferior to those that do not. The primacy the ethics of care assigns to needs over desires can give voice to many who have none under neo-liberalism. A business ethic based on the ethics of care can be used to challenge the neo-liberal paradigm. Additionally, it can be used to defend the claim that humans have the right not to be used as resources since this inevitably involves the creation of dominant relations and institutions. Many business issues that are treated as peripheral by traditional business ethics can thus take central stage when viewed from a business ethic based on the ethics of care. Business ethics thus construed is not just an ethical code of business conduct but a way of life.[19]

References

Baier, Annette C. 1994. The need for more than justice. In *Moral prejudices: Essays on ethics*, 18–32. Cambridge, MA: Harvard University Press.

Bakan, Joel. 2004. *The corporation: The pathological pursuit of profit and power*. New York, NY: Free Press.

[19] I am grateful to Giorgio Baruchello, Douglas Woods, and an anonymous referee for helpful comments.

Baruchello, Giorgio. 2008. Capitalism and freedom: The core of a contradiction—an essay on Cornelius Castoriadis and John McMurtry. *Nordicum-mediterraneum: Icelandic e-journal of nordic and mediterranean studies*.
Baruchello, Giorgio. 2011. Your money or your life John McMurtry and Martha Nussbaum on the for-profit assault upon life-capabilities. *Journal of Philosophy of Life* 1 (1): 13–48.
Bauman, Yoram, and Elaina Rose. 2009. Why are economics students more selfish than the rest? In Department of Economics, University of Washington, WA. Working Papers Series.
Cobb, John B. Jr. 2007. Towards a just and sustainable economic order. In *Environmental ethics: An anthology*, ed. Light Andrew, and Holmes Rolston III, 359–370. Oxford: Blackwell.
Cookson, Clive. 2008. Poverty mars formation of infant brains. *Financial Times*, February 16.
Copp, David. 2006. *The oxford handbook of ethical theory*. Oxford: Oxford University Press.
Daly, Mary. 2002. Care as good for social Policy. *Journal of Social Policy* 31 (2): 251–270.
Daly, Herman E. 2005. "Economics in a full world. *Scientific American* 293 (3): 100–107.
Daly, Herman E., and Townsend Kenneth N. 1993. *Valuing the earth: Economics, ecology, ethics*. Cambridge, MA: MIT Press.
Denis, A. 2005. The invisible hand of god in Adam Smith. *Research in the History of Economic Thought and Methodology* 23 (1): 1–32.
Duska, Ronald F. 2006. *Contemporary reflections on business ethics*. Springer.
Fraser, Nancy, and Linda Gordon. 2006. "Dependency" demystified: Inscriptions of power in a keyword of the welfare state. In *Contemporary political philosophy: An anthology*, ed. Robert E. Goodin, and Philip Pettit, 591–606. Oxford: Blackwell.
Friedman, Milton. 1982. *Capitalism and freedom*. Chicago, IL: Chicago University Press.
Fryer, David. 2006. Insecurity, and restructuring of unemployment and mental health. In *Unemployment and health: International and interdisciplinary perspectives*, ed. T. Keiselbach, A. H. Winefield, C. Boyd, S. Anderson, 21–34. Australia: Australian Academic Press.
Gelfand, Scott D. 2004. The ethics of care and (capital?) punishment. *Law and Philosophy* 23: 593–614.
Groenhoul, Ruth E. 2004. *Connected lives: Human nature and an ethics of care*. Oxford: Rowman & Littlefield Publishers.
Held, Virginia. 1993. *Feminist morality*. Chicago, IL: Chicago University Press.
Held, Virginia. 2006. *The ethics of care personal, political, and global*. Oxford: Oxford University Press.
Loy, David R. 1997. The religion of the market. *Journal of the American Academy of Religion* 65 (2): 275–290.
Maguire, Daniel C. 2010. *Ethics: A compete method for moral choice*. Minneapolis, MN: Fortress Press.
McMurtry, John. 1999. *The cancer stage of capitalism*. Sterling, VA: Pluto Press. London.
McMurtry, John. 2005. Principles of the good life: The primary theorems of economic reason [Unpublished manuscript circulated amongst EOLSS contributors to the encyclopedia entitled *Philosophy and World Problems*].
Nelson, Richard R. (ed.). 2005. *The limits of market organization*. New York, NY: Russell Sage Foundation.
Nicholls, D. 1992. The invisible hand, providence and the market. In *The values of the enterprise culture*, ed. P. Heelas and P. Morris, 217–36. New York: Routledge.
Nozick, Robert. 1974. *Anarchy, state, and utopia*. Oxford: Basic Books.
Nürnberger, Klaus. 1998. *Beyond marx and market: Outcomes of a century of economic experimentation*. New York, NY: Zed Books Ltd.
Pickersgill, Gary M., and Joyce E. Pickersgill. 1974. *Contemporary economic systems: A comparative view*. Englewood Cliffs, NJ: Prentice-Hall.
Pizarro, David. 2000. Nothing more than feelings?: The role of emotions in moral judgment. *Journal of the Theory of Social Behavior* 30: 355–375.
Rawls, John. 1971. *A theory of justice*. Cambridge, MA: Harvard University Press.
Rousseau, Jean-Jacques. 1986. *The first and second discourses and essays on the origin of languages* (trans. and ed. Victor Gourevitch).

Schmitt, John. 2009. Inequality as policy: The United States since 1979. *Real-World Economics Review* (51): Online journal.
Schweickart, David. 1980. *Capitalism or worker control? An ethical and economic appraisal.* New York, NY: Praeger Publishers.
Schweickart, David. 1992. Economic democracy: A worthy socialism that would really work. *Science and Society* 56 (1): 9–38.
Schweickart, David. 1996. *Against capitalism.* Boulder, CO: Westview Press.
Shaw, William H. 2011. *Business ethics: A textbook with cases.* Wadsworth Publishing (7th edition, 2010).
Singer, Peter. 1994. The famine relief argument. In *Social and political philosophy*, ed. Elizabeth Smith, and H. Gene Blocker, 456–465. Englewood Cliffs, NJ: Prentice-Hall.
Slote, Michael. 1998. Justice and caring. *Social Philosophy and Policy* 15: 171–195.
Smith, Susan J. 2005. States, markets, and an ethic of care. *Political Geography* 24: 1–20.
Sollenius, Jan. 2000. *Humane economy.* Stockholm: Almqvist and Wiksell International.
Tronto, Joan C. 1996. Care as a political concept. In *Revisioning the political: Feminist reconstructions of traditional concepts in western political theory*, eds. Nancy J. Hirschmann, and Christine Di Stefano, 139–155. Boulder, CO: Westview Press.
Varian, Hal R. 2000. What use is economic theory? In *Variants in economic theory: Selected works of Hal R. Varian.* 352–360. Nothhampton: Edward Elgar Publishing.
Waldron, Jeremy. 2006. Superseding historic injustice. In *Contemporary political philosophy: An anthology*, eds. Robert E. Goodin, and Philip Pettit. Oxford: Blackwell.
Wilber, Charles K. 1998. Trust, moral hazards, and social economics: Incentives and the organization of work. In *Economics, ethics, and public policy*, ed. Charles K. Wilber, 93–105. Oxford: Rowman & Littlefield Publishers, Inc.
Wolff, Richard D., and Stephen A. Resnick. 1987. *Economics: Marxian versus neoclassical.* Baltimore, MD: John Hopkins University Press.

Part II
Corporate Decision Making

Chapter 5
Care Ethics and Stakeholder Theory

Daniel Engster

Introduction

When considering the implications of care ethics for business affairs, few questions have more immediate and practical importance than those concerning the responsibilities of firms to their investors, employees, customers, and other individuals. How firms—or more precisely the managers of firms - conceive of their ethical responsibilities to others will determine in large part whether they recognize any obligations to their local communities, the attention they give to worker and product safety, their attitudes toward employee wages and benefits, and other similar matters. Classical liberal theorists argue that the only ethical responsibilities firms have are to increase their profits, provide stockholders with high returns on their investments, obey the law, and avoid deceptive business practices.[1] Care ethics presumably expects firms to do more than just fulfill these minimal responsibilities, but how much more? What in practical terms does it mean for a firm to conduct business in a caring manner?

Over the last few decades, many business ethicists have drawn on stakeholder theory to identify the ethical responsibilities of firms.[2] In contrast to classical liberal

[1]The stockholder view described here is most famously defended by Milton Friedman (1970).

[2]The main concepts of stakeholder theory and even the term "stakeholder" existed prior to the 1980s, but the origins of contemporary stakeholder theory are generally associated with the publication of R. Edward Freeman's *Strategic Management: A Stakeholder Approach* (1984). For a brief account of the pre-history of stakeholder theory, see Freeman and Reed (1983), Freeman (1984), and Friedman and Miles (2006). The literature on stakeholder theory is by now quite extensive. R. Edward Freeman's works have continued to hold a central place in this theory (See Freeman 1994, 2004; Freeman and Reed 1983; Freeman and Evan 1990; Freeman and Gilbert 1992). A collection of important writings on stakeholder theory can be found in Zakhem et al. (2008). A comprehensive survey is provided by Friedman and Miles (2006).

D. Engster (✉)
Department of Political Science, University of Texas, San Antonio, TX, USA
e-mail: Daniel.Engster@utsa.edu

M. Hamington, M. Sander-Staudt (eds.), *Applying Care Ethics to Business*, Issues in Business Ethics 34, DOI 10.1007/978-90-481-9307-3_5,
© Springer Science+Business Media B.V. 2011

economic thought, stakeholder theory suggests that businesses have an ethical responsibility to consider the interests and attend to the needs of all individuals and groups who are affected by their policies and operations, including employees, consumers, suppliers, the local community, and others. In developing stakeholder theories, several business ethicists have specifically identified care ethics as a fruitful resource for elucidating the responsibilities of firms to their stakeholders (Burton and Dunn 1996; Freeman and Gilbert 1992; Freeman and Liedtka 1991; Hendry 2001; Liedtka 1996; Machold et al. 2008; Wicks, Gilbert, and Freeman 1994; White 1992). Brian Burton and Craig Dunn (1996), in particular, have most fully developed the principles of care-based stakeholder theory with the goal of providing managers with ethical guidelines for conducting their everyday business operations according to caring values (134).

While Burton and Dunn offer important insights for applying care ethics to business affairs and identify some useful guidelines for a care-based stakeholder theory, their theory nonetheless suffers from a number of weaknesses. They do not offer a very convincing philosophical justification for their care-based stakeholder theory, for example, or provide very clear accounts of who should count as a stakeholder or how managers should prioritize different stakeholder claims. As a result, their argument is vague in crucial areas and fails to provide managers with the concrete practical guidance they set out to define.

In this article, I build upon the work of Burton and Dunn in order to extend and clarify a care-based stakeholder theory. My central aim is to elaborate a more cogent and concrete care-based stakeholder theory that spells out more fully what it means for a firm to conduct business in a caring manner. My argument also, however, has a broader purpose. Stakeholder theory in general suffers from some of the shortcomings I point out in Burton and Dunn's theory. Critics have noted that many stakeholder theories offer only broad and vague definitions of who should count as a stakeholder and do not explain very clearly how managers should make decisions when the interests of different stakeholder groups come into conflict (Goodpaster 1991; Hasnas 1998; Marcoux 2003). By addressing the weaknesses in Burton and Dunn's argument, I hope to show how a care-based stakeholder theory can overcome these problems and contribute to the viability of stakeholder theory in general. In the next chapter, Daniel Palmer and Mary Lyn Stoll further show how care ethics can supply a richer account of moral agency to support stakeholder theory.

I begin by discussing Burton and Dunn's article on care ethics and stakeholder theory and highlight a number of shortcomings with their argument. Since many of the shortcomings of Burton and Dunn's theory stem from their underdeveloped account of care ethics, I next offer a fuller account of certain elements of this theory. In the third section, I develop a stakeholder theory based upon my revised account of care ethics. I conclude by highlighting the various ways in which a care-based stakeholder theory can help to address some of the central criticisms that have been leveled against stakeholder theory generally.

Care Ethics and Stakeholder Theory: Foundations

While the stakeholder concept has long existed, R. Edward Freeman is generally credited with developing the first full account of stakeholder theory.[3] In *Strategic Management: A Stakeholder Approach* (1984), Freeman defined a stakeholder as "any group or individual who can affect, or is affected by, the achievement of a corporation's purpose" (vi, 46). Initially, Freeman outlined his stakeholder theory as a management tool to help executives manage their organizations more effectively. In his later works, however, he turned his attention to the normative implications of this theory (Evan and Freeman 1988; Freeman 2004; Freeman and Evan 1990; Wicks, Gilbert, and Freeman 1994). In "A Feminist Reinterpretation of the Stakeholder Concept" (1994), he and his co-authors singled out a care-oriented feminist theory as an especially valuable resource for drawing out the normative insights of stakeholder theory and providing ethical guidance to business activities.

In "Feminist Ethics as Moral Grounding for Stakeholder Theory" (1996), Burton and Dunn developed this idea of a care-based stakeholder theory. They begin by noting that stakeholder theory rests on a very different vision of business activity from the dominant liberal view. Rather than seeing business transactions as a series of discrete voluntary contracts, stakeholder theory sees business transactions as existing within a larger web of (stakeholder) relationships. In this regard, they note that stakeholder theory shares a natural affinity with care ethics. Like stakeholder theory, care ethics makes existing relationships the starting point for moral thinking, and as such, Burton and Dunn claim that it represents a fruitful source for developing a stakeholder theory (136). Drawing on the works of Carol Gilligan (1982) and Nel Noddings (1984), Burton and Dunn next define care ethics as a moral framework that gives priority to sustaining relationships and avoiding harm to others. In contrast with Noddings's theory, they nonetheless argue that care ethics need not eschew all justice principles. By their account, care ethics can identify some general principles or guidelines for business activity, and in this way, serve as a more useful guide to ethical business practice.

From these premises, Burton and Dunn develop their care-based stakeholder theory. They argue most generally that care ethics supports a "more cooperative, caring type of relationship" in business: "Firms should seek to make decisions that satisfy stakeholders, leading to situations where all parties involved in a relationship gain" (140). Specifically, they claim that firms should be primarily concerned to satisfy the interests and needs of individuals and groups with whom they have established relationships. In a care-based stakeholder theory, it is not a matter of dealing with " 'competitors,' 'suppliers,' 'buyers,' and other firms in abstract terms" but with "this supplier or that product, raw material, or service. The question is the type of effect your decision has on that particular supplier, not 'suppliers' in

[3] A brief history of stakeholder theory can be found in Freeman and Reed (1983), Freeman (1984), and Friedman and Miles (2006).

general" (140–141). Burton and Dunn further maintain that a care-based stakeholder theory also gives some value to our emotions when making business decisions. We should pay attention, for example, if we feel badly about some decision since this may be a sign that our proposed course of action violates important relational values. Moreover, a care-oriented manager will communicate with stakeholders about important business decisions and involve them whenever possible in the decision-making process (141).

While the above rules offer some general guidelines for conducting everyday business affairs in a caring manner, Burton and Dunn acknowledge that they do not provide clear guidance about what a manager should do when faced with difficult decisions. In order to address these hard cases, they specify an additional set of moral rules for resolving conflicts among stakeholder interests. The first rule, which they borrow from Wicks, Gilbert, and Freeman (1994), is the "rule of consensus:" "First, the attempt is made to find win-win solutions to the issue confronting the firm and its stakeholders. If this seems impossible, communication is urged to encourage understanding of others' positions and eventual acceptance of a 'second best' result" (142). While consensus decision-making should be used whenever possible to mediate stakeholder conflicts, Burton and Dunn admit that it may not always be practical. Consensus decision-making can be time consuming and easily undermined if even just a few individuals are not committed to reaching consensus with others. Thus, Burton and Dunn offer a second, more practical rule for resolving conflicts: "Privilege those with whom you have a close relationship" (142–143). When trade-offs must be made and consensus cannot be reached, managers should favor those individuals and groups with whom the firm has the closest relationship. Yet, Burton and Dunn note that this rule, too, can be problematic. This relationship rule would seem to justify a company's shipping hazardous waste materials to other countries with weak environmental and worker safety regulations for the sake of protecting and promoting the interests of its own employees, stockholders, and local community. Burton and Dunn argue that this action is wrong because it harms individuals "who will suffer more from harms than the more advantaged in society" (144). Drawing on Rawls's difference principle, Burton and Dunn thus suggest a third decision-making rule: "special attention [should] be given to the least advantaged members of the moral community." They formulate this third moral rule as follows: "Care enough for the least advantaged stakeholders that they not be harmed; insofar as they are not harmed, privilege those stakeholders with whom you have a close relationship" (143–144). Altogether, then, Burton and Dunn argue that: (1) companies should never harm more vulnerable individuals for the sake of favoring their close relations; and (2) companies should favor their close relations over others when harming the least advantaged is not an issue. In choosing a supplier, for example, we should "give our business to the supplier with whom we have a close relationship—a relationship built upon trust, experience, and mutual accommodation over the years" (144). Even if other suppliers may suffer from our decision, Burton and Dunn argue the relationship principle justifies our decision.

Burton and Dunn's article represents an important contribution to the literature on feminist business ethics. They not only provide a general account of a care-based stakeholder theory, but also offer some specific rules for applying care ethics to particular management decisions. There are nonetheless a number of weaknesses in their theory that ultimately undermine its practical usefulness. First, their theory offers only a vague explanation for why businesspeople should embrace care ethics and a care-based stakeholder theory in managing their firms. Aside from noting that Noddings believes a caring attitude is universally accessible to human beings, Burton and Dunn offer no justification for why businesspeople should conduct their operations in a caring manner. Secondly, although Burton and Dunn suggest that businesspeople should privilege their close relations, they do not very clearly define what they mean by a "close relationship." At one point, they do write that a close relationship is one based on "trust, experience, and mutual accommodation over the years" (144). But these characteristics provide only loose criteria for determining which stakeholder interests should be prioritized. Thirdly, Burton and Dunn's relationship rule seems an overly blunt instrument for guiding many management decisions. Burton and Dunn suggest that we should give our business "to the supplier with whom we have a close relationship—a relationship built upon trust, experience, and mutual accommodation over the years" (144). Presumably, this rule would hold even if another supplier were to offer us a higher quality product at a significantly lower price. But this is problematic. Maintaining our relationship with the existing supplier in this case might mean lower profits for our stockholders, lower wages for our workers, and lower quality products for our consumers. In fact, this principle could easily become a justification for cronyism. At the very least, then, a more nuanced account of a firm's different obligations to different stakeholders seems necessary for developing a more viable care-based stakeholder theory. Finally, Burton and Dunn do not clearly define the idea of the "least advantaged" stakeholder. In discussing the case of the hazardous materials, Burton and Dunn simply assert that workers in less developed countries are the least advantaged stakeholders and thus should be given special consideration. Yet, we are never told why exactly these workers are the least advantaged. Surely it would be disadvantageous for these individuals to work with hazardous materials under unsafe conditions, but it might also be disadvantageous for the firm's stockholders, employees, and customers if the firm were to dispose of these materials at home. Suppose, for example, the firm could safely dispose of the hazardous materials at home but, because of the costs involved, would have to lay-off ten workers from their jobs. Who, then, is the least advantaged stakeholder? Both the firm's employees and the foreign workers have much to lose. Burton and Dunn fail to give any indication of the criteria that managers should use to identify the least advantaged stakeholder, and consequently leave a key concept in their theory undefined.

Care Ethics Revised

Many of the problems with Burton and Dunn's care-based stakeholder theory can be traced back to their definition of care ethics. When Burton and Dunn published their article, care ethics was still a relatively new theory, and Gilligan's and Noddings' approaches to care ethics still dominated the field. As numerous critics have noted, however, Gilligan's and Noddings' early definitions of care ethics were ambiguous.[4] They did not provide a very clear definition of what it means to care for others, offer plain criteria for distinguishing good forms of care from bad, or indicate explicitly which relationships generate responsibilities to care and which do not. Some of this ambiguity underlies Burton and Dunn's theory as well.

Since the mid-1990s, numerous theorists have developed more rigorous definitions of care ethics that largely avoid these problems (Bubeck 1995; Clement 1996; Engster 2007; Fineman 2004; Held 2006; Kittay 1998; Noddings 2002; Slote 2001, 2007; Tronto 1993; Walker 1998; White 2000). While there is still no single universally agreed upon definition of care ethics, there is a good deal of consensus about its core aims. When we care for individuals, we usually aim to help them to meet their basic needs, develop or maintain their basic capabilities, or alleviate their pain and suffering (Engster 2007, 21–36). A number of activities that are usually understood as caring, including parenting, teaching, nursing, counseling, and elder care, all pursue these goals. Since the precise nature of an individual's needs usually vary from person to person, situation to situation, care theorists further emphasize the importance of attentiveness, responsiveness, and respect in caring for others. Unless we attend to the particular circumstances of others, respond to their particular needs and preferences, and show them some respect, we usually will not be able to care for them effectively. Most generally, then, care ethics may be defined as a theory that associates moral action with meeting the needs, fostering the capabilities, and alleviating the pain and suffering of individuals in attentive, responsive, and respectful ways.

In addition to more clearly defining the aims and virtues of care ethics, recent care theorists have also identified some principles for the distribution of care (Engster 2007; Friedman 1993; Held 2006). Since we cannot care equally for everyone, care ethics must be able to identify some priority rules for determining how we should distribute our always limited caring resources (time, energy, money, etc.). Without some priority rules, care ethics would collapse into a general exhortation for everyone to care for everyone, and hence lose any specific action-guiding value. Burton and Dunn touch upon this point in explaining how managers should address conflicts among stakeholders, but as noted above do not very fully develop any distributional guidelines. Based on the definition of care ethics offered above, three guidelines can be identified for the distribution of resources:

(1) *The proximity principle*: We are generally justified in (a) caring for ourselves before others; (b) caring for individuals who are geographically and temporally close to us before those who are far away; and (c) caring for individuals in our own culture or state before those in foreign cultures or states (Engster 2007). The justification for this principle follows from the notion that we should

[4]For other criticisms of Gilligan's and Noddings' early theories, see Bubeck (1995), Card (1990), Flanagan and Adler (1983), Goodin (1996), Tronto (1993).

generally aim to put our always limited caring resources to the best possible use. Since we can attend more directly to individuals who are close to us and usually have a better understanding of their circumstances, customs, and needs, we can usually care better for them than for distant others. Our limited resources are therefore usually best used in caring for individuals who are in some way close to us before attempting to care for distant others.

(2) *The relational principle*: We are usually justified in caring for individuals with whom we have a close personal relationship over others. Burton and Dunn also appeal to this relational principle but do not very clearly define it. Although there is no simple way to define a "close relationship," one relevant criterion rooted in the definition of care ethics provided above is the dependency of one party on the other for his or her survival and functioning, particularly when the dominant party bears some responsibility for the other's dependency. Parents have a close relationship with their children and special responsibilities toward them in part because their children are radically dependent on them. When parents take children under their direct care, they further signal to others that they will meet their children's needs so that others need not concern themselves directly with them. Parents thus have an obligation to give priority to their children's needs before others because if they do not do so there is a high probability their needs will not be met. The parent-child relationship represents, of course, only one form of close relationship. Close relationships can also be forged through friendship, pledges, contracts, and so forth. What makes a close relationship especially morally salient from the perspective of care ethics, however, is one party's dependency on the other for meeting his or her survival and developmental needs. These sorts of close relationships deserve priority under care ethics because they are so closely tied up with the goals of caring itself.

(3) *The urgency principle*: We are also justified in caring for those individuals who have more urgent needs over those with less urgent needs. The urgency of a need can be judged by the effect that meeting or not meeting it would have on a person's survival and functioning. If a person is likely to die or have his or her life blighted without our help, he or she may be judged to have a particularly urgent need. In expending our caring resources, we should thus consider how grave or urgent the different needs of different individuals are, and give some priority to the needs of those individuals who will not survive or function without our care. Even though parents have special responsibilities to meet their own children's needs, for example, they would be justified or even morally required by care ethics to temporarily set aside some educational activity that they were engaged in with their own child for the sake of saving another child from drowning.[5]

[5] While each of the distributional guidelines outlined above indicates when it is permissible to favor one individual or group over others, they cumulatively generate binding obligations. The combination of proximity and relationality, proximity and urgency, or relationality and urgency usually places an obligation on individuals to meet an individual's or group's needs before attempting to care for others.

The three priority rules will often pull us in different directions. We might find ourselves conflicted about whether we should devote our caring resources to individuals in our local community, helping a close relation in need who now lives far away from us, or meeting the urgent needs of a distant stranger. Much here depends upon the particular details of the situation, and there may not always be one best solution. The above principles nonetheless do provide some guidance and justification for the distribution of our care resources. We are, for example, justified in meeting (or even obligated to meet) the urgent needs of a close relation or someone in close proximity to us before attempting to address the urgent needs of distant others (Engster 2007, 54–64).

Care Ethics and Stakeholder Theory: Revised

The account of care ethics outlined above can support a stronger and clearer account of a care-based stakeholder theory in a number of ways. To begin with, the revised account of care ethics provides a stronger philosophical justification for why businesspeople should orient their business practices and decisions around care ethics. Most generally, the moral and social value of business activity, including productive work, may be said to stem from the support it provides to human life. We farm, mine, manufacture, transport, and buy and sell goods most fundamentally in order to produce and obtain the goods necessary for our survival and functioning. Caring, in turn, is the activity that we engage in when we put the goods generated and obtained through business activity directly to use to support human survival and functioning. As defined above, caring includes all those activities that we engage in to directly meet the basic needs, develop the basic capabilities, or alleviate the pain and suffering of individuals. When we use food products to meet our needs for nourishment, use clothes products to cover and protect ourselves and others, or use books or educational products to develop our own capabilities or those of others, we are caring for ourselves and others. The moral and social ends of business activity and productive work are thus mediated by care. Care translates the products of business activity into usable goods that can support human life and functioning. As such, the most fundamental moral and social purpose of business activity may be said to lie in supporting care (Engster 2007, 119–127). Inasmuch as business activity supports the ability of human beings to care for themselves and others, it helps to sustain human life and society and may be considered good. Inasmuch as business activity undermines or impedes the ability of individuals to care for themselves and others, it thwarts human survival and reproduction and may be considered bad.

The intimate connection between productive work and caregiving provides one reason why businesspeople should consider the impact of their activities on the ability of people to care. If the fundamental moral and social purpose of business activity is to support caregiving, then it would seem wrong by the moral and social logic of business activity itself to engage in activities that controvert this goal. When business practices thwart caregiving, they undermine their own internal moral and social justification. Even worse, they corrode the basic social practices and relationships necessary for the reproduction of human life, society, and business activity itself. It might be claimed that businesspeople can best support caregiving by single-mindedly pursuing their own self-interest and profits, since such activity will ultimately generate the greatest supply of goods for caring. Given the distributional principles outlined above, however, we are generally required to care for those who are in close proximity to us or directly dependent on us before concerning ourselves with distant or abstract others. When the pursuit of profits and production of goods directly interferes with the abilities of individuals who are close to us or dependent on us to care for themselves and others, it violates caring values. In order for business activity to fulfill its fundamental social and moral purposes, businesspeople thus need to take account of the impact of their actions and policies on the ability of individuals who are most directly affected by them to care for themselves and others. Business practices that lose touch with this goal can be rightly condemned as immoral and antisocial.

In addition to providing a stronger justification for a care-based stakeholder theory, the revised account of care ethics can also provide a clearer definition of who should count as a stakeholder. Burton and Dunn say very little about how we should determine who counts as a stakeholder. For the most part, they simply take over from other stakeholder theories the standard list of stakeholder groups: stockholders, employees, the local community, customers, suppliers, and others. Standard stakeholder theories, in turn, tend to define stakeholders very broadly. Freeman (1984), for example, originally defined a stakeholder as "any group or individual who can affect, or is affected by, the achievement of a corporation's purpose" (vi, 46). Based on this definition, he included government regulatory agencies, the media, public interest groups, and others as possible stakeholders in firms. The revised account of care ethics provides sharper focus to the definition of stakeholders. Given the definition of care outlined above, stakeholders may be defined as any groups or individuals whose ability to care for themselves or others is directly dependent upon a firm's actions or decisions. The media, government agencies, and other groups who are sometimes included in lists of stakeholders thus fall out of this definition. Care ethics directs managers to give their attention strictly to groups and individuals whose capacities for care are in some way directly tied up with their firms' activities.

Among traditional stakeholder groups, care ethics thus identifies two groups as deserving special moral consideration: stockholders and employees. Both groups are privileged in a care-based stakeholder theory because both are directly dependent on firms for the resources necessary to care. The stockholder-firm relationship is based on an explicit agreement whereby the stockholder provides the firm with capital (or more usually takes over the capital loan from another party) in exchange for a fair return on his or her investment. The firm's special obligation to stockholders stems in part from this agreement, which establishes the terms of their relationship, but more basically from the stockholders' dependence on the firm for financial resources. While few investors would go hungry without a significant annual return on investment from any particular firm, many people do depend on their investments in general for a significant share of their income or as insurance in case of emergencies. Many people also have pension funds and personal retirement accounts that are heavily invested in stocks, and most of these individuals will eventually depend on their investments to support themselves during old age, sickness, injury, and other periods of need. Care ethics thus suggests that managers generally should give some priority to stockholder interests in making corporate decisions because stockholders depend on their firms for the resources necessary to support their care.

The employee-firm relationship is also based on an explicit contract: the firm agrees to pay an employee a certain amount of money in exchange for a certain amount and type of labor. From the perspective of care ethics, however, the employee-firm contract implies more than just a voluntary exchange of wages for labor. A number of other responsibilities are implicit in it. First, firms have a responsibility to provide their workers with a safe and healthy workplace environment, meaning that workers should not be exposed to unnecessary or unreasonable risks or harm in carrying out their work responsibilities. Free market advocates sometimes argue that any worker who finds the health or safety conditions of a particular workplace inadequate should look for another job. The ethical grounding for this position is, however, highly dubious. It abstracts economic activity from its most fundamental purpose: provisioning for human life. It further assumes a degree of freedom, voluntariness, and information on the part of workers that they often lack. Care ethics suggests that firms have a duty to make sure that their work processes and conditions meet high health and safety standards on the grounds that any work processes or conditions that unnecessarily or unreasonably endanger the lives or health of their workers are contrary to the fundamental normative purposes of business activity. The only case where some dangerous or unhealthy productive activity might be tolerated is when it is absolutely necessary to support caregiving, and even then, every reasonable precaution should be taken to protect the workers.

Care ethics further suggests that employers have an obligation to pay their workers at least a living wage, meaning a wage sufficient to meet their basic needs and sustain their functioning. Work that does not pay even a living wage falls short of the fundamental purpose for which work exists, and thus may be seen as immoral and antisocial. Employers should likewise make sure that their workers have adequate time to care for themselves and others by setting reasonable limits on daily and weekly work hours, not requiring overtime, providing workers with vacations, and offering a number of paid sick days each year. If workers lack the opportunity to care adequately for themselves and others, the ultimate purpose of productive work is once again undermined. Finally, a caring firm should foster a work environment that allows workers to exercise their basic capabilities for reason, imagination, communication, and sociability, and avoid assigning mind-numbing or back-breaking work that erodes workers' basic capabilities. While some theorists (O'Brien 2005) have gone further and argued that care ethics requires establishing a system of worker ownership and control over the workplace, this reform would appear to be neither necessary nor sufficient to achieving the goals of a caring workplace. Caring managers can create conditions for meaningful work outside a system of worker control, and worker control does not necessarily guarantee that workers will implement workplace reforms that will enrich production methods. Managers nonetheless should do what they can to enhance the nature of work for their employees within the constraints of their work processes.

Any further responsibilities that firms may have toward their employees depend on a number of circumstantial factors, such as the amount of time an employee has worked for a firm and the nature or an employee's work. These factors determine the closeness of the relationship between the firm and an employee, and thus the responsibility of the firm to the employee. Individuals who have worked for the same firm for a long period of time or developed specialized skills for a highly specific job may find it difficult to find another job. A firm has special obligations to look after these workers' job security because they are highly dependent on the firm for their livelihoods and the firm is at least partially responsible for this dependency—via the type of work it has assigned them and the length of time it has employed them. This does not mean that firms can never legitimately fire or lay-off workers. It means only that the more dependent a worker has become on a particular firm for a job, the greater the firm's responsibility to retain the employee or help him or her to find another job.

While firms generally have the strongest responsibilities to stockholders and employees, they also have some important but more limited responsibilities toward two other stakeholder groups: the local community and customers. Much of a firm's impact on the local community will take place through its relations with its employees. Yet, firms also some moral responsibilities to members of the local community based on their close proximity to the firm. For example, firms can have a significant impact on the survival and functioning of individuals in surrounding communities through their environmental practices. Harmful emissions or waste materials can cause birth defects, sickness, and death. Just as firms have a responsibility under care ethics to look after their workers' health and safety, so they also have a responsibility to make sure their production or disposal methods do not negatively impact the health and safety of community members. Production methods that cause sickness and death once again violate the basic purposes for which business activity exists. When local communities invest significant public resources in firms—by building access roads, providing free land, offering tax incentives or exemptions—firms may also be said to have a close relationship with the communities similar to their relationship with stockholders. At least until they have repaid the communities' investment, these firms have strong responsibilities to consider the local community's interests in making business decisions.

The main responsibility that firms have to their customers is to provide them with safe and reliable products or services and truthful information. When customers buy a product or service, they can generally be expected to understand the main trade-offs involved: a small, cheap car is likely to be more fuel efficient but less safe than a bulky, four-door model. It is not the firm's responsibility to dictate to consumers what they should want based on some preconceived idea of what is best for them, but rather to respond to their preferences and needs. It is nonetheless incumbent upon firms to provide accurate information to customers about their products or services and to make sure their products and services meet at least minimal safety requirements and do not have any hidden dangers or flaws. Marketing a dangerous or flawed product can inflict harm or death on consumers or cause them serious inconvenience and loss. A caring firm will therefore be forthcoming about the products and services they offer and produce and sell only goods that are reasonably safe and reliable.

Most stakeholder theories suggest that firms have responsibilities to a number of other groups. Burton and Dunn particularly focus on the responsibilities that firms have toward their suppliers, but the grounds for this special relationship seem questionable. A firm stands in relation to its suppliers much as a customer stands in relation to a firm. The firm no doubt depends upon its customers for its continued existence and success, but this does not obligate customers to continue buying from it. Customers have much stronger obligations to care for themselves, their families, their friends, and others than they have to continue buying any product from any firm, and may in any case come to regard a particular product or service as unsuitable to their needs because of quality, price, or personal tastes. The same considerations apply to the relation between a firm and its suppliers. If a firm can buy better quality or lower priced goods from a new supplier, it would seem permissible, and perhaps even obligatory, for it to do so given its stronger obligations to its stockholders, employees, and customers. There may be exceptions to this general rule. If a firm has taken actions to make a particular supplier highly dependent on it for its survival by pledging, for example, to continue buying a certain product for some number of years, then it would bear some special responsibility to continue to buy goods or services from this supplier and phase out its relationship only over time. In most cases, though, firms may be said to have only weak responsibilities to their suppliers that are usually trumped by their much stronger obligations to stockholders, employees, customers, and local community members.

An interesting question arises as to whether competitor firms should be considered stakeholders. One firm certainly can affect the sustainability and success of competitor firms through its decisions and actions. However, competitor firms are not directly dependent upon one another, but instead rivals for market share and goods. Moreover, based on the relationship principle outlined above, the managers of a firm always have much stronger responsibilities to their own stockholders, employees, local communities, and customers than to other firms. Indeed, in a competitive market system, the primary responsibility of all managers is to promote the success and profitability of their own firms.[6] If the firm fails, its stockholders, employees, and others may all face difficulties in obtaining the recourses necessary to care for themselves and their dependents. Managers nonetheless do have some general responsibilities to competitor firms. Inasmuch as a competitive market system can be justified under care ethics, it is because the market represents an efficient and flexible system for the production and distribution of goods and services necessary for care. Managers are therefore under a general obligation

[6] I discuss elsewhere the question of whether a competitive market is consistent with care ethics (Engster 2007, 134–140).

to avoid illegal or unfair business practices (e.g., collusion, sabotage) that might undermine fair market competition.

Firms have one other important general responsibility under a care-based stakeholder theory. Although firms need not continue purchasing goods or services from existing suppliers, they nonetheless do have a responsibility to ensure that whichever suppliers they purchase goods or services from follow at least minimally caring business practices. When a firm purchases products or services from a supplier, it becomes partially responsible for, or complicit in, the employment, safety, and environmental practices of the firm. In effect, it becomes the indirect manager of these firms. Consistent with the aims and values of care ethics, firms therefore have some responsibility to make sure their suppliers act responsibly toward their employees and local communities in the areas of worker health and safety, wages, and responsible environmental practices. Burton and Dunn propose the notion of the least advantaged stakeholder to explain why it is wrong for managers to contract out work to firms that exploit their workers or expose them to harm, but one need not resort to this special principle to reach the same conclusion. Even if a firm does not directly oversee the work processes of its suppliers or partners, it is still responsible in part for their workplace and environmental practices. Contracting with a firm that exploits its workers or exposes them to unhealthy work conditions is wrong for the same reasons it is wrong to treat one's own workers in this way.

While the above discussion provides a sharper focus for stakeholder theory, some key issues still remain to be clarified. In particular, there still remains the question of how firms should deal with conflicts among stakeholder interests. Which specific stakeholder interests should have the highest priority when there are conflicts among them? As a general rule, managers should orient their decisions around protecting and promoting the success and continuation of their firms. If the firm fails, stockholders lose their investments, workers lose their jobs, the local community loses a source of employment, and so forth. Thus, the goal of staying in business has high priority. As long as this first goal can be met, firms should aim to balance the interests of their main stakeholders: providing fair returns to their stockholders; guaranteeing their workers a safe and healthy work environment, a living wage, and adequate time to care for themselves and their dependents; making sure production methods and emissions meet safe environmental and health standards; offering consumers a reasonably safe and reliable product or service; and buying products and services only from suppliers that conduct their businesses in reasonably caring ways. When conflicts arise among these different interests, care ethics dictates that the highest priority be given to the health and safety of employees, community members, customers, and others. Indeed, these interests trump even the importance of the firm's survival. Since the firm exists at root to promote the survival, health, and functioning of its stakeholders, any action that directly infringes on these goods falls outside the scope of moral business activity. While a strong commitment to worker health and safety and high environmental standards may result in lesser profits for investors and possibly even the loss of jobs for some workers, individuals are likely to suffer much greater and immediate threats to their survival and functioning when health, safety, and environmental standards are compromised.

For similar reasons, if managers must choose between cutting jobs or reducing profits, they should generally favor jobs over profits, at least in the short term. Even though stockholders depend on their investments to support themselves, workers are usually much more dependent on the income from their jobs to support themselves and their dependents. There are, however, obvious limits to this policy. Over the long term, a manager who consistently favored jobs over profits would likely endanger his or her own job and perhaps the solvency of the firm. Thus, when some cuts are necessary, managers should resort to the "rule of consensus" discussed by Burton and Dunn (1996, 142). The rule of consensus has two elements: (1) managers should try to find solutions to stakeholder conflicts that are acceptable to all; and (2) managers should communicate with stakeholders both by explaining proposed solutions to them and soliciting alternative proposals from them. Suppose, for example, a firm is losing money in part because of high payroll costs. The best solution would be to increase productivity and profits without job or pay cuts (Bulger and Gessner 2001).[7] Alternatively, managers might consider gradually reducing payroll costs by leaving jobs vacant after employees voluntarily leave or retire. If more immediate or radical cuts are required, managers might propose a variety of options to workers in an effort to retain jobs: pay reductions, pay freezes, shorter work hours or weeks, job sharing, voluntary leaves of absence, or early retirement programs. They might also see if the workers have any cost-cutting proposals of their own. Finally, if layoffs are unavoidable, managers should follow the relationship principle outlined above. If an employee is essential to a firm's success, he or she would have to be retained regardless of age or experience. Otherwise, managers should try to protect the jobs of individuals who might have difficulty finding work elsewhere or transferring their skills to a new firm.

The Value of a Care-Based Stakeholder Theory

The care-based stakeholder theory outlined above leaves a number of questions unanswered. What exactly is a fair return on investment for stockholders? What are reasonable standards of workplace health and safety? These are important questions that unfortunately cannot be addressed here. Another set of questions relates to the sorts of benefits a firm should provide to its employees: Do firms have a responsibility to provide their employees with health insurance, pension programs, and paid parental leaves? Ultimately, I think these sorts of programs are best supported by the state rather than individual businesses. However, I cannot pursue this argument here.[8]

My goal in this chapter has been to develop a care-based stakeholder theory that can clarify in general terms what it means for a firm to conduct business in a caring

[7] A number of the following solutions are taken from Bulger and Gessner (2001).

[8] Requiring businesses to pay the costs of these programs for their employees unfairly burdens them with a general social responsibility and further provides a disincentive to hire new employees.

way. While my theory incorporates insights from Burton and Dunn's discussion of care ethics and stakeholder theory, I have extended their argument in several ways. In particular, I have provided a stronger explanation for why managers should consider the impact of their business decisions on their stakeholders, offered a narrower and more concrete definition of who should count as a stakeholder, discussed the precise nature of a firm's obligations to different stakeholders, and outlined some rules for prioritizing stakeholder interests. In this way, I hope to have provided a more practically-useful and applicable set of ethical guidelines for managers interested in conducting their firms' activities according to care ethics.

Beyond just elaborating a clearer care-based stakeholder theory, my argument also contributes to the general literature on stakeholder theory in a number of ways. One important weakness of traditional stakeholder theories based in Kantian, utilitarian, or other traditional moral principles is that they do not provide any rationale based in business affairs themselves for why managers should conduct their affairs according to stakeholder guidelines. If a manager is a confirmed Kantian or utilitarian, then he or she might be persuaded to follow stakeholder ideals; otherwise not. Care ethics provides a justification for stakeholder theory rooted in the moral and social aims of business activity itself. The most fundamental aim of business activity is to generate the resources necessary to supporting caregiving. Managers should therefore pay attention to the effects of their actions on their stakeholder's ability to care for themselves and others because the moral and social integrity of business activity itself depends on it. While this argument may not convince all businesspeople to conduct their affairs according to stakeholder theory, it at least engages them on their own terms to a far greater degree than Kantian or utilitarian principles do.

Existing stakeholder theories also have suffered from the lack of a clear account of who should count as a stakeholder and how different stakeholder interests should be ranked. Many definitions of stakeholders (e.g., those of Freeman) tend to be very broad, and most stakeholder theories offer little guidance about which stakeholder interests should matter most. This has led to a common misunderstanding about stakeholder theory. Many critics have argued that stakeholder theory demands that managers should treat all stakeholder interests equally and impartially, which in most cases is both impossible and undesirable (Friedman and Miles 2006, 61; Hasnas 1998; Humber 2001, 116; Marcoux 2003, 126). The care-based stakeholder theory outlined above provides clearer guidelines on who should count as stakeholders and which stakeholder interests are most important. Individuals or groups are considered stakeholders in this theory if their ability to care for themselves and others, survive and function, is directly dependent on or tied up with firm decisions. A stakeholder's dependency can be gauged, in turn, by their proximity to the firm, the closeness of their relationship with the firm, and the urgency of their claims. Thus, the interests of stockholders and employees are generally more important than those of other stakeholders, but the urgency associated with the health and safety of workers, customers, and other individuals means that these interests should always receive the highest priority.

Finally, traditional stakeholder theories have been criticized for being unrealistic. Critics have charged that existing stakeholder theories fail to give sufficient attention to the firm's goals of making profits and providing investors with fair returns on their investments (Goodpaster 1991; Hasnas 1998; Marcoux 2003). As a result, they claim that stakeholder theory does not give adequate attention to the practical constraints that most managers labor under in a competitive capitalist system. A care-based stakeholder theory is more sensitive to these concerns. As emphasized above, one of the central responsibilities of managers under a care-based theory is to ensure the firm's continued survival and prosperity. One of the manager's main priorities further consists of providing investors with a fair return on investments. These responsibilities do not override all others. Managers would be remiss if they approved the sale of defective products or neglected health and safety standards in order to increase profits or generate higher dividends. But traditional business goals do find a central place in a care-based stakeholder theory. In fact, care ethics does not see the traditional goals of business activity as necessarily opposed to its own concerns, but rather as supportive of them. Business pursuits must succeed in order for care to flourish. Managers simply need to keep in mind the ultimate moral and social purposes of their activities.

Burton and Dunn took some important initial steps toward developing a care-based stakeholder theory. My goal in this chapter has been much the same as theirs: to offer a care-based stakeholder theory that can serve as "a viable option for those managers interested in operating according to moral principles" (134). To this end, I have offered a fuller justification of a care-based stakeholder theory and provided clearer guidelines for business decision-making. Most generally, I have attempted to demonstrate that business practices and care activities are not nearly as opposed as one might initially suppose. In the final analysis, there is no deep conflict between business success and care ethics. Real business success involves contributing to and supporting the caring activities that sustain and propagate human life. A care-based stakeholder theory can provide managers with the ethical guidelines for achieving just this sort of morally and socially responsible business success.

References

Bubeck, D. 1995. *Care, gender, and justice*. Oxford: Clarendon Press.

Bulger, B., and Gessner, C. 2001. Sign of the times: implementing reductions in force. In *Business ethics*, eds. M. Snoeyenbos, R. Almeder, and J. Humber, 218–224, 3rd edn. Amherst, MA: Prometheus.

Burton, B., and C. Dunn. 1996. Feminist ethics as moral grounding for stakeholder theory. *Business Ethics Quarterly* 6: 133–147.

Card, C. 1990. Caring and evil. *Hypatia* 5: 101–108.

Clement, G. 1996. *Care, autonomy, and justice*. Boulder, CO: *Westview Press*.

Engster, D. 2007. *The heart of justice: Care ethics and political theory*. Oxford: Oxford University Press.

Evan, W., and R. Freeman. 1988. A stakeholder theory of the modern corporation: Kantian capitalism. In *Ethical theory and business*, eds. T. Beauchamp, and N. Bowie, 101–105, 3rd edn. Englewood Cliffs, NJ: Prentice-Hall.

Fineman, M. 2004. *The autonomy myth: A theory of dependency*. New York, NY: The New Press.

Flanagan, O., and J. Adler. 1983. Impartiality and particularity. *Social Research* 50: 576–596.

Freeman, R. 1984. *Strategic management: A stakeholder approach*. Boston, MA: Pitman.
Freeman, R. 1994. The politics of stakeholder theory: some future directions. *Business Ethics Quarterly* 4: 409–421.
Freeman, R. 2004. A stakeholder theory of the modern corporation. In *Ethical theory and business*, eds. T. Beauchamp, and N. Bowie, 7th edn. Upper Saddle River, NJ: Prentice Hall.
Freeman, R., and W. Evan. 1990. Corporate governance: A stakeholder interpretation. *Journal of Behavioral Economics* 19: 337–359.
Freeman, R., and D. Gilbert Jr. 1992. Business ethics and society: *a* critical agenda. *Business and Society* 31: 9–17.
Freeman, R., and J. Liedtka. 1991. Corporate social responsibility: a critical approach. *Business Horizons* 34: 92–98.
Freeman, R., and D. Reed. 1983. Stockholders and stakeholders: a new perspective on corporate governance. *California Management Review* 25: 88–106.
Friedman, M. 1970. The social responsibility of business is to increase its profits. *New York Times Magazine* September 13.
Friedman, M. 1993. What are Friends For? Feminist Perspectives on Personal Relationships and Moral Theory. Ithaca: Cornell University Press.
Friedman, A., and S. Miles. 2006. *Stakeholders: Theory and practice*. Oxford: Oxford University Press.
Gilligan, C. 1982. *In a different voice: Psychological theory and women's development*. Cambridge, MA: Harvard University Press.
Goodin, R. 1996. Structures of political order: the relational feminist alternative. In *Nomos XXXVIII: Political order*, ed. R. Hardin, and I. Shapiro, 498–521. New York, NY: New York University Press.
Goodpaster, K. 1991. Business ethics and stakeholder analysis. *Business Ethics Quarterly* 1: 53–73.
Hasnas, J. 1998. The normative theories of business ethics: a guide for the perplexed. *Business Ethics Quarterly* 8: 19–42.
Held, V. 2006. *The ethics of care: Personal, political, and global*. Oxford: Oxford University Press.
Hendry, J. 2001. Economic contracts versus social relationships as a foundation for normative stakeholder theory. *Business Ethics: A European Review* 10: 223–232.
Humber, J. 2001. Why I am not a normative stakeholder theorist. In *Business ethics*, eds. M. Snoeyenbos, R. Almeder, and J. Humber, 3rd edn. Amherst, MA: Prometheus.
Kittay, E. 1998. *Love's labor: Essays on women, equality, and dependency*. New York, NY: Routledge.
Liedtka, J. 1996. Feminist morality and competitive reality: a role for an ethic of care? *Business Ethics Quarterly* 6: 179–200.
Machold, S., Ahmed, P., and Farquhar, S. 2008. Corporate governance and ethics: A feminist perspective. *Journal of Business Ethics* 81: 665–678.
Marcoux, A. 2003. A fidicuiary argument against stakeholder theory. *Business Ethics Quarterly* 13: 1–24.
Noddings, N. 1984. *Caring: A feminine approach to ethics and moral education*. Berkeley, CA: University of California Press.
Noddings, N. 2002. *Starting at home: Caring and social policy*. Berkeley, CA: University of California Press.
O'Brien, R. 2005. *Bodies in revolt: Gender, disability, and a workplace ethic of care*. New York, NY: Routledge.
Slote, M. 2001. *Morals from motives*. Oxford: Oxford University Press.
Slote, M. 2007. *The ethics of care and empathy*. New York, NY: Routledge.
Tronto, J. 1993. *Moral boundaries: A political argument for an ethic of care*. New York, NY: Routledge.
Walker, M. 1998. *Moral understandings*. New York, NY: Routledge.

White, T. 1992. Business ethics and Carol Gilligan's "two voices". *Business Ethics Quarterly* 2: 51–61.
White, J. 2000. *Democracy, justice, and the welfare state*. University Park, PA: Pennsylvania State University Press.
Wicks, A., D. Gilbert Jr., and R. Freeman. 1994. A feminist reinterpretation of the stakeholder concept. *Business Ethics Quarterly* 4: 475–497.
Zakhem, A., Palmer, D., and Stoll, M. 2008. *Stakeholder theory: Essential readings in ethical leadership and management*. Amherst, MA: Prometheus.

Chapter 6
Moving Toward a More Caring Stakeholder Theory: Global Business Ethics in Dialogue with the Feminist Ethics of Care

Daniel E. Palmer and Mary Lyn Stoll

Introduction

Within the field of business ethics, stakeholder theory has become one of the main theoretical tools for articulating the moral responsibilities of business. However, applying stakeholder theory gives rise to a number of thorny issues, particularly at the level of understanding how business persons can properly discern and respond to stakeholder interests. In the context of global business, this issue is even more pressing, as many of the relevant stakeholders are widely dispersed and the nature of the relationship between stakeholders is often tenuous. If stakeholder theory is to provide for vigorous moral responses to the ethical interests of all persons affected by business activity in a global economy, and not merely reify the status quo, stakeholder theory needs to appeal to a richer account of moral agency than it has hitherto done. In this paper, we appeal to several elements of the ethics of care in order to provide just such an account. Supplementing stakeholder theory with an ethics of care, we argue, provides for a more complete account of business obligations in a global context.

The paper is divided into three main sections. In the first section, we delineate the essential features of stakeholder theory as a normative theory of business ethics. We also explain what we take to be an important lacuna in the development of stakeholder theory as of yet. In the next section of the paper, we attempt to show how certain insights from care ethics might, if properly developed, address this lacuna in the deployment of stakeholder theory. While the ethics of care was originally developed in a context or relationships that many have seen as antithetical to the kinds of relationships found in business, we argue that the ethics of care appeals to considerations that can, and should, be carried over to the context of business.

D.E. Palmer (✉)
Department of Philosophy, Kent State University, Kent, OH, USA
e-mail: dpaler1@kent.edu

M.L. Stoll
Department of Philosophy, University of Southern Indiana, Evansville, IN, USA
e-mail: mlstoll@usi.edu

M. Hamington, M. Sander-Staudt (eds.), *Applying Care Ethics to Business*, Issues in Business Ethics 34, DOI 10.1007/978-90-481-9307-3_6,
© Springer Science+Business Media B.V. 2011

In this sense, we argue that the ethics of care develops areas of moral analysis that stakeholder theory has largely left untouched, and that a synthesis of the theories is thus not only possible, but will lead to a more robust version of stakeholder theory. In the final section, we offer a brief example of the kind of moral analysis that such a synthesis would generate, and the kinds of ethical responses it would support.

Stakeholder Theory and the Current State of Business Ethics

The "stakeholder" concept is now widely appealed to in discussions of business ethics in both academia and, perhaps more importantly, within the business community itself. While the term stakeholder can be found in management literature going back to the 1960s, it was with the 1984 publication of R. Edward Freeman's *Strategic Management: A Stakeholder Theory* that stakeholder theory began to be articulated as a comprehensive theory of management. Elsewhere we have traced the trajectory of stakeholder theory as it developed over the years after the initial publication of Freeman's *Strategic Management* in some detail (Palmer, Stoll, and Zakhem 2008). Rather than fully repeating that account here, we will instead focus upon only those aspects of stakeholder theory that are essential for understanding its current status within the field of business ethics.

In many ways the stakeholder concept as articulated by Freeman and other stakeholder theorists is designed to both appeal to and play off of the idea of the role of shareholders in corporate management. In particular, proponents of neo-liberal views of the firm such as Milton Friedman had maintained that as shareholders were the "owners" of a corporation, managers had a fiduciary obligation to run corporations solely in pursuit of shareholder interests, which were taken to be equivalent to the pursuit of profits. While even Friedman acknowledged a basic moral responsibility on the part of mangers to obey the law and common moral rules in pursuing shareholder interests (Friedman 1970), most proponents of the shareholder view tended to accent the responsibility toward shareholders to such an extent that a consideration of the interests of any other parties in the activities of management was overshadowed. The resulting shareholder theory of management was thus often taken to amount to the dictum that the corporation's only responsibility was to pursue profits for shareholders in any manner possible.

Freeman's initial articulation of the stakeholder idea was thus meant as a corrective to what he saw as a problematically narrow view of strategic management (Freeman 1984). Given that many other persons can be affected by management activity, Freeman argued that firms that failed to pay attention to other parties who had a "stake" in corporate decisions put their companies at risk. Articulating the concept of a stakeholder, Freeman proffered that "a stakeholder in an organization is (by definition) any group or individual who can affect or is affect by the achievement of an organization's objectives" (Freeman 1984, p. 46). Stakeholders, in this sense, could include employees, shareholders, customers, competitors, community members, and a host of other potential parties. As discussed by Engster in an earlier chapter in this work, the stakeholder theory of the firm thus viewed corporations in terms of a vast network of relationships to various parties that can be affected by, and affect, management activities.

As noted by Goodpaster (1993) and others, an important distinction within the literature on stakeholder theory quickly arose between stakeholder theory taken as a merely instrumental theory of management versus stakeholder theory viewed as a normative theory of business ethics. While instrumental versions of stakeholder theory merely assert the strategic value of tending to stakeholder relations in promoting long term corporate goals, normative versions of stakeholder theory assert that corporations have a moral responsibility to take stakeholder interests into account. Our concern in this paper is solely with the normative versions of stakeholder theory, which tend to be the focus of debates within the literature of business ethics. The primary idea behind the normative version of stakeholder theory is that in so far as stakeholders could be affected, either negatively or positively, by management activities, management has a moral obligation to take account of their interests and rights in making corporate decisions (Freeman and Gilbert 1988).

While there is certainly ongoing debate about the viability of the normative version of stakeholder theory within the field of business ethics, it is undeniable that stakeholder theory has obtained a place of prominence within the field. Indeed, it would probably not be an exaggeration to claim that it is the dominant theory in business ethics today. Without going greatly into the details as to why this is so, we would suggest that there are both theoretical and practical reasons for this that are telling. At the theoretical level, stakeholder theory provides for a holistic view of corporate activity that accounts for the numerous kinds of relationships that sustain and are sustained by that activity and that acknowledges the potentially diverse array of moral claims that such relationships can create. At the practical level, it provides managers and other interested parties with a straightforward and plain manner of speaking about moral issues that is easily accommodated into the vocabulary of management. Indeed, the ease with which the language of stakeholders can be carried over to discuss the nature of various organizational relationships goes far in explaining why talk of "stakeholders" is now ubiquitous not only among the leaders of for-profit corporations but in a multitude of other organizational contexts.

In Chapter 5 in this volume Daniel Engster details many of the generic features of normative versions of stakeholder theories, so we will limit our discussion of stakeholder theory here to a discussion of some yet unresolved issues in the development of stakeholder theory. First, however, we would note that on our view stakeholder theory is intended as what might be termed a mid-level ethical theory that is designed to articulate, within a specific practical arena, how certain moral relationships might be articulated and responded to in a pragmatic manner, and not as a complete or fundamental moral theory. This explains both why there are different versions of stakeholder theory, as which relationships and which interests are counted can be carved up somewhat differently, and why the element common to all versions of stakeholder theory, that corporations have some obligation toward various stakeholders other than shareholders, has been defended by appeal to a number of different fundamental moral theories. In regards to the later point, various attempts to ground stakeholder theory have been made by to appeals to fundamental ethical theories as divergent as Kantianism (Evan and Edward Freeman 1993) Ross-style moral pluralism (Palmer 1999), critical theory (Reed 1999), and even feminism (Burton and Dunn 1996; Wicks, Gilbert, and Freeman 1994). While some might see this situation concerning the relation of stakeholder theory to more fundamental moral theories as deleterious for stakeholder theory, we see the need for mid-level theories as determined largely by pragmatic considerations. As long as such mid-level theories appeal to a wide range of general moral interests that would have to be accounted for in any more fundamental moral theory, mid-level theories can be implemented independently of a complete theoretical account of the foundations of morality. One can engage in moral dialogue and moral analysis at the pragmatic level by appealing to a wide range of normative, conceptual and empirical considerations that are found in ordinary discourse. On our view, mid-level theories such as stakeholder theory are designed precisely to aid ordinary persons in carrying out such dialogue and analysis, independently of a complete theoretical account of the foundations of morality. This differentiation also allows us to argue that one can reject certain articulations of stakeholder theory, mainly those that are made in conjunction with problematic views of moral status or moral reasoning, while still retaining the fundamental idea of stakeholder theory. Indeed, this is the general tactic we will take in this paper.

By and large, most discussions of stakeholder theory have focused upon two elements of stakeholder theory: stakeholder identification and stakeholder analysis (Goodpaster 1993; Johnson-Cramer 2008; Palmer, Stoll, and Zakhem 2008). Stakeholder identification involves determining which parties have interests as legitimate stakeholders in corporate decisions, while stakeholder analysis involves determining how to balance various stakeholder interests in order to arrive at morally defensible courses of action in cases of stakeholder conflict. As discussed by Engster earlier in this volume (Chapter 5), both issue give rise to significant questions that have dominated much of the recent literature on stakeholder theory.

However, while developing these two main elements of stakeholder theory have garnered the greatest attention within the literature, we wish to suggest that there is another aspect necessary to their proper development of stakeholder theory that has so far been largely neglected, and that here considerations taken from the ethics of care might offer a way of resolving some of the difficulties in implementing stakeholder theory properly. On our view, what stakeholder theorists have not been able to offer as of yet is what we would call a moral phenomenology in which to situate its account of either stakeholder identification or stakeholder distribution. We shall use the term moral phenomenology to refer to the analysis of the psychological or affective states exhibited in moral agency as well as the various internal states that characterize the manner in which moral agents come to appreciate and respond to moral demands. While there have been some studies into the moral phenomenology of business persons, for instance some elements of such a phenomenology are to be found in Robert Jackall's book *Moral Mazes* (1988), little appreciation has been given to issue of moral phenomenology in explicating stakeholder theory itself. We maintain that this lacuna is problematic, since as a pragmatically geared mid-level theory stakeholder theory needs to account for the phenomenology of moral agency if it is to properly articulate the nature of the moral relationships that it describes.

What is significant about the ethics of care, to our mind, is precisely that it is a moral theory grounded in a significant treatment of moral phenomenology. Indeed, the ethics of care provides a powerful critique of the failure of certain formalistic moral theories to account for the phenomenology of lived moral experience.

The basic problem then, as we see it, is that stakeholder theory so far has had little to say about how managers and other decision makers in business are made aware of morally significant relationships or the means by which they do, and should, incorporate such moral considerations into their decision making. Or, when such accounts are offered, they generally presuppose an anemic picture of moral agency. Lacking a more complete account of moral agency stakeholder theory can easily degenerate into a formulaic set of generalities that fails to take seriously the very moral import of the relationships that the theory was designed to articulate. In this sense, both stakeholder identification and stakeholder distribution presuppose the ability of moral agents to discern properly and respond to the moral interests of others. This piece of the puzzle, a rich account of the phenomenology of moral agency, is what stakeholder theory has of yet to offer. Indeed, lacking such an account, stakeholder theory often assumes a picture of deliberation that sees reasoning as a purely rule governed procedure that can be specified in terms of isolated deliberators and their individual abstract interests. Ironically then, while stakeholder theorists generally reject the classic or neo-liberal view of corporate responsibility, they often appeal to the very picture of rational and moral agency that such theories presuppose. Doing so, we maintain, leaves stakeholder theory unable to motivate a real appreciation for, or implementation of, the very moral considerations that it maintains are central to business ethics. As such, we argue that stakeholder theory needs to be supplemented with a proper account of the phenomenology of moral agency, and that insights from the ethics of care offer a fruitful possibility in this direction. While there have been a few isolated attempts to examine the potential relationship between stakeholder theory and an ethics of care (see, for example, Simola 2007), our account attempts to do so in a manner that accents the unique way in which insights concerning moral agency provided by the ethics of care can overcome the central difficulty with stakeholder theory discussed above.

Appealing to an Ethics of Care in Developing a Global Stakeholder Theory

As noted by a number of commentators, including Engster (Chapter 5) earlier in this volume, there is a basic similarity between stakeholder theories and the ethics of care that is suggestive of the possibility of bringing them into dialogue. After all, just as stakeholder theories of corporate obligations are articulated in terms of a web of relationships, so too an ethics of care focuses primarily upon relationships that give rise to moral obligation. Unlike many applications of stakeholder theory, however, an ethic of care accents the notion of moral responsiveness in action as an underlying presupposition of real moral agency. This notion of moral responsiveness is grounded in the emotional connections between persons (Groenhout

2004) by which persons become aware of and respond to the needs and interests of others. These connections are crucial to motivate ethical behavior, since abstract considerations alone, such as the notion of formal duties or rights, are rarely psychologically compelling enough to overcome other psychologically affective states (such as self-interest, feelings of loyalty, or other concrete motivational sources). An ethics of care also maintains that understanding the motivational source of action must begin with a perception of the particularity of the situation or an understanding of the concrete situations in which the perceived need for moral action arise (Lindemann 2005).

This attentiveness to the role of both emotional connections and our awareness of the particularity of situations calling for moral responsiveness is characteristic of the ethics of care. On our view, such an account provides a better understanding of the moral phenomenology of agency than is typically found in discussions of stakeholder theory. Stakeholder theory's picture of moral agency will remain flat and unmotivated without an account of the ties that bind these relationships and the particularities of the realities that generate them. To understand how an ethics of care can supplement stakeholder theories with a more robust account of moral obligation, a fuller analysis of the nature of the ethics of care and its relation to both traditional ethical theories is needed. It is this task we turn to next.

Many traditional moral theories have focused primarily upon basic obligations of justice or upon fundamental moral rights. Such theories typically treat moral agents in terms of some universal trait that gives them moral status. For example, in Kantian ethics, individuals gain moral value solely in virtue of their capacity to think rationally, a capacity which is shared by every other moral agent. Rationality and autonomy are understood in terms of what is abstractly shared by all moral agents. The morally permissible action is the action premised upon a maxim, or principle, which could, at least in principle, be adopted by all moral agents. The focus is upon the general nature of rationality, not upon the specific nature of the persons or situations under consideration. Similarly, utilitarian ethical theories, despite their fundamental disagreement with Kant over the fundamental principle of ethics, share the same core approach to understanding the basic nature of moral duty. For utilitarians, one has moral value simply in virtue of the fact that one can experience pleasure or pain, or that one is sentient, or that one can have preferences that might be either satisfied or thwarted. Ultimately, for utilitarians right actions are those which maximize the pleasure, or preference satisfaction, or whatever is taken to be the primary feature of moral consideration, for everyone affected. John Stuart Mill, certainly one of the most historically prominent utilitarians, states in this regard that a utilitarian should strive to judge the morality of a situation as an impartial spectator (Mill 1981). Again, the focus is upon an abstract concept, the general utility to be achieved, rather than upon concrete situations or the specific unique relationships between moral agents.

While there are obviously significant and very important differences between Kantian ethics, utilitarian ethics, social contract theories of justice, and various rights based approaches to morality, for the purposes of this discussion we will refer to these accounts all as rights based or justice focused accounts of morality.

The reasons for this are two-fold. The first reason is simply that care ethicists traditionally have referred to such theories in a common manner in their critiques of traditional ethical theory. While they have used a number of different monikers in doing so ("male ethics," "justice", and "rights based moral theory" to name just a few), it is useful to have a standard way of referring to such theories, in contrast to theories such as the ethics of care that begin with an analysis of particular moral situations. Secondly, the critique offered by proponents of the ethics of care applies to all of the aforementioned theories insofar as they each presuppose that moral decisions can be made in relative isolation by moral agents striving for maximal impartiality. We do not intend, however, to suggest that all versions of each of these theories are equally susceptible to the critique advanced by the ethics of care. Onora O'Neill's neo-Kantian ethic, for instance, explicitly rejects the notion that we ought to think of moral agents as acting in isolation. She also insists that we ought not to assume all moral agents are the same, especially since persons living in poverty in the global South are far more vulnerable than rich individuals of the global North (O'Neill 2004). As with any attempt to generalize about a wide range of theories or positions, such critiques at times oversimplify in their characterizations. While we should avoid strawman representations of rights based theories, there does nonetheless seem to be a contrast, at the level of moral phenomenology, between these two basic ways of viewing the starting point for moral theory. Proponents of an ethics of care typically begin by focusing upon specific relationships between persons in order to discern the concrete moral responses found in such relationships, whereas rights based theories typically begin with more abstract considerations of principles.

A second, but related, feature of the ethics of care is the focus upon the differences that characterize persons as opposed to their abstract sameness (Groenhout 2004). As Daryl Koehn notes in this regard, an ethic of care strives not to repress difference but to embrace it (Koehn 1998). Whether it be differences of class, gender, ethnicity, or a host of other identifying features, the ethics of care demands that we pay attention to how these differences affect our perception of the situation and the interests of those involved (Lindemann 2005). Again, we should not think that traditional ethical theories were completely unaware of such factors. The difference though, can be seen as one of accent, and, again on our view, the ethics of care is not meant to completely displace other moral theories so much as to provide a balance that can contribute toward a richer account of our moral world. Thus, a complete moral phenomenology needs to acknowledge that while our similarities have moral significance, so too do our differences. The tendency to equate moral significance with common features can also lead us to assume that we understand the situation of others better than we really do, or that their preferences and interests are simply equivalent to our own. Such assumptions can lead to moral hazard if left unchecked. An ethic of care recognizes this risk and strives to balance more abstract ways of organizing moral judgment with more emotionally grounded accounts that are sensitive to the differences in our situations and how those differences can alter what really matters, from a moral point of view.

The idea of viewing the ethics of care as integrative as compared to oppositional to other moral theories has been articulated by philosophers such as Virginia Held,

Marilyn Friedman, and Annette Baier, who all argue that care ethics and justice focused theories are consistent and might be integrated (Slote 2007). Held, for instance, argues that particular relationships give rise to moral reasons that are not impartial even if we can find impartial reasons for adhering to partiality as a rule. For example, although we can give strong impartial reasons for letting biological parents care for children (provided that doing so does not violate some other important moral duty, such as keeping a child safe from a parent who molests the child), the motivation to care for one's own children likely does not come from the impartial reasons one might provide. While Held believes that impartial moral reasons have their place, she also argues that it is important not to reduce all of morality to considerations which could be explained in terms for which we can provide impartial reasons (Postow 2008). A son would likely find his father morally lacking if his primary reason to care for his child was that there was impartial justification for doing so. Held also rejects the idea that justice can be taken as the moral minimum and considerations of care equated with superogatory duties that are morally good, but not requisite. There might also be a moral minimum for our duties of care as well (Postow 2008).

Michael Slote, a prominent contemporary care ethicist, believes that we must all choose between justice and care at times, but he believes that an ethic of care should develop an independent account of justice (Slote 2007). The upshot is that regardless of how one sees the relationship between an ethic of care and more abstract approaches to morality, one ought not assume that either the ethics of care or rights based accounts of moral theory must take precedence. In fact, there is no need to assume a simple either/or hierarchy between an ethics of care and more abstract accounts of moral duty. The theories, for instance, could be taken as complementary treatments of different areas or aspects of the moral realm, as opposed to competing accounts of the same domain. This approach, which we adopt in this paper, sees the goal of the ethics of care as supplementary and at times corrective of traditional moral theories, rather than as necessarily oppositional to such approaches. While sorting out the precise connection between an ethics of care and more traditional theories may be a difficult task, there is no need, in principle, to suppose that it cannot be done.

Indeed, on our account it is the moral phenomenology of an ethic of care that offers the richest possibilities for supplementing more traditional approaches to moral theory, which at times neglected robust explorations of the moral psychology of human experience. The work of Carol Gilligan (2008) and other early pioneers in the development of the ethic of care were able to demonstrate the importance of attending to the psychological underpinnings of moral judgment. On our view, what is essential about Gilligan's work was her sensitivity to the moral phenomenology of concrete experience and the extent to which such a phenomenology was necessary to providing a robust account of moral agency. Care ethics emphasizes relationships, empathy, and compassion over the appeal to generalizable principles, not because it necessarily sees such principles as worthless, but because an exclusive focus on such principles fails to make sense of how people actually respond to ethical situations. This does not mean that rules, rights, or consequences are of no moral import. The point is simply that there is more to morality than just that.

Gilligan sees justice and care as existing in a dynamic and potentially harmonious relationship (Hamington and Miller 2006).

Of course, while care ethicists have often criticized more traditional ethical theories for being too abstract, critics of the ethics of care have often pointed out the potential problems in developing an ethical theory that is too particularized. In particular, if the account of our moral phenomenology stems solely from a consideration of our most concrete relationships, an ethic of care could easily produce an account of morality that resulted in a kind of "moral blindness" to the needs of others with whom we did not have significant personal contact. To our mind, this objection is significant, and we agree that many accounts of the ethics of care have tended to overemphasize certain kinds of personal relationships in their account of our moral phenomenology.

To our mind, if such relativistic concerns are to be overcome, we need to develop an account of the ethics of care that does not assume that the relationships so important to care ethics are always simple relationships between a single pair of persons. Because the ethics of care places special emphasis upon the concrete exigencies of daily life, it cannot ignore that we have shared communal relationships as well as dyadic relationships with single individuals. While some care ethicists, such as Nel Noddings (1984), tend to see relationships largely in terms intensely singular and personal relationships, other care ethicists allow for broader kinds of relationships. Such theorists argue that the interconnectedness of persons entails that the ethics of care must also consider relationships shared in public life. Joan Tronto (2006), for instance, argues that we cannot create a society of equality (precisely the focus of justice and rights-based accounts of morality) without socializing care. She states, in this regard, that "when unequal citizens only care privately, they deepen the vast inequalities and the exclusion of some from the real prospect of being full citizens" (p. 3).

To better see this point, consider a person Megan who cares deeply for whomever she sees suffering, but who only interacts with and recognizes her relationships with the people in her middle class suburban neighborhood. She notices her neighbor is glum on a rainy day and heads to the mall to buy a gift to cheer her up. But as a result, Maria, who lives in the city and works in the sweatshop that provides Megan with affordable fashionable accessories that Megan gives to neighbors as gifts, finds her position of inequality further entrenched. Megan cares privately, but in expressing this care through the purchase of sweatshop made commodities she only deepens the inequalities between citizens. As a result, sweatshop workers such as Maria are actually made worse off as their position of subjugation becomes further entrenched. In order to avoid care deficits such as the one faced by Maria, Tronto (2006) suggest the following as an adequate account of the meaning of care: "a species activity that includes everything we do to maintain, continue, and repair our "world" so that we can live in it as well as possible. This world includes our bodies, our selves, and our environment, all of which we seek to interweave in a complex life-sustaining web" (p. 5).

Further, if care is defined as a primarily private activity, this entails two grave moral risks. First, work traditionally understood as women's work occurs privately and is undervalued as a result. This both contributes to gender inequality and undermines the ability of women to care for themselves and their families as they are more likely to be unable to care for themselves and others if they are trapped in situations of special vulnerability that are economically induced. In many ways, globalization simply replaces the housewives of the past in the global North with the mothers of the global South who can no longer stay with their own children and instead travel abroad to care for the children of others (Hochschild 2002). Because Megan can afford to pay others to care for her children, make her clothing, cook her food, etc. she can have the illusion of full autonomy and not realize how dependent she is upon the care of unrecognized others. The myth of market choice obscures relationships of interdependence. Secondly, viewing care as a completely private activity encourages what Tronto calls "unsympathetic disregard"—it makes it easy to feel that others are not entitled to your care. Say for example that Megan does come into contact with Maria but sees that she never takes her children to the park to play. Megan might judge that Maria is an unfit mother not deserving of her care, even though Maria may well not have the time to take her children to the park because she must sew enough garments to make rent (Tronto 2006). With a more social conception of care, the connections between care and justice become clearer. A social ethic of care also lends itself more easily to analyses of business obligation since business is not a private matter. A social ethic of care can thus ground the moral obligations of business in specific relationships with an awareness of the limitations faced by corporate decision makers, while at the same time refusing a status quo in which some party's real needs and interests are never acknowledged. In this regard, an ethic of care is also sensitive to questions of how background conditions can shape those relationships in a way that more traditional accounts of business ethics have often left unexamined.

Another way of seeing this point is by considering the dual sense of the infinitive "to care." On the one hand to care for someone means to have an emotional connection to the person; caring in this sense designates an affective relationship with another. This sense of caring is often what is picked up in accounts of the ethics of care, as such accounts begin with the moral phenomenology found in our day to day relationships with our friends, relatives, and others with whom we routinely interact. The richness of the ethics of care is that it allows us to see how our moral phenomenology is typically grounded in the awareness of others that stems from such caring relationships. However, the danger of the ethics of care is that it would privilege such particular relationships to the point of obscuring the extent to which our actions impact the lives of others with whom we have less direct emotional connections. In this sense, a morally robust account of the ethics of care must be attentive to a wider range of relationships as in Tronto's account of caring for the complex web of relationships that sustain our existence. The question that remains is how to ground the normativity of such a broader account of caring within the moral phenomenology of an ethic of care.

Here, we believe that the second sense of the infinitive "to care" can be illustrative. For in the second sense, "to care" for someone or something means to tend to that person or thing; in this sense caring involves a commitment to responsiveness. As those working within the ethics of care have pointed out, caring manifests itself in our moral phenomenology as a call to the needs of the other. In this sense we see caringness as rooted in a basic moral responsiveness that lies at the heart of all of our relationships. This is crucial on our view, because we conceive of the moral phenomenology of care as including an essential and irreducible normative component: one cannot care for anything without first recognizing a fundamental recognition of our duty to respond to the needs of those outside of ourselves. The goal of a robust ethics of care is to cultivate that sense of responsiveness in recognition of the many sorts of relationships that sustain us socially, economically, politically, and environmentally. Caring in this sense involves tending to all of our relationships and being responsive to the full range of needs and interests found in these relationships. Responsiveness to the other is essential to a morally justifiable account of caring.

Both stakeholder theory and the ethic of care are fundamentally relationally based moral theories. Stakeholder theory, to our mind correctly, maintains that businesses have an ethical responsibility to account for the moral interests of all parties affected by their activities. What an ethics of care can provide to supplement the stakeholder account of moral norms in business is an account of the moral phenomenology that underlies those relationships and their moral significance. Caring stems from an emotional acknowledgement of the moral interrelatedness of our lives and demands responsiveness to the moral needs of others. Of course, not all relationships demand the same kind of responsiveness, and we would not argue that business relations can be conceptualized along the same lines as many personal relationships. Nonetheless, persons involved in business, no less than any other kind of relationship, must tend to the elements of those relationships that call for moral responsiveness.

While following a somewhat winding path, we would like to conclude this section by outlining a few of the ways in which we maintain that an ethics of care might contribute to stakeholder theory. First, if both stakeholder theory and the ethics of care are viewed, as we have argued they should be, as supplementary accounts of different aspects or levels of moral thinking, then there is no reason to view either of them as theoretically incompatible with either more traditional ethical theories or with each other. This entails that there is no reason to think that the two theories are inherently incompatible. Second, the main difficulty, we have argued, in successfully applying stakeholder theory has been that it has lacked a proper account of moral agency in which to articulate its conceptual account of stakeholder relations. Such a lacuna has resulted in a failure to provide an adequate grounding for business persons to understand the significance of their relationships to stakeholders. Third, we have argued that the ethics of care proffers an account of the phenomenology of moral agency that correctly accents the role that emotions, concrete relationships, and moral recognition of the other play in both motivating and guiding our responsiveness to moral situations. Fourth, there is reason to think that the notion of caring can be extended to cover a wider variety of moral relationships than those found in the private sphere, and thus that such accounts might be as applicable to business relationships as to more personal forms of relationships. However, we have yet to articulate precisely how the ethics of care might better illuminate the nature of business relationships so as provide for a more robust account of moral agency in stakeholder relations than is typically found in stakeholder theory. To better understand how an ethics of care might actually work in practice in order to more fully flesh out the moral responsiveness called for in stakeholder theory, we thus conclude with an examination of sweatshop labor from such a mixed perspective as an example of how such a concrete analysis might operate.

Analyzing Sweatshops from the Perspective of a Caring Stakeholder Theory

An adequate ethic of care combined with stakeholder theory must work to ensure that both justice and care are given due moral consideration. Iris Marion Young argues that liability accounts of global justice fail to question background structures that are themselves unjust because they focus upon obligations of justice owed between discreet actors and fail to question systemic structural injustice (Young 2006). Because care ethics requires an account of moral responsibility that recognizes specific social, political, and economic positions of moral agents, a care ethic demands that agents recognize these background conditions. A liability account of moral responsibility only holds agents culpable that have intentionally and voluntarily caused the harms for which reparations are sought. In many cases, the liability model will suffice to account for moral responsibilities in terms of basic stakeholder relations. For instance, if a company clearly violates local labor laws and the government holds them liable for the harms incurred as a result, then the liability account will be able to explain the moral and legal duty towards reparations. Typically, stakeholder identification and analysis accounts of business ethics are articulated in relation to such basic norms governing the relationships among individuals within specified areas of business. Engster's account of stakeholder theory and the ethics of care earlier in this volume examines many of the features of such a basic account, as well as of some ways in which an ethic of care might support basic models of stakeholder theory.

However, we wish to argue that an ethic of care can also supplement stakeholder in a more radical manner. In particular, we maintain that the liability account that often underlies stakeholder theory is inadequate to explain the rich moral texture of many kinds of stakeholder relations and the responsibilities embedded in those relationships. This can be considered by examining the manner in which companies often disregard certain kinds of morally significant relationships within a competitive situation. Here we use the example of sweatshops as an example of such a moral conundrum. As long as stakeholder relations are articulated at a level of individual responses to the contingencies of already established moral norms, stakeholder theorists will fail to appreciate properly and tend to the moral relationships inherent in such activities.

For instance, a company may argue that it cannot afford adequate sanitation or ventilation if it is to be competitive in the global market place. Thus, the decision to employ sweatshop workers in unsanitary conditions is insufficiently voluntary for the factory managers and owners to be culpable for harms caused as a result. Sweatshop managers can defend decisions that cause direct and foreseeable harm to workers on the grounds that their choices are insufficiently voluntary given the nature of competition in the global market place. Similarly, those who contract the sweatshop to do work can claim that they had no knowledge of poor working conditions and that they stipulated local labor safety requirements be met. By claiming a lack of knowledge, the GAP, for instance, can say that it too is not liable for harms incurred. And, they can also argue that in having a source of income, sweatshop workers are better off than they would have been anyways. One cannot be responsible for the conditions of stakeholders if one is unaware of those conditions and their effect on the needs and interests of those stakeholders. Nearly all the actors involved believe they are relatively free of blame for the conditions of the relevant stakeholders because they lack either requisite knowledge or their actions are insufficiently voluntary. Yet is should seem obvious that those conditions are embedded in the very relationships that sustain these actors. Such backhanded justifications view stakeholder relations as merely existing between isolated individuals rather than as already embedded in a set of relationships that call for responsiveness. What an ethic of care would demand in such cases is that a full moral phenomenology of the kinds of relationships involved be articulated before considering the nature of the stakeholder obligations involved. By tending first to the moral responsiveness called for in such situations, a sphere of alternative opportunities for moral actions arise.

An ethic of care also questions background assumptions about the justifiability of an economic system that regularly creates and reinforces harm to sweatshop workers. Young suggests that we look at the relationships in which we stand to others. As Young argues, according to a social connection model of responsibility:

> individuals bear responsibility for structural injustice because they contribute by their actions to the processes that produce unjust outcomes. Our responsibility derives from belonging together with others in a system of interdependent processes of cooperation and competition through which we seek benefits and aim to realize projects. Even though we cannot trace the outcome we may regret to our own particular actions in a direct causal chain, we bear responsibility because we are part of the process. (2006, p. 119)

While no one person is to blame for sweatshop induced harms, this does not mean that all who participate are free of moral blame. Notice how Young incorporates one of the key requirements of an ethic of care: recognition of interdependency. Our hypothetical liability minded managers and government officials pointed to interdependency as an excuse for their participation in injustice. Young points to that same interdependency as an argument for greater accountability. Few actions are perfectly voluntarily, but that does not excuse moral agents from seeking to change a system that encourages injustice. Young argues that we cannot assume that the status quo is minimally just. Rather, we must work together to create a morally adequate status quo. Young's social connection account of responsibility helps to make it clearer how an account of justice would be balanced by an ethic of care. By attending to specific relationships and the varying degrees of causal exigency each brings to bear, moral blame does not simply disappear when injustice is collectively perpetrated.

So how would our purchaser at the GAP apply a stakeholder theory that was informed by an ethic of care? She would likely begin by refusing to accept the status quo as morally adequate, in part by demanding an emotionally honest appraisal of the conditions of the people involved. Few persons could be emotionally comfortable coming face to face with consequences of supporting sweatshop labor for apparel, and it is only by emotionally distancing themselves that they can come to the conclusion that their situation is not one that calls for moral response. While there are sweatshops in the global North, the vast majority are in the global South and employ primarily women and girls, often as young as thirteen or fourteen. Sexual harassment of these women and girls is rampant and many often do have to work forced overtime all night long to make a late order in time. Often workers are not permitted to use the bathroom and, even when they are, sanitation is poor. Sweatshops are also notorious firetraps, often lacking adequate ventilation and so overcrowded that when fires do occur it is impossible to evacuate everyone safely. Workers who complain or who attempt to form a union are regularly blacklisted, harassed, or even killed (Young 2006).

While an abstract account of stakeholder relations might allow managers to rely upon the oft repeated sophisms that "since I can not fix the whole system, there is nothing to be done" or "they are still better off than they would have been," the ethics of care demands that stakeholder interest be truly appreciated, which involves becoming emotionally attuned to their situation, and responding in a manner that reflects an appreciation of the particularities of their situation. A business manager operating under such a stakeholder model would be strongly motivated to look for ways of satisfying the real needs of stakeholders in creative manners. She would carefully examine both her own relationship to potential producers and to her employer as well as the relationship of her company to sweatshop conditions. If her employer is a large company, the greater power of a large company to affect change industry wide entails a greater responsibility to do just that. If she has great power within the organization to effect change, she would also realize her responsibility is also greater. If her employer is small or she simply lacks the power to change policy for the entire organization, she could try to enlist factories, in cases where she has the power to do so, that are monitored by the Workers Rights Consortium, an independent monitoring organization that works with laborers, including off site interviews, to ensure adequate work conditions are met.

The ethical manager would also have to be careful to avoid paternalistic measures as well, since real caring must be responsive. As such, under such a stakeholder theory, it will be important to listen to what workers themselves say is most the most pressing concern. For instance, while an ethical manager might be tempted simply to refuse to source apparel in a country without strong labor law enforcement mechanisms, a discussion with workers in the factories would help her to understand that a boycott of an entire nation might makes things worse rather than better. By examining not only the limitations but the potential power for transformation that her position within her organization provides, an ethical manager using care ethics stakeholder theory can find a way to work towards showing care to those who produce goods and services. Of course this is only a minimal sketch of what might be possible under a stakeholder theory informed by the ethics of care, but it should illustrate the way in which such a melding could provide stakeholder theory with a much more robust understanding of the moral phenomenology of the relationships involved and a better sense of moral agency in responding. Our hope would be that those who deploy stakeholder theory "on the ground" would thus develop responses to stakeholders that are both more sensitive and more responsive to the moral complexities of the situations in which those stakeholders are embedded.

References

Burton, Brian K., and Craig P. Dunn. 1996. Feminist ethics as moral grounding for stakeholder theory. *Business Ethics Quarterly* 6: 133–147.

Freeman, R. Edward. 1984. *Strategic management: A stakeholder approach*. Boston, MA: Pitman.

Freeman, R. Edward, and Daniel R. Gilbert Jr. 1988. *Corporate strategy and the search for ethics*. Englewood Cliffs, NJ: Prentice Hall.

Evan, W., and Freeman, R. Edward. 1993. A stakeholder theory of the modern corporation: Kantian capitalism. In *Ethical theory and business*, eds. Tom Beauchamp, and Norman Bowie, 75–84. Englewood Cliffs, NJ: Prentice Hall.

Friedman, Milton. 1970. The social responsibility of business is to create profits. *New York Times Magazine* September 13: 32–33, 122, and 126.

Gilligan, Carol. 2008. Moral orientation and moral development. In *The feminist philosophy reader*, eds. Alison Bailey, and Chris Cuomo, 467–478. Boston, MA: McGraw Hill.

Goodpaster, Kenneth. 1993. Business ethics and stakeholder analysis. In *Applied ethics: A reader*, ed. Earl R. Winkler, and Jerrold R. Coombs, 227–248. Oxford: Blackwell.

Groenhout, Ruth E. 2004. *Connected lives: Human nature and an ethics of care*. New York, NY: Rowman & Littlefield Publishers.

Hamington, Maurice, and Dorothy Miller. 2006. Introduction: A modern moral imperative. In *Socializing care: Feminist ethics and public issues*, eds. Maurice Hamington, and Dorothy Miller, xi–xxii. New York, NY: Rowan & Littlefield.

Hochschild, Arlie R. 2002. Love and gold. In *Global women: Nannies, maids, and sex workers in the new economy*, eds. Barbara Ehrenreich, and Arlie R. Hochschild, 15–30. New York, NY: Henry Holt & Co.

Jackall, Robert. 1988. *Moral mazes: The world of corporate managers*. New York, NY: Oxford University Press.

Johnson-Cramer, Michael E. 2008. Stakeholder theory. In *Encyclopedia of business ethics and society*, vol. 4, ed. Robert W. Kolb. 1992–1999. Thousand Oaks, CA: Sage.

Koehn, Daryl. 1998. *Rethinking feminist ethics: Care, trust and empathy*. New York, NY: Routledge.

Lindemann, Hilde. 2005. *An invitation to feminist ethics*. New York, NY: McGraw-Hill.

Mill, John Stuart. 1981. *Utilitarianism*. Indianapolis, IN: Hackett Publishing.

Noddings, Nel. 1984. *Caring: A feminine approach to ethics and moral education*. Berkeley, CA: University of California Press.

O'Neill, Onora. 2004. Global justice: Whose obligations. In *The ethics of assistance: Morality and the distant needy*, ed. Deen K. Chatterjee, 242–259. Cambridge: Cambridge University Press.

Palmer, Daniel E. 1999. Upping the stakes: A response to John Hasnas on the normative viability of the stockholder and stakeholder theories. *Business Ethics Quarterly* 4: 699–706.

Palmer, Daniel E., Mary Lyn Stoll, and Abe J. Zakhem. 2008. Introduction. In *Stakeholder theory: Essential readings in ethical leadership and management*, eds. Daniel E. Palmer, Mary Lyn Stoll, and Abe J. Zakhem, 15–22. Amherst, NY: Prometheus Books.

Postow, Betsy. 2008. Care ethics and impartial reasons. *Hypatia* 23: 1–8.

Reed, Darryl. 1999. Stakeholder management: A critical theory perspective. *Business Ethics Quarterly* 3: 453–483.

Simola, Sheldene. 2007. The pragmatics of care in sustainable global enterprise. *Journal of Business Ethics* 74: 131–147.

Slote, Michael. 2007. *The ethics of care and empathy*. New York, NY: Routledge.

Tronto, Joan. 2006. Vicious circles in privatized caring. In *Socializing care: Feminist ethics and public issues*, eds. Maurice Hamington, and Dorothy Miller, 3–25. New York, NY: Rowan & Littlefield.

Wicks, Andrew C., Daniel R. Gilbert, and R. Edward Freeman. 1994. A feminist reinterpretation of the stakeholder concept. *Business Ethics Quarterly* 4: 475–497.

Young, Iris Marion. 2006. Responsibility and social justice: A social connection model. *Social Philosophy and Policy* 23: 102–130.

Chapter 7
Elucidating the Role of Care in Ethical Decision-Making and Action

Sheldene Simola

Introduction

During the last 25 years, multiple conceptual models of ethical decision-making in business have been proposed (Dubinsky and Loken 1989; Ferrell and Gresham 1985; Hunt and Vitell 1986; Treviño 1986). A common feature of these approaches is that they build either implicitly or explicitly on the foundational stages articulated in Rest's (1986) four-component framework of moral problem-solving (Jones 1991), including recognition that an ethical issue has emerged; judgment about what would comprise a morally "right" course of action; the formation of intention to give precedence to moral values; and, actual implementation of ethical action.

The ethical decision-making framework articulated by Rest (1986, 1994) is primarily behavioral in nature. Not only does it describe four stages of ethical decision-making and action, but it also implies a range of individual, organizational, or issue-related factors through which *between-person* performance *within* each stage, or, *within-person* performance *across* each stage might vary (Rest 1986; Jones 1991). Indeed, substantial amounts of empirical research have investigated the role of such factors relative to each of Rest's (1986) four phases of decision-making and action (O'Fallon and Butterfield 2005; Treviño, Weaver, and Reynolds 2006).

In contrast to Rest's (1986, 1994) behavioral approach to ethical decision-making is a moral philosophical one. Within the moral philosophical method, certain theoretical perspectives such as consequentialism, deontology and virtue ethics (Buchholz and Rosenthal 2001; Donaldson and Werhane 1996; Treviño and Nelson 2006) are applied to business dilemmas in order to help evaluate and distinguish ethical courses of action. Notwithstanding the potential benefits that might be associated with more pragmatic efforts to resolve ethical dilemmas (Gioia 2002; Pamental 1991), the application of moral theory is highly valued because it moves the problem-solving process away from the use of ad hoc, idiosyncratic or

S. Simola (✉)
Department of Business Administration, Trent University, Peterborough, ON, Canada
e-mail: ssimola@trentu.ca

M. Hamington, M. Sander-Staudt (eds.), *Applying Care Ethics to Business*,
Issues in Business Ethics 34, DOI 10.1007/978-90-481-9307-3_7,

© Springer Science+Business Media B.V. 2011

opinion-based strategies toward more systematic and rigorous forms of reasoning through which morally justifiable decisions can be made (Buchholz and Rosenthal 2001).

Although the behavioral and philosophical approaches to ethical decision-making are not necessarily mutually exclusive, efforts aimed at their integration have been quite limited. In particular, moral philosophical approaches have commonly been understood to have relevance only to the second of Rest's (1986) four components, that of moral evaluation or judgment (Treviño and Nelson 2006; Wotruba 1993). There has been virtually no systematic exploration of the benefits of specific moral theories across all four stages of ethical decision-making and action. The dearth of research exploring such possibilities is lamentable given that efforts to bridge the moral philosophical and behavioral approaches could not only enhance our understanding of the practical and applied aspects of various moral theories, but could also deepen and broaden our conceptions of the components comprising Rest's (1986, 1994) decision-making framework.

The purpose of this article is to systematically consider the implications of one particular moral perspective as it applies across all four stages of ethical decision-making and action (Rest 1986, 1994). Specifically, this article will elucidate the implications and benefits of care ethics for each of the four stages comprising Rest's (1986, 1994) framework. It contrast to common assertions that moral theoretical approaches are differentially and primarily relevant only to the processes of moral evaluation or judgment comprising Rest's (1986) second phase of ethical decision-making (Treviño and Nelson 2006; Wotruba 1993), it will be argued here that certain distinctive features of contemporary care ethics not only have implications for every phase of the ethical decision-making process, but also, that these features of care can enhance individual performance within each phase.

In order to accomplish its purpose, this article will be structured in the following way. First, a brief review of the nature and defining characteristics of care ethics will be provided (Porter 1999). Second, each component of Rest's (1986, 1994) ethical decision-making framework will be considered in turn, and the implications of a care perspective for enhancing individual performance within each stage will be described. Brief examples from within the field of business ethics will be offered. Finally, directions for future research will be provided.

Nature and Characteristics of Care Ethics

Despite the diverse theoretical roots of care ethics (Baier 1985; Gilligan 1977, 1982; Noddings 1984; Ruddick 1984; Tronto 1993; Whitbeck 1983), certain defining characteristics are widely recognized among care theorists (e.g., Clement 1996; Gatens 1998; Porter 1999). These distinctive features of care include responsive engagement with the subjective, particular and concrete needs of individuals within given situations (Porter 1999; Tronto 1993); use of emotion in understanding and responding to dilemmas (Tronto 1993); focus on human interdependence and the activation and maintenance of relationships among individuals (Clement 1996; Gatens 1998); and, creative efforts to simultaneously fulfill seemingly conflicting responsibilities to more than one individual (Gilligan 1982).

Although historically care was seen as relevant to the private (i.e., familial) as opposed to the public (non-familial) sphere (Clement 1996), a number of theorists have demonstrated the usefulness of care for decision-making in much broader organizational or political arenas (Held 2006; McLaughlin 1997; Sevenhuijsen 1998; Tronto 1993). Indeed, care ethics have become an important theoretical perspective in ethical decision-making as it occurs in a number of disciplines, including business and management (French and Weis 2000; Liedtka 1999; Reiter 1996; Sama, Welcomer, and Gerde 2004; Simola 2003, 2005). However, as with alternate moral theoretical approaches, there has been a dearth of research on the implications of care ethics for various stages of ethical decision-making and action. Therefore, consider each of Rest's (1986, 1994) four stages of ethical decision-making, below, and the potential implications and benefits of care ethics within each stage.

Moral Awareness

The first stage of Rest's (1986, 1994) ethical decision-making framework is moral awareness, which refers to the recognition that a moral or ethical concern has emerged and that one has a choice about how to respond to this issue (Rest 1986). In behavioral terms, moral awareness is thought to be related to characteristics of both the individual and the ethical situation itself (Jones 1991; Treviño 1986). Although empirical research within the management field has demonstrated that both individual factors such as training and experience and issue-related factors such as degree of social consensus and magnitude of potential consequences (Jones 1991) are positively related to recognition of a given issue (O'Fallon and Butterfield 2005; Treviño, Weaver, and Reynolds 2006), substantially less attention has been given to the implications of moral philosophical perspectives in ethical awareness or recognition.

For example, in their review of empirical research on the components of ethical decision-making in business, O'Fallon and Butterfield (2005) identified only two studies focused on the relationship between philosophical orientation and moral awareness, both of which found negative associations between ethical relativism and sensitivity to ethical issues. Indeed, when it comes to the application of moral philosophical approaches to ethical decision-making stages, management scholars have noted that such approaches tend to be predicated on the assumption that Rest's (1986, 1994) first stage of moral recognition has already occurred, even though this might not be the case (Treviño and Nelson 2006).

Despite the dearth of management research on the implications of particular moral theories for Rest's (1986, 1994) first stage of moral recognition, scholars outside of management disciplines have attended to this question, particularly as it pertains to care ethics (Held 2006; Jaggar 1989; Little 1995; Tronto 1993). Two interrelated areas in which care ethics are instructive for Rest's (1986, 1994) first stage of moral recognition are attentiveness to the particular, subjective experiences of others and the epistemic value of emotion for moral awareness.

Although conventional moral theories have eschewed the cultivation and use of emotional skills in favour of a detached and rational approach to moral deliberation (Tronto 1993; Wicks, Gilbert, and Freeman 1994), a defining characteristic of care ethics is authentic engagement with and responsiveness to the subjective, particular and concrete *feelings* and needs of individuals in a given situation (Gilligan 1982; Held 2006; Tronto 1993). Furthermore, although conventional moral theories rely on distant and dispassionate deliberation in order to promote clarity and fairness, several contemporary theorists have argued persuasively that emotions in both one-self and others have epistemic value in moral recognition and deliberation (Jaggar 1989; Little 1995; Tronto 1993).

For example, Little (1995) argued that attentiveness to a range of emotions in oneself and others is not simply useful but also necessary for discerning a broad range of moral concerns. Drawing upon Ruddick (1987) now classic exposition of care ethics in the private (i.e., familial) sphere of mothering, Little (1995) delineated the inadequacy of a conventional and dispassionate "observational vigilance" for moral recognition in other spheres. Little (1995) argued that individuals who are *affectively* attuned to the subjective and particular needs of those around them will necessarily be more sensitized to a broader range of relevant issues as well as primed for the early recognition of even subtle emotional signals of impending risk or harm. In contrast, individuals relying on detached, distant and "objective" (Tronto 1993) forms of observational vigilance will necessarily be less sensitive to the subjective and particular feelings of those around them which may comprise early and subtle signals of potential moral violation or harm.

It is argued further that not only might emotional signals of potential violation or harm go unrecognized by those invoking purely rational perspectives, but also, that the seemingly "objective" criteria against which such concerns are evaluated within more "distant and detached" approaches might well be conflated with, or reflective of, the interests of those with power, thereby rendering less visible the needs and concerns of relatively disenfranchised stakeholder groups (Tronto 1993). Indeed, in their critical reinterpretation of the stakeholder concept, Wicks and colleagues argued that the western predilection for impersonal rationality "detaches us from the identities, emotions, needs, and perceptions of particular individuals" in ways that "erode their legitimacy as agents who deserve a 'voice' in corporations" (Wicks, Gilbert, and Freeman 1994, 481–482). They pointed out, however, that alternative approaches including care ethics activate our sensitivity toward the needs, feelings and perceptions of others in ways that strengthen their legitimacy as stakeholders.

When considering the epistemic value of emotions in care ethics, it is important to note that it is not simply the conventionally "positive" and "acceptable" emotions such as compassion or empathy that direct the attention of a moral agent to the plight of others, but also, the conventionally unacceptable emotions such as anger and disdain that can alert individuals to wrong-doing (Held 2006; Jaggar 1989; Little 1995; Lurie 2004). In particular, to the extent to which emotions such as anger signal the occurrence of injustice, carelessness or violation (Spelman 1989), then emotions such as anger also signal the ethically concerning dimensions of a situation. Hence, care ethics, with their emphasis on attentiveness to and responsive engagement with the subjective, particular and concrete feelings and needs of others can enhance our sensitivity to and (early) recognition of emergent ethical issues.

One example of the epistemic value of emotion in moral awareness or recognition is in the area of leadership. In her discussion of care ethics in leadership, Ciulla (2009) highlighted the importance of emotional attentiveness to the subjective needs of followers as one mechanism through which to offset the disproportionate emphasis on objectivity and rationality that can unwittingly result in leadership failures involving the disregard or neglect of others.

Additionally, the use of emotion in moral recognition as advocated within care ethics is also gaining attention in other areas of ethics research. For example, Henrik (2008) noted that despite the emotionally charged nature of many organizational whistle-blowing occurrences, emotion has been largely overlooked as a contributing factor to the decision to engage in whistle-blowing, thereby leading whistle-blowing behavior to seem quite irrational and surprising to managers or other onlookers. Henrik argued that the absence of emotion in conventional models of whistle-blowing could be one reason why these models are weak in predicting whistle-blowing behavior. In contrast to these conventional models, Henrik (2008) demonstrated how various behavioral actions would be expected to *follow* from the specific emotional reactions of prospective whistle-blowers, thereby identifying an important role for attentiveness to emotions in early recognition of ethical concerns.

Moral Evaluation

Rest's (1986) second stage of ethical decision-making is moral evaluation or judgment. Within business disciplines, research on this component is concerned with the influence of two main factors, including cognitive developmental stage of moral reasoning through which moral judgment occurs (i.e., Kohlberg 1969), and, the moral philosophical perspectives through which ethicality of various courses of action is assessed (e.g., Brady and Wheeler 1996; Davis, Andersen, and Curtis 2001).

As previously indicated, and by definition, Rest's second stage of moral evaluation is also the component of ethical decision-making for which moral philosophical frameworks have been seen to be differentially and primarily relevant (Treviño and Nelson 2006; Wotruba 1993). Indeed, a review of empirical research on ethical decision-making in business indicates a large number of studies on the relationship between various philosophical theories and the nature of ethical judgments made (O'Fallon and Butterfield 2005). Just as a range of other moral theoretical perspectives have had specific implications for ethical evaluation or judgment (Buchholz and Rosenthal 2001; Donaldson and Werhane 1996), so too would care ethics, as described below.

In his ground-breaking book on *The Ethics of Care and Empathy,* the influential philosopher Michael Slote (2007) considered the underlying mechanisms or rationale through which individuals using care ethics evaluate moral dilemmas, and examined how individuals determine the type and degree of duty they have toward others. Slote (2007) argued that empathy is the process underlying the initiation, activation and maintenance of relationships central to care ethics, as well as the criterion against which potential courses of action relative to moral dilemmas are judged.

In elaborating the role of care ethics as a philosophical form of moral evaluation or judgment, Slote (2007) also identified the importance of psychological development for enhancing the empathic maturity underlying more advanced stages of care reasoning. For example, just as research in the Kohlbergian tradition (1969) has demonstrated that higher levels of cognitive moral development are associated with enhanced abilities in justice forms of ethical reasoning, so too has research on socio-emotional development indicated that more mature forms of empathy are associated with enhanced abilities in care forms of ethical reasoning.

Drawing on Hoffman's (2000) review of empirical research on the development of empathy in individuals, Slote (2007) identified how differences in the level and strength of empathic development can account for the level of care deemed appropriate to show to others. It was argued that as cognitive skills become increasingly complex and differentiated, so too do imaginative skills in relation to the plights of others, including occurrences that are current or future, distant or near, and, with related or unrelated others. It is through the facilitation, exercise and encouragement of this "inductive" imagining of the experiences of a range of others (including those who are distant, unrelated and at risk of future versus current suffering) that an empathically driven morality becomes infused in individuals. Thus, within care ethics, potential courses of action are judged to be "right" or "moral" through the extent to which the courses of action are motivated by and reflective of a receptive form of inductively-mediated empathy toward other individuals (Slote 2007).

Classic examples of care ethics in which courses of action were evaluated by the extent to which they were motivated by and reflective of empathy toward others include certain organizational crises (Simola 2003). This was true of the response of McDonald's executives to the 1984 shooting tragedy at the San Ysidro restaurant when an individual unrelated to McDonald's went on a shooting rampage that resulted in the deaths of 21 people at that franchise. McDonald's personnel made an explicit decision to judge their own prospective responses not according to legal standards, but rather, according to compassion for the families who were affected by the tragedy. For example, McDonald's suspended its national advertising campaign out of respect of the families, flew in families of the victims, paid hospital bills of the wounded, worked sensitively with community leaders in the dismantling of a shrine and the disposition of the property on which the tragedy occurred, and stood in solidarity with the community when it opposed a proposed docudrama about the massacre (Salvá-Ramirez 1995; Starrman 1993). Indeed, McDonald's personnel were explicitly instructed by then VP and General Counsel Don Horowitz "I don't want you people to worry or care about the legal implications of what you might say. We are going to do what's right for the victims . . ." (Starrman 1993, 309). The use of compassion and empathy as standards against which to evaluate corporate decisions was not only consistent with a care approach (Simola 2003), but also, turned out to be a highly effective and much lauded method of managing the crisis (Salvá-Ramirez 1995).

Moral Intention

The third component of Rest's (1986) ethical decision-making framework occurs when individuals form an intention to give priority to moral values (e.g., integrity, fairness, honesty, care) over other values in the resolution of the ethical dilemma. As indicated by Rest (1986) the formation of moral intention involves not only the decision to give precedence to moral values, but also, the decision to do so even when this could result in personal loss or suffering for the decision-maker.

Empirical research by management scholars on the nature of moral intention and its link to moral behavior has been relatively limited (O'Fallon and Butterfield 2005). Notwithstanding conceptual arguments (Ferrell and Gresham 1985; Haidt 2001; Treviño 1986; Treviño and Nelson 2006) and emerging empirical evidence (Blasi 2005; Lapsley and Narvaez 2004) suggesting that moral action can (but does not necessarily) follow directly from either moral recognition or evaluation in the absence of explicitly and consciously formed moral intention, one other possible explanation for the relative under-development of the conceptual basis of moral intention is a broader tendency within traditional moral philosophy to differentially focus on conscious rationality, with limited attention to the role of internalized *desire* in moral motivation (Little 1995; Lurie 2004; Tronto 1993). However, within care ethics, desire plays an important underlying role in intentional behavior.

For example, Fine's (1988) work on the "missing discourse of desire" in conventional approaches to human development is instructive on the importance of desire to intentionality in care ethics (Tolman 1991). In her care-based assessment of adolescent girls' development, Tolman (1991) echoed earlier concerns that oftentimes, societal conversations or discourses tend to be discourses of "don't" rather than discourses of "desire" (Fine 1988). In discourses of "don't," individuals are given sets of socially accepted conventions about situations to avert or actions from which to refrain. However, by adhering to such conventions, individuals using discourses of "don't" tend to make reactive decisions, by *default*, based on movement away from things one ought *not* to do—rather than proactive decisions, by *desire*, based on movement toward those things that will result in authentically responsive interconnections with oneself and others. Within care ethics, decisions by default are considered problematic in that they imply reactive avoidance of rule violations rather than proactive promotion of and engagement with health sustaining relational processes (Tolman 1991), including ethical ones.

In management terms, one example of care-based, proactive movement toward an ideal, as opposed to reactive compliance with regulatory requirements would be in the area of environmental and social sustainability. As indicated by Hart (2005), the mid-1940s to 1960s were characterized by corporate denial of the detrimental environmental impacts of pollution. During the 1970s and 1980s, adherence to environmental regulations was a compliance issue to which many organizations reactively responded. By the mid-1980s to 1990s, "greening" became prominent as many firms achieved incremental improvements on their own environmental performance. However, during the last two decades, there has been a reorientation and internalization among many firms of the values and capabilities needed to proactively move toward strategies that are truly sustainable not only in economic terms, but also in environmental and social ones (Hart 2002). The emphases on actively establishing organizational culture by design rather than default (Bhide 1996/1999) and on proactive movement toward deeply held core values are not only consistent with environmentally caring and sustainable practices, but also, central to longer-term prosperity and resilience in the business world (Collins and Porris 2000).

Moral Action

The final stage of Rest's (1986, 1994) ethical decision-making framework is the implementation of moral action. Although large numbers of empirical studies have investigated various individual and organizational factors associated with propensity to implement ethical action (O'Fallon and Butterfield 2005), the role of philosophical theory in enhancing propensity toward ethical action has been left largely unexplored. This is particularly concerning given the rather pressing need to consider how individuals can become better equipped with the practical skills that will help them translate their ethical awareness, judgment or intentions into action within complex corporate settings.

For example, the Ethics Education Task Force [EETF] of the Association to Advance Collegiate Schools of Business [AACSB] (2004) noted that there have been multiple occurrences in which otherwise principled individuals fall short when faced with ethical dilemmas in organizational contexts. It was argued that "simply saying "no" to a request to behave unethically ... may not be enough" (p. 13). Consider, therefore, the ways in which the use of care ethics might better equip individuals toward ethical action in ways that move beyond simply saying "no" to unethical requests.

Implicit in the assertion that "simply saying no" to unethical requests "may not be enough" (AACSB, 2004) is the notion that zero sum (win-lose) approaches associated with simply saying "no" may be quite inadequate. In particular, although one could achieve a personal ethical win by simply saying "no" to unethical requests, this "win" of acting in accordance with one's own ethical values could still be problematic if it is perceived to be a loss by and for the other party. The other party that is simply told "no" in response to an unethical request might experience disappointment, anger, frustration or shame at the outcome. This could in turn lead to negative career repercussions for the individual that denied the request. Given these risks associated with simply saying "no," it is not unsurprising that individuals often have difficulty translating their ethical judgments or intentions into ethical action (Treviño and Brown 2004).

Note, however, that skills in creatively identifying non-zero sum (win-win) solutions to ethical problems could alleviate the negative consequences associated with win-lose approaches, making ethical action more likely. Although non-zero sum approaches might not always be possible in corporate contexts, their use, when appropriate, could support more skilled ethical action in which potential for reprisal when acting on one's ethical values is reduced. Interestingly, care ethics promote the use of non-zero sum approaches to moral problems.

For example, Reiter (1996) contrasted conventional ethical problem-solving frameworks in business to those reflected by care ethics. She pointed out that within conventional problem-solving frameworks individual decision-makers are encouraged to choose *between* different options reflecting the *positions* of various stakeholders. Reiter identified that such approaches are inherently zero sum in that one party's win will be the other party's loss.

Reiter (1996) therefore offered an alternative approach derived from care ethics (Gilligan 1982). She argued very persuasively that because care ethics focus on simultaneously and creatively fulfilling *seemingly* conflicting responsibilities to more than one person, that care ethics intrinsically focus on non-zero sum solutions. By attending to the subjective and particular *underlying interests* and needs of different stakeholders, those using care ethics can also expand the array of options available for resolving ethical dilemmas such that creative, non-zero sum (i.e., win-win) solutions can be found (Reiter 1996). Moreover, to the extent to which individuals implement creative non-zero sum solutions, they will also be able to avert the potential for relational strain or other negative repercussions that could result from "simply saying no" to unethical requests. Hence, facility in developing the type of non-zero sum solutions advocated within care ethics could increase the likelihood that one would actually implement ethical decisions.

Interestingly, Reiter's (1996) use of care ethics for promoting creative, non-zero sum solutions to ethical dilemmas is reminiscent of classical work by pioneering management scholar Mary Parker Follett (1924/1951). Follett's work on "integrating interests" in organizational behavior and ethics was prescient not only to several streams of contemporary management thought (Drucker 1995; Kanter 1995), but also and most notably here to contemporary theories of care (Burnier 2003; Fletcher 1999; Morton and Lindquist 1997).

For example, Follett (1924/1951) argued that "when differing interests meet, they need not oppose, but only confront each other" (p. 256). She argued that when one "confronts" differing interests among individuals, one of four outcomes results. These four outcomes include voluntary submission of one party; struggle followed by triumph for one party; compromise between the two parties; or, an integrative outcome that creatively meets the needs of more than one party.

Each of the first two outcomes is inherently a zero sum, win-lose solution likely to result in negative feelings for at least one party. Interestingly, the third outcome, of compromise, is also seen as problematic because it too involves concession or loss to one or both parties. Follett (1924/1951) therefore advocated not for the use of compromise, but rather, for the use of creative ingenuity, through which the fourth outcome could be achieved. She indicated that the fourth outcome represents a qualitative shift in thinking toward finding integrative solutions in which the underlying interests of various parties are met, as opposed to a quantitative loss in which one or both sides sacrifice their underlying interests. This shift toward integrative solutions in behavioral and ethical problem-solving is consistent with requirements within care ethics to creatively find ways of fulfilling seemingly conflicting responsibilities to a range of stakeholders. Moreover, this use of integrative solutions also averts the concerns expressed by the AACSB (2004) EETF about the problems associated with "simply saying no" to unethical requests. Because such creative, integrative solutions simultaneously support the underlying interests and needs of more than one stakeholder, they decrease the risk of negative repercussions for the decision-maker, thereby enabling implementation of ethical action.

One micro-level example of creatively fulfilling multiple but seemingly conflicting ethical responsibilities to different stakeholders can be derived from the teaching case study "*Is the Customer Always Right*" by Pfeiffer and Forsberg (1993). In this useful (but somewhat dated) case, a customer asks a mechanic to disconnect the car's catalytic converter. In this way the customer could use leaded gasoline and achieve better gas mileage. The mechanic points out it would be illegal (not to mention environmentally unfriendly) to do as requested and is also concerned about losing his job or getting a bad reputation. However, the mechanic knows the task could be completed in a discrete way and the customer has said he will go elsewhere both to achieve the disconnection of the catalytic converter and for all of his repairs if the mechanic turns him down.

On the surface this dilemma seems to have two obvious choices for the mechanic; (1) comply with the customer's request at the potential expense of job loss, reputational damage and negative environmental impacts, or (2) decline the customer's request at the potential expense of significant lost revenue and customer annoyance. Each of the two seemingly obvious solutions is inherently win-lose. One party's gain will be the other party's loss. However, creative efforts to identify ways of simultaneously fulfilling seemingly conflicting responsibilities could result in a third, more integrative option. In this case, the mechanic could identify alternate ways of meeting the customer's underlying need of achieving better gas mileage. For example, ensuring appropriate tire pressure, replacing worn spark plugs or ensuring a clean fuel injection system. Use of this third approach that simultaneously addresses the specific underling needs of both the customer and the mechanic enables a non-zero sum, win-win solution that can enable ethical action.

On a macro-level, perhaps the most common contemporary examples of creative and integrative solutions consistent with a care approach are those found in companies seeking to use the "triple bottom line" (Elkington 1997) in their approach to business. Within this approach, environmental and social sustainability are not necessarily incompatible with profitability. Rather, firms that are sustainability in environmental and social terms can also be profitable (Hart 2002). In fact, environmentally and socially sustainable business models might be even more profitable in developing economies than conventional transnational approaches (Hart and Christensen 2002; Prahalad and Hart 2002).

Summary and Directions for Future Research

The purpose of this article was to consider the implications and benefits of care ethics across each of Rest's (1986, 1994) four behavioral stages of ethical decision-making and action. In contrast to conventional assumptions that moral philosophical frameworks are differentially and primarily relevant only to Rest's (1986) second stage of moral evaluation or judgment (Treviño and Nelson 2006; Wotruba 1993), it was demonstrated here that such frameworks can and do have clear implications for each of the four stages comprising Rest's (1986) decision-making framework. In particular, it was argued that care ethics—with their emphases on sensitivity and attentiveness to emotions in oneself and others, on using empathy as a criterion against which to evaluate the appropriateness of potential courses of action, on using discourses of desire rather than discourses of default in order to proactively promote health-sustaining relational practices, and, on creatively achieving non-zero sum solutions to dilemmas—can enhance individual performance across Rest's (1986) four stages of moral awareness, moral judgment, formation of moral intention, and, implementation of moral action, respectively.

Future research in this area could consider more closely the implications of other moral philosophical approaches across each of Rest's (1986, 1994) four stages of ethical decision-making and action. Similarly, more detailed consideration of various elements of a given moral philosophical approach within each decision-making stage would be helpful. For example, within care-ethics, how might a deeper philosophical understanding of various emotions in oneself and others, including the so-called "outlaw emotions" such as anger (Jaggar 1989) enhance moral awareness or recognition. Or, how might use of specific discourses of desire enhance moral intention even when there are risks associated with giving precedence to moral values in given situations. Finally, although the current article focused on Rest's (1986) dominant behavioral approach to ethical decision-making, consideration of the relationship between various moral philosophical perspectives and emerging social intuitionist approaches (e.g., Haidt 2001) would also be worthwhile.

References

Association to Advance Collegiate Schools of Business International (AACSB). 2004. Ethics education in business schools. http://www.aacsb.edu/eerc/EETF-report-6-24-04.pdf. Accessed 23 Jan 2008.

Baier, A. 1985. What do women want in a moral theory? *Nous* 19: 53–63.

Bhide, A. 1999. The questions every entrepreneur must answer. In *Harvard business review on entrepreneurship*, 1–28. Boston, MA: Harvard Business School Press (Original work published 1996).

Blasi, A. 2005. Moral character: A psychological approach. In *Character psychology and character education*, eds. D.K. Lapsley, and F.C. Power, 67–100. Notre Dame: University of Notre Dame Press.

Brady, F.N., and G.E. Wheeler. 1996. An empirical study of ethical predispositions. *Journal of Business Ethics* 16: 927–940.

Buchholz, R.A., and S.B. Rosenthal. 2001. A philosophical framework for case studies. *Journal of Business Ethics* 29: 25–31.

Burnier, D. 2003. Other voices/other rooms: Towards a care-centered public administration. *Administrative Theory & Praxis* 25 (4): 529–544.
Ciulla, J. B. 2009. Leadership and the ethics of care. *Journal of Business Ethics* 88: 3–4.
Clement, G. 1996. *Care, autonomy and justice*. Boulder, CO: Westview Press, A Division of HarperCollins Publishers Inc.
Collins, J.C., and J.I. Porris. 2000. *Built to last: Successful habits of visionary companies,* 3rd edn. London: Random House Business Books.
Davis, M.A., M.G. Andersen, and M.B. Curtis. 2001. Measuring ethical ideology in business ethics: A critical analysis of the ethics position questionnaire. *Journal of Business Ethics* 8: 855–862.
Donaldson, T., and P.H. Werhane. 1996. *Ethical issues in business,* 5th edn. Upper Saddle River, NJ: Prentice-Hall.
Drucker, P. 1995. Introduction: Mary Parker Follett: Prophet of management. In *Mary Parker Follett: Prophet of management*, ed. P. Graham, 1–9. Boston, MA: Harvard Business School Press.
Dubinsky, A.J., and B. Loken. 1989. Analyzing ethical decision making in marketing. *Journal of Business Research* 19 (2): 83–107.
Elkington, J. 1997. *Cannibals with forks: The triple bottom line of the 21st century business.* Stony Creek, CT: New Society Publishers.
Ferrell, O.C., and L. G. Gresham. 1985. A contingency framework for understanding ethical decision making in marketing. *Journal of Marketing* 49 (3): 87–96.
Fine, M. 1988. Sexuality, schooling and adolescent females: The missing discourse of desire. *Harvard Educational Review* 58 (1): 29–53.
Fletcher, J. K. 1999. *Disappearing acts: Gender, power, and relational practice at work.* Cambridge, MA: The MIT Press.
Follett, M. P. 1951. *Creative experience.* New York, NY: Peter Smith (Original work published, 1924).
French, W., and A. Weis. 2000. An ethics of care or an ethics of justice. *Journal of Business Ethics* 27: 125–136.
Gatens, M. 1998. *Feminist ethics.* Brookfield, WI: Ashgate Dartmouth.
Gilligan, C. 1977. In a different voice: Women's conceptions of self and morality. *Harvard Educational Review* 47 (4): 481–517.
Gilligan, C. 1982. *In a different voice.* Boston, MA: Harvard University Press.
Gioia, D. A. 2002. Business education's role in the crisis of corporate confidence. *Academy of Management Executive* 16 (3): 142–145.
Haidt, J. 2001. The emotional dog and its rational tail: A social intuitionist approach to moral judgment. *Psychological Review* 108 (4): 814–834.
Hart, S.L. 2005. *Capitalism at the crossroads: The unlimited business opportunities in solving the world's most difficult problems.* Upper Saddle River, NJ: Pearson Education.
Hart, S.L., and C.M. Christensen. 2002. The great leap: Driving innovation from the base of the pyramid. *Sloan Management Review* 44 (1): 51–56.
Held, V. 2006. *Ethics of care: Personal, political, gobal.* Oxford: Oxford University Press.
Henrik, E. 2008. Mad as hell or scared stiff? The effects of value conflict and emotions on potential whistle-blowers. *Journal of Business Ethics* 80: 111–119.
Hoffman, M. L. 2000. *Empathy and moral development: Implications for caring and justice.* Cambridge, UK: Cambridge University Press.
Hunt, S.D., and S. Vitell. 1986. A general theory of marketing ethics. *Journal of Macromarket* 6 (1): 5–16.
Jaggar, A. M. 1989. Love and knowledge: Emotion in feminist epistemology. In *Gender/body/knowledge*, eds. A.M. Jaggar, and S.R. Bordo, 145–171. London: Rutgers University Press.
Jones, T. M. 1991. Ethical decision making by individuals in organizations: An issue- contingent model. *Academy of Management Review* 16 (2): 366–395.

Kanter, R. M. 1995. Preface. In *Mary Parker Follett: Prophet of management*, ed. P. Graham, xiii–xix. Boston, MA: Harvard Business School Press.
Kohlberg, L. 1969. *Stages in the development of moral thought and action*. New York, NY: Holt Rinehart & Winston.
Kohlberg, L. 1976. Moral stages and moralization: The cognitive-developmental approach. In *Moral development and behavior*, ed. T. Lickona, 31–53. New York, NY: Holt Rinehart & Winston.
Lapsley, D. K, and D. Narvaez. 2004. A social-cognitive approach to moral personality. In *Moral development, self and identity*, eds. D.K. Lapsley, and D. Narvaez, 189–213. Mahwah, NJ: Lawrence Erlbaum.
Liedtka, J. 1999. Linking competitive advantage with communities of practice. *Journal of Management Inquiry* 8 (1): 5–16.
Little, M. O. 1995. Seeing and caring: The role of affect in feminist moral epistemology. *Hypatia* 10 (3): 117–137.
Lurie, Y. 2004. Humanizing business through emotions: On the role of emotions in ethics. *Journal of Business Ethics* 49 (1): 1–11.
McLaughlin, J. 1997. An ethic of care: A valuable political tool? *Politics* 17 (1): 17–23.
Morton, N.O.'R., and S.A. Lindquist. 1997. Revealing the feminist in Mary Parker Follett. *Administration & Society* 29 (3): 348–371.
Noddings, N. 1984. *Caring: A feminine approach to ethics and moral education*. Berkeley, CA: University of California Press.
O'Fallon, M.J., and K.D. Butterfield. 2005. A review of the empirical ethical decision-making literature: 1996–2003. *Journal of Business Ethics* 59: 375–413.
Pamental, G. L. 1991. The course in business ethics. Why don't the philosophers give business students what they need? *Business Ethics Quarterly* 1: 385–393.
Pfeiffer, R.S., and R.P. Forsberg. 1993. Is the customer always right? In *Ethics on the job*, eds. R.S. Pfeiffer, and R.P. Forsberg, 144–145. Belmont, CA: Wadsworth Publishing.
Porter, E. 1999. *Feminist perspectives on ethics*. New York, NY: Longman.
Prahalad, C.K., and S.L. Hart. 2002. The fortune at the bottom of the pyramid. *Harvard Business Review* 80 (9): 48–57.
Reiter, S. 1996. The Kohlberg-Gilligan controversy: Lessons for accounting ethics education. *Critical Perspectives on Accounting* 7: 33–54.
Rest, J. R. 1986. *Moral development: Advances in research and theory*. New York, NY: Praeger.
Rest, J. R. 1994. Background: Theory and research. In *Moral development in the professions: Psychology and applied ethics*, eds. J.R. Rest, and D. Narvaez, 1–26. Hillsdale, NJ: Lawrence Erlbaum Associates.
Ruddick, S. A. 1984. Maternal thinking. In *Mothering: Essays in feminist theory*, ed. J. Trebilcot, 213–230. Totowa, NJ: Rowman and Allanheld.
Ruddick, S. 1987. *Maternal thinking: Towards a politics of peace*. New York, NY: Ballantine Books.
Salvá-Ramirez, M.-A. 1995. The San Ysidro massacre—Ten years later. *Public Relations Quarterly* 40 (1): 38–43.
Sama, L.M., S.A. Welcomer, and V.W. Gerde. 2004. Who speaks for the trees? Invoking an ethic of care to give voice to the silent stakeholder. In *Stakeholders, the environment and society*, eds. S. Sharma, and M. Starik, 140–165. Northampton, MA: Edward Elgar.
Sevenhuijsen, S. 1998. *Citizenship and the ethics of care: Feminist considerations on justice, morality and politics*. New York, NY: Routledge.
Simola, S. 2003. Ethics of justice and care in corporate crisis management. *Journal of Business Ethics* 46: 351–361.
Simola, S. 2005. Concepts of care in organizational crisis prevention. *Journal of Business Ethics* 62: 341–353.
Slote, M. A. 2007. *The ethics of care and empathy*. New York, NY: Routledge.

Spelman, E. V. 1989. Anger and insubordination. In *Women, knowledge, and reality: Explorations in feminist philosophy*, eds. A. Garry, and M. Pearsall, 263–273. Boston, MA: Unwin Hyman.
Starrman, R. G. 1993. Tragedy at McDonald's. In *Crisis response*, ed. J.A. Gottschalk, 309–321, Detroit, MI: Invisible Ink.
Tolman, D. L. 1991. Adolescent girls, women and sexuality: Discerning dilemmas of desire. In *Women, girls & psychotherapy: Reframing resistance*, eds. C. Gilligan, A.G. Rogers, and D.L. Tolman, 55–69. New York, NY: Harrington Park Press.
Treviño, L. K. 1986. Ethical decision making in organizations: A person situation interactionist model. *Academy of Management Review* 11 (3): 601–617.
Treviño, L.K., and M.E. Brown. 2004. Managing to be ethical: Debunking five business ethic myths. *Academy of Management Executive* 18 (2): 69–81.
Treviño, L.K., and K. Nelson. 2006. *Managing business ethics: Straight talk about how to do it right,* 4th edn. New York, NY: Wiley.
Treviño, L.K., G. Weaver, and S.J. Reynolds. 2006. Behavioral ethics in organizations: A review. *Journal of Management* 32 (6): 951–990.
Tronto, J. C. 1993. *Moral boundaries: A political argument for an ethic of care*. New York, NY: Routledge.
Whitbeck, C. 1983. A different reality: Feminist ontology. In *Beyond domination*, ed. C.C. Gould, 64–88. Totowa, NJ: Rowman and Allanheld.
Wicks, A.C., D.R. Gilbert Jr., and R.E. Freeman. 1994. A feminist reinterpretation of the stakeholder concept. *Business Ethics Quarterly* 4 (4): 475–497.
Wotruba, T. R. 1993. A framework for teaching ethical decision making in marketing. *Market Educational Review* 3: 2–8.

Chapter 8
Care Ethics and Unintended Consequences

Daryl Koehn

Introduction

Unintended consequences regularly occur in business and professional practice and often are devastating. Although social scientists have devoted some energy to identifying such consequences, ethicists rarely speak of them. This oversight is particularly unfortunate because thought needs to be given to how we should think and act in a world fraught with unanticipated effects. Simply having good intentions does not suffice to make us responsible agents. To the extent that some unforeseen effects are nonetheless in principle foreseeable, we ought to hold ourselves accountable for trying to identify them when making choices. Moreover, if some ethical theories are better than others in coping with unintended consequences in business and professional spheres, we ought to be using these better theories more extensively, especially in applied ethics.

This paper is an attempt to remedy this neglect of an important dimension of ethical thinking. Part 1 defines just what an unintended consequence is. Part 2 gives examples of various types of unintended consequences in business and elsewhere and discusses why some are in principle foreseeable. Part 3 argues that an ethic of care is well-suited for both helping us to anticipate foreseeable unintended effects in business and for dynamically coping with them as they emerge. Part 4 provides some reasons for thinking that an ethic of care is better adapted for dealing with unidentified consequences than either utilitarian or deontological moral theories.

Definition of an Unintended Consequence

What is an unintended consequence? An unintended consequence is an unenvisioned and unwilled effect of an action, law, or policy to which human beings

D. Koehn (✉)
Department of Ethics and Business Law, University of St. Thomas,
Minneapolis, MN, USA
e-mail: koehnd@stthomas.edu

M. Hamington, M. Sander-Staudt (eds.), *Applying Care Ethics to Business*,
Issues in Business Ethics 34, DOI 10.1007/978-90-481-9307-3_8,

© Springer Science+Business Media B.V. 2011

and other organisms adapt their behavior. Although we certainly adapt to natural events—for example, after a hurricane, we may decide to move out of a storm surge area—, social scientists and political theorists reserve the category of "unintended consequences" for adaptive responses to purposive human action. This restricted usage makes sense, because we typically are most interested in those consequences over which we have some degree of control. I argue in Part 2 that unanticipated and unhappy adaptive responses to policies and courses of actions sometimes can, in fact, be foreseen and avoided.

In what follows, I take unintended consequences to result from actions traceable to a cause (choice, emotion, desire, policy) that, in principle, lies within the control of the agent. In other words, my focus will be on cases where individuals responsible for bringing about unintended consequences could have acted other than they did. These undesired outcomes are not the result of some instinctual drive, biological tropism, or conditioned reflex outside the control of human agency.

Unintended consequences sometimes result from the best of intentions. Scientists devised a project to combat hunger in the Okavango delta. Beef cattle were substituted for native wild animals. In addition, efforts were made to eliminate the tsetse fly. At first, the cattle thrived, and the people had plenty of meat. Over time, however, the cattle overgrazed the land, leaving natives far worse off. Their land, which initially was habitable, turned into desert, and they starved.

Unintended consequences may be positive or negative. When the company Danone initiated its "1 Liter for 10 Liter" bottled water program to support the digging of new wells in dry areas of Africa, university students participating in the program felt that they were acting nobly and compassionately. If new wells were established, Africans would have fresh clean water. Some wells were dug, but it quickly became apparent to village elders that building several wells in their village would not be feasible. Neighboring village leaders watched jealously as one village chosen by UNICEF and Danone got a well. Why, these elders wondered, weren't their villages chosen as beneficiaries? Leaders of the chosen village worried that, if they were to get several new wells, their neighbors might attack them in an effort to acquire water for themselves. If building a new well were to lead to a sustained local war, the villagers might end up worse off than they were before they got the well. The project did have one apparently desirable but unintended outcome. The new well provided by Danone meant that young girls no longer had to travel so far to get fresh war. Freed from the traditional female duty to carry water, these girls were able to enroll in the local schools and continue their education.

Note that an unintended consequence is not merely a surprising result of a trigger event. If that were the case, every historical contingency would qualify as an unintended consequence and there would be little to analyze. The most we could say is that historical events do not follow immutable laws or, more poetically, "fortune governs events."[1] The unintended consequences that fascinate economists and sociologists—and that should interest ethicists more—are not simply contingent

[1] The Scotsman Dunbar quoted in Berry (1997), 45.

effects or instances of good or bad luck. Instead they are unforeseen adaptations to some human alteration of the natural or social landscape.

Pervasiveness of Unintended Consequences in Business

Policy-making provides many examples of decisions that increase the costs borne by employers, producers or consumers. These groups alter their behavior in order to reduce costs, sometimes bringing about perverse results. These effects, while unforeseen by the regulators or policymakers who increased costs, could have been anticipated because we know that individuals generally try to minimize their costs. Consider the effect that the Americans with Disabilities Act (ADA) has had on business employers and employees. Employers believed, rightly or wrongly, that the ADA would make it more expensive to hire disabled workers. Corporate managers were spooked by the prospect of having to alter facilities, provide specialized equipment, or redefine job responsibilities. Fearing lawsuits from disabled workers, employers hesitated to hire them. For both reasons, firms hired fewer men with disabilities after the ADA went into effect. While most firms did not shed current disabled workers already on the payroll, they did refrain from hiring any additional disabled workers.[2] Employment data suggest that this legislation aimed at protecting the disabled dimmed, rather than improved, these workers' job prospects. In this case, a significant number of businesspeople consciously chose to amend their hiring practices in response to what they perceived as a legislated increase in their cost structure.

Let us take another case of an adaptation to increased costs, this example drawn from automobile manufacturing. Fuel economy legislation in the 1980s (Corporate Average Fuel Economy or CAFE) aimed at encouraging the production of smaller cars. The legislation phased in different standards for cars and trucks with a view to favoring the manufacturing of more fuel efficient cars. Model year 1985 cars were to get 27.5 mpg, while trucks needed to average only 19.5 mpg. This difference in standards persists. Model year 2006 manufactured trucks had to meet an average of 21.6 mpg, while passenger cars faced a 27.5 mpg hurdle.[3] Seeing the looser standards for trucks, manufacturers avoided increased compliance costs by ramping up production of small trucks and SUVs. Consumers bought millions of these non-fuel efficient vehicles. As a result, mileage per gallon actually declined after the fuel-economy law was passed. In 1987, cars and trucks together averaged 26.2 mpg. By 2004, the average had fallen to 24.6 mpg.

Foreign as well as domestic laws have generated perverse unintended consequences by increasing costs. In order to protect contract employees from exploitation, the Chinese government revised its labor law in 2007. The new law requires employers to hire contract workers as regular employees if the firms wish to

[2]Thomas DeLeire (2000, 21–24).

[3]See table of standards in NHTSA (2003).

continue to use these workers. The law permits contract workers to work for two fixed contractual periods (often 5 year periods, but sometimes shorter). Workers may not be hired for a third such period unless the contract worker explicitly states that he or she prefers to continue as a fixed contract worker rather than to become a full-time employee.[4] In the absence of such explicit consent, the worker must be offered an open-term employment contract. The new law also stipulates that employees who have already worked for a company for 10 years or more without a contract must be offered an open-term (i.e., quasi-permanent) contract if this firm wishes to retain them. Open-ended contracts are considerably more expensive (up to 40% more costly) than fixed term arrangements.

The Chinese government and its leaders did not adequately evaluate the possible effects of this new labor law, a law which creates a clear incentive for employers to dump contract workers after two terms and to start anew with a fresh set of cheaper contract workers. Although no formal studies have yet been done quantifying the effects of this law, some academics in China believe that the layoffs prompted by the new legislation have been substantial. Forbes reported that layoffs appeared to increase dramatically in response to the new law:

> As trickles [of layoffs] turned into tidal waves, China's media and analysts started to find a common denominator in these mass layoffs, pinpointing the high-risk groups: certain temporary workers, whom employers now must sign on at a greater cost, and staff that have served long tenures, who will soon receive almost ironclad terms of employment, all thanks to a new national labor law, effective January 1, 2008 ... Huawei and LG Electronics, not coincidentally, targeted for job cuts those staff members who were approaching the ten-year limit.[5]

The famous Exxon Valdez spill provides yet another example of an unintended consequence resulting from legislation that increased producer costs. After the 1989 disaster, many states along the East and West coasts passed laws assigning unlimited liability to tanker operators. One or two companies (e.g., Conoco) voluntarily adopted double-hulled ships to reduce the risk of horrific spills. Other oil companies (e.g., Royal Dutch Shell) responded to this mandated increase in costs by outsourcing US oil deliveries to independent shipping companies. These independent firms often had little or no insurance and used tankers that were older and far more likely to leak than the ships used by the larger, better established multi-national oil firms. While it is true that the number of large oil spills has steadily declined over the past 50 years, the fact is that huge spills were never that common and were already on the decline prior to the passage of the tanker laws. Most oil gets spilled in small accidents or in the form of steady leaks. The post-Exxon Valdez state laws inadvertently but foreseeably worsened the environmental situation by creating financial incentives for firms to switch to older, leakier tankers.

The above examples involve changes to employer or producer cost structures. In other cases, unintended consequences arise because agents perceive that some

[4] Grieve and Dickinson (2000).

[5] Chen (2007).

policy, rule or choice is saddling them with greater risk. In general, people do not assume greater risk without the prospect of greater reward. If we alter the amount of risk people are expected to bear, we should expect that they will demand higher compensation or refuse to serve altogether. Even before the passage of the Sarbanes-Oxley (SOX) law, prudent observers predicted that the law, by imposing more personal liability on board members, would make it more difficult and expensive for firms to recruit and retain competent board members. Audit committee members would be especially vulnerable to lawsuits by disgruntled shareholders who would infer that the board should have known that the company was in severe trouble or even cooking the books.[6] These observers' prediction came true: Audit committee candidates adapted to the increased risk and responsibility by demanding greater compensation to serve on boards. This demand was a rational, foreseeable, and even predictable response to the change in the law. However, the legislators and regulators did not anticipate this SOX effect, because they did not consider how directors likely would view their liability under the new law. The consequence was unintended insofar as those responsible for the law did not set out to make it more difficult for corporations to recruit directors. Nevertheless, this outcome, I would argue, was foreseeable because we know how individuals typically respond to heightened risk.

Not all foreseeable unintended consequences derive from legislation. The private sector has produced its share of such effects. In the 1980s, Harvard's Michael Jensen and other finance professors urged firms to compensate board members using stock options. The professors maintained that the board's interests would be more closely aligned with those of the firm if the directors prospered only when the firm did. Alignment was supposed to encourage board members to discharge their fiduciary duties of care and loyalty to the firm in a more mindful way. Hundreds of firms rushed to adopt stock option plans for directors. As it turned out, finance professors and corporate governance experts were overly optimistic about directors' integrity. They forgot that board members might be tempted to overlook wrongdoing by management when a significant proportion of their own paychecks was linked to the firm's financial performance.[7] When board members of a company hold hundreds of thousands of dollars worth of that company's stock, they are in danger of losing independence and falling to discharge their duties. If corporate management appears to be corrupt, directors may have a duty to disclose possible wrongdoing to regulatory authorities and law officials. However, going public with these problems usually depreciates the value of board members' holdings. Directors who are paid cash retainers pocket the cash regardless of how the company does. By contrast, directors paid with stock options are left holding virtually worthless pieces of paper if the stock price falls. Options-paid directors have a substantial incentive to turn a

---

[6]Expansion of director duties documented in Vera-Munoz (2005, 115–127).

[7]The possibility that compensating directors with stock or stock options might create a moral hazard was foreseen by a few people. See, e.g., Kristie (1999), in which he asks: "Why does stock ownership by directors enhance their independence, but stock ownership by auditors makes them less independent? What is the board but an 'auditor' of management?"

blind eye to fraud in order to preserve their income stream. As some ethicists foresaw, many directors adapted their behavior in line with this huge financial incentive. In this case, the attempt to achieve better director performance through alignment produced the exact opposite effect. It worsened director performance by creating incentives that severely compromised board member independence.

Why Care Ethics Helpful in Coping with Unintended Consequences

I want to shift gears now and provide some reasons for thinking that care ethics may be better than some other types of ethics in either anticipating or at least coping with unintended consequences.

An ethic of care emphasizes that human beings are inter-dependent. We are embedded selves, not free floating atoms. This ethic enjoins us to act in ways that honor and develop healthy relationships. Articulated largely by women psychologists and feminists, the care ethic is not rule-based. On the contrary, many women view rules with suspicion because precepts are typically laid down and enforced by those in power. The powerful, who are usually men, are not, care ethicists contend, sufficiently sensitive to the needs and concerns of those who are subjected to rules.

Moreover, rule-making tends to extol and promote autonomy, logic, and rationality at the expense of interdependence and feeling. Therefore, the care ethics stresses not rules but rather the cultivation of empathy, sympathy, trust and other states or sensibilities that enable people to co-exist in mutually nurturing ways. In the words of Carol Gilligan (who was one of first to propose the idea of a distinctively female ethic of care), the

> moral imperative ... [for] women is an injunction to care, a responsibility to discern and alleviate the "real and recognizable trouble" of this world. For men, the moral imperative appears rather as an injunction to respect the rights of others and thus to protect from interference the rights to life and self-fulfillment .... The standard of moral judgment that informs [women's] assessment of self is a standard of relationship, an ethic of nurturance, responsibility, and care .... Morality is seen by ... women as arising from the experience of connection and is conceived as a problem of inclusion rather than one of balancing claims.[8]

Since the care ethic's focus is on sensibility rather than rules, it is, in theory, more flexible than rule or maxim-based ethics. It asks us to think about the larger effects of our action on all people with whom we are in relationship. We are not locked into rigid, rational rules but can use our imagination to make various possible effects present to us. This freedom may help us anticipate undesirable outcomes of policies and decisions.

The more empathetic we become, the more we will be able to view the world from other people's perspectives, thereby transcending our limited egoistic

[8]Gilligan (1982, 100, 159–160).

perspective. Indeed, if we are really serious about developing our empathy, we need to get into the habit of reaching out and listening to people whom we may inadvertently victimize:

> The significance that others find in our words and deeds tends to increase in proportion to the amount of power we have over their fate. What may seem to be a casual expression or an inconsequential indulgence can, and often does, have tremendous consequences for the less powerful individuals affected by such an action. We can, of course, make an effort to be sensitive to the unintended consequences of seemingly inconsequential actions. But, given our lack of omniscience, no one can recognize all of these consequences of her actions. Thus a whole range of harmful consequences will be apparent only to those whom they victimize. We will learn about these harmful consequences only if we listen to the voices of the individuals who feel victimized by our words and actions. These individuals may frequently look for victimizers even when none exist; but they also have insights into the harmful consequences of public actions we can get from no other source.[9]

As I argued in Part 2, many unintended consequences, while not planned, are nevertheless foreseeable. However, we will not be inclined to devote the effort to anticipate such consequences unless we are genuinely committed to promoting the welfare of other people and to being a good steward of the world. Care ethics requires that we make such a commitment. It implicitly asks us to consider early on in our deliberations how changes in risks, compensation, and costs might unintentionally harm others, especially those at the margin or those who have little or no voice.

The following example from medicine, which is increasingly thought of not as a profession but as a business, illustrates how the care ethic could help us head off adverse effects of a proposed policy change. Many supporters of health care reforms are pushing for "pay-for-performance" programs. These programs compensate health care professionals only when good or acceptable outcomes are attained. On the one hand, these new incentives might make for better care if they can be properly aligned with physicians' professed goal of promoting the health of patients. On the other hand, insofar as such incentives are tied to outcomes connected with a single disease, doctors may reduce people to "the liver in bed 6" and cease to attend to the whole patient. Elderly men and women with several difficult to treat chronic conditions may be shunted aside in favor of more treatable younger patients with fewer maladies. In education, we are hearing many concerns about how outcomes assessment has led teachers to "teach to the test." In medicine, the proposed payment system might encourage what some have termed "playing to measures."[10] Performance might even be damaged if physicians risk heroic measures or take shortcuts in order to produce ostensibly good results faster.

Care ethics would ask direct our focus away from payment mechanisms and outcomes to the well-being of the whole individual, the cared for patient. A patient with a debilitating disease might not be curable, but he still can be cared for in better and worse ways. How should doctors proceed in order to be most caring? The

[9]Yack (1991, 1334, 1342–1343).

[10]For a sustained discussion of possible disadvantages of "pay-for-performance" programs, see Snyder and Neubauer (2007).

care ethics would invite us as well to reflect upon the possible effects that pay for performance measures might have on the professionals as well as on the patients. Doctors and hospital administrators would likely feel under even greater pressure to produce results and might start to feel rage toward those patients who cannot be readily and quickly healed.

The care ethic does not let us cast "difficult" patients or employees aside. An ethic of care insists that, since we are born and die as relational selves, we have no choice but to remain engaged and concerned with others throughout our entire lives. The ethic implicitly requires that we continue to monitor the consequences of our choices for as long as these choices impact our family, neighbors, and members of the larger community. In this respect, it could be said to be more sensitive to unfolding unintended consequences than ethical systems that focus on single choices, render judgment on those choices, and then move on to the next issue. Let's face it. Human choices are messy things. Although we may initially believe that a choice was sound, as surprising and perhaps negative outcomes of that choice begin to emerge, we must be willing to reconsider its goodness. While an ethic of care is not as tidy or elegant as some more algorithmic ethics (see Part 4), this ethic may be more suitable for coping with the somewhat chaotic reality of human choice. As Virginia Held has put it, "Caring, empathy, feeling with others, being sensitive to each other's feelings, all may be better guides to what morality requires in actual contexts than may abstract rules of reason or rational calculation, or at least they may be necessary components of an adequate morality."[11]

As I have argued elsewhere in a detailed analysis of the various causes of unintended consequences, one major contributing factor is our "master of the universe mentality." Using an ethic of care, some feminists have argued against an anthropocentric, dominating and universalizing mindset in favor of a more ecological perspective. Although care ethicists are often criticized for substituting partial caring for impartial justice, such partiality begins to look more defensible once we admit the reality and pervasiveness of unintended consequences. Ecologists increasingly realize that our perspectives to be true may have to be quite limited and partial. What occurs in one ecological niche may not be reproducible in any other. Just to see what is going on in a rather constrained niche takes great sensitivity coupled with humility, perception, and open-mindedness, exactly the traits that an ethic of care emphasizes. Instead of pretending that we know the effects of our actions on an entire system and all of the people and organisms whom we do not and cannot know directly, we should concentrate on the difficult task of accurately assessing what is going on in the niche we occupy.

The empathy fostered by ecological caring can sharpen our perceptions and alert us to the possible unintended suffering and widespread damage that corporate choices and economic policies are causing not only to other human beings but also to other living creatures and to the environment that we all share:

> The care approach to animal ethics consists of an empathetic way of understanding the plight of individual animals in patriarchal and capitalistic institutions. Proponents maintain

[11] Held (1990, 332).

> that sympathetic responsiveness, compassion, and care can and should inform our ethical understanding as to why we have a responsibility to free non-human animals from human domination. Our treatment of the natural world is another matter. Part of the reason why our world is characterized by injustice, lack of care, and huge socioeconomic disparities between different people is that we treat the natural world with indifference and sometimes even contempt, say ecofeminists. We stockpile weapons of mass destruction, consume energy resources as if they were infinite, dump waste into our waters, and slaughter animals for meat we really do not need to eat. In so doing, we manifest our belief that it is our right to control nature to create a better world for ourselves. But we are suffering from a delusion in our feverish attempt to dominate nature ... Nature is rebelling and the human species is setting its own annihilation in motion as it detrees forests and extinguishes animal species. . . .[12]

Care ethics' fostering of empathy serves to combat this hubristic master of the universe mentality. It has another important advantage: it encourages introspection. Ever since Carol Gilligan wrote the groundbreaking book *In A Different Voice*, care ethicists have emphasized the importance of talking with and listening to other people. When we speak openly and candidly with others, we sometimes get painful feedback. We may be told that we have prejudices of which we were not aware. An ethic of care requires that we take such feedback seriously and examine our attitudes to see whether we are indeed biased. Such introspection can make us more cognizant of biases that may create unintended but nonetheless harmful outcomes for other people.

Why Care Ethics Deals Better with Unintended Consequences than Other Ethics

I want to close by arguing that an ethic of care is better equipped than some other standard moral theories to cope with unintended consequences. In particular, it is superior to both utilitarian and deontological moral systems.

Utilitarianism maintains that an action, policy or rule is morally good if and only if it produces the greatest net benefit (or smallest net loss) for the largest number of people when compared with alternative actions, rules or policies the choosing agent might have endorsed. Since it is impossible to calculate the effects of proposed alternatives with respect to every single person in the world, utilitarians typically focus on classes of relevant people whose utility is likely to be affected in some significant way by the proposed action. The fact that there are unintended consequences poses difficulty for even this more restrictive approach.

The agent must first identify alternative courses of action and then perform a cost-benefit analysis comparing each course's benefits and costs. This comparison presupposes that the agent is able to specify in advance the consequences of each of the evaluated courses of action. If an unintended consequence is of the foreseeable type; and if we assume that the utility evaluator possesses finely-honed foresight,

[12] Tong (2009).

he or she may be able to factor these unintended consequences into account when engaging in the moral calculus. However, there is still a danger that tne utilitarian will be blinded by some unexamined prejudices, psychological investments, or biases. As we have seen, insofar as care ethics requires that choices grow out of engagement and dialogue with others who can challenge our perceptions and assumptions, care ethics offers a way for us to become more prudent, far-sighted and less biased. By contrast, utilitarianism offers no account or mechanism by which agents become less in denial or more mindful over time. Doing cost-benefit calculations in some cubicle will not in and of itself make someone more prudent. If the evaluator is already favoring one outcome, then doing the calculations typically turns into a self-validating exercise that confirms the initial bias. Consequently, it is likely that even foreseeable unintended consequences will slip through the utilitarian net of calculations, because many utilitarians will not, in fact, refine their faculty of foresight.

Deontological moralities do not fare much better when it comes to dealing with unintended consequences. A deontological morality, such as that offered by Immanuel Kant, stipulates that a course of action is morally good, or at least morally permissible, if and only if the maxim of the action does not involve the agent in a logical contradiction. The agent must be able to will the maxim or practical description of the envisioned action in a logically consistent way. Only actions that do not involve us in a contradiction and that thus accord with our rational nature are truly morally respectful of human nature. In Kant's language, only when we act in a non-contradictory way do we treat people as ends in themselves, rather than as means.

It is not, according to Kant, morally permissible for an agent to say, "I will make it my maxim to commit suicide because I will be better off if I kill myself than if I go on living." In this formulation, the would-be suicide inconsistently projects the self into the future, imagining herself as continuing to live and to reap benefits even after she has killed herself. There is no "I" who could be better off dead than alive. As Kant puts it, the suicide's maxim is not consistent with a system of nature organized around the idea of self-preservation through self-love: if we analyze the maxim, then we see at once that "[this system of nature] ... would contradict itself and would therefore not subsist as nature" understood as a system of self-love[13] (4:422). Since the suicide's maxim cannot be consistently willed, her action is morally wrong. By contrast, if a manager of a firm proposes, "I will make it my maxim to pay the firm's employees the highest wage I possibly can while providing appropriate returns to all other stakeholders," there is no obvious contradiction in the maxim itself and so this action would qualify as morally permissible.

The difficulty with the deontological approach is that formulating the maxim correctly requires insight into the meaning of the proposed action. If the agent lacks a highly refined sense of the possible consequences of the action, the maxim of the action will not capture the action's true practical significance. Suppose we wonder whether it is morally permissible to introduce some organism into an environment to

[13] Kant (1998, 32).

counter a threat to human life posed by another organism. We hope and intend that the introduced counter-pest will prey upon or in some way eliminate the original threat to human beings. If human life is, as Kant insists, "beyond price," sacrificing some predators (or perhaps even an entire species of animal) perceived to be a threat appears to involve no logical contradiction and thus seems to qualify as a morally permissible course of action. Put another way: It seems that we can consistently say, "I make it my maxim to introduce counter-pests in the environment to remove another pest posing a serious threat to human life." But will the artificially induced change to the environment, in fact, preserve human life in the long run? The counter-pest may ultimately pose a much greater threat to human beings than the organism we initially feared. Introducing new predators or prey into an ecosystem inevitably causes organisms to adapt their behavior in response to new opportunities or threats. Therefore, instead of using the neutral-sounding term "counter-pest," we may discover in hindsight that we should have formulated our maxim to read, "I will make it my maxim to introduce another potentially human-threatening organism into the environment in order to remove a serious threat to human life." In that form, a contradiction emerges, and the action ceases to be morally permissible. The problem is that we know the correct terminology or phrasing of the maxim only after we have acted in accordance with our seemingly good initial maxim and have experienced the unintended destruction of much of the human race. It is of dubious moral value that remaining survivors can tell themselves: "Well, at least our maxim seemed to be consistent at the time we willed the action, even though the effects of the action showed our maxim was actually radically inconsistent."

Unless we have some implicit sense of the consequences of the envisioned actions, we will neither be able to formulate our maxims well nor will we be able validly to assess their consistency. To the extent that unintended consequences are frequent, widespread, perverse, and sometimes completely unforeseeable, it is doubtful whether any single individual has the requisite foresight needed to anticipate these effects and to build them into his or her maxims. Even if we grant that the more prudent among us are better able than rash peers to formulate maxims capturing the full import of proposed actions, that concession will not save deontological reasoning. Two problems remain. First, deontologists do not base their morality on prudence. Instead, they claim, as Kant does, that being moral is within the reach of everyone whose reason is intact. Any rational being can correctly formulate and then adequately assess maxims. Second, even the most far-sighted person in the world will not anticipate on his or her own all unintended consequences. There will always be cases where an action initially deemed to be straightforwardly morally permissible on deontological grounds will appear, after the fact, to be either outright immoral or at least possibly so. Deontology involves us in a profound paradox: our action is morally permissible only up until the point we act and bring about unintended consequences. We are moral only up to the moment we act in a supposedly moral way.

Unlike deontological ethics, an ethic of care does not ask us to come up with a single pristine maxim encapsulating the essence of a proposed action. Instead, it commits us to the less elegant, hard slog of considering various perspectives and numerous possible standards with a view to ascertaining what is best in this particular case here and now. It recognizes that we will inevitably make false starts and have to rethink earlier choices. That recognition can help us keep from getting wedded to prior decisions that are not working out as we had hoped. The moral mandate is less one of getting it right than of staying engaged.

Making and sustaining a commitment to care for the world is especially relevant today, given the power we human beings now possess to destroy it. Care ethics requires that we move beyond mere prescriptive rules. We need to rethink our entire master of the universe mindset. As Hans Jonas has cautioned,

> [S]o formidable and potent have the new technologies at humanity's disposal become that they have rendered obsolete 2,500 years of ethical discourse. Heretofore, humankind's interventions in the natural world were limited in scope, and their consequences were readily foreseeable. For this reason, the balance between humanity and nature was never fundamentally in doubt. No such assurances can be provided concerning the impact of modern technology, which, contrary to all precedents, has already permanently altered the earth's biosphere in numerous respects and which continues to do so in ways in whose consequences have yet to be fully determined .... Traditional approaches to ethics—Aristotle's "phronesis," Kant's "categorical imperative"—were accustomed to dealing with human action that fell within well-defined and familiar parameters .... Under the radically changed situation inaugurated by technological modernity, however, ethical prescriptions that are merely oriented toward "the good" (Aristotle), or that rest content to treat persons as "ends in themselves" (Kant), might well prove defenseless in the face of the worst case scenario of ecological catastrophe.[14]

Much more could be (and should be) said about how ethical theories ought to incorporate the problem of widespread unintended consequences. I make no claim here to have resolved this issue once and for all. The above analysis should be read as a first attempt to kickstart a crucial (and likely messy!) discussion. This discussion needs to commence sooner rather than later if we are to care for our shared world—as it really is. For

> [i]t is all too easy to think that what morality really requires of us is to avoid intentionally doing harm to one another, to avoid deceiving, stealing, letting down, assaulting, libeling one another, and so on, and that, in general, what really counts in moral assessment is what one aims at or intends... That might all be very well if we lived in a world where the unintended consequences of our actions did not materially affect the conditions under which others pursued their objectives .... But the world is not like this ....[15]

References

Berry, Christopher J. 1997. *Social theory of the Scottish enlightenment.* Edinburgh: Edinburgh University Press.

Chen, Shu-Ching Jean. 2007. Mass layoffs? In booming China? Forbes.com, November 13, www.forbes.com/2007/11/13/china-mass-layoffs-markets-econcx_jc_1113markets02.html

---

[14]Wolin summarizing Jonas' view of technology in Richard Wolin, (2003, 117–118).

[15]Dower (1998, 166).

DeLeire, Thomas. 2000. The unintended consequences of the Americans with disabilities act. *Regulation* 23 (1): 21–24.

Dower, Nigel. 1998. *World ethics: The new agenda*. Edinburgh: Edinburgh University Press.

Gilligan, Carol. 1982. *Gilligan, in a different voice*. Cambridge, MA: Harvard University Press.

Grieve, A., and S. Dickinson. 2000. China's new labor law. www.chinalawblog.com/2008/05/chinas_new_labor_contract_law_1.html

Held, Virginia. 1990. Feminist transformations of moral theory. *Philosophy and Phenomenological Research* 50: 321–344 (supplement), (Autumn).

Kant, Immanuel. 1998. *Groundwork of the metaphysics of morals* (trans: Gregor, M.J.). Cambridge: Cambridge University Press.

Kristie, James. 1999. A delicious irony in governance ideology. *Directors & Boards* (Summer).

NHTSA. 2003. Automotive fuel economy program: Annual update calendar year 2003. www.nhtsa.dot.gov/cars/rules/cafe/FuelEconUpdates/2003/index.htm

Snyder, Lois, and Richard L. Neubauer. 2007. Pay-for-performance principles that ensure the promotion of patient centered care—an ethics manifesto. http://www.acponline.org/running_practice/ethics/issues/policy/p4p_ba.pdf

Tong, Rosemary. 2009. Feminist ethics. *Stanford Encyclopedia of Philosophy*. May, revision, http://plato.stanford.edu/entries/feminism-ethics/

Vera-Munoz, Sandra C. 2005. Corporate governance reforms: Redefined expectations of audit committee responsibilities and effectiveness. *Journal of Business Ethics* 62 (2), December: 115–127.

Wolin, Richard. 2003. *Heidegger's children*, 117–118. Princeton, NJ: Princeton University Press.

Yack, Bernard. 1991. Injustice and the victim's voice. *Michigan Law Review* 89 (1334): 1342–1343.

Part III
Case Studies

Chapter 9
The Changing Face of Ethics in the Workplace: Care and the Impact of Immigration Enforcement

Jill Hernandez

Introduction

Remnants of the Bush-era immigration policy continue to impact many aspects of business within the United States, as the Obama administration attempts to find its footing amidst diverse voices in the immigration debate. Even after the results of a Department of Homeland Security review of worksite immigration raids were announced in May 2009 by Secretary Janet Napolitano, the policy of widespread raids has been kept intact.[1] Both Napolitano and President Obama have iterated their mutual commitment to criminalizing employers for hiring undocumented workers (*San Antonio Express-News*, May 2009), but they have chosen to continue to use immigration raids on businesses as their enforcement tool. The implementation of this policy creates a tangle of ethical issues for business owners, administrators, and workers.

At root, the ethical and existential climate for employers and employees has devolved as "aggressive interior enforcement activities" are pursued by the Immigration and Customs Enforcement (ICE mission statement 2010). Rather than taking any particular side on the immigration debate, or focusing on the ethical impact of undocumented workers on business, this paper addresses the palpable ethical effects on business that result from enforcing immigration policy through worksite raids, and the need for an ethics of care to mitigate those effects. My contention will be that the true costs to business (an increase in unpaid dependency workers (Schutte 2002), a rise in redistribution expenditures aimed at helping working-class families (McCluskey 2002), and the environmental pressures of living under the constant fear of the government (Buff 2008) require new methods of theory and practice to be overcome. This paper will argue that classic cost-benefit utilitarianism is inadequate to address the thorny ethical dimensions

[1]Napolitano said, "Make no mistake, we will be doing worksite enforcement. There will be employees, as well as employers, who ultimately are picked up in those enforcement actions." Associated Press (2009).

J. Hernandez (✉)
Department of Philosophy, University of Texas, San Antonio, TX, USA
e-mail: jill.hernandez@utsa.edu

M. Hamington, M. Sander-Staudt (eds.), *Applying Care Ethics to Business*, Issues in Business Ethics 34, DOI 10.1007/978-90-481-9307-3_9,
© Springer Science+Business Media B.V. 2011

facing employers, brought on by aggressive immigration enforcement, because it cannot take into consideration the compelling moral significance of "attending to and meeting the needs of the particular others" affected, whether the needs of the employer or employee (Held 2006, 14–21). As political tensions increase over the immigration debate, and real consequences are faced by employers, employees, families, and communities, this issue needs to be approached with a more nuanced cache of ethical tools, including those provided by an ethics of care: the reconceptualization of public and private, a relational and interdependent sensitivity to needs, and a broader moral framework into which justice fits.[2]

Towards that end, I will use the Marshalltown, New Bedford, and Postville examples to demonstrate that aggressive immigration enforcement through worksite raids relies upon an outmoded ethical opposition in business between economic growth and social equity, which especially exploits the interests of documented workers. These three cases will show that an ethics of care could help assuage the problems facing businesses—and the families employed by them—because of its emphasis on community response to need (Kittay 1998, ix). If businesses could draw upon ethics of care principles, and if the ICE refocuses its enforcement efforts (for example, to their Criminal Alien Program), the result would be that American businesses and their employees would be better able to respond to needs, work with clear focus on the job, and begin to once again pump money back into their communities without fear.

Immigration Policy Enforcement in Business by the Obama Administration

In order to understand the ethical groundwork and implications of immigration raids on business, it is important to first underscore the current administration's policies and practices surrounding immigration raids.

In May 2009, a policy switch was to be announced in which President Obama would distance himself (at least in theory) from the immigration raids actively pursued by the previous administration. Bush-era immigration raids were the result of the National Fugitive Operations Program, created in 2003, which had the mission of apprehending and deporting fugitives who were national security or public safety threats (Ruiz 2009, 37). Prior to election, however, candidate Obama projected that an overhaul to the immigration system—including immigration raids—would be a part of the package of policy changes he would bring to Washington. "Immigration raids are not a long-term solution," White House spokesman Nick Shapiro stated in early February 2009, "The real answer to our broken immigration system is to fix it. The president has said that we will start the immigration reform debate this year, and this continues to be the plan" (Dinan 2009, A01).

[2] I agree here, with Friedman (2008, 540), Gilligan (1995), and with Engster (2007), that a successful ethics of care accommodates a notion of social justice.

There has not, however, been a change in the use of immigration raids to enforce employment policies for businesses. Since Obama took office, major immigration raids on business have been performed in Arizona, California, Oklahoma, Washington, and Texas (Castro 2009). Instead of a change in using immigration raids for policy enforcement on businesses, the administration has altered the expressed targets of the immigration raids. Ms. Napolitano noted that the focus of ICE actions at worksites was no longer to be on undocumented workers, but on "employers who intentionally and knowingly exploit the illegal labor market." (Gorman 2009, A13). In July 2010, the White House announced that the changes in policy enforcement underscored key differences in immigration enforcement priorities that would "boost confidence in the administration," and cited, "new guidelines directing immigration agents to target employers who hire illegal immigrants rather than simply arresting undocumented employees" (Gorman 2009, A13). In tandem with the Obama administration's announcement, in 2010, DHS notified more than 650 businesses of plans to audit their employment records.

The purpose of auditing employment records is to identify businesses whose employees use I-9 documents that either cannot be verified as their own or have conflicting (and possibly, fraudulent) information. The pragmatic difficulty in assessing the veracity and efficacy of the policy shift, however, is that the audits are often enforced by immigration raids, and the aim of the immigration raids on businesses is the detainment and termination of employees.[3] In early October 2009, for example, ICE raided American Apparel in Los Angeles, which was not under suspicion of violating health, safety or labor laws, but was under suspicion of employing workers who had improper employment documentation. As a result of the raid, 1800 workers of American Apparel were detained and, later, fired after federal immigration authorities concluded their employment documents were illegitimate or out of order. John T. Morton, the head of ICE appointed by President Obama, commented on the American Apparel case that, "the administration intends to change the practices of American employers as a class" (Rutten 2009, A29).

It remains unclear as to whether the intent of the administration is to change the practices of business owners as a class, or to change the face of business altogether. From a fiscal perspective, the federal government has prepared to use immigration raids as an increasingly significant arm of the ICE. Congress in 2009, for example, directed ICE to spend $127 million on workplace operations, $34 million more than requested by the Bush administration (Hsu 2009). And from a jurisprudential point of view, the Obama administration successfully argued over the course of 2009 that employees who use—knowingly or otherwise—documentation that is not their own are guilty of the felony of identity theft, even if the documentation that is used is not

[3]Common concerns are racial profiling and due-process complaints. One recent court case pits US citizens who are employees of a Maricopa, Arizona business, against the US government. The citizens were arrested and detained, with alleged force, because they could not prove their citizenship during the raid. The legal argument contends that open-ended warrants allow federal officials to detain large groups of individuals without prior identification of those individuals. (*Mora, Mora, et al v. Maricopa County* 2009.)

actually assigned to any United States citizen. Recent court cases (see, for example, *Flores-Figueroa v. United States*), reversed the 2008 *United States v. Mendoza-Gonzalez* case, which required proof in identity theft cases that defendants knew "that the means of identification that he or she unlawfully transferred, possessed, or used did, in fact, belong to another person" (see also *Greenlaw* 2009; *Spears v. United States* 2009; *United States v. Ingram* 2009). The full consequence, then, of the shift in justification for immigration raid policy is not simply a governmental interest in increasing the number of arrests for business owners, but in making felons out of those who have or use improper documentation for employment.

One more interesting upshot of the change in policy should be noted for the ICE. Prior to the recent shift from *Mendoza-Gonzalez*, one of ICE's main directives was the Criminal Alien Program, which hones in on aliens who are in the country illegally and are felons, have outstanding warrants for narcotic crimes, or who have a history of violent crimes. Included now in the Criminal Alien Program are new felons who do not have the proper documentation for employment (ICE 2010). The result is that for the first time in 20 years, the government is targeting almost exclusively those immigrants who are working in particular labor sectors and have irregularities with their papers, rather than deportable immigrants who are ensnared in the criminal justice system (Cox and Rodriguez 2009). ICE has created a new enforcement tool[4] called the Document and Benefit Fraud Task Force, whose primary task is to focus solely on document and benefit fraud (ICE 2010). The DBFTF's largest operation to date has been to notify over 1000 companies in November that they would be audited for hiring immigrants, and so could be subject to immigration raids (Lewis 2009).

The Justification for the Immigration Enforcement in Business

There are pragmatic and moral reasons that are given for the current enforcement policy of the immigration standards in business. From a pragmatic standpoint, immigration raids are justified for their potential to deter employers from hiring illegal immigrants. ICE contends, "effective worksite enforcement plays an important role in the fight against illegal immigration in protecting our homeland" (ICE 2010). If business owners face fines and federal charges when they employ individuals who do not have proper documentation, they will be less likely to run the risk of doing so. The bigger implication is meant to be, that if employers do not hire undocumented workers, people will not risk coming to the country

[4]Along with the Department of Justice, U.S. Citizenship and Immigration Services (USCIS), Department of Labor Office of Inspector General, Social Security Administration Office of Inspector General, State Department Office of Inspector General, State Department Bureau of Diplomatic Security, U.S. Postal Inspection Service, U.S. Secret Service. "Document fraud" refers to the manufacture or use of documents that are tied to one's identity. "Benefit fraud" is the use of those documents to obtain a benefit (like employment) that is reserved for US citizens.

illegally. According to ICE (2010), "Worksite enforcement investigations often involve egregious violations of criminal statutes by employers and widespread abuses, and by uncovering such violations, ICE can send a strong deterrent message to other employers who knowingly employ illegal aliens. These worksite enforcement cases often involve additional violations such as alien smuggling, alien harboring, document fraud, money laundering, fraud, or worker exploitation."

The positive values of justice and national security serve as the given moral ground for the justifying rigorous enforcement of immigration policy enforcement in business. A democratic government has the responsibility to protect its citizens from risks, and if there are illegal aliens employed in jobs that can have an impact on national security, then it can be argued that the government has a duty to engage in any enforcement activities that will prevent national security risks. As DHS notes, "We will direct every resource available toward prevention and preparedness, and empower Americans to live in a constant state of readiness, not a constant state of fear" (DHS 2010).

Aggressive enforcement of immigration policy in business, however, undermines the values that the immigration raid model seeks to protect. The Marshalltown, New Bedford, and Postville raids underscore that aggressive policy enforcement relies upon an obsolete ethical opposition in business between economic growth and social equity, which especially exploits the interests of businesses and of legal, documented workers. The cases together show an evolution in federal immigration enforcement policy in business, and they work together to demonstrate the desultory logical effects the raids have: the raids were once performed to send a message to illegal immigrants, they now are performed to send a message to business owners and managers, but the raids have produced an increase in dependency workers, redistribution in the economy, and fear, all of which are consequences that require long-term intervention from the government to offset. These three cases will show that an ethics of care could help assuage the problems facing businesses—and the families employed by them—because of its emphasis on community response to need (Kittay 1998, ix).

Three Cases: Marshalltown, Postville, New Bedford

Marshalltown, Iowa

Responding in part to criticism that Homeland Security had done little interior enforcement since the department's 2003 creation, ICE was able to infiltrate the employment practices of a large meatpacking plant owned by the national company Swift & Company in Marshalltown, Iowa (Seper 2006). In 2006, an informant working for ICE was able to tape human resource workers and union officials advising new employees at Swift on how to obtain and protect false identities (Hsu 2008). Partially on the basis of the informant's information, ICE conducted a raid on the Swift and Company's holdings, and detained nearly 1300 employees, of which 274

Iowan workers were criminally charged, and more were charged on administrative immigration violations (Seper 2006 and Petersen 2009).

It was not just the ratio of employees detained versus those arrested that caused a controversy over the raid. During the raid, ICE asked the workers specific questions about how they obtained their identifications, and ICE's strategic practice in the raid was to round up every employee and arrest those who were unable to provide on-the-spot proof of immigration status (Aldana 2008). Additionally, prior to the raid, Swift & Co. had received ICE scrutiny over employment records, and responded by proposing a phased enforcement action that would allow the business to identify and incrementally dismiss unauthorized workers from its plants (*Lozano v. Hazelton* 2007). In fact, Swift & Co. initially responded to the investigation without notifying ICE by interviewing approximately 450 suspect employees at several of its plants and found that 90–95% were ineligible to work, which resulted in 400 of the workers quitting or being terminated (Injunctive Order, Swift & Co v. ICE 2006). After Swift & Co.'s preemptive actions, ICE was unable to determine how to charge the workers that left.

The Marshalltown raid is interesting philosophically not just for the scope of the raid, but for its focus. Swift management and ownership was never under scrutiny legally, and they distanced themselves immediately from legal culpability. "Swift has never condoned the employment of unauthorized workers, nor have we ever knowingly hired such individuals," Chief Executive Officer Sam Rovit said, noting that the eligibility of all job applicants is checked through a federal database before hires are made (Seper 2006). Their efforts were successful. "The company was not charged in today's action," said Homeland Security Assistant Secretary Julie L. Myers, the head of ICE at the time of the raid, "Today's action is against the individuals who have stolen identities of U.S. citizens and who are here working illegally."

New Bedford, Massachusetts

In New Bedford, Massachusetts, Michael Bianco Inc. (MBI), a company that specialized in the manufacture of leather goods, was the focus of an immigration raid in March 2007. Five hundred employees were detained, and 361 were charged for possessing or using fraudulent employment documents. The New Bedford raid was motivated by "egregious hiring practices, widespread use of fraudulent documents and blatant disregard for the rule of law," said then-Homeland Security Assistant Secretary Julie L. Myers (Seper 2007). The national debate over illegal immigration quickly used the New Bedford raid as a flashpoint, however, largely because over two-thirds of the workers who were detained (and many, later deported) were women who had children at home (Wadhia 2008). That number contrasted with the stated focal target of the ICE New Bedford raid (that of upper-level management and ownership, who were also arrested on charges of conspiring to encourage or induce illegal aliens to reside in the U.S. and conspiring to hire illegal aliens).

Another significant aspect of the New Bedford raid was the tie MBI had to the Department of Defense. According to affidavits in the case, MBI held Defense Department contracts worth $10 million between 2001 and 2003 to manufacture products for the U.S. military, and it received another defense contract in 2004 worth $82 million. As a result of those contracts, MBI increased its work force from 85 in 2003 to more than 500 at the time of the raid (Seper 2007). The affidavits stated that although MBI required prospective employees to produce proof of their identity and their eligibility to work, the company was aware that many employees had obtained fraudulent Alien Registration Cards and were using fake Social Security cards to receive their paychecks. In addition, MBI management allegedly instructed prospective employees on how to obtain fraudulent documents.

Postville, Iowa

On May 12, 2008, more than 500 federal immigration authorities in helicopters, buses, and federal vehicles descended on Agriprocessors Incorporated in Postville, Iowa to conduct "one of the largest single-site raids in U.S. history" (Leys 2009). As a result of the raid on Agriprocessors Incorporated's meatpacking plant, Immigration and Customs Enforcement detained 389 employees under warrants for both civil offenses (for those suspected of being in the United States illegally) and criminal offenses (for those suspected of felonious identity theft). ICE reported that none of those arrested had authorization to work in the United States (Petersen 2009). The plant was forced to close by November 2008 after Agriprocessors declared bankruptcy (Dinnen 2009).

The Postville raid signaled an important change in the tactics ICE used to enforce immigration policy at places of business. Prior to the Postville raid, ICE typically removed unauthorized workers from the country through administrative deportation hearings, and criminally prosecuted only those workers who committed additional crimes, but the Postville raid marked the first time in U.S. history that officials criminally charged and prosecuted such a large number of detainees (ICE Postville Press Release). Of the 389 employees who were detained under civil warrants, 305 were arraigned on criminal charges of using false documents and unlawfully reentering the United States (ICE Postville Press Release). Of the 305 who were arrested on criminal charges, 265 workers were sentenced to federal prison—each for 5 months—for a total of more than 110 years of imprisonment. The Postville raid was also unique because it was the first time that the section 1028A "identity theft" statute was applied to criminalize employees who used improper documentation. What is perhaps even more startling from a law enforcement perspective is that none of the 389 people who were detained had even a simple misdemeanor conviction between them (*United States v. Ingram*). The Postville cases were the toughest application to date of criminal charges against illegal immigrants whose main offense was that they were working without authorization (Preston 2009).

Postville also set a precedent for using an immigration raid as a medium to establish ground for arresting business owners and managers with employment violations. Agriprocessor's chief executive, Sholom Rubashkin, was arrested on multiple charges, including bank fraud, and his lead manager, Laura Althouse, pled guilty to aggravated identity theft after prosecutors accused her of helping illegal immigrants gain employment at the plant by using documents that she knew were false (Friesen 2008; US vs. Agriprocessors 2009). (It should be noted that on November 19, 2009, all of the immigration-related charges against Rubaskin were dropped, although he was convicted on the bank charges. See *United States v. Sholom Rubashkin*. In addition, a federal judge allowed Ms. Althouse to withdraw her guilty plea after she successfully argued that she had not been aware that the documents that Agriprocessor employees presented to her were fradulent. See Preston 2009.)

Finally, the Postville raids were significant in terms of the effects the raid had on the community of Postville. Nearly 1/3 of the town's 2400 residents were arrested during the raid, and the Agriprocessor slaughterhouse was the largest employer in the town (Friesen 2008). The local elementary school immediately lost 1/3 of its students, as nearly all of the workers who were arrested were also deported, and many had children in the school (Preston 2009). The legal battles, as well, continue. In 2009, the Supreme Court ruled that to win convictions for identity theft, federal prosecutors have to show that illegal immigrants who use fraudulent documents know that the false identification they use actually belongs to another real person (*United States v. Ingram*). As a result of the ruling in *Ingram*, the immigration lawyers' national bar association called on the Justice Department to dismiss the guilty pleas of the workers from Agriprocessor, although to date the Court of Appeals for the Eighth Circuit covering Iowa upheld the interpretation of the identity theft law that prosecutors applied to the immigrant workers from Postville (Preston 2009).

The True Cost of Policy Enforcement on Business

The Marshalltown, Postville, and New Bedford raids demonstrate a crucial aspect of the true impact of using immigration raids for immigration policy enforcement on businesses. An increase in dependency workers, financial redistribution expenditures, and the economic and psychological ramifications of living in fear are all factors that mitigate against an unrestricted use of cost benefit utilitarianism to justify immigration raids on business.

Dependency Workers

An unintended impact of the recent and polarizing immigration raids is that it has led, essentially, to children becoming temporary orphans, as their parents are taken away from them. Detained parents can be separated from their children for months as they await movement in their legal hearings (Zounes 2007). The New Bedford raid, for example, resulted in hundreds of children being stranded and separated from their parents (Sacchetti and Bailou 2007), especially because more than 200 of the detainees were sent to detention centers in Texas and New Mexico to await their hearings, and none of them were asked about their childcare needs (Mishra and Ballou 2007). Of the suspected undocumented workers sent to other states, childcare arrangements had to be made by the state for at least 35 children (Rhor 2007 and Shulman 2007). DSS Commissioner Harry Spence said that, although he had been told of the raid prior to its execution, social workers were actually denied access while the raid was carried out (Weber 2007).

A supporter of immigration raids on businesses might argue that, even though poor execution of a large-scale immigration raid (like that which occurred in New Bedford), could unintentionally result in numbers of children being without care, that should not serve as the basis for rejecting the use of immigration raids to enforce policy. Such an argument, however, misses two important points. First is that the enforcement of immigration policy through immigration raids on businesses will *necessarily* produce large numbers of dependent children who will need care. That hundreds of children will require care by workers who are not their parents cannot be avoided if immigration raids are the vehicle by which an administration enforces their policy. In fact, the fear that is generated by the raids often leads to more dependent children who need care. Consider that detainees are frequently not initially honest with ICE investigators who inquire about their families, often because the detainees are afraid that their children will also be taken into US custody, even though many of the children are citizens of the United States (Abraham 2007). And after the detainees admit they have children, they are given the choice of taking their citizen-children out of the United States with them (in which case there is an administrative scramble to secure passports for them), or of being separated from their children permanently in hopes of giving them better opportunities (Abraham 2007). Those children who stay behind then become even more vulnerable to exploitation, since those who depend on the care of others and cannot get that care from a direct relative often suffer more from a lack of care (Bubeck 2002).

The second point that is missed by those who suggest that the New Bedford raid was an anomaly in its impact on children, is that, regardless of whether the consequence of having increased numbers of children who need care is intended or not, the system of policy enforcement on business through immigration raids has a damaging impact on the children it leaves behind as well as the communities involved in the immigration raid. Interestingly, prior to his oath of office, then-candidate Barak Obama appeared to understand the intrinsically negative impact immigration raids have on children, parents, families, and businesses. In a speech to the National Council of La Raza during his presidential run, Obama said, "When communities are terrorized by ICE immigration raids, when nursing mothers are torn from their babies, when children come home from school to find their parents missing, when people are detained without access to legal counsel, when all that is happening, the system just isn't working, and we need to change it" (Ruiz 2010). Prior to his death, Sen. Edward Kennedy commented specifically on the New Bedford raid, arguing that "the immigration system is broken and the government has no effective plan to identify and help the children who would be left alone"

(Sacchetti and Bailou 2007). The systemic indifference to the needs of children has the (morally and economically ironic) result that the typically unpaid domestic work of caring for children (frequently performed by the spouse, parent, or siblings of the worker), now has to be paid by the state, whether the cost is foster parents, temporary custody, legal hearings, or deportation. Apart from the economic cost to the state, the community suffers the burden of an increased need of dependency workers. As Schutte (2002) points out, a society simply cannot function without dependency work, but in economic terms, dependency work tends to be costly since it requires that the time spent on unpaid care work will disenfranchise the dependency workers from the income they could have secured had they been free to engage in paid employment. Even for children who end up cared for by other, non-parental relatives, the economic and existential burden for the care of the child shifts, so that the one who had been staying with the child must go to work or must pay for someone else to be with the child.

Redistribution of Finances

In the dominant liberal political theory, autonomy is the key to both a free state and a free market, whereas dependency is relegated to the family (McCluskey 2002). Immigration raids are used, in part, by the state as a demonstrative example of the government's ability to regulate how free markets can operate but they also create (as has been shown above) an increase in dependency relations that ends up impacting not just the family, but the state. An increase in dependency relations strains the community and businesses by taking workers out of the already-strained workplace to take care of their new charges, but it also can lead to problems in supporting the needs of caretakers, which ultimately has a deleterious effect on state finances. This consequence not only can be disastrous for communities, but it runs counter to the recent federal move away from long-term funding and social support for human services. For those states that make jobs a legitimate condition for the receipt of public assistance, even the detainment of a working family member can become an insurmountable economic hurdle.

The economic impact of displaced families through these raids is borne by the government, but the overall result of using immigration raids to enforce employment laws is that a cycle of dependency has been created by the state that also must be funded by the state. By taking away an alternative to wage work for immigrant parents of US-born children, families who depend on wage work to avoid poverty must then forgo productive labor market opportunities by seeking state subsidies just to survive.[5] The needs of the family are redistributed to the state, at the same time that the ability for businesses to eviscerate dependency costs are impeded by the loss of workers. It should be noted, as well, that the fiscal redistribution burden added to the state as a result of this cycle is potentially incredibly high. There are

---

[5]McCluskey (2002) gives a fascinating treatment of the relationship between the need for dependency workers and the economic interests of the state.

many varieties of mixed-status families who could need to rely on welfare (or some other state-sponsored subsidy), given that approximately one in five children in the United States live in a family in which at least one parent is an immigrant (Federal Interagency Forum on Child and Family Statistics 2007).[6] Children in immigrant families form, "the fastest growing segment of the United States child population", and if current demographic trends persist, "children of immigrants will represent at least a quarter of all U.S. children by 2010" (Thronson 2008). The staggering numbers of children potentially impacted by workplace raids, as well as the numbers of families who could potentially be caught in a web of financial displacement should give us pause when thinking about whether the pragmatic reasons for immigration raids in business are actually justified.

A report by the Urban Institute found that the actual impact of these raids on communities is so damaging that it far outweighs any potential benefit received from conducting the raid in the first place (Capps 2007, 68). Public schools carry the burden of caring for children whose parents are detained as well as normal educational duties, and this strain increases when the parent that is removed from the home is the primary wage earner, which is typically the case (Capps 2007, 41). In addition to the burdens on schools, families, and children, the workplace raids have a lasting negative consequence for the members of a community as a whole. In Postville, for example, community respondents said that the aftermath of the raid was akin to "disaster relief", and in all three of the major raids discussed in this paper, churches and other faith-based organizations were the primary responders to the crisis, but soon faced infrastructure and staff limitations that impeded the ability to provide sustaining, lasting relief (Merritt 2009). The cycle of dependency that requires fiscal redistribution through the state is not just a possibility, then, but has become an actuality for communities devastated by immigration raids.

Fear

The implementation of immigration enforcement through worksite raids has the final consequence of creating an atmosphere of fear for every level of business and the community, which then undermines one of the specific goals of immigration enforcement: to encourage job growth for American citizens and legal permanent residents (DHS 2010). At a fundamental level, ICE raids cannot be successfully achieved without racial profiling, and the profusion of racial profiling at the federal level can breed a reluctance for business owners to hire, especially, Latinos (Cox and Rodriguez 2009). An atmosphere of fear has been bred throughout every level of business as a result of immigration raids: employers fear "Gestapo methods of enforcement", sanctions, and significant financial losses that come with a loss of employees and production (Capps 2007); employees fear being detained even if

[6]More specifically, "15 percent of all children in the [United States] were native-born children with immigrant parent(s)," and "4 percent of children were foreign-born children with at least one immigrant parent" (Thronson 2008).

they are legal (as has been the practice of the ICE since the Marshalltown raid); and the communities fear losing workers, gaining groups of children without parents or primary earners, and, ultimately, watching business become bankrupt and leave town (as was the case for Agriprocessors[7] and Swift in the Iowa raids).

Without warrants that name specific individuals to detain, workplace raids must depend upon racial profiling for their success. A surprise raid on Micro Solutions Enterprises in Van Nuys, CA in early 2008 provides a troubling example. About 238 employees of MSE were swept up in the raid, including more than 100 US citizens and legal residents. Perhaps not surprisingly, none of those detained were Caucasian, and all of those who were not Caucasian were required to show proof of citizenship, and if they could not, they were arrested on the spot (Bazar 2008). Rep. John Conyers, D-Michigan., has posed an interesting counterexample when questioning the efficacy of workplace immigration raids, "When dealing with Anglo identity theft suspects, is federal law enforcement going to start cordoning off white neighborhoods or workplaces, handcuffing and detaining everyone, and only then sort out the accused?" (Reyes 2008).

If worksite immigration raids could be performed without racial profiling, or without instilling economically and psychologically debilitating fear in the people upon whom the national economy depends, there might at least be stronger pragmatic reasons to accept the continuation of its practice. But ICE agents often work from internally assigned "administration warrants" which give them broad discretion in the execution of the raid, and also work under pressure to fill certain detention "quotas" during worksite raids (Schumacher-Matos 2009). It is simply easier (and loosely, it is legal) to detain individuals who are not white than to require ICE agents to confirm that those who are working at a particular place of business are, in fact, working illegally and, even more difficult, to confirm that business owners intentionally are hiring undocumented workers. Enforcement practices that instill a top-to-bottom fear will damage businesses (and so, it will negatively impact job growth and production), even though the immigration raids are supposed to protect legal business practices and to encourage the development of jobs for American residents. Worksite raids are, once again, contrary to their purpose, and so their justification should be reevaluated.

True Cost Requires New Methods to be Overcome

Economic, political, and existential factors all come to bear on the debate over using immigration raids as policy enforcement in business, but there are also moral reasons to assess the efficacy of immigration raids on business. Policy enforcement that depends upon immigration raids for its success, but results in the disastrous

[7] Agriprocessors in Postville went bankrupt only after they hired homeless individuals to take the place of their workers, but the experiment went awry with a rise in crime, public drunkenness, and a run on food banks (Reyes 2008).

consequences noted above requires moral reasoning that is different from the cost benefit model, which cannot quantify certain "human" aspects of this issue (community impact, for example, or the influence of racial profiling and perhaps, most especially, the logical and pragmatic contradictions that come with policy enforcement through worksite raids). The difficulty, however, in refocusing the moral justification for immigration enforcement in business is that doing so requires a review of the relations between business owners, employees, and those who enforce policy. This difficulty is assuaged, however, if an ethics of care is used as justification for policy enforcement, since it grounds moral reasons in how people are related to others. An ethics of care, if used as a new method of moral reasoning for policy enforcement, reconceptualizes what is public and private, it provides for a relational and interdependent sensitivity to the needs of others, and it sustains a broader moral framework into which justice fits (which, if applied to the immigration issue in business, will allow a focus on criminal activity beyond the identity theft clause). An ethics of care allows for both the recognition that we are tied to each other and that those relations need to serve as a basis for moral decision-making when there is injustice that results in those relations (Mahowald 2006, 180).

The enormous impact of immigration raids on business, and the disconnect of reasons from the human condition upon which it depends, requires that a different model of moral reasoning constrain immigration enforcement. For business interests, employees, and the goal of federal enforcement, an ethics of care can serve as an effective moral theory to guide policy enforcement, especially since the American economy depends in practice upon the intricate social and business relations between employees, business, and the government. Worksite immigration raids invert what is private (like dependency care) and what is public (such as the legal status of business managers, owners, and workers). Policy enforcement that is both consistent and effective should include as its justification the crucial relations in the workplace upon which an effective economy depends.

Care as a normative base speaks at least to the dissociations which can abrupt an employee's ability to work effectively. Gilligan notes (1995, 125) "the vibrations and resonances which characterize and connect the living world" are "numbed by the types of dissociations that present themselves when care is not present." Grounding the bottom line in the mutual care of employees ensures that corporate interests (even for small businesses) depend upon the proper treatment of workers, and that the success of the workers on the job depends in part on the business model used. All employees are in a subordinate relation to their employees, businesses are subordinate to federal law, and when employees and businesses can produce without fear, they are in a position to contribute to the maintenance of their connection (Smeyers 1999, 236), which for the purposes here, can then foster immigration reform in business that does not have the deleterious effects immigration raids have. Rather than assuming, as do the dominant moral theories, that moral relations are to be seen as entered into voluntarily by free and equal individuals, the ethics of care is developed for the realities of unequal power relations (Held 2004, 143), such as the ones that exist between businesses and the government and businesses and their employees. The ethics of care is not limited, then, to private contexts. Employees are not objects to be manipulated, but instead are free beings who should be valued—if nothing else—for their intrinsic tie to the success of the economy, and so for the government. What the employees (as those cared-for) give to the relation serves to prevent the business interest from being subverted to simple survival of the business. Care is a value that is universal, since it refers mainly to the social relations upon which we rely, it cannot be dispensed practically and morally from social relations, such as those in business (Mahowald 2006, 178).

If the conception care ethics has of persons as "relational and interdependent" is correct, then ethics must start with the moral claims of particular others (Friedman, 2008, 541). If moral justification for actions is grounded in the claims of those we are tied to, then justification for actions is essentially second-personal. An ethics of care, then, is essentially second-personal, because it contends that we have a compelling moral interest in attending to and meeting the needs of others for whom we take responsibility (Held 2006, 10–14). On the basis of the second-personality of care ethics, moral rules (like that upon which cost benefit utilitarianism depends) are less compelling than the claims of others, because they are wholly independent from the agents the action will impact. Second-personal care claims, then, constrain other moral rules. (This doesn't mean that businesses should abandon the cost/benefit calculus as an appropriate practical business model, or that governments should not use reasoning other than an ethics of care, but instead for ethical judgments, cost benefit moral reasons should be informed by and constrained by an ethics of care.) If the pragmatic and moral aspects of life depend upon the connection of others' interests, then moral reasons must be tied to that connection to be successfully justified.

Especially in the wake of an economic crisis like the one we are now suffering through, economic gain is made the highest priority of policy, and every social element is considered to be a fungible commodity (Held 2004, 148). The fact that immigration raids put communities in the position of supporting families as well as businesses should factor in to the economic justification for immigration raids. In the atmosphere in which we desire stronger markets and more jobs, actions (like worksite raids) that negatively impact the economy should be avoided. But, if market practices are constrained by an ethics of care, we can have both an improvement in market conditions, effective and humane policy enforcement, and an avoidance of critical consequences brought on by immigration raids. Institutions that erode the care relation are pragmatically and morally malignant, but applying an ethics of care can encourage just business and personal relations.

It is logically consistent, on the one hand, to use as the moral foundation of actions that affect people who have mingling interests, a moral theory that is itself based on relations in which people have shared interests (Held 2004, 144). It is, on the other hand, practically consistent for businesses to assume their workers understand their responsibility to the company within the context of a relationship they have to the company. An ethics of care allows for both, since responsibility is equated with the need to respond to those with whom we are connected, and the moral imperative to care obligates us to alleviate troubles for others (Kroeger-Mappes 1994, 109). Business owners and managers respond to their workers, and workers in turn take care of the job; similarly, the government ensures its actions and policy enforcement techniques appropriately respond to the needs of communities and those in need.

A critic might contend that immigration enforcement is not a matter of morality, but of public policy. But such a view denies the human costs that are important to the rationale behind enforcing immigration policy through immigration raids on businesses, and it obfuscates the dependency of our economy on meeting the needs of employees—or in the very least, of allowing employees the freedom to be able to meet their own needs. Engster notes that care theories, "start with the individuals already existing in society and dependent upon one another for their survival, development, and social functioning, and highlights the unchosen obligations we all have toward others by virtue of our interdependency," and our mutual dependency means that, "all capable individuals have obligations to care for others in need regardless of our explicit or tacit consent" (Engster 2007, 7–8). The scope of care must be extended to injustices within communities, and so within business, since caring is fundamentally about concern for others (Smeyers 1999, 236). Grounding the bottom line for immigration policy enforcement as well as for the economy in the mutual care of communities and employees ensures the business interests and the needs of the employees are inextricably related. Care, then, is the wider moral framework into which justice for employees and businesses (and, let it be said, economic development as well) can be fit.

Conclusion

This paper set out to perform a unique task: to evaluate the pragmatic and moral consistency of the current administration's continued use of immigration raids on business to enforce immigration policy, without taking a particular stance on the immigration debate itself. I have not argued for any specific view on the immigration debate at all. Even more, this paper did not argue that immigration enforcement should not occur at all at the worksite.

Instead, this paper looked at the role that immigration raids are meant to perform for this administration, and I weighed its purported role against the practical and moral results that immigration raids at worksites necessarily produce. There are logical consequences of this inquiry: Proponents of immigration raids as policy enforcement for businesses cannot consistently plan for economic growth for the communities in which the raids are performed. Neither can one consistently maintain that immigration raids protect business interest by ensuring that only properly documented workers are employed, since immigration raids on business create an increase in the need for dependency workers, a cycle of dependency which must be funded by the government, and an atmosphere of fear that undermines the very impetus for immigration raids. An inquiry into three significant immigration raid cases in business both shows these to be true, and motivates a change in a moral point of departure.

Not all is lost, however. If we use an ethics of care to inform our policy making and enforcement, the pragmatic and moral contradictions can be overcome. An ethics of care can inform, and then, constrain how we respond to certain difficulties, like the impact of illegal immigration on the bottom line of business. Actions that are rooted in an understanding of our mutual dependence, and of the relation between the economy and the worker, can more consistently and effectively be performed and maintained. In addition, the government is able to seek out policy enforcement that ensures the preservation of the dignity of its residents and gains authenticity with those impacted by the policy enforcement.

References

Abraham, Y 20 March 2007. As immigration raids rise, human toll decried. *Boston Globe*, online edition. http://www.boston.com/news/nation/articles/2007/03/20/as_immigration_raids_rise_human_toll_decried/. Accessed 31 January 2010.

Aldana, R. February 2008. Rights and Remedies: Of Katz and "aliens", privacy expectations and the immigration raids. *University of California-Davis Law Review* 41: 1081.

Associated Press. 26 April 2009. Two Iowa towns, 2 perspectives on immigration raids.

Bazar, E. 25 June 2008. Citizens sue after being detained in workplace. *USA Today*, final edition, news, 1A.

Bubeck, D. G. 2002. Justice and the labor of care. In *The subject of care: Feminist perspectives on dependency*, eds. Eva Kittay, and Ellen Feder. New York, NY: Rowman & Littlefield.

Buff, R. 2008. The deportation terror. *American Quarterly* 60 (3): 523–551.

Capps, R. 2007. Paying the price: The impact of immigration raids on America's children. The Urban Institute. http://www.urban.org/UploadedPDF/411566

Castro J. 2009. Second-class citizens: the Schism between immigration policy and children's health care. *Hastings Constitutional Law Quarterly* Fall 37: 199.

Cox, A., and Rodriguez, C. December 2009. The president and immigration law. *Yale Law Journal* 119: 458.

Department of Homeland Security. 2010. http://www.dhs.gov/xabout/responsibilities.shtm. Accessed 30 Jan 2010; Fact Sheet, http://www.ice.gov/doclib/pi/news/factsheets/worksite_strategy.pdf. Accessed 8 Feb 2010.

Dinan, S. 2 February 2009. Raid on immigrants dismays Obama Backers. *Washington Post,* Page One, A01.

Dinnen, S. 31 May 2009. How an immigration raid changed a town. *Christian Science Monitor*, 17.

Engster, D. 2007. *Heart of justice*. Oxford: Oxford University Press.

Federal Interagency Forum on Child and Family Statistics. 2007. *America's Children: Key National Indicators of Well-Being* 8. http://www.childwelfare.gov/systemwide/statistics/wellbeing.cfm

Flores-Figueroa v. United States. (4 May 2009). U.S. 129 S. Ct. 1886, 173 L. Ed. 2d 853, 2009 US Lexis 3305, WL 1174852.

Friedman, M. September 2008. Care ethics and moral theory. *Philosophy and Phenomenological Research* 77 (2): 539–555.

Friesen, J. 24 May 2008. Hardening the line on illegal works. *The Globe and Mail*, A16. International News; Weekend Special: Canada.

Gilligan, C. 1995. Hearing the difference: Theorizing connection. *Hypatia* 10: 120–127.

Gorman, A. 26 July 2009. Obama sets the priorities on immigration. *Los Angeles Times*: Part A, 13.

Greenlaw. 2009. U.S. 128 S. Ct. 2559, 171 L. Ed. 2d 399, 2009.

Held, V. 2004. Care and justice in the global context. *Ratio Juris* 17 (2): 141–55.

Held, V. 2006. *The ethics of care: Personal, political, and global*. Oxford: Oxford University Press.

Hsu, S. 21 July 2008. In immigration cases, employers feel the pressure; but critics fault laws as ineffective. *Washington Post,* Met 2 Edition, A-Section, A01.

Hsu, S. 31 March 2009. Proposed immigration raids delayed. *The Boston Globe National News,* 5.

Injunctive Order at 7, Swift & Co. v. ICE, No 2:06CV-314-J (N.D. Tex.7 December 2006). http://www.aif.org/lac/clearinghouse122106 ctorder.pdf

Kittay, E. 1998. *Love's labor: Essays on women, equality, and dependency*. New York, NY: Routledge.

Kroeger-Mappes, J. 1994. An ethic of care vis-à-vis an ethics of rights. *Hypatia* Summer 9 (3): 108–131.

Lewis, N. 20 November 2009. In search for illegal workers, immigration officials will audit more companies. *The New York Times,* Late Edition, Final, Section A, Column 0, National Desk, 14.

Leys, T. 28 August 2009. Critics tie scant new charges to wariness after Iowa raid. *Des Moines Register,* 1A.

Lozano v. City of Hazelton. 2007. U.S. Dist LEXIS 17118 (M.D. Pa., Mar 9, 2007), at P4.

Mahowald, M. 2006. Review: Ethics of care: personal, political, global. *International Journal of Feminist Approaches to Bioethics* 2: 1.

McCluskey, M. 2002. Subsidized lives and the ideology of efficiency. In *The subject of care: Feminist perspectives on dependency*, eds. Eva Kittay, and Ellen Feder, 115–137. New York, NY: Rowman & Littlefield.

Merritt, N. Winter 2009. The conflicting interests of labor demands and employer based immigration laws. *The Scholar: St. Mary's Law Review on Minority Issues* 11 Scholar 281.

Mishra, R, and B. Ballou. 9 March 2007. DSS to check on detainees sent to Texas: Some workers' children may lack care, officials fear. *Boston Globe,* A1.

Mora, Mora et al. vs. Maricopa County. 2009. US District Court for the State of Arizona, 29th U.S. District Lexis 101403, No. CV-09-1719-PHX-DGC, 28 Oct 2009.

Petersen, C. November 2009. An Iowa immigration raid leads to unprecedented criminal consequences. *University of Iowa Law Review* 95: 323.

Preston, J. 26 May 2009. Dismissal of guilty pleas is sought for immigrants. *New York Times,* Late Edition, Final, Section A, Column 0, National Desk, 19.

Reyes, R. 8 August 2008. What are ICE raids accomplishing? *USA Today,* Final Edition, News, 9A.

Rhor, M. 12 March 2007. Immigration raids split kids from moms. *Seattle Times,* A1.

Ruiz, A. 31 January 2010. Immigration reform dies in 36 words. *Daily News (New York),* 37.

Ruiz, A. 8 February 2009. Obama takes positive steps towards reform. *Daily News (New York)*, 37.

Rutten, T. 3 October 2009. Stripped of jobs by Obama. *Los Angeles Times*: Part A, 29.

Sacchetti, M., and B. Bailou. 11 March 2007. DSS teams arrive in Texas to interview detained immigrants. *Boston Globe*, B3.

San Antonio Express-News. 1 May 2009. From AP reports.

Schumacher-Matos, E. 1 August 2009. When law flies out the door. *Washington Post*, Regional Edition, Editorial Copy, A15.

Schutte, O. 2002. Dependency work, women, and the global economy. In *The subject of care: Feminist perspectives on dependency*, ed. Eva Kittay, and Ellen Feder, 138–158. New York, NY: Rowman & Littlefield.

Seper, J. 13 December 2006. Agents raid job sites for illegals; identity theft prompts effort. *The Washington Times*, Nation, 03.

Seper, J. 8 March 2007. ICE to query 500 workers in illegals probe. *The Washington Times,* Nation, A04.

Shulman, R. 18 March 2007. Immigration raid rips families: Illegal workers in Massachusetts separated from children. *Washington Post*: A06.

Smeyers, P. 1999. "Care" and wider ethical issues. *Journal of Philosophy of Education* 33 (2): 231–255.

Spears v. United States. 2009. US 129 S. Ct 840, 172 L. Ed. 2d 596.

Thronson, D. 2008. Creating crisis: Immigration raids and the destabilization of immigrant families. *Wake Forest Law Review* 43: 391.

US Immigration and Customs Enforcement. 2010. www.ice.gov., http://www.ice.gov/document-benefit-fraud/, Criminal Alien Program, http://www.ice.gov/criminal-alien-program/, Postville

Press Release: http://www.ice.gov/news/releases/0805/080520waterloo.htm, http://www.ice.gov/news/library/factsheets/cap.htm, Accessed 31 Jan 2010.

United States v. Ingram. 2009. No. CR 07-4056-2-MWB, 613 F. Supp. 2d 1069; 2009 U.S. Dist. LEXIS 40075; 79 Fed. R. Evid. Serv. (Callaghan) 735, 11 May 2009.

United States v. Mendoza-Gonzalez. 2008. 520 F.3d912 (8th Cir) 2008.

United States vs. Agriprocessors, Inc., Sholom Rubashkin, Brent Beebe, Hosam Amara and Zeev Levi. 2009. No. 08-CR-1324-LRR, U.S. District Court for the Northern District of Iowa, Eastern Division, 2009 U.S. Dist. LEXIS 65165, 28 July 2009.

United States vs. Sholom Rubashkin. 2009. No. 08-CR-1324-LRR, US District Court for the Northern District of Iowa, Eastern Division, 2009 U.S. Dist. Lexis 109115, 20 November 2009.

Wadhia, S. 2008. Emerging issues in immigration law: Immigrants' rights and the rule of law. *University of Memphis Law Review* 38: 853.

Weber, D 11 March 2007. Delahunt says congress will investigate immigration raid. *Boston Globe*. http://www.boston.com/news/local/massachusetts/articles/2007/03/11/delahunt_says_congress_will_investigate_immigration_raid/

Zounes, S. 2007. Current development: Children without Parents: An unintended consequence of ICE's worksite enforcement operations. *Georgetown Immigration Law Journal* Spring 21: 511.

Chapter 10
Taking Care of Business: Caring in Competitive Corporate Structures

Bill Puka

MEMO: TAKING CARE OF BUSINESS

To:	Upper, Middle-level, lower level Mgt., staff—All Personnel
From:	Bill Puka
Re:	Compassionate Ordering Around

The "Bullet"

- *Question*: Exactly how can a kindly ethic like "caring" enhance business practice when it is so tenderly ill-suited to competitiveness, and aimed so high above the bottom line?
- *Answer*: Caring is a skill-ethic that does not put ethics and practicality at odds. It views the two as overlapping parts of the same activity: partners in excellence.
- *Problem*: Caring is an ethical model or theory, not a plan of action. It is meant to explain ethical beliefs and observations, not concretely guide them. More, care shows obvious shortfalls even in that role. How can a flawed general theory solve concrete problems?
- *Remedy*: Reversing the theory-building process, we can identify the particular beliefs, insights and rationales that went into care generalization. The stronger ones can be selected, with the weaker ones left behind. Then the strengths can be refit for practical use.
- *Recommendation:* Reformat care as an ethical "tool box" from which we draw whichever care features we need, and also as a problem solving process for concrete problems.
- *Implementation:* ASAP (See Part II)

This is the path our discussion will follow, and is addressed to business folk interested in being ethical at work, or not so much ethically interested as set on being competent.

B. Puka (✉)
Department of Philosophy and Psychology, Rensselaer Polytechnic Institute, Troy, NY, USA
e-mail: billpuka@gmail.com

M. Hamington, M. Sander-Staudt (eds.), *Applying Care Ethics to Business*, Issues in Business Ethics 34, DOI 10.1007/978-90-481-9307-3_10,
© Springer Science+Business Media B.V. 2011

Clearing Our Desks—The Trouble with Care

When I first encountered an ethic called "care," the word "bullshit" popped into mind. If you work in a no-nonsense business setting—in a competitive industry, needing serious management tools—your reaction may be similar. "Caring in business" may not be as bad as *Lead with Love* (a recent management book title). But one wouldn't want to do a board presentation on it, especially given one of its volume-length presentations "Caring—*a feminine approach to ethics*" (Noddings 1984).

Even the most broadminded female executive may blanch at the stereotype-affirming ruse seemingly at work here—care, a "Virginia-Slim" ethic for women, not like the "fat" ethics that men develop and use. Caring is a highly personal, intimate, and familial notion, not designed for the often contentious, rough-and-tumble world of business sharks and barracudas.

Truth be told, however, the care "logo" has seen a spectacular run in the corporate world, becoming a virtual mantra of TV and print ads. There are caring banks, caring car companies, caring life-insurance companies (with whom we are "in good hands") and of course, caring healthcare organizations—a no brainer. "While the big banks couldn't care less about your small business, we at X Inc. care about every customer, sharing his dream." "What if something was to happen to you [like dying for instance] what could show you care more than assuring your children's financial security?" There is money to be made in caring, or at least spent.

Showing customers you care is believed to enhance customer loyalty and word-of-mouth interest, which is measurable in sales. And this is not because the word is sweet and can be put in a catchy tune. It's because people care about being cared for. Likewise, showing concern for employees increases bankable benefits like higher productivity, fewer sick days, less turnover, less pilfering or internal sabotage on the "factory floor." Studies back these beliefs up as well. Employees work more and have higher morale as well as loyalty to a company in which they feel well-treated. (Koh and Boo 2004).

"Windowdressing" is the least costly form of care for business. So it is with any ethical innovation. But there are two types: one based totally on appearance—suggestion and tissue boxes, strategically located near the hand sanitizers with happy faces designating them. A second involves instituted rituals, like the little celebrations such as when an employee's productivity is recognized by personnel applauding it by his desk, similar to restaurant wait-staff singing to a "birthday boy." For better or worse, this sort of simple reinforcement works, and is little trouble. Nobody "goes out of their way" to deliver this kindness.

Asking Too Much

Common knowledge also has it that to be caring, kind, or generous means going beyond the call of duty. It means being minimally fair and respectful first, a stretch in itself for some, but then it also involves going an extra mile. (The stretch is termed "supererogation" in ethical lingo.) Benevolence thus puts extra moral burdens on us that invariably outstrip any spontaneous kindly sensibilities we feel inside. Even having to listen to someone go on and on about their problems represents a significant self-sacrifice to some of us—less preferable than a root canal. I often think of comedian Jack Handy's "deep thoughts" on the matter: "If trees could scream, would we be so cavalier about cutting them down? We might, if they screamed all the time and for no good reason." Here merely doing our duty (not to kill) comes to seem supererogatory due to its extraordinary burdens.

Believing that no reasonable person should be *obliged* to extend themselves this far for others, we view generous behavior as largely discretionary. When indexed to the competitive nature of business, going beyond the call of duty has the additional disadvantage of inefficiency—unaffordable inefficiency. Efforts that could be placed on doing good business itself, with business interests in the lead, are spent on extraneous distractions. From a business perspective, ethical tenets and practices that tie closely to legal issues make sense—decreasing law suits, avoiding a bad image for the company. But ethics with no business payoff simply does not make sense from a profit motive. "We're in business to do business, and our business is not ethics," nor presumably, is it caring. But if what is true in principle often does not fit practice, matters can go the other way—what seems a stretch conceptually may not be when you try it. Most of the ways we interact with people in modern society is in words. This is especially so in the workplace through memos and phone calls. And it is remarkably effortless to work up kind and encouraging words where neutral or curt phrasing is habitual. More, it didn't require much "faking-it" even from the start—it's not as if we don't have a well of positive words of *comments* in our verbal repertoire. The collegial payoffs here are enormous: it's hard not to feel better about a colleague or boss who compliments us, offering support or praise when it's not completely merited. It's hard not to feel better about oneself and one's interactions when being such a better person in them. And this is not difficult. Changing verbal habits from curt to kindly is like moving a paper clip from one side of one's desk to the middle. There are even business manuals for doing it, such as *How to Say it.*

More, if caring at times requires going the extra mile, we can reduce the effort needed and the distance seemingly traversed, through training—a few hours each week at the ethical gym. Obviously if we could upgrade our caring sensibilities a bit, then engaging them more wouldn't be a stretch. Common belief has it, however, that changing inner traits or habits is even more difficult than changing outward behavior. And even a few minutes at an ethical gym taxes some employees' resolve. Personality change is no easy trick for the employee—how does one even try, or start to try to change one's character? How does a company focused on performance make this change? Our psychologies are designed to resist the imposition, as is the "fair-work" employee in us. Job training is one thing, required character-development, is another—it's too invasive, as well as too much to ask.

But research in social psychology has shown the common belief that one cannot change one's motives through behavior modification to be wrong. The data vindicates the discredited motivational theory that acting a certain way—insincerely, without "feeling it,"—actually creates the very intentions thought needed to motivate it (Meyers 2005). And this process is NOT difficult, nor something that requires great effort, with one's nose to the psychological grindstone. Go figure, it turns out that Aristotle, Confucius and William James were right on this point all along.

Inner traits, personal virtues, and character are best trained from the outside. The key is to keep it up through a regular exercise routine, which having a peer group and institutional setting to reinforce the change helps assure. Those arranging marriages for their children knew this was a good way to help them fall in love. Centuries of distastefully authoritarian moralism also had it right. Get the kids to conform—to do the parents' and teacher's bidding—and they will eventually bid themselves. When you came to the office, you were not your office self. You got to be a manager, executive or other sort of employee by acting like one. And you may recall, thinking back to the first week, exactly how you faked it.

Of course, forcing people to marry, or indoctrinating them to learn is hardly the moral way. And while "faking it" and acting "as if" one is competent, to become so, involves no coercion, it seems hypocritical, and can deceive others. But as an office-wide policy, with everyone knowingly participating, that problem diminishes. (Sports like football or hockey are exercises in assault and battery. Mutual consent makes them mutual fun instead.) The process is like trying to accommodate to open-designed work-spaces or cubicles after having offices with doors that closed. Strangely, the change involved not only occurs psychologically, through so-called "dissonance reduction," but deep in the brain apparently, as fMRI research has indicated, where resistance to change is found also (Meyers 2005). The brain, like the mind, moves to remove inconsistency. If it can't stop us from behaving as we don't feel genuinely motivated to, it will change or create appropriate motivations to suit. This is why mental hospitals "force" severely depressed patients to "jump up" in the morning, gingerly make their beds, and so forth, so that the brain will respond, "Hey, we must be happy and energetic!"(Braiker 2001) The instituting of care policies here promises little pain, but tremendous gain.

Here we have automatic and unconscious forces doing the work of character development for us. Learning to care, then, is not an exercise in sweat and tears, like dieting or working one's way up the corporate ladder, rather it is relatively easy to accomplish.

Un-Caring Is No Slouch Either as an Asset in Business

There are a group of managers and supervisors who find that being tough and being feared for ruthlessness are delicious pleasures. "I'm not someone to mess with, and everybody knows it." They're reliable protections as well for one's turf and career. Granted, uncaring can work, and some people may have a flair for it. Risking that feared reputation for the sake of feely-touchiness is anything but a pleasure for such folks, if it's even possible: the last thing a shark wants others to think is that s/he is toothless, an old softy or pushover.

Yet from a care ethical view, there are faulty assumptions at work here, just as when we assumed changing habits was difficult in practice. Fear seems the best deterrent only when not compared to more sustainable, long-term alternatives. Care is not a failure to exercise other strengths or competences well—intimidating ones—but a set of strengths and competences in itself, that nurture accountability and respect in different ways. But, more, care competences need not supplant other competences like being no-nonsense with co-workers, and demanding about what is required. They can work alongside. Obviously, showing significant concern for employees can get one taken more seriously than dressing them down, humiliating them in front of co-workers or "not suffering fools lightly" in general. Not suffering fools is a disability, not just a strength. (Some people can do it, why not you?) Using tough methods basically exposes us as fools, after all, of the petty tyrant variety, not deserving to be taken seriously except on the surface. We become threats. And how do people handle threats when there is an opening? Some parents hits kids to get them to "behave." Pre-school kids "use their words" to do so, with peers. Who's the more able manager?

Few seem interested in nailing a caring colleague even in retaliation for a past offense. Being a "bastard" makes one a target, setting on a perch, to be schemed against, knocked off, and then preyed upon by a workforce turned to vultures. Although being a feared "Godfather" can work in many business contexts, being an admired leader, a respected and admired colleague, and perhaps even a beloved boss may work a good deal better. My consulting at many firms seems to paint this picture. Admittedly, your experience may be different and superior. Success can come in many forms, including incompetence. But traditional authoritarians at work also are in general the last to change when others are open to it. Authoritarianism and resistance to change are part of the same mindset. And this stance of stubborn authoritarianism seems a road to doom in modern business culture.

Practicality

Caring is arguably more about people skills than ethical capabilities. Empirical research (Gilligan 1982) and, ironically, criticisms of caring as an ethic (Kohlberg et al. 1983) both support this argument. This obviously recommends care strongly to management in itself, rendering care's ethical externalities pure gravy. Care was at first termed "relationality" or "relational caring" with the "ethical" left out. But its "being good with people" works both ways, ethically too. And this also makes care a far more proven ethical approach than all of its theory-derived alternatives. Nothing can match that "on the market" because nothing was designed to. The most popular ethical views were designed not for how we act, but how we *should* act, and fail to. They are "ethically distinctive," meaning they counter pose themselves to the practical or personally "interested," aiming to push back these dubious "temptations." Doing business would be one of these temptations.

Care is one of the rare non-distinctive ethics. It derives from a tradition that asks, "If being ethical is not the best way to act, period, why should it be preferred to amoral or immoral activities that succeed?" Doing good business, and doing good business well, must include ethical excellence or ethics is simply not excellent here, and should be overlooked. One business volume after another, however, takes the opposite, traditional perspective, putting ethics in the way of high productivity and profit. The recent *Good Value: Reflections on Money, Morality and an Uncertain World*, by banker Stephen Green, Chairman of HSBC, highlights this opposition from the first sentence forward. How in the world can anyone sell this ethical stuff? What's the pitch? Do what doesn't work well? What hampers the basic aims of the organization and enterprise? Have I got a product for you!

But the gentle tones and tender sensibility of care are equal parts pragmatism and staunchness. (This is partly what their feminist connections are about.) Care is pro-ideals, but not idealistic in an airy sense. As it does not require sacrificing for others nor forego reciprocity—return on caring investment. Care is committed to not letting others take advantage of it. It is aware and opposed to doormat syndrome, offering its key offset: "balancing self-care with care for others."

Ironically, benevolence has gotten a bad rap in theory, that is belied in practice. Even working at soup kitchens principally means making soup, not "saving the poor and destitute." (Then you clean up together.) Feeding the world's hungry, even up close and personal, means loading canned goods onto trucks, or driving the trucks, or unloading and opening the cans with a can opener. Or it means paying others to do these not very difficult things, via donations. All real work is practical, useful, including ethical work. And ethical work is judged primarily by its results, not its intentions. Mother Teresa carried water, cleaned gurneys, changed diapers, and made baby formula all day long. She delivered it with a loving smile, yes, but didn't sit around conveying anguished sympathy or beatific facial expressions. "If a man is hungry you give him a piece of bread" (Petrie and Petrie 1986).

Ethics of a business-opposing sort is not just a hard sell, it should be greeted as a "no sale" by any business that has its head screwed on right. Countenancing such ethics would put firms at odds with the very purpose of their pursuit. No wonder "window-dressing" is the role assigned them for their utopian purposes.

Accenting the Feminine?

"Business" and "management" have been discussed so far in traditional male terms. Over the decades (centuries?), women employees have accommodated to those terms and, more recently, added some new and better terms. But care is not primarily an ideology designed to promote a feminine approach to business, or to anything else. In fact it has attracted criticism from feminist writers for reinforcing traditional sexist stereotypes (Senchuk 1990) and for over-generalizing the outlook of white middle-class women, primarily, to women of color, working class immigrants and the like (Toinette 1990). (I am one of care's most virulent and sustained critics, incidentally (Puka 1993) but I'm still able to make its practical case here, despite its conceptual flaws—it's that good. And I found its strength chiefly in practice.)

Caring was originally described as a "female ethic" because the shortfalls researchers noticed in the moral problem-solving of male subjects and how it was compensated for by female subjects. It found these shortfalls, however, primarily because females were so under-represented compared to males in research samples. As research continued, the data showed both males and females using care strategies, and to good effect. (The same holds for non-empirical accounts of care, drawn from common observation.) Females tend to use more care largely because they are socialized to do so in most cultures, being accorded the roles of caretaker and child-rearer. Male socialization, by contrast, actually inhibits care development. In fact, males are socialized to denigrate female skills and sensibilities as weak, passive, indecisive and over-emotional: unfit for the workplace. (This outlook dominated recent confirmation hearing for Supreme Court Justice Sonya Sotomayor, when President Obama had the "effrontery" to suggest that compassion with real people's concerns was a desirable trait in a judge. Glenn Beck attributed empathic tendencies to the Nazi "final solution.")

Caring is a cross-gender ethic. For males, it represents the "other-half" of human skill denied them—their "better half" in a sense. And where women have been unwittingly blessed with care by sexism, males can overcome their reverse-sexist debilities by strengthening what care sensibilities were allowed them. Here "exploiting" female business potential is crucial. The current business arena still pressures women to play traditional male roles in traditional male ways, *Damned If I Do, Damned If I Don't, Nice Girls Don't Get the Corner Office 101* (Dindia and Canary 2006). This is a hackneyed plot in sexism—using a male standard as the objective or factual standard for any enterprise. It minimizes the participation and would-be contribution of businesswomen. A care ethic empirically shown to utilize female excellences and skills promises to remedy this sizable inefficiency.

Bullish at Work, Clueless at Home

One's of care's greatest tests at work is dealing with "big-idea" men" in executive positions, bent on "shaking things up." Care shines at parrying this "bull in a china shop" syndrome." BCS is the female-recognized phenomenon of new (male) managers coming into a firm, bent on making their mark through sheer bravura and "know-it-all-ness." They set out to change everything without getting much information on anything first, especially what already works and what is essential to existing corporate culture. The only listening they do is prelude to proving others wrong. Such managers dominate every social meeting with tales of past business exploits, and stubbornly push and hold their ground despite all indications that their style is alienating and disruptive. Do you see yourself here, or someone you work under?

Applying crude slash and burn tactics to a delicate parsing project, wracking havoc on the employees who actually do the work and know how the organization runs, is not care's way, even if it appears to work. Care avoids scars, bad feelings, resentments or resignations in key people because it is both humane and efficient, avoiding the "office is down" time needed to absorb blows and clean up the mess. Of course, this doesn't prevent the next assault and wasted time of educating a new incoming blowhard, movers-and-shaker in organizational dynamics. Installing caring office practices, would, however.

Female caring is well-versed on BCS because female "secretaries" are more impacted by it than the "golden boys" causing it. Women are still the greater percentage of underlings, and a practical ethic must be in the know and savvy in dealing with whatever comes, especially in a subordinate position. In harm's way, caring neither confronts nor defers to bullying strategies. Neither does it mimic the beta-male tactic of buttering up the boss. Caring has spine, but usually shows it in subtle ways—by deftly leaning to the side, letting the storm blow by, rechanneling it (tai chi style) so that it unwittingly blows in better directions, modeling more effective strategies and their results and carrying them on beside imposed ones. Its resolve searches out mutually beneficial partnership among opposing sides. It gets movers-and-shakers, and actual doers on the same side of the table, externalizing the problems caused by one of them and working on it together. Rather than digging its heels against, care affirms those traditional (male) strategies that work, and works to complement them, compounding their effect. Care is a partner ethic by nature, not a helpmate, but equal partner. The spectacularly successful "Getting to Yes" strategies are "care-lite" by comparison, suggesting how much farther care can go. After striking accords, with smiles all around, it seeks out the hosts of lingering resentments and dissatisfactions that "yes-yes" can mask, letting them air out, not simmer.

What care can do in the office is more than matched by its performance after hours. Care serves as a revelation at home for male employees and employers, and a salvation for female counterparts. This is especially true for males who've taken to the old or new machismo they have been fed continually by the media—in school hallways, in locker rooms and bars. "What do women want?" Care is what women want. It is one of the best depictions of women's gender orientations available, in a nice tidy package. Notions about women being inscrutable, unable to be figured out are dissipated by care understanding in one fell swoop, along with the follow-up notion, "Can't live with them, can't live without them." Women are caring, this is what should be figured out, and they can be easily lived with if a one sometimes thinks relationally, not egocentrically—being attentive, listening carefully, dialoguing, working to make the relationship better and closer, using the relationship to address issues faced together, seeking consensus, not victory, not looking for clear answers in absolute terms in order to walk away from the struggle and have a beer.

To the most obnoxiously rhetorical, male-to-male question, "Do you want to be right or married?" care poses better questions, "Do you only wish to be right, and at any cost—to win your point for your side, even when there is no point to doing so but creating bad feeling and alienation each other?" Might you not wish to peer through your smugness and confrontation at times to see whether your partner is even playing your game, contesting your point, resting on the other side of anything?"

Nuts and Bolts

Care at Work

Now that we've sung its praises, we focus on how care functions. The following case-applications provide enough information for you to experiment on your own. Its seemingly minor steps are most detailed here to capture care's subtlety and contrast to typical ethical approaches. Though formatted in steps, care is not merely a recipe, but something like an orientation to the kitchen, the cooking equipment, the feel for food needed to carry off an excellent meal. It orients its user to caring ways of seeing and reacting. These are interdependent. The order chosen for them here, while flexible, has a logic to it.

Care's main features can be listed as a set of dos and don'ts.

DOs: Taking a relational (not separated) orientation toward others, showing attentiveness (listening, observing), natural (spontaneous) response to what is observed, engaging response-abilities—dialoguing, empathizing, building relation where possible, also using the relation established to address issues (to problem-solve), negotiating toward consensus, showing understanding and compassion-toward-need or concerns, sharing positives and aspirations, helping, supporting, nurturing or empowering, reaching accommodation.

Continuing Resolves: Concentrating on not hurting or harming, on balancing self-care with other-care, on being flexible and tentative (more than decisive or unilateral), on thinking on a continuum of better and worse, (not right versus wrong) and on seeking shades of gray (not black-and-white answers). These resolves guide every step of the way.

DONT'S: Coming into a situation set on one's position beforehand, pre-judging and being judgmental, dismissive, personally aloof, and over-assertive—being strongly interventionist and unilaterally so (imposing one's will, one's outlook). Avoid blaming, being calculative, formulaic or legalistic in decision making, or righteous and inflexible.

Rights and Responsibilities: In making ethical judgments, it is especially crucial not to use rights as clubs against others or conceive responsibilities automatically as burdens to restrictions place on people. These are moralistic or Puritanical features of traditional ethics that make it a punitive, "gotcha" enterprise, not an inspiring one. They are themselves ethically questionable, harboring a view of humanity's inherent sinfulness or animality that seems unjustified by psychological research or history.

Taylorist Concerns. This list of "don'ts" characterizes certain dominant approaches in management—the vestigial offspring of Taylorist authoritarianism. Their success cannot be ignored, nor their hold on some minds. As noted above, however, these ("pre-pre-school") methods can be seen for present as likely less able interpersonal skills, a problem if we presume that managers should strive toward excellence. Pushing people works where a manager has great power and his supervisees are sheepish, but not well elsewhere or over time, with exceptions. The concrete care applications here should be able to back this relative assessment.

Ethically, pushing people around fails sufficiently to grasp their radical difference from objects and tools in being able to shape and take responsibilities for their own work projects. Thus it is also less able to call out and utiliize the full productive potential of employees.

Three Directives: (a) Carers need not apply every step of care to every problem. (Because every care-giver differs in their caring experience or ability, it is understandable that they may stop at different points along care's path.) (b) Caring occurs by degrees of more and less, better and worse. (c) Not caring "to the max" is not wrong, blamable or shameful and need not be avoided.

Performance Evaluation: Care only expects us to do what we can, the best we can in a particular situation. It does not abide by some external evaluation standard as right and wrong does. The fact that we are trying to care shows that we are moving in an admirable direction. With time and practice, we are likely to go farther, getting better. Why this happens is not primarily because we must, because we are under company obligation or provided incentives. It is because we wish to—because people tend to do what they are good at, preferring what they are best at. They get maximum satisfaction from a job very well done, as was known since Aristotle. This is a very important motivational difference between skill or virtue ethics and a should or obligation ethics. Employees demand (extra) pay for "have-tos." Obligation ethics require, care enables; obligation ethics sanction, care ethics equips. Managing care in the workplace should follow suit.

The Steps of Care

To err is human, to blame someone else shows management potential.

Relational Perspective: Adopt a (Moral) Point of View that Emphasizes our Connection and Interdependence with Others Rather than our Distinctness from Them

The first step of caring concerns outlook and sets the perspective needed for all the rest. For some (who define themselves in relation to others) this "step" has already been taken spontaneously, and frames their outlook toward other people. Those of us who are not such "relational types" must consciously adopt this outlook, alongside our spontaneously individualized one, until relationality becomes habitual. Research shows that everyone has both perspectives available to them. But males and male psychological types tend to be more spontaneously "individualistic." We define ourselves in contrast to other people, distinguishing ourselves by our special accomplishments, beliefs and values.

Moms generally see themselves within their family, relative to their children and their spouse. (Traditional) males see themselves as living their lives and then "acquiring" a job, wife, and family along the way. (Ever play "The Game of Life?"). But good "dads," as opposed to "fathers," become moms in outlook.

Individualized perspectives speak ethics as follows: "Do I want to get involved here or not? Actually, this is none of my business (fault), and not really my responsibility. If I choose to jump in, might I be sorry later?" (One can see why concepts like individual rights and "getting one's due" serve this perspective. They protect one's privacy and freedom to refuse.)

The caring perspective starts out involved, at least potentially. It leans automatically in the direction of getting involved, which feels like merely actualizing potential relation. Other people's concerns are care's concerns to an extent. This is because others are not really inherent strangers—are not really "other" to us; neither are strangers "strange." We are connected. We are moral familiars, but for our not yet having been introduced. When someone approaches us, or their situation somehow calls out to us, to "not get involved" is actually to "sever" relation and existing connection.

Why should we see things this way? The answer is partly that ethics, like business faces facts. Not to see our relationality is to ignore half of our social reality. But also, if we look at things relationally, factual or not, caring predicts, things will work out better. Interpersonal relations and their ethical qualities will be handled more artfully. Why is relationality the "other half" of our social truth? Look around. Move around. Consider how much that you are looking at, standing on, using was your doing——made by you. Turn on the lights, get a glass of water from the tap. It's all produced and provided by others, as what you do provides others.

Practicality

Obviously, it is not going an extra mile simply to regard people as connected to us, and feel that we are not uninvolved at our own office, and righteously so. The same is true for the next step, being attentive. More, everyone need not get constantly involved in everyone else's situation at work or elsewhere. Being reasonable and realistic, care sees that there are far more people than we can directly care for even in small-scale situations. Some are closer to each other than others—closer to others than to us—and more apt to reach out. They're in a better position to do so as well, and other expect them to. So rarely must we jump in also to help.

In addition, there's always a balance to strike between self-care and other-care. It may be unduly tipped if we are too other-directed. Striking many balances is part of reasonable living. These are among one's response-abilities in caring—care's abilities to respond.

Case Application

You hear someone tell a co-worker at the desk next to you that the boss is hopping mad about something s/he did. And you know that the employee is new, young and therefore extremely intimidated. A relational orientation pulls you to say something reassuring to buck the employee up. At the least you look over, signaling that you are available to them so that if they wish to vent, you can listen and then react. What you avoid is to lead by offering an opinion. "Here is what I would do." It's not about you; even helping them is not about you. But here's the relational rub, it's not about them either. It's about "us," or an "us" on the way to becoming. That involves the person who carried the tale as well.

If not approached by the co-worker, a caring person might ask a question, making sure the co-worker isn't hesitant to seek help because s/he thinks it would be an intrusion on you. "Did that worry you? I can't believe s/he blurted that out about the boss." The carer then attends to what the co-worker answers, and responds to that, perhaps with another question. The idea is to let the other person express his or her worries. Caring volunteers an ear.

Say the co-worker goes to the boss and takes his medicine, then returns from the corner office with tales of threats made by the boss or blame being shifted to the co-worker unfairly, by another employee. Now we might be seriously tempted to intervene. That's a consequence of a relation being established. But a caring intervention would start only by supplying context for the co-worker: "That's how this place works sometimes I'm sorry to say. I've been there." The problem is not about you, but the co-worker. You're there to care, and in supplying context here, the carer responds to the person's reactions and feelings, not really trying to convey something about "the place" per se. (Notice that someone not taking the relational perspective might go off on a long tangent about the place and past events as if that were the point, it happens all the time.)

What represents a sensible intervention beyond this response, depends on you and the context. The key is that doing nothing, remaining silent, keeping one's head down is not an option for care. That would be actively turning away. And that's not what someone in relations to someone does, even to avoid the hot water they are in. But how far need care's relationality go? There's no way to say in general. As in any art, practice and experience reveals such answers. Perhaps the exchange of a few words, even a concerned look is involved, and that's the end of it. If caring more would be a real burden at that moment, we consider stopping, even if going a bit farther would be better in some abstract sense—abstracted from who we are, and how things are in the situation. It wouldn't be better for *us*, perhaps, so why is it automatically better if it's better for them? Here is where you are up to on the caring road. Becoming more able will get you farther, as will getting better at your job skills and career.

Attentiveness: Stop, Look and Listen. Put your Observational Powers in Gear and Don't Miss a Trick

We spoke above of listening carefully to our co-worker. That already gets us into the second care step, attentiveness. While attentiveness comes naturally to relational types, just about everything but comes naturally to individualized types. This includes thinking we're attending when we are not.

As noted, offering one's opinions and advice from the get go comes naturally to the individualist type—"If I were you I'd . . ." In the face of an injustice done someone, you might be tempted to act in their behalf, or at least to judge the situation the way you see it. This is not care's way; caring does not take someone's situation away from them, even to help. (But of course, care doesn't expect anyone to go *only* care's way.) To care, it's not even what happened or what is going to happen in the situation that counts most, it's what'd happening in the person you're connected with, and in the connection. At most one partners, making the other's situation partly "our" situation. Having made real connection should naturally lead to paying attention—letting the apparent victim vent, perhaps, in our co-worker case, or inviting them to do so, neither judging nor taking control. We don't actually *know* the real situation, do we, when you think about it? We've heard about second or third-hand others' interpretation of it. Our situation is how the apparent victim is reacting to it.

Attentiveness is how we *gather information*, mostly about the object of our attention. It may show us that the problem is not what it appears, not how it is being relayed to us. Attentiveness is also a *showing of respect and concern* in itself. It's not brushing someone off, but taking time to focus on their concerns, deeming them important enough to occupy our awareness. In any context, however, this simple courtesy may have to be put off due to the rigors of a busy schedule at work. But wanting to devote one's attention can be communicated. One can set a later time, soon, for actually doing it. Showing attention also further realizes or *builds the relation* between you two. You may not desire more of a relation with this particular person, and that's fine. This is another thing one can learn by simply focusing, without distraction—"I don't like this person, we don't hit it off."

Case Application

In the present instance, you may find that the co-worker only needs to vent their worries or sense of betrayal, and there's no need for you to do anything further. Congratulations, you've solved an ethical problem.

You may find that you're dealing with a complainer, and you may not want to become their ongoing confidant, conspiring in this whining approach to work. You might find that the co-worker is grossly misinterpreting what happened. With a few clarifications you can help them disperse the problem in their mind. You two solved it together, here you get an assist. The co-worker may seem to be asking for advice from you, but doesn't really want it. Being attentive helps one notice that—to notice that they never listen or respond to any advice you offer. Or it may be possible to give valuable advice that helps them make fewer mistakes in future, including trusting the co-worker who made them look bad. Much can be accomplished here by simply noticing, and spicing it up with a little dialogue in response. Twenty seconds, and case closed. How hard was that? You also likely have won a supporter in the process, also enhancing your office reputation. Credit caring.

Have you ever stood talking to someone about something important to you whose face showed their mind scanning many ideas in their head at the same time, eyes darting everywhere at passerby, fidgeting, hiking up their pants or skirt, brushing their hair back from their forehead or ears? Hopefully they're not texting simultaneously. You may see clearly that they are following the thread of the conversation in some sense. But they are not paying attention; they are not paying attention to *you*! A caring person stops, turns to you, looks unswervingly, and observes, filling their awareness with you and putting other thoughts to the side. That's the Caring version of attention, excellence or artfulness in attention. And this "full" attention can make all the difference in practice. Do you know someone who does this with you? They turn and devote their whole mind to you? That reaction can even make you feel, "Why did I even mention this matter, it's not important enough to even have this friend focus on I now see." We can solve problems with a steady glance.

Natural Response: Let Your Emotions and Thinking Go, Unrestricted, Reacting in Whatever Way They Wish, Calling Up Associations, Past Experiences Without Judging their Appropriateness

What you observe, when being really attentive to someone, sets off a range of inner responses off, some of which we rarely notice. The attentiveness shown above to the co-worker should now go to yourself as well, noticing these reactions. Noticing, but not judging, at least not out of the box. Whether what we observe says something bad about the co-worker or produces a good reaction in us, perhaps saying something generous about ourselves that surprises us, our natural response usually does not come with an evaluation. It is simply a set of experience with information to convent, with lessons to teach us. It offers suggestions about what to do next, if anything, and about how to in a caring and responsible way next.

Case Application

You may feel sympathetic to this co-worker. But you may feel angry also, that they were blamed unfairly, or that they are taking it lying down. By contrast, you may feel suspicious about whether the apparent victim may actually be pointing fingers at others, not the other way around. Maybe they really are the one to blame, only claiming that they are being blamed unfairly. You may feel very impatient with the way they talk about their dilemma, perhaps in a whiny, over-resentful way. Or they may bluster about it without thinking about it—"They not going to get away with this." Over time they may constantly make such threats about this or that but never carry through. And this may make you sorry you talked to the co-worker in the first place.

Our pre-caring conscience will jump to judgment at this point, getting down on us for these negative feelings and may urge self-recrimination. Care does the opposite. If you're feeling negative or impatient, watch out, care remarks inside: this may be warning you against getting involved, for better or worse. You may say something to worsen the situation if you try to involve yourself further, something you'll regret. End it here, extricate yourself.

Suppose you have all sorts of tender responses, compassionate feelings, a desire to help. Those can be especially helpful for caring. But past experience may warn you that you're over-sensitive to other's situations, blowing everything up into a big problem. Or by trying to help, you typically disempower others, interfering with their helping themselves. All of this gets taken into account when thinking of the caring response to make, if any. This is another way that care is to practical. It doesn't blame for thought crimes and doesn't expect you to just ignore or overcome them, as if this were really possible.

Let's switch things around. Assume that you were the one called on the carpet, finding that you were apparently blamed by a different co-worker for a mistake they made. But also, you're not sure if it was them or you. Your natural response is defensiveness perhaps ("Who are they to say ... it's just not true that ... the boss just believed them before ..."), You may also feel resentment, anger against the boss and the other co-worker. Perhaps a little fear or anxiety mixes in ("I'm on the boss's bad side now") with a little self-blame ("I screwed up again") and a sense of resolve ("That was fair criticism, I can do better"). You may have other feelings you can't put into words, a knot in your stomach or, chaos, and conceptual reactions that you realize are rationalizations. Caring attends to each, considering what they might signal and teach. We always have time to judge them later on.

Responsibility and Knowhow: Time to Act, Meaning to React, Most Likely. We Now Use Our Particular Reactions in This Situation, Relevant Prior Information and Past Lessons in Our Personal Experience and Observation, Along with Our Knowhow to This Point. Responsibility Is Not Born, or Taken on—It Is Response-Ability, Exercising Our Abilities to Respond

Other ethics tell us to do the right thing at this point, perhaps guided by a precept or rule, fulfilling the obligations it sets—treat them the way we'd like to be treated, engage the right virtue—honesty, prudence or forgiveness. Care bids us to react out of our natural reactions, selecting those that fit conventions of caring behavior—supporting, showing concern, helping—guided by all the other factors in how, and how much to show them. This process occurs in a flash. It is rarely reflective or deliberative. To us it seems like going with our gut or following our intuitions. We know ourselves, we have developed habits—knowhow—and a readiness to care. We have social conventions and observations at hand for how care is shown, and a readiness to care among other reactions. And of course we "never walk alone." Caring partners with those related to, which is handy if one carries a significant load. Certainly there hasn't been any load to speak of so far.

This implicit integration process may seem as murky and indecisive as "problem-solving" can get. What is the guarantee that it will be caring, or good? There is no guarantee only a likelihood, just as there is with being fair or respecting someone's rights, which we always can get out of by rationalizing justifications. The truth is, though, that there are many ways to go, each equally fine. And the issue is how *you* should act (with those related to you) in this particular situation at this time. It is not how "one" should act in general in situations of this sort. Nonetheless, care is not a situational or relativist ethics. It merely ties to context and the realities of our moral development, also the reality that we are affected by what we do, both in its effects and in the doing of it. The person acting can only do what is ethically sensible for *her* at this time, to the best of her caring ability. We all make our contribution. And we don't have to make the ideally right contribution to each person in each situation all the time.

Case Application

If we were called on the carpet we may be tempted to run from the boss's office right to the offending co-worker and confront him—perhaps in front of others. As a co-worker, we may yearn to do that same favor for the egregiously wronged new guy, after his chewing out. Alternatively, we may vow a vendetta—"He just made a very big mistake and he'll pay . . . all in good time" my pretty. (These are traditional macho approaches.) By contrast, we may be the sort of person who feels mortally wounded, either by being betrayed or seeing a co-worker betrayed. We're already composing e-mails in our head asking, "How could you do that to me?" confessing our hurt, or bringing in some home-baked cookies the next day for the new guy to share.

If we have our relational perspective and attentiveness in gear, however, we'll more likely notice that we've heard nothing from the co-worker who supposedly turned on us or the new guy. The boss may have found out through a different source, or made up the tale of your mistake to see if we would affirm it. There may have been a third "party" involved that caused this—a video or e-mail monitor. If the other co-worker did say something that seemed to shift the blame, we don't know why. But what's for sure is that going to someone with presuppositions about what they did is not the most able way to function in (potential) relationship, or to build relationship. In fact, it's a good way to fracture a relation, working against it, creating enemies to boot. Caring gives us pause. Such responses are not able, given the relationality of our perspective and aims of relationships in later care steps.

If we're angry, and perhaps legitimately so, we need to vent. But is it best to vent on someone at a particular place and time that anger chooses? Not likely. We know better than that. We may know something additional about ourselves, that we're not good at getting rid of anger. We also tend to be very judgmental. Once we target someone as an enemy, we never seem to get over it. So, at the least, care might recommend, "It's time for lunch," or a very brisk walk outside with very loud music playing on our iPod. Once properly "chilled" we decide, "Okay, that's done, time to schedule a little talk with so-and-so to get to the bottom of this." How should such a talk go? Answer: first, relationality, then attentiveness—listening more than talking—then natural response, and so forth.

What about while we are on the carpet, if we were called in, or if we decided to accompany the new guy for his chewing out? A notable Clark Gable line may come to mind while watching the boss's lips move, "Frankly my dear, I don't give a damn." I've said this endless times though I'm not sure a carer can ever say, I just don't care, unless it's meant as a distracter from doing something worse—tirading back. Caring values militate for making points more civilly. Once off the carpet, on which you bit your tongue, sage words may occur to you that could have stopped the boss in his tirading tracks, sapping the yell out of him. It's too late now, but Care files these for use next time.

Dialogue and Empathy: Engage in Conversation that Involves Genuine Inquiry and Mutually Self-Expressive Exchange, Aimed to Elicit Mutual "Feeling with" Each Other and Your Situations

Dialogue is what people do in relationships—getting a feel for where the other person is at the moment, where they are coming from, and working things out. Dialogue is a more explicit, tangible form of mutual attentiveness that invites further attentiveness. And as attentiveness, it is also a form of respect—taking the time and energy to engage. Dialogue can gather as much, or more information about a situation than listening or observing, especially if conducted artfully. To be avoided is a trading of non-mutual self-expressions—I think this, well I think this other—familiar to *Seinfeld* viewers. ("I think I'll go down the coffee shop," says George, "Where did I get this mark on my arm?" says Kramer in "response.") More, dialogue can help us check on whether we are perceiving the situation correctly, or as our conversant does. This helps us put ourselves in her or his shoes. But more, it helps us feel for her, or share his reaction, as s/he experiences it. Honestly, when we talk things out with someone we also learn what we think as well—what we didn't know we thought until we said it. Dialogue also lets us try out different ways to feel.

Caring dialogue selects among natural responses to capture primarily caring ones. (Again, we generally know the difference, no ethics education required. Being sarcastic, putting people on the spot—these are not among them. By contrast, inviting others to vent, offering encouragement and support, these care, boosting relation, beneficial reciprocity and the like.) Still context is crucial. Some people like when others lay it on the line, and find "looking out for their feelings" condescending. Sharing comments over pizza together may work like a charm, by comparison, guaranteeing empathic like-mindedness. "Can you believe the sauce they put on this?" And it can avoid unprofessional intimacy in the work setting. Empathy is like sharing the same idea or belief with someone, but with experiences or emotions. It need not involve painful emotions, suffering, need and the like, or the sharing of verbal tears—Ohhhh, that's so terrible for you dear." Sometimes learning to share someone's joys is more important.

Typical dialogue styles reveal troublesome gender differences. As females often see it, the male tendency is to intervene actively through words, addressing a problem by handling it for themselves and others in one swoop. They're typically surprised when accused of imposing their view and solution, since they assume that anyone would find their decision the right one, objectively. Traditionally males don't actually dialogue, but tell. While others speak (females especially) they wait impatiently, not really listening, for an opening to tell. If not agreed with they respond by defending or bolstering their position or attacking the alternative. Studies show that women tend to ask questions more, to give and take responsively. Men often feel grilled by such questioning and stymied by talking around a problem, not solving it. Both genders can engage in conversation that carries on separate lines of thought. Talking past each other comes in endless varieties compared to the real give and take of sharing.

Caring empathy suffers even more from gender differences. We are all familiar with cognitive role-taking (putting ourselves in another's place). It involves conceptualizing how someone else is thinks about a situation, then trying to conceptualize it that way oneself. Unfortunately, we often simply overlay our own perspective on another's, imagining how we'd think in their position and thus putting ourselves there. "Feeling with" someone is quite different, usually occurring spontaneously, no mental acrobatics involved. We perceive an apparent feeling, and our heart goes out to the person, seeming to reproduce the feeling involved. My male students have found it very difficult to fully grasp the distinction, but once they do some note, "If that's what empathy is, I'm not sure I ever felt it." Many feminists find that scary, especially given the male tendency toward violence at home and in the conference room—verbal warfare between two male lawyers, for example.

If a mother sees her child get injured, or another mother hear her tell of it, she literally winces in pain. Some fathers show a like empathy when feeding an infant; the father's lips move as if he were taking the food in himself. But women's experience with the phenomenon starts early in life and continues through adolescence and adulthood. "You got your hair streaked, he proposed? I'm so excited." "You didn't get the job? Oh my God Elli, that's horrible." A popular beer commercial plays on the sex difference, showing a woman's female friends celebrating her enormous clothing closet in a new house, only to be matched by male friends of the husband sharing emotional ecstasy over his new "beer closet." While sexist, it's funny because men don't share joy that way. Caring empathy works hand and hand with cognitive role-taking when solving problems. This is one of the most crucial ways caring complements other approaches.

Case Application

What do we say in our different case scenarios to promote dialogue and empathy, or to show it? Previously we considered offering words of support to comfort our novice co-worker. Such words aren't particularly meant for dialogue. They'll often get a simple "Thank you" in return. But if the co-worker is upset, they can make for a fine opening. (The words we'd choose for a male versus female co-worker might be different, for better or worse.) Saying, "I heard the boss yelling at you, you should have told him off," or "You should have just walked out on him" does not do it. They judge and give post-hoc advice, to no purpose but self-expression. Still, if we're the type of person that shoots off our mouth in this way, it could be a conversation starter. "You're right, I wish I could have yelled back or walked out, but the guy intimidates me." The two of you then talk from there. A better way to get conversation going, as our own knowhow tells us, is to key in on the unspoken concerns of the co-worker, "So that must have been real pleasant for you. Nothing like a monthly chewing out to boost morale, eh?" This opens the opportunity to vent while also seeking some light in the tunnel. "Ah, so I'm not the only screw-up?" "No, not at all, let's see, how many times did I get my turn on the carpet."

Imagine opening dialogue with the boss, before his tirade really gets going. How about this starting line? "I think you're right. And I'd bet you don't want to waste your time dealing with these screwups. I'd also rather avoid being lamed any more than I've been blaming myself all week. So can we figure a way for me not to screw this up in future? Obviously I want to do the best job I can and give you what you need. I try, and it should work. Why isn't it, what's getting in the way?" That could work for starters, even if his response was "You're stupidity and incompetence" is getting in the way" or "You're supposed to figure that out, not me." It sometimes helps to go heavier on the pain and punishment component, clarifying how much you deserve it. (Notice how we feel shortchanged when a public official merely apologizes for a mistake, or a national leader apologizes 100 years later for, say, slavery or genocide, to descendants of the victims.)

In a prison course I once taught, inmates posed opening remarks for dialogue, then played the position of those that they were talking to. It was a revelation to them to see how often their previous remarks "pissed them off" as listeners. "No wonder we're always getting into fights," several noted, "we have a knack for provoking and egging people on even without trying." Notice that care hasn't had much to say about ethics in particular during this step or the ones before. More skilled or effective dialogue generally turns out to be more respectful and caring dialogue as well. The more effective the dialogue, the more respectful and caring it is as well.

Enhancing Relations Through Care by Nurturing, Enabling, Directing Compassion Toward Need, Sharing Joy, Building Relations, and Striving for Justice

The next several steps of care—helping, supporting, building relationship—are further guides for how to dialogue caringly while providing companionship as well. Dialogical care is good company, a way to create intimacy, holding hands with words. Professional versions can include exchanging memos, revealing to a colleague where you bought that tie or those shoes. As social conventions and socialization provide so much guidance in these areas I'll offer only a few caring highlights here. Helping sounds like altruism, going out of one's way to aid others, often at one's own expense. But as noted earlier, regarding kind words, no expense at all may accrue. More than that, kindness can be seen as a fortunate conspiracy of self-interest. How do we show kindness but by catering to someone else's desires? And doing so usually brings reciprocation. Reciprocity seems to be a deep motivational law or "reflex" in our species, bolstered by bolstered by socialization and sanctioning (Cialdini 2001). In the work setting especially, failures to reciprocate earn a bad reputation and a certain degree of ostracism.

Support is easier to offer than aid. It requires little more than one's presence and verbal agreement. "Yes, you make a good point." "Right, they shouldn't have done that to you." It builds relationship, reputation, and alliance, promising reciprocity as well, but at lower cost. Still if we are allergic to whining, it might prove more toxic to our sensibilities than helping. This calls for know-how, learning to support then shut the door on more, without seeming abrupt.

Nurturance and empowerment take more skill. But it's rare that they will be needed. They're usually only appropriate with younger or novice co-workers, which bring personal rewards of feeling more in the know, and a mentor. Parents usually have plenty of experience and wisdom in these arts. But it's also easy to figure them out by watching others who are good at them. The same applies to showing sympathy or compassion, and sharing joy so long as we are not extremely competitive and envious people. If we are, time to skip a few steps, letting others provide. The main reason care emphasizes this joyful step is to lighten the woeful focus on compassion. "Not everything is a problem," as someone once said to me when I showed constant solicitousness.

Strengthening bonds of relationship is the next step of care, already advanced by all the foregoing steps. Why build bonds? Because they're good in themselves. Affiliation is one of our deepest needs, even if we are introverted and hermit-like in our personal style. Affiliation brings a sense of belonging, adding meaning to our activities, struggles and accomplishments. It is a guard against feeling alienated and lonely, even among co-workers, and is a source of fun and potential aid from co-workers when needed. But relationships are also crucial when solving our own problems. When problems and conflicts arise at work, being able to fall back on a history of relationship can help resolve them with surprising ease. "Look Tom, we've known each other for years, Have I ever...." "You can trust me, and you know it, remember that time when...." Every previous step of caring invests in relationship-building, and it's not for me to tell business people how crucial personal relationship is in most dealings with clients, suppliers and potential hirers should a job change seem necessary.

The ideal of justice is to render each what s/he deserves. Sometimes it involves having a neutral party decide on a fair distribution. The problem is that fair decisions often leave everyone dissatisfied due to the evils of compromise. Some are left seething by fair decisions feeling that their voice was heard, but then overridden—the wages of majority rule. On occasion, justice actually harms and seems to punish people though designed for the opposite. Care's overriding orientation is not to harm, physically, psychologically, and especially not ethically. Care finds it damning for other ethics that they cannot keep this pledge. This is why care aims at consensus, and uses relationship to achieve it. The key here is not simply to give everyone something, but to assure that no one leaves feeling resentful or ill-treated. Only relationship has the power to actually change what we want and what we're looking for in resolving a conflict. Once we change out interest, the need to compromise is gone. When people get on our side, in addition, they have a way of changing our mind. In relationships, when you give, you receive. Going with what others wish need not be a sacrifice, a giving up, but a moving up. That's what a relational perspective allows. Parents who love their children end up wanting (for themselves) what the children want, coming to identify with their children's welfare. This is the key to consensus, not some utopian hope of universal agreement on an issue despite near-universal conflict of wants.

Giant Strides

Some steps of care straddle the rest, guiding their direction as part of each. These are *not harming, acting contextually, making only tentative and flexible decisions (where possible) and making choices by shades of gray, not in black-and-white terms*. This often means aiming for better—not best, not right versus wrong. Again, I offer only highlights, distinctive of care.

Hurting and Not Hurting

Getting what you deserve, but only what you deserve, can be a deflating experience. Merit can be rated by output, but what about the effort you put in, working nights and weekends. What about the morale-building you've contributed and the overall loyalty you've shown the firm? To be fair, we say that hiring and firing should be based solely on qualifications. But what if a close friend and all-around nice guy is in competition with a brash newcomer who produces by stepping on toes? Won't the friend feel slighted, even misused if not preferred? Isn't that feeling legitimate whether it's considered fair in some abstract sense or not, whether other considerations conflict with it? Closer relations breed special responsibilities and legitimate expectations of preferred that care does not ignore. How to balance them with fairness is the issue, like balancing self-care with care for others.

Being show the greatest respect, or making the best business move, still may lack human concern or compassion. On the receiving end especially it can feel cold and aloof, even harsh. Consider how you feel when others tolerate you. Is it generally enough to be tolerated? Consider how you're kids feel when you react to their bickering over a play item, "Now neither of you gets to play with it. I told you that if you didn't share or take turns you'd lose your privileges; didn't you agree to that? "

Firing staff right before major holidays can be a shrewd business move that saves a lot more money than waiting. Holidays mean paying for zero productivity after all—an excuse to "pick a man's pocket every December 25th" as Scrooge put it. But it's cruel. At my Institute a senior vice-president won a business award for firing scores of support staff right before Winter holidays, earning the undying ire of the faculty. Caring is especially sensitive to pain caused even by the best of intentions or principles. It does all it can to mitigate it, even when there's no way to avoid causing it. Care moves gently, and gives hope as much as possible in such circumstances. At the very least it "shares your pain," which it would have avoided causing if it could. This show of empathetic humanity matters to people.

Care looks for ways to avoid confrontation, usually by pre-empting it, and sees this as a mutual strength, not personal weakness. Care tries to make others feel comfortable and well-treated, not pressured by having their feet constantly held to the fire. There are other ways to motivate people. If none seem better to us, the fault is likely a lack of imagination and ingenuity. Caring empathizes with the anxieties of potential employees at job interviews or current employees, come evaluation time. It helps employees foresee problems in the pipeline before they explode—company set-backs that may translate into lay-offs. For example, caring urges us to ask employees for their suggestions on how to deal with financial setbacks—would they prefer firings to furloughs or across the board cuts in salary to save jobs? It would promote and help facilitate employee dialogue on the matter as opposed to majority-ruled votes.

Caring cuts co-workers slack on occasion, doing a nice thing for someone whether they deserve it or not. A boss might say, "Just take a day off; it's obvious you're stressed." What's really the cost here? Obviously, exploiting others' vulnerabilities is not the caring approach. Nor are the other Samurai or Machiavellian tactics taught at some business schools, with the prime directive, "to win." But even in trying to out-compete a rival, one can find caring ways to relate without giving an inch.

Balancing Self and Other Caring

Caring is NOT about self-sacrifice or martyrdom, as other benevolence ethics are. This is one reason it is so practical and motivating. You have to look out for yourself. After all, you are a person too, with comparably legitimate interests, needs and aspirations. You shouldn't be any more un-caring to yourself than you'd be to others, and you shouldn't be un-caring to others. In fact, you have a special relationship to yourself—a most intimate one. And where there is special relationship there are special responsibilities and grounds to show preference. (Not all preference is bias.)

But there's a crucial distinction here. Caring takes looking out for one' *self*, literally, as opposed to one's interests alone. Interests usually have their own agendas, some of which are very dangerous and destructive to their possessors. To care for oneself goes beyond self-*interest*; it sees ourselves in the third person as well as the first. We should do ourselves favors, see to our comfort and safety, our *best* interests and longer term welfare. Our actual interests often push us around. Care doesn't. And it doesn't let us take ourselves for granted just because we're "doing it willingly" or "by choice." Choice under pressure—even the pressure of our own wants or ideals—is not always free, and not always ours.

Contextuality

Care bids that we approach every situation differently, also adjusting responsively to changing dynamics of the situation unfolds. Don't stick to the game plan if the game changes. Care recognizes however that other ethical themes may thrive on standing pat and staying the course, however. This may be obvious to a seasoned business negotiator. But it is a lesson many in business, (and business ethics) learn the hard way, if ever. Some of us adopt certain staid practices and policies—"Always go into a meeting assertively, firm handshake, get the," "It's all about power—who has it and how to get it." "Affirm everything someone contributes at the meeting before you say what's wrong with it, nodding and smiling—'Good point.' " This is why thousands of management books sell that start with a number—ten ways to close a deal, six ways to be promoted. Caring avoids a steadfast commitment to formulae.

Those who only know how to bull through a new situation, creating a splash, often leave one job situation after another, frustrated with the supposed "sluggishness" of the organization and its "incapacity to change." Those who focus on "doing the work" and "doing a good job" often are frustrated by their lack of promotion, caused by failing to promote their visibility to top management. One must finesse the balance between actual work and self-promotion. Caring finesses everything, but in an unusually genuine or authentic way.

Applied ethics show a dichotomy between tailoring general principles to concrete cases and deriving particular tenets from situational particulars. The latter approach must try to generalize its tenets somewhat to show that they are not arbitrary and relativistic. The former must make sure a situational choice fits its rationale despite the many peculiarities involved. Care's contextualism is of a different sort entirely because care ethics is a knowhow process, not a conceptual structure. Care engages different working strategies to produce certain types of effects. Its steps are used, reused, retooled, or dropped depending on the results of their implementation. The results yielded create new demands that other care components are employed to address. While care components, working together, form a theme each component only works on the particulars of the situation. In a particular case, some may never be called on despite being conceptually related to others. Not so with a general principle.

Flexibility and Tentativeness

Being decisive is especially prized in the business world. And there are certainly important places for it. Some things must be written in stone, if not blood, and strictly honored. Laws or contracts are not for bending. But there is a laughable arrogance in thinking we can know the right or best thing to do on any occasion and into the future. This is especially true if the policy relies on the prediction of future events or motivations. Care does not pretend that complex matters can be captured in simple rules and regulations. Being realistic requires being tentative and flexible. We have to foresee change, especially in our informal expectations of each other. Following rules and regulations, formulae, calculations, strict prohibitions and the like is for people who do not know how to be ethical. Because they have not learned how to respond and treat people carefully, they have to carry around a map, with explicit directions.

Caring Continua—Better and Worse

Even where we treat certain actions as wrong and intolerable, there are degrees of better and worse involved. Theft is less bad than rape, and rape is less bad than murder, though all three are incontestably wrong. (There are metaphors for all three crimes in business activities, often in cutthroat competition with other firms.) Also, pilfering office supplies or even embezzling a small amount of profits from one's company is less bad than Ponzi schemes.

As much as we'd like to judge actions in absolute terms, this is not a realistic conception. Actions don't occur in a vacuum. Why we do them—our personal situation at the time, the particular business context involved, and all sorts of unseen factors—shape our perception and action choice. As much as we'd like our choices to be "right on the money," they're more likely partly wrong, partly pro and partly con. This is another reason to be flexible and tentative in our choices. But it is also grounds for preferring a continuum to a dichotomy—better and worse.

In caring we aim at the higher end of this continuum. Why? Because we care; because we seek competence. But we're not likely to score much higher than usual for any instance, because we aspire to. "Have that report to me tomorrow morning, 8 A.M. sharp—no excuses." One can order anything, but increased pressure may not help the order get carried out. What's psychologically possible or likely isn't easily known. Care wishes us to do better each time. Still, it does not hold us to an absolute standard, seeing everything below par as unacceptable. Such caring toleration may allow some slacking. But it makes caring much more feasible, especially in an ethically unwelcoming environment. Absolute standards also allow slacking off. The report is there, but what's been hidden and left out unseen?

Take Away—Implementing Care

In my experience, a good way to start caring is to pick one step or small cluster of steps at a time. Relational perspective and attentiveness are my favorites. I believe the whole moral world can tilt 90 degrees on this turn. Watch, look, listen, try out, test, and practice these steps. We already care to some degree, in some contexts, research shows. Perhaps home life is our favored caring context. The task then is to build on what we already do, trying to make room for more caring in this much more systematic way, a step or two at a time, in the thicket of less-caring practices. Alerting ourselves to ways we commit the "don'ts" of care can be most helpful. I continually tried to highlight ways in which I wrongfully tend to judge at the outset, intervene instead of listening and partnering, and order instead of dialoging. It was a revelation, and a big help. Once implemented and practiced, progress on caring goes faster than one would expect.

References

Braiker, H. 2001. *Getting up when you're feeling down*, Part 4. Kirkwood, NY: Putnam Press.

Cialdini, R. 2001. *Influence: Science and practice*. New York, NY: Allyn and Bacon.

Dindia, K, and D. Canary. 2006. *Sex differences and Similarities in Communication*. Matwah, NJ: Laurence Earlbaum Press.

Gilligan, C. 1982. *In a different voice*. Cambridge, MA: Harvard University Press.

Green, S. 2010. *Good value: Reflections on money, morality and an uncertain world*. New York, NY: Atlantic Monthly Press.

Koh, H., and E. Boo. 2004. Organization ethics and employee satisfaction, commitment, and turnover. *Management Decision* 42 (5): 677–693.

Kohlberg, L., C. Levine, and R. Hewer. 1983. *Moral stages: A current formulation and response to critics*. Basel, Switzerland: Karger.

Meyers, D.C. 2005. *Social psychology*, chapters 4, 6. New York, NY: McGraw-Hill.

Noddings, N. 1984. *Caring—A feminine approach to ethics*. San Francisco, CA: California University Press.

Petrie, A., and J. Petri. 1986. *Mother Teresa* (documentary film).

Puka, B. (ed.). 1993. *Caring voices and women's moral frames*. New York, NY: Garland Publishing.

Senchuk, D. 1990. Listening to a different voice: a feminist critique of Gilligan. *Studies in Philosophy and Education* 10 (3): 233–249.

Sims, R., and K. Kroeck. 1994. The influence of ethical fit in employee satisfaction, commitment, and turnover. *Journal of Business Ethics* 13: 939–947.

Toinette, E. 1990. Sometimes I feel like a motherless child: The call and response for a liberational ethic of care by black feminists. In *Who cares? Theory, research, and educational implications of the ethic of care*, ed. M. Brabeck, 45–62. New York, NY: Praeger.

Van Veen, M., M. Krug, J. Schooler, and C. Carter. 2009. Neural activity predicts attitude change in cognitive dissonance. *Nature Neuroscience* 12 (11): 1469–1474.

Chapter 11
Bumfights and Care Ethics: A Contemporary Case Study

Matthew Brophy

Introduction

Dr. Phil, television host and psychologist, kicked a guest off his show in December, 2006. The guest was Ty Beeson, a producer of Bumfights: a DVD series depicting homeless "bums" engaging in degrading, violent, and dangerous acts—all for the amusement of video viewers. Clips include a homeless man paid a dollar to drink Windex. Others are given money to run head-first into walls, fight each other, have a tooth pulled out with pliers, eat a raw frog, set their hair on fire, among other dangerous and demeaning acts. The producers paid these homeless men a pittance: sometimes in cash, sometimes in food, sometimes in alcohol.

Exploiting the homeless has proven a lucrative business enterprise: Bumfights is the fastest selling independent video series to date. But is the Bumfights enterprise ethical? Our intuitions tell that there is something morally wrong with Bumfights as an entrepreneurial venture. Yet traditional business morality condones such homeless exploitation. Two parties freely and openly contract with one another. No one is directly coereced, deceived or defrauded. No one's negative rights are being violated. And the Bumfights producers could even defend their enterprise as a "win-win," as homeless participants might be benefiting from the transaction.

Bumfights represents a simple business case that exposes the moral myopia from which traditional business morality suffers—a morality predominantly focused on contracts and agreement. Such a narrow focus misses a world of ethical dimensions that we intuitively recognize. Care ethics, however, succeeds in keeping faith with our moral intuitions in such cases. The Bumfights case, as well as other more conventional cases in business ethics, evinces that care ethics is an essential addition to traditional business morality, to help cure its ethical blind spot.

To demonstrate care ethics as a critical supplement to traditional business morality, I will allude to a few well-known cases in the business ethics canon. Through the Bumfights case and these others, I will show that care must counterbalance

M. Brophy (✉)
High Point University, High Point, NC, USA
e-mail: mbrophy@highpoint.edu

M. Hamington, M. Sander-Staudt (eds.), *Applying Care Ethics to Business*, Issues in Business Ethics 34, DOI 10.1007/978-90-481-9307-3_11,
© Springer Science+Business Media B.V. 2011

contracts; vulnerability must counterbalance autonomy; and cooperation must counterbalance competition.

Overview of the Bumfights Case

Ryen McPherson (2002), a 22-year-old aspiring filmmaker, conceived of and co-produced with friends the first Bumfights video in 2001, "Bumfights: A Cause for Concern." They dubbed their company, "Indecline Films." The DVD sold for $19.95 off of their website. McPherson and his cohorts at Indecline, sold the rights for $1.5 million to two producers in Las Vegas, who have since produced three sequels. Bumfights is alleged to be the fastest-selling independent video series to date.

Bumfights showcases footage of homeless on the streets of San Diego and Las Vegas. One "star" of Bumfights, Rufus Hannah (aka "Rufus the Stunt bum"), recalls being paid $10 at the most for each stunt. His performed his first stunt after McPherson offered him $5 to run headfirst into a stack of milk cartons, outside of a grocery store. Rufus was later pushed in a shopping cart down a flight of stairs. Other stunts in the series include a homeless person jumping off a building into a dumpster, defecating on the sidewalk, getting "branded" with a Bum Fights tattoo, being severely spanked and hit with sex whips across the buttocks and genitals, and other demeaning and/or dangerous acts. Rufus recalls running hard into steel doors, which sparked his now chronic condition of epilepsy. Perhaps the most regretful of Rufus' stunts was the brutal fight with his best friend, also homeless, Donald Brennan, which broke Brennan's leg in two-places.

While might suspect that the Bumfights producers were acting illegally. The producers were acquitted of all criminal charges, except for staging an unlicensed fight. For this, they were sentenced to 250 hours of community service and 3 years of probation.

Business as Poker

Albert Carr's (1968) canonical article, "Is Business Bluffing Ethical?" promotes the metaphor of business as a game of poker. Autonomous individuals sit at the (business/poker) table together, where they compete and negotiate with each other. There are winners and losers at the business game, but there are no "victims," where one can claim to have been treated unjustly.

After all, like poker, business has its own set of moral rules: neither should not be unfairly condemned by the morality you find in church, have in your personal life, or are taught in kindergarten. For instance, in our ordinary life—say, in relation with our neighbors –we should be honest and cooperative: whereas in business—among competitors—"bluffing" is a morally accepted norm of competing in the business "game."

Unfortunately, this nearsighted poker metaphor betrays a myopia afflicting the paradigm of traditional business morality: its tendency to mischaracterize all adults as equally autonomous, rational, and informed. The reality is that individuals are on a spectrum in regard to these morally relevant characteristics. This poker metaphor, which I will further examine later, succeeds in aptly illustrating how the normative rules of business practice may differ from those in other aspects of life.

Should we really consider homeless persons to be like poker players, who elect to negotiate with other players at the business table? As we will see, Carr's metaphor seems ill-equipped to capture the situational context of homeless persons. The Bumfights case, however, is merely representative of a broader range of cases in business where care ethics is needed due to the particular circumstances of vulnerable individuals. In effort to illuminate this broader application of care ethics, I will appeal to additional cases beyond Bumfights—cases both classic and contemporary—where care ethics can do the ethical work that traditional business morality cannot.

Traditional Business Morality

Carr's poker metaphor epitomizes what I'm calling "traditional business morality" (TBM), which denotes the day-to-day moral perspective dominating the contemporary practice of American business and elsewhere. TBM represents a paradigm best characterized by the ethical theory, entitlement theory; the business view championed by Milton Friedman (1970) known as stockholder theory; and the political theory of libertarianism—all three of which set the cornerstone of morality as the duty not to interfere with the rights and liberties of others. The locus of all three are property, trade and contracts.

This "contract view" of traditional business morality deems business practices as morally legitimate if it meets the following criteria: (1) The is practice in accordance with laws, rules and regulations (2) No one is directly harmed (3) No one's negative rights are violated (4) It is a "free and open transaction" between adults, without any direct coercion, deception or fraud (5) It is mutually beneficial transaction for all parties involved.

If the business action passes the five required criteria above, the business action is morally validated. While a business action needn't pass all of these criteria to be morally permitted by TBM—for instance a business transaction needn't be mutually beneficial—TBM would dismiss any moral objections to a business action if that action passes all five criteria. After all, if two adults reach open and voluntary mutual agreement and both parties benefit, what moral objections can there be?

Will Fight for Food: Homelessness and Choice

Bumfights is a business enterprise premised on coaxing homeless persons to engage in self-demeaning and injurious behavior for a pittance of payment. Traditional business morality condones such exploitation, characterizing both sides of the transaction as autonomous, free participants that reach a mutually beneficial agreement without coercion or fraud. By these lights, it's not exploitation: it's just business.

Craig Walton, a professor of ethics and policy studies at the University of Nevada, Las Vegas, points out, "Even if the homeless aren't forced to perform, it's inaccurate to describe people without adequate shelter, food or clothing as having choices" (Squires and Casey 2002).

Homeless persons tend not to be equally autonomous in comparison to the average person. They lack autonomy in terms of health, background, and circumstance. According to The National Coalition for the Homeless, assorted health ailments include serious mental illness or disability (22%), chronic physical ailments (46%), or substance abuse problems (30%). Homeless person's circumstances are bleak: 58% report difficulty finding food; 55% have no health insurance; 50% receive less than $300 per month (NCH, 2007).

It's all too easy to rationalize that the homeless landed in their downtrodden positions themselves, though some poor life-choice. However, a large percentage of homeless appear to be homeless through tragic circumstances that contributed to their situation: 21% were homeless during some point in childhood; 25% were physically or sexually abused; 27% were in foster care or similar care as children; 23% of homeless are veterans. And while it's a comfortable rationalization to imagine the homeless as lazy, 44% report having worked within the last week (NCH 2007).

Desperation: A Difference in Kind

Jackass, the popular MTV series (Knoxville, Jonex, and Tremaine 2000–2002), purveys similar content to Bumfights. Several young male twenty-somethings stage pranks, engage in injurious and demeaning acts for the amusement of viewers and each other. How is *Jackass* different from Bumfights? In answer, one might point out that Jackass is a cooperative venture, where the profits are shared among the participants. Another salient difference is that the participants in Jackass are not circumstantially desperate: they have the essentials necessary to live a minimally dignified life.

Desperation pervades the lives of the homeless. Bereft of the essentials of life—food, shelter, medical care—homeless persons live day-to-day in precarious circumstances. The homeless featured in the Bumfights videos do not demean themselves out of elective choice between reasonable alternatives: they demean themselves because they have no alternatives. If they do not accept the producer's offer, it's possible they will not be able to afford to eat that day.

The Bumfights producers take advantage of the desperation of the homeless: moreover, the desperation is presented as part of the entertainment (e.g., see what crazy things a bum will do for half a pastry!). The producers' offers of food, money, etc. to the homeless are, of course, not coercive in the traditional sense: after all, they are not forcing homeless persons to agree to the terms of the transaction. However, we must recognize the "circumstantial coercion" that frames the transaction.

While there is no figurative gun-to-the-head of the homeless person in Bumfights, where an analogy to a mugger might apply, the situation is still coercive, even if not directly so. A more faithful analogy would be that of a drowning person, victim of a shipwreck, who agrees at the behest of his potential helper on dry land to transfer all wealth to the saver—or even to agree to become a slave to the saver—in order to be extended a branch to be brought safely to shore. Both analogies, direct and circumstantial coercion respectively, represent unethical examples of coercion. Taking advantage of one's coercive circumstances is not ethically ok, just because the exploiter didn't create those circumstances.

The desperation of the homeless is a difference in kind from the lives most of us live. As such, we should be careful not to compare the nature of their decisions with our own. For example, I might imagine that if someone offered me $20 to pull out a tooth, I would refuse; however, if they offered me $20,000, I would likely accept. I might infer from this that the two cases are alike: it's just that $20 to a homeless person is equivalent to what $20,000 is worth to me. And just like me, the homeless person is electing to accept the disfiguring transaction because of what it's worth to them. This comparison is a mistake, however, as it ignores salient factors. The $20,000 to me would be superfluous to my dignity and well-being: I'd probably use it to fix some things around the house, upgrade some appliances, perhaps buy a fancier car, and so forth. The $20 to a homeless person, though, would be essential rather than superfluous: it might help shore up his deficits, as he languishes underneath a humane minimum. Our two positions are incommensurate: only I could just as easily refuse the offer, and yet still walk away just as well-off in terms of my basic human welfare. I would still possess the essentials necessary to living a minimally hospitable and dignified life. I have food, shelter, clothes, and access to medical care. The homeless person does not. The homeless person is below a minimally decent living circumstance, and as such is not free to "elect" to participate: they are forced to participate through the hostile circumstances in which they're situated.

In sum, there is no multiplier that makes a proffered payment to me a coercive one, where it is circumstantially coercive to the homeless person. Desperation is a difference in kind, where choices I would make as an autonomous individual are incommensurate to the choices a homeless person must make. I have a choice in a real way that the homeless person does not.

One tragic instance of such circumstantial coercion involves homeless veteran, Donald Brennan. Brennan was offered $200 to get the tattoo "Bum Fight" etched in his forehead. In his desperation, and at the persistent urging of the producers, Brennan put himself under the needle, and now wears a baseball cap with shame, to cover the logo. Brennan did not have a truly "free" choice to refuse the money, but permitted the producers to treat his forehead as a billboard to market their product. Brennan retells his decision with tears welling in his eyes.

Sex for Money: Prostitution and Autonomy

To further examine the ethical blindness of traditional business morality toward stark differences in autonomy, consider the simple business transaction of sex for money. First, consider low-end prostitution that occurs in an impoverished country, like

Singapore. Imagine that "Helena" is a poor female in Singapore who, on her 18th birthday, submits herself to the prostitution trade, legal in that country. Helena is cognizant of the rough life of prostitution: the inevitable damage to her physical, mental, emotional and spiritual well-being. Unfortunately, as for many girls her age, prostitution is the only way she can make a living wage.

Contrast Helena's all-too-common story with that of Ashley Dupre, the high-end prostitute involved in the sex scandal with Eliot Spitzer, former Governor of New York. After being slipped a business card for a high-end escort service, Dupre describes her decision to become a prostitute as an opportunity, "You don't mean to make those choices but you're put in a situation and, you know, you have an *opportunity* to do it" (Sawyer 2008). Dupre also says that she viewed her escort career as comparable to dating. After the scandal broke, Dupre was offered many lucrative deals, from reality shows to $1 million to pose in *Hustler* magazine. Dupre refused all of these offers, explaining: "You stop and think, but that's not who I am . . . And that's not what I want to do" (Sawyer 2008).

Traditional business morality would uniformly describe both cases of prostitution (provided both were legal), as voluntary and open transactions, free of coercion and fraud, where no one is being unjustly treated. Therefore, for TBM, the two cases are identical, and no moral questions remain. One might argue that Ashley Dupre was indeed an autonomous contractor in the business game: trading sex for money. Yet can one argue similarly in the case of Helena? It seems Dupre is autonomous in a way Helena is not. Dupre is electing to take advantage of the "opportunity" to become a prostitute; Helena seems to have no reasonable alternative. Dupre views her prostitution as harmonious to her authenticity and life-goals: she can even refuse $1 million dollars to pose naked in Hustler magazine. Helena has no other reasonable choice, and is circumstantially forced to prostitute her body, ultimately undermining her well-being.

The failure of TBM in these two cases lies not in its possible validation of prostitution, but in the fact it treats both cases of prostitution as morally identical. It views Helena and Ashley Dupre as equally autonomous, yet Helena is victim of tragic exploitation whereas Ashley Dupre is an elective opportunist. Any moral view that fails to see such stark differences in autonomy is a deficient view. An adequate moral view needs to acknowledge the differences in the vulnerability of individuals, and the desperation of their circumstances. Such factors will alter the playing field, when it comes to morality of business transactions involving vulnerable individuals.

Our Most Vulnerable Citizens

Homeless persons are vulnerable, as they struggle at the margins of existence. As such, they are appropriate subjects of our care. This is not to say that the homeless have claims of being "deserving" or "entitled" to our care: care is extra-dimensional to well-trafficked concepts of desert and rights.

To evince our care obligations, let us enlist Peter Singer's famous example utilized in his article "Rich and Poor" (Singer 1993). A child is drowning in a shallow pond, where we could easily save the child by merely wading in, knee-deep, and bringing the child to safety. Unfortunately, to do this, we would need to muddy our clothes and sacrifice some of our time. Virtually everyone who considers this example affirms that it would be immoral to walk past the child, rather than stopping to save the child, even if this means we'd have to sacrifice some morally insignificant things to do so. Yet the serendipitous savior of the child would not likely cash out their moral obligation in terms of rights or entitlements. The child had no claim upon the passerby to save him from drowning. The child's rights would not have been violated by the passerby if she decided simply to walk on by without helping. Nonetheless, despite the nonappearance of any rights and entitlements onto the scene, the savior still acknowledges that she ought to save the child. Why? Simply because the child is vulnerable and needs saving, and the individual is in a particular position to provide that saving at little expense to herself. It seems the very proximity of the child is sufficient to necessitate the passerby act with care.

Similar to the drowning child, homeless persons perhaps have no claim to "entitlement" or "deservingness" of help from other private citizens, yet the moral onus may still be upon such citizens to help them due to care obligations. While the Bumfights producers failed to positively care for the "drowning" homeless persons that they were in relations with, this seems a moderate failure in comparison to the fact that the producers moreover callously exploited the very situation of desperation and helplessness in which the homeless persons struggle. The producer's failure is not a failure of passive omission, but rather of active exploitation.

One type of exploitation by the Bumfights producers is their frequent use of alcohol (as well as illicit drugs, allegedly) to prey upon the vulnerabilities of the homeless, thereby coaxing them to engage in degrading acts or injurious stunts that they otherwise might refuse. Brennan, for example, claims that the producers took advantage of his alcohol dependence to get him to agree to the "Bum Fight" tattoo on his forehead. Knowing that Brennan was dependent on alcohol, the producers allegedly sought to impair his autonomy further, by offering him liquor in order to gain his compliance.

Maternal Ethics and Business Morality: Care vs. Contracts

Maternal ethics presents one paradigm for care as represented by the mother-child relationship, upon which other care relationships might be modeled. This contrasts the predominant contract view in traditional business morality, which views ethical obligations arising from mutual negotiation and agreement. On the care view of maternal ethics, an individual ought to nurture and care for a subject on the basis of her relationship to that subject, as well as from the subject's vulnerability and need for nurturance. Eva Kittay argues that each human being has an inalienable entitlement to being recognized as "some mother's child" (1998). This contrasts the atomistic view of traditional business ethics, where individuals are conceived of as unrelated objects in space, with no relationship or responsibility to each other, except for not violating each other's negative rights. According to the care ethics view, however, each individual's existence depends on human interconnection as a fundamental feature for survival. We are not atoms in space: we are an ecosystem of human networks.

The contract view, characterizing TBM, holds that while it would be *nice* for an individual to care for a needy stranger, it is not her responsibility, rather such care is supererogatory: morally good to do, but not wrong not to do to. Imagine, for example, that it's lunchtime and I am walking to my car, whilst polishing off the first half of my sandwich. Let's say that I'm full, and I seek to discard the remaining half of my sandwich. I see a trashcan to my left, and a homeless woman to my right with a sign pleading for food. According to the contractual view, I can just as rightly throw into the trash the remaining sandwich half rather than give it to the woman. After all, I do her no injustice by throwing away my sandwich: it is *my* sandwich, and she has no claim to it.

In such situations as passing panhandling homeless persons, we tend to make up a comfortable story about their laziness, voluntary sloth, karmic desert, irresponsible addiction, or inability to be helped. These rationalizations are employed to evade our moral obligation to care for them. Such rationalizations, by their very rigorous employment in such circumstances, seem to betray what we'd otherwise acknowledge: that, all else being equal, human beings have a moral obligation to care for other vulnerable human beings if it's at little cost to ourselves.

Care Ethics in Christianity

Care ethics, though nested within the feminist ethics paradigm, is implicit in some religious ethics. Similar to Kittay's "placing" of each individual as "some mother's child," one could view religious ethics as acknowledging each individual as "some god's child," in virtue of which that individual has an origin, identity, dignity, and worth.

Christian ethics, particularly, espouses an ethics that derives from care. While Christian ethics tends to predominantly focus on faith and salvation, a powerful secondary impetus of Christian ethics, salvation and faith aside, is that we ought to emulate Christ as the moral ideal concerning how to regard and treat the vulnerable. Putting aside the controversial question of divine ancestry, it's clear that Christ represents a moral exemplar in his care for the downtrodden of society. He is admired as a moral figure not just for his actions, but for his caring attitudes toward the desperate, diseased, and disenfranchised.

The appreciation of Christ is not merely in admiration of his virtues, but also his recognition of others as appropriate ends of care. In the book, *Compassion: Reflections on a Christian Life*, Jesus' care is poignantly expressed, such as when

Jesus met those suffering, "He became lost with the lost, hungry with the hungry, and sick with the sick. In him, all suffering was sensed with perfect sensitivity" (McNeill, Nouwen, and Morrison 1982).

The New Testament portrays Christ as morally perfect in his care for the vulnerable. "When [Jesus] saw the multitudes, he was moved with compassion on them, because they were harassed and helpless, like sheep without a shepherd" (Holy Bible, 1989. Matthew, 9.36). "When he saw the blind, the paralyzed, and the deaf being brought to him from all directions, he . . . experienced their pains in his own heart" (Holy Bible, 1989. Matthew, 14:14).

One might object to moral exemplars, such as Christ, as representing an appropriate model for a business person. Christ, after all, would not make a good CEO. As Carr might say, business is a competitive context in which Christian ethics does not and should not apply. Christ's care was singular and supererogatory: morally good and admirable, and yet business persons are not morally deficient by "failing" to reach such heights of compassion.

In response, one might concede that while perfect compassion is not the responsibility of a business person, surely some degree of care is a minimal responsibility of a business person toward other stakeholder groups vital to the business. Consider the infamous case of the Ford Pinto. After rushing toward production their Pinto, Ford realized that the Pinto's shoddy gas-tank construction would cause, upon moderate-speed rear impacts of 40 mph, the tank to rupture, making it very likely that the car would catch fire, injuring or killing its occupants (Birsch and Fielder 1994). Ford executives sent out an internal memo calculating the cost of retrofitting for a safer gas-tank versus the out-of-court settlements for death, injury and burned out cars. They concluded that it would be much cheaper to send the Pinto to market with the explosive gas tanks, and just pay these settlements. Reading this Pinto memo, where lives of customers are cashed out in terms of dollars and cents, one could rightly conclude that the Ford executives manifested an almost sociopathic lack of care toward their customers—many of whom would later die due to the cold calculation that their dying was the most "cost-effective" for Ford. The contract view of traditional business morality would also condemn Ford's decision as committing coercion—by not informing customers of the safety defect prior to purchase—yet it seems Ford's unethical decision can also be rightly cashed out in terms of a deficiency in care.

Surely the exploitation of human beings in such a way exposes a deficiency in care. And while one certainly needn't rise to the heights of Christ's compassion, Gandhi's, or that of Mother Teresa's, we ought to aspire toward such moral exemplars rather than wholly dismiss them. One cannot wholly insulate themselves from morality with the pat rationalization, "It's just business," where morality doesn't apply. Certainly this would not morally justify the decision of Ford regarding the Pinto. A business person, after all, is still a *person,* and playing the putative "get-out-of-jail-free" card of "it's just business" is a vacuous claim that overly relies on the business context to license any negligence of care to fellow "contractors" in business transactions. Business persons must show some minimal level of care toward their stakeholder groups.

Rationality: Knowing the Rules of the Game

Advertisers cannot market to children during Saturday morning cartoons, without significant limitations on what their commercials can present. Such regulations acknowledge that children are not fully rational: they cannot adequately separate fact from fiction, sufficiently know relevant background information, nor understand long-term consequences.

Many of the homeless possess similar deficiencies, and as such require similar protections. They are not equal players at the poker table of business: knowledgeable of the game and all of the rules. Surely Rufus was not cognizant of the possible long-term injuries he could sustain when he acquiesced to certain stunts, where one resultant concussion left him with epilepsy. The homeless persons do not typically know what they're signing when they sign forms releasing the producers from liability. Nor were Rufus or Brennan aware of their rights from promotions featuring their likenesses. As a witness during the criminal trial of the Bumfights producers, Rufus Hannah could not understand the questions being asked by the defense attorneys, was unable to recall events over a year ago, and provided contradictory answers. Meanwhile, the four defendants—co-producers of Bumfights—were scolded by the Superior Court judge for smirking and giggling during Hannah's testimony.

Deficiencies in rationality must curtail business enterprise. Consider the notorious Nestle case, where, in the early 1970s, Nestle heavily marketed their baby formula to mothers in impoverished communities in developing nations (Baker 1985). Nestle treated the third-world mothers as fully rational. The women, however, were not rational in the context of the business game in which they were unwitting players. The mothers could not separate fact from fiction: they were not cognizant, for instance, that the rosy-cheeked babies in the billboard ads were the "puffery" of marketing (aka "business bluffing"). Instead, these uneducated mothers unwisely took such portrayals as truth in advertising. They did not realize the consequences of their actions, and so many of them "stretched" the formula or mixed the powder with polluted water, both of which caused malnutrition and infant death. These mothers were unaware of relevant background knowledge, such as what germs are, the studies that showed at the time that breast milk was considered as good if not superior to formula, and the fact that their breast milk would dry up soon after Nestlé's promotional free samples did.

In such cases of uneducated persons, it would be gross negligence to apply Carr's "business game" metaphor to business interactions with such vulnerable groups. Business is a game that requires literacy of things we often take for granted. The Nestle mothers did not understand marketing as a competitive game, where the Nestle representatives were not looking out for the well-being of themselves and their babies, but rather for company profits at the possible expense of such well-being.

The "bums" in Bumfights likewise did not understand the context of the business interaction. They thought that the producers were their friends, when they were not. They thought that Bumfights might make them famous, where it did not (at least not in the way they were promised, envisioned, or desired). Many of the "bums" were uneducated, mentally ill or impaired, or under the influence of drugs or alcohol. In addition, the day-to-day malnourishment many of them faced likely exacerbated the cognition necessary to play the business game and make autonomous, rational decisions.

"Bum-Vertising": Exploitation or Empowerment

Homeless exploitation for profit is not limited to Bumfights, unfortunately. One distasteful marketing innovation in twenty-first century has been dubbed "bumvertising." The term and practice was created and trademarked by Ben Rogovy, a 22-year-old University of Washington graduate (Rowe 2005). Rogovy sought a cheap means by which to advertise his online poker website. His eureka moment occurred when he realized he could tape his website advertisement to the bottom of the cardboard sign desperate homeless persons held at the corner of busy intersections.

Critics of "bumvertising" deem it exploitation, citing the use of "bum" as degrading to the homeless person and perpetuating the myth that homeless persons are lazy. It portrays the homeless as societal throwaways, presenting them as if signposts rather than human beings. Certainly this innovative exploitation of panhandling homeless has garnered some chuckles and admiration for entrepreneurial "thinking outside the box."

We might try to surmount these obvious ethical objections, though, and attempt to see if "bumvertising" could be turned into something empowering rather than exploitative, where it is mutually beneficial to the homeless persons and to marketers, while not being demeaning to the homeless person.

I would proffer the following three criteria as requisite to turn "bumvertising" into an ethically legitimate business practice:

(1) the homeless person should be paid a minimum wage, a wage similar to an independent contractor performing similar work, or a wage other street advertisers receive
(2) the marketing should not be negatively predicated upon the homeless person's identity (for example, an advertisement for a job search website with the slogan "Need a job like this guy?").
(3) the trademarked name of "bumvertising" be renamed something less demeaning

If "bumvertising" were recast in such a way, the homeless person's employment of marketing a product or company would no longer be (as) exploitative, but would seem similar to other persons standing on street corners, twirling advertisements for local businesses. If the entrepreneur were employing the homeless person as a bona fide street-corner advertiser, this form of marketing might actually be seen as a true symbiotic solution to both some homeless persons' unemployment, and to certain business's marketing challenges.

Cooperators or Adversaries: Is Business a Zero-Sum Game?

Albert Carr's poker metaphor for business asserts general morality doesn't apply to certain contexts. Bluffing, for example, is an expected and accepted strategy in both business and poker, but not in "normal" life outside those contexts. Likewise, typical morality, for instance, prescribes doing unto others as they'd do unto you. Business, in contrast, is a game of gaining advantage over the competitor before they gain advantage over you. To apply ordinary morality to business would be like applying the "do unto others" rule to professional boxing.

Certainly there are rules in business, poker and boxing. But beyond adhering to the basic rules of the game, you try to overpower, outwit, and outperform your peers. Carr's poker metaphor exemplifies the traditional, masculine model of business: namely, that business interactions between stakeholder groups are to be adversarial rather than cooperative in nature.

Carr's poker metaphor succeeds in illuminating that ethical obligation is contextual, yet what is most illuminating about the metaphor is its limitations. In poker, all parties are fully voluntary participants, not coerced—whether directly or circumstantially—to the table. In poker, all parties are fully rational and aware of the rules. In poker, each player starts "negotiations" on relatively equal footing. Relatively equal freedom, rationality, and power among all "players" may be the case in many business scenarios, but many interactions fail in one if not all three of these regards.

In the case of Bumfights, the homeless are not fully voluntary: they are circumstantially coerced to the business table. Second, the homeless participants may not be fully rational or autonomous, nor are they likely aware of their rights (or ability to negotiate at all for treatment/payment). Third, and most certain is the unequal footing in the preposterously unbalanced negotiating positions between the producers and the homeless.

Carr's metaphor fails when misapplying it to business cases where there is a vast disparity in bargaining power. Consider, for example, Wal-Mart's titanic leverage over small suppliers. Wal-Mart can demand access to the supplier's financial books, and can thereby subsequently pirate away the supplier's profits, leaving the supplier with a razor-thin margin of revenue. Due to this great disparity in negotiating power, many Walmart suppliers have gone bankrupt. To characterize Walmart and such suppliers, especially small to mid-size suppliers, as two poker players negotiating at the business table is to be obtuse to morally relevant differences in power.

In regard to Bumfights, the homeless are vulnerable persons that certainly are not equal or effective negotiators at the business table. When business enterprises or transactions involve vulnerable parties, such as the homeless, Carr's poker model is ill-suited to capture the situation. In such cases, Carr's adversarial metaphor must be abandoned, and we must seek metaphor that is more cooperative.

Consider mainstream sports as a similarly masculine metaphor closely paralleling Carr's adversarial poker metaphor. In sports, competitors start in equal positions, competing to overpower, outwit, and outperform. There are a few rare and notable instances in sports history, though, when this adversarial paradigm is broken through. For instance, consider a moving story in college baseball history. Sara Tucholsky finally hit her first ever homerun, clearing the center-field fence, only to twist her knee, trying to tag first base. Sara collapsed, no longer able to stand. Two players of the opposing team picked her up and carried her around the rest of the bases, to help her complete her three-run homer, even though it contributed to that opposing team's own elimination from the playoffs. Mallory Holtman, one of her carriers, explained, "In the end, it's not about winning or losing so much ... it was about this girl. She hit it over the fence and was in pain, and she deserved a home run" (Associated Press 2008).

Other similar stories of cooperation in sports history show that "winning" at times is better achieved through cooperation over competition. At times, a player needs to show care for his purported opponent, in recognition that the competitor is not the enemy. We need to be aware of this possibility and need to be cognizant of the value of winning together rather than alone. We need to be able to think outside the boxing ring, and identify cooperation and collaboration as valuable in addition to competition.

Care Beyond Contracts

Both Rufus Hannah and Donald Brennan are veterans, who bravely served our country and were honorably discharged. The US Army decorated Brennan with a Purple Heart and a Silver Star. While citizens have no contractual obligations toward veterans of wars long ago, we still tend to recognize that we bear moral obligations of respect and care toward our nation's veterans. This reciprocal duty of care is aside from any contract. Such care obligations might parallel the moral obligations one would recognize to their elderly parent, guardian or caregiver, even if there were no legal obligations to them. We may have care obligations to others due to our relationships to them, in addition to any vulnerability of those persons.

Reciprocal altruism, in business, is regarded as a sound long-term strategy rather than as an ethical duty. It's ethically ok, for instance, if a dedicated, long-serving employee is trivially fired for some minor interest. It's just business. But showing care toward those who have sacrificed in order to benefit us, is ethically appropriate, even in a business context.

Beyond what is contractually required of our actions toward veterans, we should query what our attitudes toward our nation's soldiers should be. If not an attitude of respect or gratitude, then certainly—at minimum—not an attitude of callousness or ridicule, manifested in a readiness to exploit their disadvantaged condition for profit by dehumanizing them to others. Veterans comprise a significant percentage of homeless persons, and while we have care obligations toward all homeless persons, one might think that, toward veterans, our care obligations become overdetermined, if they are not additionally extensive.

The contract view of TBM fails to recognize reciprocal duties of care beyond mere contractual obligations. The Bumfights producers would owe no respect toward Rufus or Brennan, according to this view, neither as humans nor veterans.

Innocent Bystanders: Innocent Consumers

At first blush, it's tempting to be amused by Bumfights: to chuckle at the wacky antics of those silly bums, performing scandalous stunts for scraps. But such an attitude of amusement is not an appropriate attitude for a human being to have toward the desperate. The contract view of TBM might exonerate the amused viewer as morally innocent: viewers cause no bad consequences, break no deontological rules, violate no one's negative rights. Still, it seems the very attitude Bumfights viewers have toward such videos is unethical: deriving pleasure from other persons' painful circumstances betrays a deficiency in care.

To illustrate this attitudinal deficiency, consider a personal story. There was fellow student in my high school, who was part of the special education program. I'll call him Nicholas. Nicholas' teachers, and other parents, did not describe him as suffering from significant retardation, but did describe him as euphemistically "slow." During our lunch period, Nicholas would goofily dance for the amusement of a crowd of "normal" students. Many students would throw change at his feet, which he would occasionally stoop to pick up. Students laughed at him, and he laughed back. He thought these people were his friends. He conceived of himself as popular. What he didn't realize, however, was that his peers were laughing at him, not with him. They were ridiculing him. They saw him as their monkey, dancing for peanuts.

These students did no harm, true. They didn't force Nicholas to do anything he didn't want to do. Nicholas even benefitted from the lunchtime transaction: money for amusement. Still, some students walked away from the spectacle, rightly commenting that it was mean to make fun of a person with mild retardation. We might parallel the Bumfights producers to those kids who first incited Nicholas to dance for change in the first place. My focus, though, is on the kids who watched Nicholas with ridiculing amusement—pointing and laughing. These are the viewers of Bumfights. Deriving pleasure from the demeaning treatment of the disadvantaged may be effectively innocuous, but it still betrays inappropriate emotional attitudes toward those disadvantaged others who warrant our care—not our amused distain. Finding the demeaning of the disadvantaged as suitable entertainment betrays attitudinal deficiencies in care.

That certain attitudes in business can be ethically inappropriate is evinced in other contexts, in addition to Bumfights. A practice referred to as "dead peasant insurance" reveals a company's inappropriate attitude toward employees. Essentially, these life insurance policies are bought by corporations, for tax breaks and possible insurance payouts, where if the employee dies, the company will profit. In most cases, neither the employee nor her family ever knew that the corporation was gambling on her life, betting to profit on her demise. One might defend such insurance policies as ethically permissible, given that no harm is done, and the company is maximizing revenue. There seems to be no downside. While such a justification might seem partially compelling, there remains some reason for moral objection: that this widespread corporate practice demonstrates the wrong attitude—callousness toward its own employees.

Win-Win: A Business Rationalization

The contract view dominates traditional business morality. Unfortunately, it lacks the tools to explain why certain business transactions and enterprises are unethical, such as the case of Bumfights. Because the typical tools in the business person's toolbox cannot explain why Bumfights is unethical, the business person may be left with a false negative—a "no" answer to the question, "Is Bumfights unethical?" The business person might then rationalize, against their moral intuitions and emotions, that Bumfights must not be unethical, since it doesn't violate property rights, involves no coercion or fraud, and is an open and free transaction that stays within Milton Friedman's "rules of the game." The individual, moreover, might find further reassurance in that the homeless person seems arguably benefited by the transaction with the producers, so it's a "win-win."

In brief, let us review the arguments that traditional business morality would present that Bumfights is ethically permissible:

(1) There entrepreneur isn't violating any law, contract, or negative rights of the exploited
(2) The exploited voluntarily accepts the open transaction, which is free of coercion/fraud
(3) Both parties benefit from the transaction: it's a "win-win"

Throughout this chapter, I have responded to the first two arguments, above, in the following way:

(1) There is more to morality than contracts or negative rights (e.g., drowning child analogy)
(2) Many homeless persons are bereft of autonomy/rationality (e.g., circumstantial coercion)

In regard to (3), I will further explore here the third argument: that a business practice is morally vindicated if it is a "win-win" where all parties benefit from the transaction. Another way of expressing this rationalization is that the exploited party would have been worse off if not for the transaction. Let us presume, for the sake of argument, that the homeless persons does in fact marginally benefit from the transaction (an allegation which can certainly be disputed). Even if the homeless persons marginally benefit from the transaction in Bumfights, it seems this "win-win" rationalization is not sufficient to justify any and all exploitation.

Consider the business practice of profiteering. Profiteering isn't always bad, as hotels often spike room rates during large conventions, vacation seasons, and so forth. But consider cases of profiteering that occurred after Hurricane Katrina, by low-end hotel owners in states, such as Texas, that saw a flood of desperate Katrina evacuees, seeking shelter. One Houston hotel reportedly raised its rate six-times: from \$50 to \$300 (Peterson 2005). This steep price increase extends beyond covering costs. Regarding this skyrocketed price, the hotel owner could claim that the hotel is his property, that the transaction was legal, open and voluntary, and that the evacuees who sacrificed $300 for a room were benefitting from the transaction (otherwise they wouldn't have agreed to the price). But does this "win-win" morally justify the hotel owner's profiteering upon their evacuee's desperation? It seems the hotel owner is deficient in care, to see a lobby full of desperate families who just lost their homes and almost everything else, and not only to fail to be moved by the opportunity to help their fellow human beings, their fellow Americans, but to exploit them by charging them six-times the normal rate. The fact the transaction is a "win-win" fails to ethically justify such profiteering upon the desperate and vulnerable. The business person must *care* at what cost the desperate individual "wins" while they try to maximize their profits.

In regard to the Bumfights case, the homeless persons could be technically labeled as beneficiaries of transactions with the producers: they often received food, shelter, or other necessities. But the paltriness of these benefits (e.g., half a pastry for a stunt) shows a lack of care for the homeless. The benefits are extraordinarily disproportionate from the profits derived from their sacrifices. There could be more equitable distribution of the profits that was cooperative rather than adversarial.

Generally, the "win-win" ethical justification appears to rely, at least partially, upon a false dichotomy, where either the empowered offers the disempowered an opportunity to marginally benefit, or he does not. Since it would be better for the disempowered to be marginally better-off than not, the empowered gets an automatic moral pass for offering this opportunity. There is, of course, a third possibility: that the empowered offers an exchange that includes fair, rather than marginal, benefits to the disempowered (e.g., a modest share of whatever profits may come from the disempowered's contribution).

Second, the "win-win" rationalization licenses the treatment of human beings as mere objects toward the end of profits. Immanuel Kant's 2nd formulation proclaims that one should not treat any persons—or herself—as a mere means to an end, but always as an ends in themselves (Kant 1785). In the case of Bumfights, the producer is using the homeless person as a mere means—a mere object toward the end of profits—and isn't acknowledging of the intrinsic value of the homeless person. The homeless person is a human being, not an object, and should not be used in a way that wholly ignores his humanity, and violates his dignity or intrinsic value. While Kantian ethics lives leagues away from care ethics, Kant's 2nd formulation can show auxiliary affirmation toward care ethics: you ought to treat others with care if you conceive of yourself as someone who ought to be treated with care. You ought to recognize and respect other's intrinsic value if you recognize it in yourself and believe you ought not to be treated by others as a mere tool toward their private interests. Kant's 2nd formulation, of course, is motivated by rational consistency, whereas care ethics is motivated by emotional care toward others. Both, nonetheless, recognize human beings as proper subjects of care. And both recognize that a "win-win" rationalization does not vindicate the exploitation of the vulnerable. Exploitation is still exploitation, even if the exploited "freely" agree to the terms.

Conclusion: Supplementing with Care

This chapter presents the Bumfights case as an example of a business enterprise that is morally objectionable. Traditional business morality, however, would condone Bumfights as a morally permissible business enterprise: after all, the transaction is a voluntary and open exchange, free of deception and fraud, which stays within the confines of the law, and benefits both parties. With this limited moral lens, TBM suffers moral myopia. In particular, the contractual view is blind to morally relevant factors, such inequalities of autonomy, rationality, and freedom—which make some persons in business transactions especially vulnerable, where they cannot be accurately and conveniently characterized as metaphorical poker players at the business table.

Vulnerable persons involved in business transactions ought to be treated with care. This care recognition needn't extend to extraordinary heights, but the business agent must at least minimally care for the well-being of the subjects with whom she is contracting. The Bumfights producers demonstrably felt no caring toward their vulnerable subjects, where not only did they fail to significantly help them, but they publicly ridiculed their vulnerability for profit. Traditional business morality would condone this callous exploitation of the vulnerable for profit, unable to recognize the enterprise as even partially unethical.

Bumfights exposes the moral myopia that blinds traditional business morality. Other business cases additionally show that a supplemental lens of "care" needs inclusion into business morality if we are to wholly apprehend all of the moral dimensions of business. Our moral intuitions tend to recognize these moral dimensions, even if traditional business morality cannot. For this reason, if business persons are to be empowered to ethically navigate through the business landscape, contemporary business morality must provide them with more than just the contract view: care ethics needs to be readily included as well.

References

Associated Press. 1 May 2008. "Unbelievable" sportsmanship in softball game. CBS News Interactive: <http://www.cbsnews.com>.

Baker, J. 1985. The international infant formula controversy. *Journal of Business Ethics* 4: 181–190.

Birsch, D., and John Fielder. 1994. *The Ford Pinto case*. Albany, NY: State University of New York Press.

Carr, A. 1968. Is business bluffing ethical? *Harvard Business Review* 46: 143–153.

Friedman, M. 13 September 1970. The social responsibility of business is to increase its profits. *New York Times Magazine*.

Holy Bible. 1989. *The Holy Bible: Containing the old and new testaments with the apocryphal/deuterocanonical books*. New York, NY: Collins, New Revised Standard Version.

Kant, Immanuel. (Trans. A. Zweig from German: 1785). 2002. *Groundwork for the metaphysics of morals*. New York, NY: Oxford University Press.

Kittay, E. 1998. *Love's labor: Essays on women, equality and dependency*. New York, NY: Taylor & Francis.

Knoxville, J., S. Jonez, and J. Tremaine (creators). Jackass (2000–2002) [TV Series]. New York, NY: MTV.

McNeill, D.P., H.J.M. Nouwen, and D.A. Morrison. 1982. *Compassion: A reflection on the Christian life*. New York, NY: Image Books.

McPherson, R. (Producer). 2002. Bumfights: A cause for concern [Video Series: DVD]. Las Vegas, NV: Indecline Productions.

National Coalition for the Homeless. August 2007. NCH Fact Sheet #3: Who is Homeless. National Coalition for the Homeless Fact Sheet.

Peterson, J. 2 September 2005. It's not just gasoline: reports of price gouging. *Los Angeles Times*.

Rowe, C. 13 September 2005 "Bumvertising" stirs debate. *Seattle Post-Intelligencer*.

Sawyer, D. 21 November 2008. Ashley Dupre: "I"ve made so many mistakes. ABC News interview with Diane Sawyer [Television Interview].

Singer, P. 1993. Rich and poor. In *Practical ethics*, ed. P. Singer, 218–246, 2nd edn. Cambridge: Cambridge University Press.

Squires, M., and J. Casey. 5 May 2002. Film cashes in on street scenes. *Las Vegas Review-Journal*.

Part IV
Corporate Culture

Chapter 12
Care and Loyalty in the Workplace

Julinna Oxley and D.E. Wittkower

Introduction

Should employees be loyal to their employers? Can employers require their employees to be loyal? The academic and public debates on these questions usually begin with the presumption that loyalty is a good thing, and that it can be a duty or a virtue. This is odd, since expressions of loyalty seem inevitably to be about showing partiality to someone on the basis that one cares for or is concerned about her, and the morality of such expression depends largely on the context. Since people can be loyal to morally problematic organizations and ideals, loyalty does not seem to be the kind of characteristic about which one can easily make universalizable prescriptions. While the appropriate relationship between an employee's personal interests and her obligations to a firm is indeed important, supposing that loyalty is a virtue or an obligation ultimately misconceives its nature and gives rise to the strange and intractable arguments that the current debate on employee loyalty has been mired in.

Understanding loyalty in business as a kind of care, and as an analog to relationships of friends and family, can provide a unique and more satisfying account of when it is morally appropriate to be loyal in business contexts. For example, we usually think that a loyal friend will help a friend who is struggling, for example, with alcoholism, even if such loyalty requires taking that person to a rehabilitation center against her stated wishes. Similarly, loyalty in business may include performing actions that are difficult and that go beyond or even against stated job requirements and the traditional law of agency. By understanding loyalty as an expression of care, we are able to explain the intuition that loyalty is neither simply a duty nor a rational requirement of the pursuit of mutual self-interest. Any duties or obligations to a corporation or to an employee are better described as requirements that flow

J. Oxley (✉)
Coastal Carolina University, Conway, SC, USA
e-mail: joxley@coastal.edu

D.E. Wittkower
Department of Philosophy and Religious Studies, Old Dominion University, Norfolk, VA, USA
e-mail: d.e.wittkower@gmail.com

M. Hamington, M. Sander-Staudt (eds.), *Applying Care Ethics to Business*,
Issues in Business Ethics 34, DOI 10.1007/978-90-481-9307-3_12,
© Springer Science+Business Media B.V. 2011

from the contractual relationship, rather than flowing from a requirement of loyalty. This is because loyalty is not just a set of actions required by a contract. Loyalty involves feelings and a disposition to go above and beyond what is already required by the contract. Approaching loyalty as a kind of care can also explain why it should be secondary to more fundamental moral requirements. If loyalty is an expression of care, we are able to make sense of the intuition that the natural development of loyalty is praiseworthy and rightly contained within our conception of the ideal employee, but at the same time is neither a duty nor a virtue, and not always an unambiguous good.

This chapter will begin by showing how loyalty has been defined as a wide range of concepts: an obligation that flows from contractual commitments, an ideal that contributes to the pursuit of mutual self-interest, a mere feeling, or an inappropriate kind of self-sacrifice. We suggest that these are impoverished conceptions of loyalty. We then develop a robust account of loyalty that is conceptually grounded in care, and explain why loyalty should be understood as an expression of care and concern. Next, we describe how this conception of loyalty can be applied in the personal aspects of business relationships and explain why loyalty as care is more recognizable when it is expressed in personal relationships, such as to co-workers. Fourth, we argue that it is also possible for an employee to be loyal to a corporation, and examine the way whistle-blowing can be an expression of critical loyalty. We conclude by examining whether loyalty as care can be *obligated*, and argue that loyalty to a corporation can be *deserved*, but never obliged, since loyalty itself involves going above and beyond duties and obligations.

Traditional Approaches to Loyalty in Business

In the academic study of business ethics, one of the most important questions regards how loyalty should be defined. There are descriptive approaches that seek to clarify what is meant when loyalty is discussed among non-academics involved in the conduct of business (e.g. Mele 2001; Herman 1992; Jensen 1987). There are normative approaches, some of which define loyalty as an obligation based upon fiduciary duties and the law of agency (Corvino 2002; Bok 1983); others of which define loyalty as a desirable virtue, based upon a commitment to social values shared or served by the corporation (e.g. Hoffmann 2006; Vandekerckhove and Commers 2004; Mele 2001); and finally, still others of which base an obligation of loyalty upon an express or implied pledge or oath which may or may not be made (Pfeiffer 1992).

Those who instead address loyalty in psychological terms straddle descriptive and normative approaches. For example, some describe loyalty as a feeling that is desirable but not obligatory (Hoffmann 2006; Rosanas and Velilla 2003; Randels 2001, and Solomon 1998, whose overall view is very similar to ours here), and others define loyalty more prescriptively, as an implicit understanding (Cavanagh 2010) or "psychological contract" (Wicks et al 2010; Hart and Thompson 2007; Werhane 1994, Argyris 1960). Authors taking a more psychological approach nevertheless claim that considerations of desert are still relevant, since "emotion and judgment are not, of course, entirely separate matters" (Ewin 1993), and claim that loyalty may be more or less "appropriate" or justifiable depending on employer reciprocation and the "worthiness" of the business (Randels 2001, Schrag 2001, Hartman 1994). While some authors (e.g. Vandekerckhove and Commers 2004; Werhane 1999; Carbone 1997) say that their approach is opposed to a "traditional" view of loyalty, the "traditional" view of loyalty varies from one author to the next. Our definition of loyalty will seek to be consistent with ordinary language and with the normative considerations that follow from an ethic of care.[1] Our view is that loyalty is an expression of care and concern for others, and that any duties of loyalty are grounded in the caring relationship.

Another difficulty in defining loyalty in the conduct of business is that there are many ways that loyalty is manifested in business. As an example, consider the diversity of this non-exhaustive list of kinds of loyalty: loyalty may be (i) an inhibiting consideration relative to whistle-blowing, (ii) a behavioral set which consumers may develop relative to a brand, (iii) a set of obligations owed to the employer by the employee, or (iv) obligations owed to employees by the employer. Moreover, there are many dimensions to business ethics, and appropriate loyalty often depends on the position adopted on other issues such as the nature of corporate agency or the nature of the particular business in question. For example, those who assume that corporations are incapable of moral agency dismiss any version of loyalty based upon reciprocal self-sacrifice (e.g. Carbone 1997; Duska 1984), but this conclusion does not as clearly follow when considering, for example, very small, family-run businesses containing personal relationships with employees. It also does not necessarily follow when the stakeholder view of corporate social responsibility—when businesses or professionals uphold values beyond profit maximization—is adopted (e.g. Duska 1992 and Mane 2005).

These conceptions of loyalty are all impoverished because they fail to acknowledge that loyalty is usually an expression of care in a personal relationship, rather than a requirement of implicit or explicit contract or obligation. Although loyalty is expressed in a variety of ways—as concern for others, as advocacy or sticking up for someone or something, through a ritual, as a kind of identification, or as an allegiance to certain beliefs—these expressions are a result of care and concern for someone, and express partiality toward that person. Our central argument is that loyalty is a form of care and concern for others, and as such, loyalty cannot be obligated—either by the corporation, or morally, all things considered. This thesis, we believe, is more consistent with a commonsense understanding of what loyalty in business consists in, and avoids the conceptual muddle that ethicists seem inevitably mired in when trying to address how loyalty can be obligated. A conception of loyalty that is rooted in care and concern for others will appropriately capture the role of loyalty in business.

[1] It is hard to see how defining the necessary and sufficient conditions of loyalty could cover these various loyalties without emptying the concept of any force since not all expressions of loyalty are "good" or moral. For example, a loyal employee might fail to become a whistle-blower when confronted with damning evidence of corporate wrongdoing, or a loyal Nike or Gap customer might willfully refuse to acknowledge allegations of use of sweatshop labor out of loyalty to the brand.

Loyalty As a Product of Care

Care ethics provides a useful framework for examining the nature of loyalty defined as a commitment to some person or thing in virtue of one's care and concern for it. If loyalty is a form of care, then it can be understood within the context of interdependence and personal relationships, as something one does for those one cares for. Let us examine the core commitments of care ethics, and develop a substantive conception of loyalty by using its ideals. Although there are different versions of care ethical theories, in general, they claim that:

(1) The language of care, care activity, and care work are central to our everyday lives.[2]
(2) The concepts, metaphors, and images associated with the practice of caring, rather than contracting, best express the dynamics of the moral life and should thus be used in ethical analysis.[3]
(3) Moral agents ought to seek to nurture and preserve the concrete relationships they have with specific others.[4]

Contemporary care ethics theories do not in general give pride of place to loyalty over other virtues or emotions, but a substantive conception of loyalty emerges while keeping in mind these core commitments. Since the ethics of care "values the ties we have with particular other persons and the actual relationships that partly constitute our identity," it emphasizes the relatedness of people to each other and the caring nature of the relationship (Held 2006). On this view, loyalty would be an expression of care for another person in virtue of an interdependent relationship, and is virtuous insofar as it contributes to the flourishing of the relationship. Loyalty to particular others naturally develops as a result of care and concern, and is a product of the caring relationship. Loyalty should thus be interpreted as a kind of *partiality* to those one cares for, justified on the basis that one cares for the other. Care ethicists would not consider it virtuous or morally desirable for an employer to

---

[2]Carol Gilligan's early research suggests that men and women discuss morality using two different "voices:" the voice of justice and the voice of care. For Gilligan, loyalty would be an expression of care to particular individuals in concrete relationships. (See Carol Gilligan 1982.)

[3]See especially Virginia Held, who argues that the concepts, metaphors, and images associated with the care involved in parenting/mothering best express the dynamics of the moral life. (Held 2006) Nel Noddings also argues that we each exist in a web of relationships, and that in these relationships of care, one should be both a care-er and a cared-for. We should seek to preserve and nurture the concrete and valuable relationships we have with specific persons. (See especially Chapters 2 and 3 of Noddings 1984.)

[4]The obligations that flow from our caring relationships are described differently by care ethicists. For example, according to Gilligan, we should exercise special care for those we are concretely in relation to by attending to their particular needs, values, and desires. Eva Feder Kittay, on the other hand, argues that we have an obligation to exercise special care toward those particular persons with whom we have valuable close relationships, particularly where the relationship is one of "dependency" such as that of a child on a parent (Kittay 1998).

exhibit loyalty simply out of concern for universal principles or because it is mutually advantageous. Rather, a care ethicist would say that an employee's loyalty is virtuous when she cares for her employer, sees that she is in an interdependent relationship with her, and seeks to care for and be loyal to her employer in a way that contributes to the flourishing of the relationship.

Simon Keller's (2007) treatment of loyalty characterizes loyalty in this way, and emphasizes that loyalty is an emotion that involves attachment to a particular object. To Keller, "whether or not you are loyal is in large part a matter of your feelings and motivations; it depends on what is going on inside your own head," and this means that demands or requirements of loyalty must be limited. He argues that "we do not have direct control over our feelings and emotions; we do not have the ability suddenly to become loyal to a specified individual. Our loyalties are not directly subject to choice, and that is a reason to doubt the suggestion that they are the subjects of duties."[5] To see why we should understand loyalty as an expression of concern or care for another that is rooted in an emotional attachment or response, let us consider whether a morally appropriate expression of loyalty could *not* spring from concern or care for another person or object.

In his distinctions of loyalty, Keller (2007) argues that while most philosophers treat loyalty as a kind of concern, he says that this concern is expressed as "prioritizing the interests of the loyalty's object." That is to say, loyalty as concern involves placing the interests of another being ahead of oneself or another person. Nevertheless, says Keller, there are several ways of expressing loyalty that do not come down to prioritizing the interests of the loyalty's object. These include loyalty as advocacy or sticking up for someone or something, loyalty expressed in ritual, loyalty as a kind of identification, and loyalty as a kind of belief. While we agree with Keller that there are types of loyalty that do not involve prioritizing the interests of the loyalty's object, and that caring for something does not always result in prioritizing another's interests, it is misleading to say that there are genuine expressions of loyalty different from "loyalty in concern," for it seems that all expressions of loyalty are an *expression of concern and care* for another's interests even if they do not result in *prioritizing* another's interests.[6] In some ways, this complaint regards terminology, for we support the idea that there are indeed different expressions of loyalty; nevertheless, our idea is that a genuine expression of loyalty is grounded in care and concern.

With this background in mind, we can now ask, how can loyalty be an expression of care in business relationships? While relationships of employment begin as contractual and maintain that character as long as the contract endures, business relations are *interpersonal* as well as contractual. It is in the interpersonal aspect of the

[5]Keller argues that the only time loyalty is a duty is between children and their parents. Children should perform loyal actions, out of loyal feelings and motives. Keller (2007), 143.

[6]In addition, Keller is right to say that not all forms of loyalty involve prioritizing another's interests, and that this is neither sufficient nor necessary for loyalty to that entity. One may prioritize someone's interest out of duty or obligation and not as an expression of loyalty, and conversely, loyalty can be expressed without prioritizing another's interests.

business relationship that there is a need for an account of loyalty as a form of care. Business relationships are interpersonal in the sense that they involve people who must work together on a personal level. Co-workers must learn to give credit where credit is due, know how to communicate effectively with their bosses, show others how to perform tasks without insulting their intelligence or offending them, learn from others without intruding on their "territory," and seek to develop relationships of respect and trust. These interpersonal relationships are central to the practice of business because they are integral to the possibility of cooperative ventures. In this regard, business is, essentially, about people working together harmoniously so that operations flow smoothly. Business relationships are interpersonally robust, and can indeed be the proper context in which to address loyalty an appropriate expression of care.

So what would care ethics recommend regarding loyalty in interpersonal working or business relationships? Let us begin with employee loyalty within interpersonal workplace relationships. We can account for many of our intuitions about loyalty as an expected trait of employees by appealing to personal relationships of interdependence within the workplace. It is evident that there are elements of care between employees, except in the coldest and most hostile work environments. Now, certainly, some elements of the give-and-take between co-workers are best characterized as legal and social contracts motivated by mutual self-interest: successful job performance may depend upon maintaining good working relationships with others on the job, and both success and happiness in the workplace can be improved if one can do some favors for others while expecting them to return the extra help when one is in need. Nevertheless, these contractual obligations do not exhaust the kind of relationship we think that a good co-worker has with her peers. We think of a good employee as being cognizant of the way in which those around her are dependent on her proper and conscientious fulfillment of her role. The role which "teambuilding" retreats play in the corporation, with their trust falls and ropes courses, is more clearly about a recognition of the *interdependence* of employees and the need for care in workplace relationships than it is about building an awareness of mutual self-interest and obligations. Put simply, a good worker is not necessarily a good co-worker, but a good employee, ultimately, is both. From the perspective of care ethics, one should be loyal to these people as friends and nurturers in virtue of the interdependent nature of the relationship to each other.

Keller also argues that one can also express loyalty through performing or participating in rituals, or participating more generally in practices that are understood to symbolize or express loyalty. Keller's classic examples include expressions of patriotism such as reciting a pledge of allegiance, saluting the flag, or standing to attention during the national anthem, but there are also ways of ritualizing loyalty in business. Some examples include going to weekend workplace-related events, attending the annual holiday party, contributing to a firm's charitable donations, or participating in company activities such as raffles or fundraisers. These are ways of symbolizing one's commitment to the firm by going through the motions of loyalty. Again, they are not required by one's contract, and thus are not a duty or obligation to the firm, but do express a kind of loyalty to the firm, department, or workplace community.

How would a virtuous *employer* express loyalty understood as a kind of care? If we can assume the possibility of something like a virtuous employer—an employer that approaches the employee in a way that goes beyond enlightened self-interest—we can say that not only is the development of a loyal disposition psychologically more-or-less likely and perhaps mutually beneficial, but morally praiseworthy as well, and the failure to develop such a disposition morally blameworthy. An example of employer loyalty can be exhibited in the idea of a virtuous manager. In a business, the manager has legal obligations and obligations of fairness, but a virtuous manager will not apply these obligations in a purely mechanical and unfeeling way. We expect managers—*good* managers, at least—to "have a heart." By this, we mean that we expect her to take circumstances and contexts into account, to be sensitive to the needs and life-projects of those she manages, and to be aware of the effects that her decisions and determination have on those who she manages. If she must discharge a long-term employee due to budget cuts, the loyal employer will not simply keep the employee on as an expression of loyalty to that person—rather, her loyalty to that person might motivate her to help her in other, more personal ways. For example, she might offer to help the person to find another job, loan her some money, or go to extraordinary measures to help that person succeed.

This is not to say that developing this kind of loyalty to an employee is morally required—we are not arguing that there is a prima facie obligation even to attempt to form such a relationship. Rather, we are suggesting that in circumstances where contractual obligations have been met, interpersonal relationships have been developed, and moral principles have been committed to, then insofar as one cares for an employee, expressing concern through loyalty is morally praiseworthy because it is appropriate given the nature of the relationship; failing to demonstrate loyalty to that individual as a person demonstrates a moral failing on a relational level. An employer that is unable to express some feeling of loyalty to a loyal employee is deserving of moral censure, not because loyalty is a "two-way street" but because a person that is unable to express loyalty toward another individual has not followed through on what naturally follows given that the nature of the relationship is a caring one.

Although it seems plausible that loyalty in the personal aspects of business and work relationships is virtuous, one might object that loyalty that flows from care and concern for another person generates unfair favoritism toward those with whom one is in personal relationship. We now turn to examining the appropriate place of loyalty in business itself.

Loyalty and Obligation in Business

Having outlined the way that loyalty may be expressed as care in business relationships, we can now examine whether loyalty (as based in care) can ever be considered a workplace duty or obligation. Although some have argued that employers[7] may

---

[7] In the preceding, we have used "employer" to refer ambiguously to the business in its role relative to the employee, in which the "employer" may be conceived of by the employee as being both the

appropriately require loyalty, it is also true that employers cannot demand loyalty as a kind of care. As we will argue here, the *requirement* of loyalty is best understood as a fiduciary duty obligated by in virtue of the Law of Agency,[8] or an express or implied contractual obligation. Our view is that these are not expressions of genuine loyalty but are instead one-sided demands better characterized in moral terms as requirements of allegiance, following simply from fiduciary duties. After showing the shortcomings of an idea of loyalty which can be obligated, we then outline a care ethic approach to loyalty which goes beyond fiduciary duties, and describe what it recommends regarding conflicts of loyalty, such as in cases of whistle-blowing.

Any view of "loyalty" that can be obligated in virtue of being an employee is better described as fiduciary duty through the law of agency or contractual obligation. For example, being a "team player" may be implied merely by our fiduciary duty as agents, "because the proper function of business *does* require a certain degree of self-sacrifice in the service of a collective goal" (Corvino 2002), but loyalty is usually taken to refer to actions and commitments beyond those required merely for satisfactory job performance. Since satisfactory job performance itself may require self-sacrifice and adopting the interests of the corporation, this *obligation* of loyalty is best understood as one that springs from the Law of Agency, even though these fiduciary duties may include actions which are outwardly similar to loyal actions, including "some degree of 'self-sacrifice without expectation of reward' " (Corvino 2002).

Sissela Bok (1983) bases loyalty on either a fiduciary duty or an express or implied contract, stating that "[i]n holding his position, he has assumed certain obligations to his colleagues and clients. He may even have subscribed to a loyalty oath or a promise of confidentiality." But arguing that loyalty is owed because it is part of an obligatory sworn oath or contract ignores the question of whether loyalty can be simply promised and whether such a promise can be required. It is question-begging to say that an employee has an obligation to loyalty based on a contractual requirement to do so. At most, an employment contract can establishes an obligation to perform specifiable actions whose outcomes are approximate those that would follow from loyalty as care. For example, employers often require employees to sign non-compete clauses and maintain trade secrets. These are requirements of

abstract legal entity of the corporation and the representatives of that abstract legal entity. Since we will now be discussing particular interpersonal relationships within business, we will avoid the ambiguous term "employer" in favor of speaking either of "corporation" or "management". By "corporation" we will mean exclusively the abstract legal entity and by "management" we will mean exclusively the group of actual people who represent the corporation in their roles as managers, supervisors, and executives.

[8] As stated in the *Restatement (Third) of Agency*, "Agency is the fiduciary relationship that arises when one person (a "principal") manifests assent to another person (an "agent") that the agent shall act on the principal's behalf and subject to the principal's control, and the agent manifests assent or otherwise consents so to act" (American Law Institute 2006). Having entered a relationship of special trust, in which the agent is taken as representative of the principal, there are special obligations to promote the ends of the principal.

loyalty that are demanded by a contract, and are not robust expressions of loyalty. Following through with these obligations is not well-characterized as loyalty—it is more like doing one's duty rather than showing personal commitment to a firm. Working weekends, abiding by a non-compete clause, and going out of one's way to consider the greater good of the business are often part of the job, but are not, in fact, genuine expressions of loyalty.

This is not to say that corporations should not require loyalty of this sort. It *does* make prudential sense to ask employees to perform actions that are in the interest of the relationship and the business, and these can be specified in a contract. As Keller (2007) emphasizes, while these agreements might privilege the interests of the corporation and *may* occur as expressions of loyalty, such actions are neither necessary nor sufficient to constitute genuine loyalty. If genuine loyalty goes beyond actions that can be captured by fiduciary and contractual duties, but is also an affective orientation, then it is incoherent for management to require loyalty. Loyalty involves feeling concern or care for an object of interest and being concerned with the relationship with that entity, and managers can really only require *allegiance* to the corporation, where the employee is expected to act loyally in limited and specifiable ways, but not to be loyal. Loyalty involves having the motivation to go above and beyond what is already required by the contract, and involves emotional motivations of care and concern.

To think that loyalty is derivative of duties and justice or contractual obligations, and to treat loyalty as a duty or obligation, mistakes the effect for the cause. Consider an analogy with interpersonal relationships. Do you have an obligation to care for a family member? As care ethicists have argued, there are certainly duties and obligations involved in family relationships, but they do not capture the extent or the core of what it is to be, for example, a caring mother. Similarly, when we describe employee loyalty in terms of duties and obligations, we capture neither the extent nor the core of what it is to be a loyal employee. While it is evident that parties have certain duties that follow from agreement to a contract, it does not make sense to say that loyalty to a company is required in virtue of a contractual relationship. We would have just as much difficulty—and difficulty of a similar kind—if we tried to argue that parents have an *obligation* to care about their children.

When the question of whether loyalty can be obligated is asked from the care ethical perspective, it turns out that obligations of loyalty to a business are like obligations of loyalty to a family member. In both cases, the moral obligations flow from the nature of the relationship. Care ethicist Michael Slote (2007), for example, suggests that our duties and obligations to others are directly correlated to the nature of the relationship and its care dimension.[9] The more one cares for another, the greater her obligations to her; the less that one cares for another, the fewer the obligations. Nel Noddings also argues that we have subordinate ethical obligations that derive from the ethical ideal of caring. On her view, there are two criteria that

[9] See Slote (2007) Chapter 1.

govern obligations of "ethical caring": "the existence of or potential for present relation, and the dynamic potential for growth in relation, including the potential for increased reciprocity and, perhaps mutuality" (Noddings 1984). When these criteria are applied to loyalty, there is no simple recipe to follow regarding how to be loyal to another person. If being loyal contributes to the possibility of growth in a relationship, and to the potential for increased reciprocity, then one is obligated to be loyal and perform actions that cultivate the caring relationship. But in absence of a caring relationship, there are limited obligations of loyalty. The extent of the obligation of loyalty is thus informed by the (more or less) caring nature of the interpersonal relationship.

This thesis regarding the obligation to be loyal in personal relationships can be applied to business relationships: the nature of the caring relationship gives guidance regarding the appropriate moral obligations and obligations of loyalty to the one with whom one is in relationship. And the way that loyalty should be expressed in these relationships is unique and highly variable.

For care ethics, then, only a limited obligation of loyalty in personal relationships can be derived from the ethical ideal of caring, since loyalty is one of many obligations we have in a caring relationship. Is the same true in business relationships? Is loyalty one of many moral obligations that arise in relation to the other? It is, insofar as obligations of loyalty can potentially conflict with other obligations to a corporation. The most important of these conflicts occurs in cases of whistle-blowing, where an employee's obligation to be loyal to an employer may conflict with her obligation to follow the law, company policies, or other moral principles such as justice. Care ethicists have been careful in addressing the relationship between obligations of care and obligations of justice and are sensitive to the idea that justice is also an important part of the moral life. Their approach is to say that care ethical principles should apply to relationships of "partiality" and the domains of family and friendship, while "universal" requirements of duty and justice should apply to the domains of law (Held 2006). When this thesis is applied the workplace, then, duties of loyalty and duties of justice apply to different domains; obligations of loyalty should be cultivated in the personal domain, while obligations of justice motivate one's response to violations of justice, etc. (Held 2006). This interpretation of care ethics would thus recommend that employees uphold duties of justice and disclose violations of justice that harm society, but cultivate loyalty to the dimension of the relationship that involves care. Employees should "blow the whistle" when they are motivated by concerns of justice, and at the same time, show care and loyalty to the person with whom they are in a caring relationship. The extent of the requirement of loyalty to the individual depends on the extent of the caring nature of the relationship. For example, if the relationship is a close family one, individuals should still seek to care for and be loyal to those others in order to promote the caring nature of the relationship. If the relationship is not a close one, and the relationship is not a caring one, the employee's obligation to be loyal to the employer is diminished. We now turn to examining the requirement of employee-employer loyalty in greater detail.

Care for and Loyalty to a Corporation

To this point we have argued that care ethics recommends a limited obligation of loyalty in business, one that is highly variable and dependent on the nature of the caring relationship. Most loyalty in the course of business is personal, and takes place between managers, employees, and co-workers and so loyalty as an expression of care in this realm is plausible. But a central issue business ethics is whether employees should be loyal to the corporation itself. We now turn to considering whether employees ought to be loyal to their employers when that employer is a *corporation*. In order to isolate the corporation itself as an object of loyalty, we will imagine a corporation of the most impersonal and least humanized form: a publicly-traded for-profit national or multi-national corporation. If we are able to provide an adequate account of loyalty to this kind of corporate entity, and if we have been successful in the above in providing an adequate account of loyalty to co-workers, employees, and managers, then we take it that all cases should be covered by either one, the other, or both at once.[10]

As captured by the Law of Agency and fiduciary duties, the employee is clearly in a position of caring *for* the corporation in a literal sense. The corporation is a legal entity, given a fictional personhood by law. The corporation is the legal property-holder, and therefore legally the principal who the employees represent as its agents—and the corporation, for its part, is clearly in a relationship of dependency relative to the employee: without its agents, the corporation cannot manufacture, trade, provide services, or engage in any activity in any way, since outside of its representatives, it is nothing but an abstract legal entity. In some cases, the *caring for* which the employees must engage in qua agents, however, amounts to nothing more than making good on contractual obligations: showing up on time, making a good-faith effort to meet performance expectations, and preserving trade secrets whenever possible. We agree with Soles's assessment that "if [this] minimalist conception of loyalty is accepted, it seems clear that employees ought to be loyal to their employers," but that "[this] minimalist view is sufficiently attenuated . . . that such a claim does not amount to much," and "does not impose upon them the sorts of obligations that often are urged in the name of loyalty" (1993). Rather than call this minimal and contractually obligated fiduciary duty a kind of loyalty at all, we prefer to reserve the word "loyalty" for something more robust.

Loyalty, as we have discussed it, is the expression of a partiality towards those one cares for, in which care and concern is shown, and through which the relationship is able to flourish. If loyalty to a corporation also fits this model, it must not be merely a dependent and fiduciary relation—i.e. that the employee is of necessity in the position of caring for the corporation—but must extend this caring-for into

[10]For example, in a small, privately-owned, family-run business, there may be little sense in speaking of loyalty to the business separately from loyalty to the owner-manager, while in most U.S. businesses, loyalty to the corporation may be quite separable, and may indeed come into conflict with, loyalty to one's co-workers or managers.

caring-about, in which care is shown for the interests of the corporation *for its own sake* rather than out of contractual obligation. This loyalty would be an expression of partiality in virtue of a caring relationship, in which the interests of the corporation are given additional weight on the basis of this relationship of care.

For the time being, let us bracket the additional teleological condition of tending towards flourishing, and concentrate on partiality which grants additional weight to the interests of the corporation, for there is a question which immediately presents itself here: are the interests of the corporation of a kind appropriate to loyalty? If these interests consist of nothing beyond profit maximization, it may be argued that our understanding of loyalty is inappropriately applied, for profit is a very narrow scope of "interests." Yet, even a corporation that subjugates all other concerns to the profit motive has a robust set of other interests, even if they are secondary and subsidiary. Corporations have public personae, products, services, and brand identity. While each of these may be adopted out of nothing other than market analysis, they impart sufficient character to the corporate entity to allow some employees to come to see the corporation as an object of care. Employees who defend their corporation's products against criticism, who actively seek to improve the corporation's public image, or who venture beyond their job description to improve efficiency perform actions that can be meaningfully called loyal, in that these actions exhibit a concern for the various direct and subsidiary interests of the corporation as a legal entity, which concern goes beyond contractual obligation or the expectation of reward. Indeed, this is all the more clearly a form of loyalty where the corporation is more narrowly concerned with profit maximization, for here the employee is less likely to expect her actions to result in gratitude or reciprocation.

We expect that the degree to which employees are able to adopt the corporation as an object of care and loyalty will vary at least in part along with the variety and richness of interests that the corporation adopts and exhibits. Compare, for example, the same employee's relationship to her bank account. If we can mean anything by the "interests" of a bank account, these interests must be exhausted by maximization of profits and holdings—and surely the bank account is similarly dependent on the employee's agency on its behalf, since it, like the corporation, is a legal entity having no independent agency. It seems strange indeed to imagine that this employee would develop loyalty towards her bank account, which, based on our model, would consist of the additional weighting of the interests of the bank account out of concern for it rather than out of the self-interested and contractual aspects of her relationship with it. Here, surely, there is a relevant difference in the independence of the interests at stake: the bank account exists for the sake of the employee, while the corporation does not. Still, at least a part of the strangeness of the idea of loyalty to a bank account has to do with the lack of a variety of aims and goals bound up with the activity of the bank account.

Conversely, employee adoption of the corporation as an object of care is more likely if the corporation has a particularly rich set of aims. Imagine that the employee believes her corporation takes a stakeholder view of corporate social responsibility. Perhaps it is an industry leader in sustainability efforts, taking financial losses and market risks in order to try to change the way that business is done within its industry. In this case, the perceived interests of the corporation go beyond profit maximization and its subsidiary goals, and the type of caring support and intervention that the employee may be able to render begins to widen.

Why are employees more likely to be loyal to a corporation that seems to have a broader view of corporate social responsibility? The established mode of debate about loyalty would chalk this up to the employee's identification with the corporation, based upon a shared set of values (Duska 1992). If we consider other modes of corporate social responsibility, such as community support or employee involvement in managerial decisions, the established debate might tie this difference back to mutual benefit and obligations to reciprocate. But the care-ethics-based account of loyalty is able to recognize that some employees are loyal even in the absence of the likelihood of reciprocation, and in the absence of an assessment of the moral worth of the corporate enterprise. Moreover, whether or not it is wise or virtuous to do so, it is uncontroversial that there are some employees who exhibit loyalty to their corporate employers simply because they are its employee, without ever asking whether the corporation's products, services, or business model are in accord with the employee's personal moral values and ends, or whether this loyalty is more likely to serve their self-interest than seeking alternate employment. Surely, though, if promoting the interests of the object of care is one way of expressing loyalty, as we have claimed, those corporations that have a more varied and robust set of apparent interests are more likely to inspire loyalty in employees. And we acknowledge that having a shared set of values and mutual self-interest might both play strong roles in the development of employee loyalty.

It remains for us to consider whether the teleological aspect of our definition of loyalty may be appropriately applied to employees' relationship with corporations. Here we can return to each of the examples just given in opposite order. First, we can begin with a corporation with a demonstrated interest in employee involvement in managerial decisions, or in employee and community welfare. Here we may easily see that the employee who pursues these interests beyond contractual obligation tends towards the flourishing of the employee-corporation relationship insofar as it is a caring relationship. Where the corporation invites employee involvement in these ends, and takes these ends seriously, employee commitment to these ends will tend to strengthen and further develop these connections. Furthermore, a corporation that is able to demonstrate an apparent awareness and appreciation of interdependence between itself and its agents is far more likely to be adopted as an object of care, since adopting policies reflecting support for and gratitude to employees causes the employee-corporation relationship to more closely resemble the kinds of personal relationships of interdependence that are typically accompanied by care and loyalty.

Next, we can consider the corporation which may have a demonstrated interest in goals other than profit maximization but not including specific commitments to employees and community, as in our example of the corporation which seeks to reform environmental practices within its industry. The employee who adopts this corporation as an object of care will be likely to pursue these environmental interests, and give them additional weight in her practical reasoning on the basis of this relationship of care. We can expect the corporation that has adopted this goal to be more likely to continue and intensify pursuit of it when employees actively contribute and commit to the goal. Since we can assume that the employee has adopted this goal because of her caring about the corporation, this likelihood of continued and intensified pursuit of the goal represents a strengthening and development of the employee-corporation relationship, which we can appropriately call a flourishing of that relationship insofar as it is a caring relationship.

Finally, we have left to consider the most extreme case: the corporation that pursues profit maximization in the most crass manner, subjugating all other interests to the bottom line. We claimed in the above that there are some employees who may exhibit care and loyalty even in the absence of any assessment that the corporation is pursuing ends which accord with the employee's personal moral values, and in the absence of any reasonable expectation of reciprocation or mutual self-interest. Can this relationship be described as a genuinely caring relationship that may flourish on the basis of that care and loyalty? From the perspective of care ethics, can and should an employee be loyal to this corporation?

There is, in principle, no reason why an employee would be unable to adopt the corporation as an object of care in this situation in the same way as she might for the corporation with environmental goals. If the corporation, for example, seeks only its own profit, and does so by attempting to corner a particular market, the employee may take on that goal on the basis of her caring about the corporation, just as, in the other case, she may take on the other corporation's environmental goals. For example, the corporation may set its proximal goal (in pursuit of the primary economic goal) as making its product the next "must-have" technological gadget. The employee may adopt and commit to that goal, beyond self-interest or contractual obligation, as a "loyalty to the corporation-with-its-function" (Ewin 1993). In this case, it is again reasonable to describe this adoption as tending to produce a caring relationship within the employee-corporation model, for both the corporation and the employee have adopted this goal, and the pursuit of this goal will tend to strengthen and develop the sense in which it is a caring relationship, based as it is upon the mutual adoption of this non-moral interest.

In fact, the care-ethical definition of employee loyalty is nicely illustrated using this example. In a distinct divergence from the idea that loyalty is based upon a set of values shared by both employee and corporation, an employee may adopt the corporation as an object of care despite significant disagreement about values, and this may motivate the employee to express loyalty in a very different way while still tending toward a form of flourishing of that relationship. Consider an employee who believes a particular corporate policy to be indefensible, but chooses to attempt to reform the corporation from within, rather than to dissolve her voluntary association with the corporation by accepting a job elsewhere. By exercising *voice* rather than *exit*, to use Hirschman's terms (1970), this employee is exhibiting loyalty by pursuing what she believes the company's true interests. In this way, the situation is similar to accounts of whistle-blowing as "the highest form of loyalty" in that she pursues the corporation's best possibilities as she sees them, rather than the corporation's own implied conception of its interests. This may be motivated out of loyalty to her co-workers, who may not have the ability to exercise the option of exit, or may be "loyalty to principles, which can lead somebody to oppose the other members of a group claiming to espouse the principles if she believes that they have really moved away from them" (Ewin 1993). However, in some cases this may also be motivated out of loyalty to the corporation as a legal entity. In this case, by adopting the corporation as an object of care, she is clearly going beyond (and perhaps even against) contractually obligated actions in order to pursue the interests of the corporation as she sees them.

This kind of critical loyalty is best explained using the model of loyalty as a product of care, in which the employee is loyal because she genuinely cares for the corporation and its well-being. The starting point is one of disagreement: the employee raises objections to the current practices of the corporation, claiming that the corporation is not properly pursuing its best possibilities. Sometimes the result of this action will be termination or discipline of the employee, but if the corporation, through its other agents in managerial and executive positions, is able to adopt additional concerns which add variety and robustness to the set of demonstrated corporate interests, not only will the relationship between this employee and the corporation flourish, develop, and strengthen, but it will be more likely that other employees will care more for the corporation and develop loyalty to it as well.

These examples, concerned with loyalty towards a corporation that subjugates all other interests to profit maximization, reveal an important difference between our definition of loyalty and those definitions that suggest that loyalty must based on the pursuit of the moral good of the corporation. In our view, it is possible for an employee to care for and be loyal to a corporation that pursues amoral interests, as in the example of the corporation pursuing the "next must-have technological gadget." In fact, our definition of loyalty includes the possibility that employees may also care for and be loyal to corporations whose interests are immoral from the care ethical perspective and from other moral perspectives as well. Like Ewin (1993), our view is that loyalty can be morally problematic from the standpoint of justice, as well as from the standpoint of care, and believe there is no reason to define "loyalty" as a term only appropriately used when it is in support of moral acts or people. It is plausible for loyalty to be directed towards immoral acts or persons, and the only apparent reason to insist otherwise is that this creates a problem for those who want to claim that loyalty is an obligation of employees. For how can loyalty be a moral obligation if loyalty can include taking immoral actions, towards immoral ends, for the sake of an immoral entity? Business ethicists must either allow that there is no moral obligation to be loyal, admitting that at least some expressions of loyalty can be morally impermissible, or must artificially define "loyalty" as applying only to the morally acceptable parts of what is called loyalty in ordinary language. We avoid this pseudo-dilemma entirely: loyalty, understood as a form of care, cannot be obliged, and is not always moral, even from the perspective of care ethics.

This pseudo-dilemma has introduced confusion into the debate about loyalty, even when it is not directly taken up as an issue. For example, Corvino (2002) seems to accept that the word "loyalty" may be meaningfully used to refer to immoral behavior, stating that "[t]he mafia underling who turns state's evidence is indeed disloyal to his boss," but that loyalty, in this case, is not good because the object of loyalty, or the values embodied by it, are not moral. But then this commonsense view is not consistent with his use, elsewhere in the same article, of phrases like "proper loyalty," "true devotion," and "tough love," which imply that the mafia underling is engaged in a form of *false loyalty* when obeying his don, and *true loyalty* when he forces his don out of a life of crime by presenting evidence against him to the authorities. But this distinction seems arbitrary—why not simply say that these are two different expressions of loyalty, only one of which is in keeping with objective moral standards? We agree with Varelius (2009) that "[a]lthough it can be morally repugnant, the idea of a loyal Nazi, a gangster who is loyal to the mafia, etc. is quite coherent." The simpler and less question-begging analysis suggests that in these different circumstances, what varies is not whether the underling is truly or falsely loyal, but instead from what perspective the underling views his boss's interests: from an immoral perspective, his best interests lie in committing crimes and getting away with it; in another moral perspective, his best interests lie in going straight, repentance, and incarceration. Using this distinction, we can respond to the resolve this discomforting moral ambivalence of loyalty by differentiating *appropriate* from *inappropriate* loyalty. There may be a satisfactory way to do this through the ethics of justice, but care ethics can also make this distinction from within its own realm by recognizing that, while loyalty is a form of care, caring for another can sometimes help the other to be more caring, and can at other times enable the other's failure to be caring.

From the perspective of care ethics, while loyalty is an expression of care for another, not all expressions of loyalty are appropriate. While people may in fact care for and be loyal to a wide range of corporations, care ethics distinguishes between *appropriate* and *inappropriate* loyalty using a criterion of care: it recommends employee loyalty to a corporation whose effects and interests are caring. In other words, the propriety of employee loyalty tracks the extent to which a corporation's interests are themselves caring. The more that a corporation's goals, interests, and practices express care for consumers, the environment, and its own employees, the more an employee should care for and be loyal to that corporation. This is *appropriate loyalty*, or loyalty that is motivated by care and tends towards the flourishing of the corporation and the employee-employer relationship. But if the corporation has a dearth of moral values and social concerns, it is not appropriate for employees to be loyal to this kind of corporation in the sense that she ought to carry out this corporation's goals and interests. If the employee genuinely cares for a corporation whose interests and practices are morally problematic, she should exercise critical loyalty, as described above, by seeking to reform the corporation's practices so that they tend toward genuine moral flourishing.

The care ethics account of loyalty is also able to explain why loyalty is an ambiguous motivation for whistle-blowing. Loyalty can motivate an employee to blow the whistle when the corporation is engaging in uncaring activities regarding its employees, the environment, or its consumers—and, here, this critical loyalty is appropriate. But loyalty can also be a motivation to attack and silence whistleblowers, when that dissent has a strong and apparent moral basis. This is inappropriately uncritical loyalty. While Larmer (1992) is right that loyalty often involves pursuit of the best interests of an object of care, his claim that "to the degree that an action is genuinely immoral, it is impossible that it is in the agent's best interest," is a non-sequitur. This is because the issue at hand for the employee's approach to her loyalty is not necessarily what is *actually* in the best interests of the object of care, but what is *perceived* as in the best interests of the object of care, and we cannot ignore that employees exhibiting loyalty can certainly at times be morally benighted, especially when in an atmosphere of conformity and groupthink. Those who argue that there is an obligation of loyalty have a strong incentive to artificially define loyalty so that it is always moral from an impartial perspective, since it is problematic to claim that we can be obligated to perform immoral actions. By arguing instead that loyalty is an expression of care, we are able to distinguish between appropriate and inappropriate loyalty without making the question-begging claim that the inappropriately loyal employee is not "really" loyal at all. This analysis more consistently shows that loyalty involves a pursuit of perceived interests which, although based on a moral element within our relationships, may take place within a misguided moral context. Insofar as loyalty can express care and concern for a corporation's well-being, then this account provides a way to resolve the apparent tension between loyalty and whistle-blowing that is both more theoretically sound and more descriptively accurate.

Desert, Care and Loyalty

Employees may care for and develop loyalty to a corporation which expresses no interest in anything beyond profit maximization, even though it is more likely that care and loyalty will develop toward a corporation that is able to demonstrate a wider and more robust set of interests, particularly when they have values and goals in common with the employee. But a view of loyalty in business must also provide some account of when loyalty is more or less *appropriate* in the sense that it is worthy of moral recommendation or discouragement. We mentioned this briefly above, but the established debate in business ethics is concerned with whether and under what conditions loyalty may become an *obligation*, and in order to address the intuition that loyalty is at least sometimes obligatory, we must give a more detailed account of appropriate loyalty. The analysis we present here shows that there is never an obligation of loyalty independent of contractual agreements, but that in some cases, a corporation is *deserving* of employee loyalty.

Even though the language of "desert" seems entirely distinct from the language of care, there is a sense in which the idea of desert is present in personal relationships of care. As we will argue here, the idea of "desert" within caring relationships is different from the idea of "desert" within relationships of obligation and contract. Our central idea here is that "desert" in caring relationships has to do with symmetry, and not justice.

To see this, consider everyday usages of "desert" in personal relationships, the most common of which might be in romantic relationships: "You deserve better than him," or "She doesn't deserve you." In the cases of certain very strong and close friendships, honorifically referred to as "true friendship," we may make similar claims, such as "she doesn't deserve a friend like you." In these examples, we use the concept of desert to emphasize the idea of symmetry in a caring relationship. We do not mean that there is some action which is obligated of the other, such as that a friend might deserve remuneration when she has lent a friend some money, or that a favor deserves to be repaid—instead, we mean that the friend who does a favor without a thought of when and whether it might be repaid deserves a friend who cares for them in the same way, and would be similarly willing to help without expectation of reward. "Desert" within an ethics of justice refers to equitable and fair treatment, whereas "desert" within caring relationships refers to similar kinds of commitment and similar willingness to move beyond equitability and fairness to altruism or selflessness. This does not mean that there is an *obligation* to care—indeed, when there is a lack of emotional attachment to the other, we are likely to say that the relationship has failed and will result in dissolution, rather than saying that one party is "not living up to his side of the agreement." Although there may be an obligation to ensure that past care cannot be regained, especially in the case of a marriage which has become loveless, the relationship is rooted in a commitment based upon, but extending further than, reciprocity or the expectation of mutual benefit. There are elements of reciprocal benefit and obligation in such a relationship, but these capture neither the core nor the extent of the commitment, which is not a first-order concern with contract and fairness, but a second-order mutual commitment to value one another and the relationship in a far more unconditional and giving way, not delimited by first-order considerations of equitability.

In romantic relationships and friendships there are elements of mutual satisfaction and partnership towards shared ends that are similar to the voluntary and economic arrangements of employment. Yet, if a relationship is pursued solely on the basis of mutual satisfaction of needs, this is a mere relationship of convenience. If this aspect of the relationship is one-sided, it seems that the more committed partner is being "used" by the partner who views the relationship as a mere mutual satisfaction of needs. The Hegelian definition of marriage as a "contract against contract" exemplifies our conception of romantic relationships as including mutual benefit and give and take, but being, in fact, based upon a refusal to take note and keep account of whether these benefits are justly distributed. Hegel claims that to view marriage as a civil contract degrades it to "mutual caprice" and "a contract for reciprocal use," while to base it on love alone makes it "exposed in every respect to contingency," and so, although marriage does include love and "begins in contract," the true basis of marriage can be neither of these, but instead " a contract to transcend the standpoint of contract, the standpoint from which persons are regarded in their individuality as self-subsistent units" (Hegel 1952 [1820]). The partner, married or unmarried, who makes an honest commitment to transcend contract and justice can be said to "deserve better" than a partner who takes such a vow while remaining a self-centered narcissist. The problem here is an asymmetry in the relationship: the one party has made a commitment based only upon contract and mutual self-interest; the other has made a far more unconditional and altruistic commitment.

The same may apply to friendships. Friendships, most of all when they are exceptionally close or long-lived, may be viewed as being "beyond" the give-and-take of obligations and favors. Favors may be viewed simply as something friends do for one another, without any accounting of whether a favor is earned or deserved. And a similar asymmetry is possible here: As in Wilde's story of *Little Hans and the Miller*, it is perfectly possible—but undesirable—for one party to maintain a commitment that "true friendship [is] quite free from selfishness of any kind" (Wilde 1915) while the other party acts in the most selfish and inconsiderate ways. But if one party acts on the basis of care, and the other does not, the relationship is asymmetrical, and according to care ethics, this impacts the nature of the obligations of each party.

When we refer to desert in our personal relationships, it does not signify whether care has been "earned" or is obligatory, but refers to an asymmetrical kind of commitment within a relationship, where one party acts on the basis of care, and the other does not. Similarly, we can speak of whether loyalty is deserved in a business relationship based on similar claims of symmetry or asymmetry within the relationship, where the employee may maintain loyalty towards an uncaring corporation, or the employee may fail to develop loyalty towards a caring corporation. In employee-corporation relationships, though, we must be even more careful to separate deserving loyalty from being owed loyalty, since in this very abstract relationship there are not clear markers of care as there are in our personal romantic and friendship relations. Corporations and employees show care in far more ambiguous ways—a corporation may support an employee during a time of need, but whether this is done out of concern or self-interest is usually inscrutable, especially when compared to a confession of love from a romantic partner, or a friend's willingness to help move a couch. Consequently, our account of desert and symmetry is largely in line with Hart and Thompson (2007), who assert that when employees and employers have asymmetrical degrees of loyalty towards one another "the misalignment in perceptions does not necessarily mean that one party is *disloyal* to the relationship, although the other may deem it to be so,"—but that "asymmetry may also be characterized as the case of two actors conceiving of different reciprocal obligations in their relationship to one another ... [and] loyalty asymmetries may occur despite good-faith efforts by both parties."

This care-based account of desert is consistent with the claim that employee loyalty is a "two-way street," not because loyalty is owed on the basis of contract or mutual self-interest, but because a party willing to move beyond these self-interested concerns in taking their partner as an object of care is deserving of receiving care from their partner in return. Since this kind of care requires subjugating considerations of fairness and obligation to the interests of the other, it makes no sense to say that this kind of loyalty can generate an obligation to reciprocate through first-order implicit agreements—loyalty is a "two-way street" regarding second-order agreements only, and those second-order agreements-about-agreements consist of a refusal to insist on requiring our first-order agreements to be a "two-way street." This is why it has been argued that, "without transcendent motives on both parts (i.e., the individual and the organization), it is not possible to feel identified with an organization, or feel loyal to it. Consequently, loyalty cannot be a gimmick" (Rosanas and Velilla 2003). Appropriate loyalty in this regard is highly dependent on the nature of the relationship between the two parties.

Understanding loyalty as an expression of care, we can conclude that the reciprocation of loyalty with loyalty in return may be deserved, without claiming that loyalty is obligatory, a claim that would lead to intractable contradictions regarding whether "loyalty" can be distinguished from considerations of justice or mutual self-interest. To say that loyalty is obligated by a business relationship or in an employee's and an employer's best interests conflicts with the idea that loyalty expresses partiality, care, and concern for the other. Loyalty is best understood as a commitment that goes beyond obligation, and is often a desirable and praiseworthy aspect of the employee-corporation relationship. Care ethical theories help to explain the intuition that, while a business has no obligation to be loyal to a loyal employee, a loyal employee does *deserve* loyalty in return, even though she is not *owed* loyalty in return. This voluntarily reciprocated loyalty could be manifested in a variety of ways. Since loyalty tends to arise from a varied and robust set of demonstrated corporate interests, a company which is able to demonstrate a valuation of employees which goes beyond contract and obligation is more likely to generate loyalty in return. Similarly, an employee who meets her contractual obligations and who acts appropriately as an agent of a corporation does not wrong that corporation if she does not demonstrate loyalty, even if that corporation demonstrates loyalty towards her. Such a corporation deserves employee loyalty, but this desert does not generate an obligation, since loyalty is a going-beyond of relationships of obligation.

From the perspective of care ethics, is it wrong for an employee to maintain loyalty to a company that does not "deserve it" in the sense that it is unable to transcend mutual self-interest in its policies and behaviors? Employees do sometimes maintain care and devotion to their corporate employers even when they are ruthless profiteers, socially irresponsible, or cut wages for the sake of overall profits. In some cases it would be appropriate to compare this situation to that of the battered wife who chooses to "stand by her man," even in the face of overwhelming evidence that he is undeserving of loyalty; in other cases we can see where this choice of "voice" rather than "exit" can be praiseworthy rather than unhealthy and morally quixotic.

In order to address this kind of case, Larmer (1992) uses an analogy with a parent's loyalty to "an erring teenager," wherein we see a loyalty to a party that actively refuses to demonstrate loyalty in return. We can easily imagine a more extreme example that more dramatically and clearly parallels the loyal employee's relationship with a corporation truly unable to recognize moral value: the parent's relationship with a child suffering from Attachment Disorder. Such children may resist or reject affection, demonstrate manipulative and sociopathic behavior, and may be unable to care for and value those around her. These are extremely difficult circumstances in which to maintain a caring relationship. And yet, while the child may not "deserve" loyalty in the same way one might in romantic and friendship relations, this surely does not mean that the parent is wrong or misguided to care for the child—he is right to believe that the child is in need of his caring engagement, for a variety of reasons: because the child is dependent on him; because he has responsibility for her; because through his caring support, she may become a better and healthier person; and because she is a thinking feeling being who is struggling and suffering.

Obviously, not all of these conditions will apply to a loyal employee's relationship with an uncaring corporation, and so the analogy is not perfect. An employment relationship is voluntary, explicitly founded on mutual benefit, and lacks the strong moral particularism and commitment appropriate to the relation between a parent or guardian and a child. Nevertheless, there are some significant similarities between a parent's relationship with his troubled child and an employee's relationship to a corporation that suffers from behaviors analogous to Attachment Disorder or sociopathy: the corporation is dependent upon its various managers and employees, and through its employees' caring intervention, the corporation may be able to realize its better possibilities, and form a meaningful attachment and caring relationship to the beings *it* is dependent upon—care for employees, for the community, and for the environment. Employees may exercise voice and stay with abusive corporations because they care enough to want things to be done differently, and by remaining loyal, those possibilities are more likely to come to be. Like a parent who cares for his uncaring child, the caring loyal person has faith in the organization's better possibilities, and will work to improve the corporation and the relationship out of loyalty to it. We should not be quick to judge an employee who maintains loyalty to an undeserving corporation, or one which has harmful or immoral policies, for there remains the possibility that her loyalty can improve the corporation in the long run, even though this relationship may be unwise or unhealthy for her to maintain.

Conclusion

Our main aim in this essay was to argue that loyalty is often based in care, explain how this is expressed in business, and show why this account provides a view of loyalty in the workplace that is preferable to the relevant alternatives. By treating loyalty as an expression of care and concern towards another, we can account for the intuition that loyalty is not just a set of actions required by a contract, but involves feelings and a disposition to go above and beyond what is already required by the contract. Moreover, care ethics captures the way that expressions of loyalty are partial, and thus highly dependent on the nature of the caring relationship. And yet, even from the perspective of care ethics, the obligation of loyalty is subordinate to substantial impartial, universalizable moral requirements. In showing that the relationship between an employee and her employer is complex and robust enough to mirror personal relationships, we argued that employees can even be appropriately loyal to large, seemingly uncaring corporations, even from the perspective of care ethics. Finally, we showed that in a caring relationship, loyalty can be deserved but not obligated, except in those situations (such as a parent-child relationship) where the caring relationship is asymmetrical but dependent.

Our analysis provides an important corrective to the dominant academic approach to loyalty in workplace relations that presumes that the requirements of loyalty can be understood as impartial and universalizable. In recognizing that loyalty to others is partial, and appropriately rooted in a relationship, we reflect the common view that loyalty is more a matter of feelings and relationships than of obligation and justice. As agents who are embedded in contractual and interpersonal relationships in the workplace, there is moral importance in responding to co-workers, management, employees, and the corporation itself as persons with whom one is in a caring relationship, although every expression of loyalty is by no means "moral." The capacity to develop caring relationships which tend toward the flourishing of mutual care is certainly praiseworthy, and the failure to develop loyalty to one deserving of it is certainly a kind of failing, but loyalty cannot be simply called moral, nor disloyalty immoral, and deserving loyalty generates no obligation. The moral ambiguity and contextual specificity of loyalty is nicely captured by care ethics, and prior attempts to generate a theory of loyalty in business have been impoverished by reducing the complexity of our personal relationships and emotional commitments to too-solid and too-objective abstract moral judgments.

References

American Law Institute. 2006. Restatement (third) of agency. In the *Restatement of the law: Third records*, American Law Institute archives, ALI.04.003, Biddle Law Library, University of Pennsylvania Law School, Philadelphia, PA.

Argyris, C. 1960. *Understanding organizational behavior*. Homewood, IL: Dorsey.

Bok, S. 1983. Whistleblowing and professional responsibility. In *Contemporary issues in business ethics*, ed. J. DesJardins and J. McCall, 295–300. Belmont, CA: Wadsworth.

Carbone, J.H. 1997. Loyalty: subversive doctrine? *The Academy of Management Executive* 11 (3): 80–86.

Cavanagh, G.F. 2010. *American business values: A global perspective*. Upper Saddle River, NJ: Pearson Prentice Hall.

Corvino, J. 2002. Loyalty in business? *Journal of Business Ethics* 41: 179–185.

Duska, R.F. 1984. Whistleblowing and employee loyalty. In *Contemporary issues in business ethics*, ed. J. DesJardins and J. McCall, 142–147. Belmont, CA: Wadsworth.

Duska, R.F. 1992. Why be a loyal agent? A systemic ethical analysis. In *Ethics and agency theory*, ed. E. Freeman and N. Bowie, 143–168. New York, NY: Oxford University Press.

Ewin, R.E. 1993. Corporate loyalty: its objects and its grounds. *Journal of Business Ethics* 12: 387–396.

Gilligan, Carol. 1982. *In a different voice: Psychological theory and moral development*. Cambridge, MA: Harvard University Press.

Hart, D.W., and J.A. Thompson. 2007. Untangling employee loyalty: A psychological contract perspective. *Business Ethics Quarterly* 17: 297–323.

Hartman, E.M. 1994. The commons and the moral organization. *Business Ethics Quarterly* 4: 253–269.

Hegel, G.W.F. (Trans. T.M. Knox) 1952[1820]. *Hegel's philosophy of right*. Oxford: Oxford University Press.

Held, V. 2006. *The ethics of care: Personal, political, and global*. Oxford: Oxford University Press.

Herman, S.W. 1992. The modern business corporation and an ethics of trust. *Journal of Religious Ethics* 20: 111–148.

Hirschman, A.O. 1970. *Exit, voice, and loyalty: Responses to decline in firms, organizations, and states*. Cambridge, MA: Harvard University Press.

Hoffmann, E.A. 2006. Exit and voice: organizational loyalty and dispute resolution strategies. *Social Forces* 84: 2313–2330.

Jensen, J.V. 1987. Ethical tension points in whistleblowing. *Journal of Business Ethics* 6: 321–328.

Keller, S. 2007. *The limits of loyalty*. New York, NY: Cambridge University Press.

Kittay, E.F. 1998. *Love's labor: Essays on women, equality, and dependency*. New York, NY: Routledge.

Larmer, RA. 1992. Whistleblowing and employee loyalty. *Journal of Business Ethics* 11: 125–128.

Mane, Hajdin. 2005. Employee loyalty: an examination. *Journal of Business Ethics* 59 (3): 259–280.

Mele, D. 2001. Loyalty in business: subversive doctrine or real need? *Business Ethics Quarterly* 11: 11–26.

Noddings, N. 1984. *Caring: A feminine approach to ethics and moral education*. Berkeley, CA: University of California Press.

Pfeiffer, R.S. 1992. Owing loyalty to one's employer. *Journal of Business Ethics* 11: 535–543.

Randels, G.D. Jr. 2001. Loyalty, corporations, and community. *Business Ethics Quarterly* 11: 27–39.

Rosanas, J.M., and M. Velilla. 2003. Loyalty and trust as the ethical bases of organizations. *Journal of Business Ethics* 44: 49–59.

Schrag, B. 2001. The moral significance of employee loyalty. *Business Ethics Quarterly* 11: 41–66.

Singer, P. 1994. *Rethinking life and death: the collapse of our traditional ethics*. New York, NY: St. Martin's.

Slote, M. 2007. *The ethics of care and empathy*. New York, NY: Routledge.

Soles, D.E. 1993. Four concepts of loyalty. *International Journal of Applied Philosophy* 8: 1.

Solomon, R.C. 1998. The moral psychology of business: care and compassion in the corporation. *Business Ethics Quarterly* 8: 515–533.

Steib, J.A. 2006. Clearing up the egoist difficulty with loyalty. *Journal of Business Ethics* 63: 75–87.

Vandekerckhove, W., and M.S.R. Commers. 2004. Whistle blowing and rational loyalty. *Journal of Business Ethics* 53: 225–233.

Varelius, J. 2009. Is whistle-blowing compatible with employee loyalty? *Journal of Business Ethics* 85: 263–275.

Werhane, P.H. 1994. Justice, impartiality, and reciprocity: A response to Edwin Hartman. *Business Ethics Quarterly* 4: 287–290.

Werhane, P.H. 1999. Justice and trust. *Journal of Business Ethics* 21: 237–249.

Wicks, A.C., R.E. Freeman, P.H. Werhane et al . 2010. *Business ethics: A managerial approach*. Upper Saddle River, NJ: Prentice Hall.

Wilde, O. 1915. The devoted friend. In *Novels and fairy tales of Oscar Wilde*, ed. H.S. Nichols New York, NY: Little & Ives.

Chapter 13
Care Ethics, Knowledge Management, and the Learning Organization

Maurice Hamington

Introduction

The idea that "caring" should be considered part of the definition of an ethical business organization is nothing new. In 1991, R. Edward Freeman and Jeanne Liedtka described the "Care Proposition" as one of the viable forthcoming approaches to business ethics. Accordingly, "Corporations are places where both individual human beings and human communities engage in caring activities that are aimed at mutual support and unparalleled human achievement" (Freeman and Liedtka 1991). A few years later, Thomas J. Donaldson further suggested that caring was intrinsic to the morality of business activity in general: "business consists of the existing practices and institutions through which men and women coordinate their activities to create goods and services. And I wish to add the moral claim that business fails unless it enhances the quality of human life, the equality of human worth and the extent of human caring" (Donaldson 1997). Other theorists contend that care ethics provides an important imaginative dimension to business ethics because it is more flexible than strict rule adherence (French and Weiss 2000; Reiter 1996) and less susceptible to game playing or legalism (Hamington 2009). Despite the strong claims about caring, the specifics regarding the role and operation of care ethics have remained largely underdeveloped except for a smattering of publications. Although social and political philosophers have begun to engage care ethics as a viable alternative to traditional moral approaches (Slote 2007; Engster 2007), business ethicists have been more reluctant to embrace care. The reasons for this reluctance are manifold but in part the term "care" evokes images of emotional attachments not commonly associated with the business community. In this chapter, I explore the overlooked epistemological aspects of care ethics, including its inherent particularism and engagement of tacit knowledge, to argue that care can and should participate in an organization's program of knowledge management en route

M. Hamington (✉)
Institute for Women's Studies and Services, Metropolitan State College of Denver, Denver, CO, USA
e-mail: mhamingt@mscd.edu

M. Hamington, M. Sander-Staudt (eds.), *Applying Care Ethics to Business*, Issues in Business Ethics 34, DOI 10.1007/978-90-481-9307-3_13,
© Springer Science+Business Media B.V. 2011

to building a robust learning organization that holistically flourishes—financially, culturally, and ethically.[1] A caring culture is a culture of learning.

I suggest that if caring is conceptualized as fostering fundamental respect, engaging intellectual inquiry, and facilitating a moral atmosphere, then perhaps a culture of care will be more palatable to business professionals who often regard "caring" with suspicion as a nonproductive emotional disposition. This chapter focuses on caring as intellectual inquiry that inspires the moral imagination in the service of creating a culture of care. A culture is a system of shared meaning held by a group of people. That meaning includes values and attitudes as well as transmitted knowledge. Much has been written about corporate culture, but little about a caring culture. In this regard, care should be distinguished from friendship. A corporate culture of care does not suggest that members of the organization must become friends or develop strong relationships. It does suggest that people are attentive to one another as part of a willingness to grow. A culture of care is the moral good which is the overriding objective of this project.

The chapter begins by addressing the relationship between epistemology and care ethics followed by a discussion of the embodied and tacit dimension of caring as well as the skills entailed. After briefly describing the field of knowledge management and the notion of the learning organization, I suggest how care ethics, knowledge management and learning might be integrated.

Epistemology and Care Ethics

Because care ethics was only clearly identified as a unique ethical approach in the 1980s, its definition is still being negotiated. The operational definition of care ethics used in this chapter is "care describes an approach to personal and social morality that shifts ethical considerations to context, relationships, and affective knowledge in a manner that can only be fully understood if its embodied dimension is recognized. Care is committed to the flourishing and growth of individuals; yet acknowledges our interconnectedness and interdependence" (Hamington 2004). This definition lacks the clarity of Kant's categorical imperative or Mill's moral calculus because traditional approaches to ethics begin with abstract, albeit lucid, rubrics which are then applied to existential social phenomena. Care ethics begins with the particulars of a situation and then the caring response comes into view.

[1] A note about the theoretical context of this chapter: In many ways, care ethics is a postmodern project without the flight from materiality often associated with postmodernism. It challenges traditional philosophical categories and the rigidity of definitions. However, care ethics also transcends modernist feminist categories such as "liberal" and "radical." Some might accuse an application of care ethics to business organizations as a cooptation of the revolutionary potential of care (Ferguson 1997). I am not inclined to be concerned about cooptation because care is so foundational to human experience that whether one is engaged in liberal reforms or radical change care has an essential moral role to play. Therefore, facilitating a corporate culture of care should not be read as an unqualified endorsement of free market capitalism or unfettered globalization.

Virginia Held describes, "the ethics of care rejects the view of the dominant moral theories that the more abstract the reasoning about a moral problem the better because the more likely to avoid bias and arbitrariness, the more nearly to achieve impartiality. The ethics of care respects rather than removes itself from the claims of particular others with whom we share actual relationships" (2006). Care starts with a general disposition of openness and caring but is ultimately animated through an experience of the other. Out of that experience a response, reflection, and thematization emerge. For much of its early development, care ethics was conceptualized as a personal ethic but theorists have begun to integrate caring into models of social and political organizations (Hamington and Miller 2006; Engster 2007). Extending care ethics to business organizations is another step in the maturity of this moral philosophy.

Recent work on care ethics has stressed its imaginative and empathetic dimensions (Hamington 2004; Slote 2007). Empathy is an imaginative process that bridges experience and moral reflection/thematization. Although not addressing care ethics directly, Patricia Werhane contends that moral imagination is a crucial component in business ethics: "Moral imagination and moral reasoning provide concrete managerial decision-making skills with which to avoid questionable activities, prevent unseemly consequences, and enable a manager or a company to create decision models that contribute positively to corporate and societal well-being" (1999). It is the process of imaginatively understanding the "other" and their context that makes caring and subsequent action possible. Imagination is a requisite but not a sufficient condition of caring. If I allow myself to find a connection with others and imaginatively perceive their plight, I *may* take caring action. However, psychological and social forces are rich and complex. Caring action may be hindered by other ethical constraints or external social disciplines. Some caring is easier than others such as the care for a child. Nel Noddings refers to familial caring as an example of "natural caring" which exists on one end of a continuum that finds "ethical caring"—caring for unfamiliar others—at the other end (1984). The work of the imagination is made easier through familiarity. Note that Werhane's definition of imagination includes the notion of skill building. Caring is a cognitive skill that engages our ability to move from particularity to thematization. Werhane describes, "Moral imagination, then, is the ability in particular circumstances to discover and evaluate possibilities not merely determined by that circumstance, or limited by its operative mental models, or merely framed by a set of rules or rule-governed concerns. In managerial decision-making, moral imagination entails perceiving norms, social roles, and relationships entwined in any situation" (1999). An intriguing implication of Werhane's analysis of moral imagination is the need for understanding particulars—the need for knowledge.

An overlooked aspect of the imagination is its requirement for experiential material to work with. Even the most abstract artist draws upon the intelligible world for inspiration. Similarly, I cannot care for that which I have no knowledge of. Sometimes, corporate leaders are criticized for the negative impact their decisions have on people or communities. This is not just a question of morality; it is also a question of epistemology. Did those leaders know, or allow themselves to know, the ramifications of their decisions? One can stunt moral imagination through disconnection from available information. The moral imagination cannot operate in a vacuum. Care ethics employs a form of particularism that favors drawing moral themes and reflection from the specifics of context rather than the application of abstract principles or rules. Knowledge, then, is the basis of caring. Philosopher Milton Mayeroff describes, "We sometimes speak as if caring did not require knowledge, as if caring for someone, for example, were simply a mater of good intentions or warm regard. But in order to care I must understand the other's needs and I must be able to respond properly to them, and clearly good intentions do not guarantee this" (1971). The implications of the epistemological dimension of care ethics are enormous. For example, do I have a moral obligation to learn about others? Can I be morally exonerated if I choose not to learn about the underground exploitation known as human trafficking? If morality is based on knowledge, it seems to throw knowledge acquisition into a new light.

Given the knowledge basis for care described above, one can characterize caring as a form of inquiry. Every caring engagement with another person has the potential to contribute to learning because caring and learning are deeply intertwined activities. The absurdity of the statement, "I care about you but I do not want to know anything about you" is demonstrative of the intimate entanglement of care and epistemology. A caring disposition is one that is open to learning about others with the potential for greater depth of understanding and thus greater care. In the process of caring, the openness and attentiveness to the other leads to greater knowledge and sometimes *visa versa*.

Care: Embodiment, Tacit Knowledge and Skill

Care may depend upon particular knowledge, but it is also rooted in embodiment (Hamington 2004). Accordingly, we care *for* other bodies and *through* our body. Moral philosophers are familiar with theorizing about ethics in a purely abstract or disembodied fashion, but it harder to ignore the corporeal dimension of care ethics. Note, for example, Daniel Engster's definition of care as "everything we do directly to help individuals to meet their vital biological needs, develop or maintain their basic capabilities, and avoid or alleviate unnecessary or unwanted pain and suffering, so that they can survive, develop, and function in society" (2007). Engster does not explicitly theorize about embodiment but the language of "biological needs" and alleviating "unnecessary or unwanted pain and suffering" is grounded in physicality. Noddings is more explicit: "caring puts a great emphasis on bodies. Bodies must be nurtured, and the spirit of dependent on tem is the locus of a suffering that goes beyond physical pain" (2002). Our initial experience of care (hopefully) is the dependence and vulnerability of childhood when others care for our physical needs. The body is also the predominant vehicle through which we care for others. Expressions and actions of care are communicated and delivered through the body. We usually have a pretty good understanding of whether someone is acting in a caring manner toward us because we are experienced at detecting the physiological cues of caring. Finally, the body is also the nexus of much of our caring imagination. Even when social barriers make others almost entirely unintelligible, the shared experience of corporeality creates a common framework for understanding. If I witness someone getting hit by a high-speed piece of equipment on an assembly line, I do not need to speak their language, know their religion, be familiar with their economic class, or understand their history to recognize that they are in pain and need care. Our shared embodiment provides sufficient imaginative knowledge for many aspects of care.

The body has significant implications for two related aspects of caring: tacit knowledge and the skill or habits of care. Tacit knowledge is the notion that we know more than we can explicitly describe. As Michael Polanyi suggests, the knowledge we are aware of does not exhaust the totality of the knowledge we possess: "we can know more than we can tell" (1966). Unlike moral principles that can be overtly known, much of caring is tacitly known in the motor skills of the body and remain so unless attended to. If, for example, a co-worker is suffering through personal trauma such as a divorce or death in the family, I can provide some level of care for them by attentively listening to them and consoling them. The range of physical activities that participate in such care are numerous including eye contact, voice inflection, posture, touch, and facial expression. I do not consciously attend to each of these muscle movements, but collectively they represent a caring bodily mode. These collective actions are a skill or what John Dewey referred to as a habit (1921). Such habits are not rote, repetitive actions but open-ended activities that allow me to focus my care and attention on the other person. Accordingly, habits represent a kind of tacit knowledge. One might comparatively think of any physical skill—riding a bike, driving a car, knitting a sweater—that requires a complex series of muscle movements. We know that we can do these things but we struggle to describe the respective elements of the skill because individual aspects have receded into the background as we attend to the whole. Care is one of these complex activities that engages many discrete components that we are not normally conscious of.

Tacit knowledge, the implicit knowledge contained in our bodies, muscle memory, and habits not only helps us understand one another, but, according to Georg von Krogh, is part of what skilled employees bring to the work place. Von Krogh goes so far as to claim that tacit knowledge is the first step in organizational knowledge creation: "Knowledge creation is a social as well as an individual process. Sharing tacit knowledge requires individuals to share their personal beliefs about a situation with other team members" (2000). For von Krogh, the sharing of tacit knowledge participates in an overall corporate culture of care that in turn enables knowledge creation (von Krogh 1998, von Krogh, Ichijo, and Nonaka 2000). A culture of care is intertwined with explicit and tacit knowledge creation.

To summarize the claims thus far, care ethics is receiving greater recognition as a significant approach to morality and has applications in social and political spheres as well as personal relations. Because care responds to particular circumstances and contexts, it relies heavily on knowledge development to facilitate the moral imagination and thus empathy. That knowledge consists of explicit propositional knowledge as well as tacit knowledge held by the body in the form of muscle memory and is expressed as habits or skills. Given this understanding of caring knowledge and moral imagination, next we will address more directly how the contemporary field of knowledge management in business organizations can incorporate care ethics.

Knowledge Management and Care as an Intellectual Asset

In 1992, just prior to the explosive growth of internet usage, Peter Drucker described a forthcoming paradigm shift to a "knowledge society." Accordingly, the principle characteristic of social organization will be the creation, transmission, and usage of information. The economic implication is that land, labor, and capital become secondary to the management of intellectual assets in the productive activity of humanity. With the advent of the knowledge society, Drucker suggested that business leaders would have to transform the definition of successful management skill: "For managers, the dynamics of knowledge impose one clear imperative: every organization has to build the management of change into its very structure" (1992). Similarly, James Brian Quinn declared, "The capacity to manage human intellect—and to transform intellectual output into a service or a group of services embodied in a product—is fast becoming the critical executive skill of this era" (1992). The work of management theorists like Drucker, Quinn, and others, combined with technological advances, spawned the development of the discipline of knowledge management in the 1990s. At first, knowledge management was a field characterized primarily by discussions of technologically maintaining and transmitting mass information but it soon matured into a complex discipline engaging the application of traditionally philosophical epistemology to business management. The field of study has vertically expanded to address the creation, transformation, transmission, and maintenance of knowledge.[2] Perhaps, it can be further expanded to include care as an intellectual asset of business organizations.

There is no consensus around a definition of knowledge management—some definitions are narrowly focused around productivity such as "Knowledge management is the identification, storage, protection of knowledge for future operational and strategic benefit of the organization; this may be implicit or explicit" (Perrott 2006). Other definitions are expansively directed at organizational growth and learning, for instance, knowledge management is "any processes or practice of creating, acquiring, capturing, sharing, and using knowledge, wherever it resides, to enhance learning and performance in organizations" (Swan, Scarborough, and Preston 1999). Ethics is not a major topic in the knowledge management literature, although it is occasionally referenced. Laszlo and Laszlo, for example, believe that "the field of

[2]There are warranted concerns that knowledge management has been theorized to a much greater extent than it has been actualized. See, for example, Frappaolo (2006) or Spender and Scherer (2007). Perhaps Drucker's full expression of a knowledge society is still to be realized.

knowledge management faces the challenge of making concrete and relevant contributions for the betterment of society and not only for promotion of competitive advantage for business" (2002). However, they foresee this as part of a mature 3rd generation of the discipline. The absence of extensive moral discussion is understandable given the traditional divide between ethics and epistemology and the roots of knowledge management in data maintenance. Nevertheless, the theoretical work in knowledge management lends itself well to the epistemological basis of care discussed above. In particular, the delineation of knowledge categories and the functions of knowledge management are fertile groundwork for the integration of care ethics.

With some variation, theorists of knowledge management often refer to a categorical hierarchy of knowledge. At the base is *data,* which is described as facts or statistics. Next comes *information*, which systemizes data. *Knowledge* is then described as thematized information that provides a framework for action. *Understanding* implies a high degree of personal engagement with the knowledge such that internalization takes place. Finally, *wisdom* has a tenuous relationship to understanding such that wisdom does not always reflect all of the facts but provides useful insight (Jashapara 2004; Laszlo and Laszlo 2002; Meadows 2001; Perrott 2006). The expansiveness and complexity of this definitional hierarchy of knowledge is significant for the inclusion of care ethics. The experiential grounding for a caring imagination includes numerous data points that appear to be just facts. However, aggregating these facts and skillfully utilizing them can transform an ordinary superficial conversation into one that conveys care. For example, knowing the family member names of a co-worker is not exceptionally caring, but taking the time to ask about them might reveal a concern that is occupying their mind. A deeper, caring conversation—one that exhibits the engagement of understanding—and may even result in unanticipated actions can take place as a result of simple knowledge skillfully employed. The empathy that stems from engaging the moral imagination requires a baseline of information.

Theorists of knowledge management have also developed important distinctions regarding the nature of managing knowledge. Stephen Drew describes a "knowledge portfolio" that relativizes knowledge to awareness:

1. What We Know We Know. Emphasizes knowledge sharing, access, and inventory.
2. What We Know We Don't Know. Emphasizes knowledge seeking and creation.
3. What We Don't Know We Know. Emphasizes uncovering hidden or tacit knowledge.
4. What We Don't Know We Don't Know. Emphasizing key risks, exposures and opportunities (1999).

Although Drew does not engage ethics in his rubric, this kind of assessment or inventory of knowledge is particularly important in creating a culture of care. Every organization has assets of care; people and systems that foster understanding and actions on behalf of others. Recognizing, communicating, and celebrating those assets is a starting point for building culture (#1). Creating a dynamic climate of caring will involve moving beyond existing assets. Development and training can serve a strategic function in infusing opportunities for obtaining new intellectual assets of care (#2). One of the benefits of emphasizing the embodied dimension of care is that everyone has the potential to develop robust caring skills and knowledge if given the appropriate opportunity (#3). Caring exists on a continuum with "perfect" caring unattainable and perhaps indefinable. Identifying potential gaps and weaknesses can help create a realistic approach to a caring culture (#4). This kind of analysis can facilitate a caring knowledge portfolio.

Viewed as an intangible intellectual asset of the corporation, caring is a strategic component of a robust organizational culture. Given the emphasis on the epistemological aspect of care, caring can also be described as participating in creating a learning organization.

The Learning Organization and Caring Inquiry

At the same time that knowledge management developed into a field of study, the notion of a "learning organization" also emerged and took hold in management studies. Often associated with the work of Chris Argyris and Peter Senge, a learning organization is a business ideal that posits a flourishing community committed to unleashing potential through collective leaning and constant transformation. One succinct definition of a learning company is "a place where employees excel at creating, acquiring, and transferring knowledge. There are three building blocks of such institutions: (1) a supportive learning environment, (2) concrete learning processes and practices, and (3) leadership behavior that reinforces learning" (Garvin, Edmondson, and Gino 2008). Much like the knowledge management movement, the literature on organizational learning only sporadically addresses business ethics. Jennifer Rowley and Paul Gibbs describe the quest for organizational wisdom as motivated by diverse environmental factors—both competitive and ethical—that challenge business to learn differently: "organizations are coming under increasing pressure not only to learn, change and adapt, but also to take actions that are ethically acceptable and sustainable, and which balance the interests of a range of different stakeholders. In other words there are increasing expectations that organizations should act wisely or with wisdom" (2008). However, whether motivated by competition or business ethical concerns, there is little disagreement about the need for fostering learning organizations. Care, perceived as inquiry in pursuit of greater understanding and possibly action, resonates strongly with the language of organizational learning.

Argyris posits a distinction between the depth of learning that separates superficial from deep commitments to learning, and by extension ineffective from effective organizations: single versus double-loop learning. Single-loop learning addresses typical knowledge acquisition that takes place in response to problems, challenges, or errors employing existing rational paradigms and assumptions. Double-loop learning goes further to challenge operant existential and epistemological ideas. Argyris describes: "Double-loop learning occurs when a mismatch is detected and corrected by first changing the underlying values and other features of the status quo. Single-loop learning remains within the accepted routines. Double-loop learning requires that new routines be created that were based on a different conception of the universe" (2003). Double-loop learning is not passive learning but an active stance that encourages a questioning attitude beyond propositional knowledge. "A double-loop learning asks questions not only about objective facts but also about the reasons and motives behind the facts" because there might be important reasons for an organization to rethink its assumptions and systems (1994).

In the following passage, Jeanne Liedtka addresses how an organization might express care for its customers. Within the caring relationship, information is shared and assumptions are challenged in a manner consistent with double-loop learning. Caring implies a depth of attention that precludes treating new information as mere facts.

> To say that I care about my customers or my employees would place them as particular others and the capabilities that they represent at the center of my attention, and to work with them to realize those capabilities. The customer, for instance, is seen here as having a set of needs and possibilities to which, as a care-giver, I must attend. It is these needs, rather than the organization's prepackaged solutions, that drive my response in a process that is part of an on-going relationship, rather than a transaction. (1996)

Liedtka suggests that the commitment to caring with its accompanying commitment to taking learning seriously, transforms business relationships. Stakeholders are no longer expendable universal or generalized others (Benhabib 1987). One cannot learn from abstract generalized others. Only particular others can be learned from and cared for.

What Argyris characterizes as double-loop learning reflects a kind of humility toward knowledge discovery. New information, rather than forced into existing rubrics of understanding, should be accorded the respect that warrants full consideration in regard to how one thinks about knowledge. In showing respect for new knowledge, one shows respect for the bearer of that knowledge, and in doing so contributes to the climate of caring. Mayeroff explicitly connects humility, knowledge, and caring:

> Humility is present in caring in several ways. First, since caring is responsive to the growth of *this* other, caring involves continuous learning about the other: there is always something more to learn. The man who cares is genuinely humble in being ready and willing to learn more about the other and himself, and what caring involves. This includes learning from the one cared for as well: the teacher learns from the student; the parent learns from the child; and the artist learns from the work of art. No source is felt to be beneath me in principle; I am not humiliated to learn from any source, including my own mistakes. An attitude of not having anything further to learn is incompatible with caring. (1971)

The learning organization as Argyris and others describe it is compatible with the notion of a caring corporate culture. Caring and learning go hand in hand. They both seek the growth and development of the one cared for and the caregiver—and, by extension, the moral and material growth of the organization.

Conclusion: The Caring Organization

The caring organization need not be an oxymoron or a naïve ideal. An ethic of care conceptualized as a form of interpersonal inquiry can foment a learning organization within a culture of care and trust. A caring culture is a moral environment that is sensitive and responsive to a broad range of stakeholders. Caring does not preclude self-interest or the profit motive but it does establish a commitment to knowing and acting on behalf of others.

Caring can be viewed as a core competency of an organization.[3] Core competencies are particular strengths or characteristic values of an organization that endure beyond the short term: "Core competency differs from product and market competency in that an organization's core competency outlives product life cycles and market swings" (Frappaolo 2006). Caring is a strength of an organization that fosters a healthy work culture, maximizes the sharing of information, seeks out new knowledge, and leverages solid relationships. One unique aspect of caring is that, similar to Socrates' notion of wisdom, it is latent in everyone. Organizations can foster the exercise of atrophied caring skills through training, modeling, leadership, and support systems—methods familiar to organizational behavior theorists as participating in culture change.[4]

How might a caring culture of inquiry be applied? Sheldene Simola offers one avenue of application. Simola argues that care ethics is a particularly effective approach to addressing contemporary demands for sustainable engagement in global business development. Simola cites Hart (2005) who claims that new approaches are needed for emerging global challenges and that leveraging "native capabilities" is crucial for success. Native capabilities are defined as "the ability to engage with, and, learn about local needs and traditions [which] facilitates the development of trust, and the "coinvention" of innovative, win-win solutions" (2007). Hart describes five competencies necessary to foster native capabilities: 1. Establishing connections, 2. Facilitating voice in those who have been traditionally excluded, 3. Attending to subjectivity, 4. Engendering trust, and 5. Establishing mutuality and creating win-win situations. (2005). As Simola points out, Hart's description maps exceedingly well onto the elements of the ethic of care. For our purposes, note how the language resonates with a corporate culture of caring inquiry. Knowledge seeking and human connection are tied together in a manner that provides the foundation for imaginative "win-win" solutions all the while fostering a moral climate. This is just one example. Caring is a flexible competency that can inform any interaction.

---

[3] In C.K. Prahalad and Gary Hamel's original work on core competencies, three definitional conditions were offered: (1) consumer benefit; (2) difficult for competitors to imitate; and, (3) ability to leverage widely to many products and markets (1990). Care does not fit condition number 2 in a strict sense. However, caring is such a rich and complex response that there is room for wide variation in how care is communicated to stakeholders.

[4] DeMoss and McCann contend that business schools are inadequately infusing care ethics into the business ethics curriculum (1997) leaving organizations desiring to create a caring culture at a disadvantage.

What might a caring corporate culture look like? In describing a caring society, Pearl M. Oliner and Samuel P. Oliner offer one glimpse (1995). They characterize the caring business as encouraging self understanding, led by managers who openly speak of care, having systems that foster care, welcoming conflict as an opportunity to learn, and envisioning the business organization as participating in caring efforts locally, nationally, and internationally. In particular, Oliner and Oliner emphasize the internalization of responsibility for care. They describe employees in a healthy caring environment as understanding that "taking care of others may be necessary at times but that practices which empower others to take care of themselves and others are generally preferable" (1995). Oliner and Oliner want to make it clear that care should not be equated with altruism or charity. Caring for others involves respecting them and their knowledge and abilities.

Georg von Krogh's vision of a caring organization is intertwined with one that enables learning. He describes knowledge creation in organizations as fragile and requiring a caring culture to flourish. According to von Krogh, a caring culture exhibits trust, empathy, helping behaviors, lenience, courage and mentorship (2000). Many of these attributes appear antithetical to stereotypes of business behavior. For example, von Krogh indicates that a certain amount of leniency in corporate rule following can foster creativity and experimentation while reinforcing relationships over formal structures. By contrast von Krogh emphasizes that internal corporate hypercompetitiveness among employees is antithetical to the caring culture that enables knowledge creation. Ultimately, von Krogh finds a caring culture to be both ideal and pragmatic: "At the deepest level, care matters for moral, ethical, and social reasons. We are not suggesting, however, that companies throw all business concerns to the wind. In a postindustrial economy in which customer loyalty, strong brands, and radical innovations often give firms the competitive edge, improving relationships among all participants, listening to new ideas, and having the courage to handle constructive criticism are absolutely necessary for effective business operations" (2000).

Whether a corporation fosters it or not, caring occurs in every business. Individuals will care for one another even under oppressive circumstances. Indeed, it is caring that makes social life possible at all. Perhaps, because caring is so basic to the human condition, it has largely gone unnoticed in ethical theorizing and in particular in business ethical theorizing. In caring, businesses have a latent asset that contribute to its knowledge, success, and ethical environment.

References

Argyris, C. 1994. Good communication that blocks learning. *Harvard Business Review* 74: 77–86.

Argyris, C. 2003. A life full of learning. *Organization Studies* 24: 1178–1192.

Benhabib, S. 1987. The generalized and the concrete other: The Kohlberg-Gilligan controversy and moral theory. In *Women and moral theory*, ed. E.V. Kittay and D.T. Meyers . Lanham, MD: Rowman & Littlefield.

DeMoss, M., and G. McCann. 1997. Without a care in the world: The business ethics course and its exclusion of a care perspective. *Journal of Business Ethics* 16: 435–443.

Dewey, J. 1921. *Human nature and conduct*. New York, NY: Henry Holt and Company.
Donaldson, T.J. 1997. Morally informed iconoclasm: A response to Ferguson's "postmodernism, feminism, and organizational ethics". In *Women's studies and business ethics*, ed. J. Larson, and R.E. Freeman. New York, NY: Oxford University Press.
Drew, S. 1999. Building knowledge management into strategy: Making sense of a new perspective. *Long Range Planning* 32: 130–136.
Drucker, P. 1992. The new society of organizations. *Harvard Business Review* 70: 95–105.
Engster, D. 2007. *The heart of justice: Care ethics and political theory*. New York, NY: Oxford University Press.
Ferguson, K E. 1997. Postmodernism, feminism, and organizational ethics: Letting difference be. In *Women's studies and business ethics* J. Larson, and R.E. Freeman. New York, NY: Oxford University Press.
Frappaolo, C. 2006. *Knowledge management*. West Sussex, England: Capstone Publishing.
Freeman, R.E., and J. Liedtka. 1991. Corporate social responsibility: A critical approach. *Business Horizons* 34: 92–98.
French, W., and A. Weiss. 2000. An ethics of care or an ethics of justice. *Journal of Business Ethics* 27: 125–136.
Garvin, D.A., C.R. Christensen, and F. Gino. 2008. Is yours a learning organization? *Harvard Business Review* 86: 109–116.
Hamington, M. 2004. *Embodied care: Jane Addams, Maurice Merleau-Ponty and feminist ethics*. Champaign, IL: University of Illinois Press.
Hamington, M. 2009. Business is not a game: The metaphoric fallacy. *Journal of Business Ethics* 86: 474–484.
Hamington, M., and D. Miller. 2006. *Socializing care: Feminist ethics and public issues*. Langham, MD: Rowman & Littlefield.
Hart, S. L. 2005. *Capitalism at the crossroads: The unlimited business opportunities in solving the world's most difficult problems*. Upper Saddle River, NJ: Wharton School Publishing.
Held, V. 2006. *The ethics of care: Personal, political, and global*. New York, NY: Oxford University Press.
Jashapara, A. 2004. *Knowledge management: An integrated approach*. Essex, UK: Pearson Education.
Laszlo, K.C., and A. Laszlo. 2002. Evolving knowledge for development: The role of knowledge management in a changing world. *Journal of Knowledge Management* 6: 400–412.
Liedtka, J M. 1996. Feminist morality and competitive reality: A role for an ethic of care? *Business Ethics Quarterly* 6: 179–200.
Mayeroff, M. 1971. *On caring*. New York, NY: Harper & Row.
Meadows, J. 2001. *Understanding information*. Munich: K. G. Saur.
Noddings, N. 1984. *Caring: A feminine approach to ethics and moral education*. Berkeley, CA: University of California Press.
Noddings, N. 2002. *Starting at home: Caring and social policy*. Berkeley, CA: University of California Press.
Oliner, P.M., and S.P. Oliner. 1995. *Toward a caring society*. Westport, CT: Praeger Publishers.
Perrott, B.E. 2006. Knowledge management in health: an evolution? *Proceedings of Knowledge Management: The Key to Innovative Health Programs*. Sydney, Australia.
Polanyi, M. 1966. *The tacit dimension*. New York, NY: Doubleday.
Prahalad, C.K., and G. Hamel. 1990. The core competence of the corporation. *Harvard Business Review* 68: 79–91.
Quinn, J. B. 1992. *Intelligent enterprise: A knowledge and serve based paradigm for industry*. New York, NY: Free Press.
Reiter, S. A. 1996. The Kohlberg-Gilligan controversy: Lessons for accounting ethics education. *Critical Perspectives on Accounting* 7: 33–54.
Rowley, J., and P. Gibbs. 2008. From learning organization to practically wise organization. *The Learning Organization* 15: 356–372.

Simola, S. 2007. The pragmatics of care in sustainable global enterprise. *Journal of Business Ethics* 74: 131–147.
Slote, M. 2007. *The ethics of care and empathy*. New York, NY: Routledge.
Spender, J.–C., and A.G. Scherer. 2007. The philosophical foundations of knowledge management: Editor's introduction. *Organization* 14: 5–28.
Swan, J., H. Scarborough, and J. Preston. 1999. Knowledge management: The next fad to forget people? *Proceedings of the 7th European Conference on Information Systems*, Copenhagen.
von Krogh, G. 1998. Care in knowledge creation. *California Management Review* 40: 133–153.
von Krogh, G., K. Ichijo, and I. Nonaka. 2000. *Enabling knowledge creation: How to unlock the mystery of tacit knowledge and release the power of imagination*. New York, NY: Oxford.
Werhane, P. 1999. *Moral imagination and management decision-making*. New York, NY: Oxford University Press.

Chapter 14
Care as a Corporate Virtue

Maureen Sander-Staudt

Introduction

Bill Gates has called for more philanthropic capitalism, noting that although there are strong mechanisms for the generation of profit in capitalism, there are few incentives to meet the basic needs of others when doing so does not seem financially profitable (Gates 2009). What is needed, according to Gates, are caring individuals to use capitalism creatively to generate broad social welfare in profitable ways. In this paper, I use a feminist care ethic to expand on Gate's suggestion in a specific way, arguing for care to be understood as a corporate virtue, or a morally admirable trait conducive to individual and social flourishing, that inclines business agents to care-about and for others. More precisely, I argue that virtuously caring corporations should support the care responsibilities of their employees, especially women, and care broadly about the welfare of those vulnerable to their policies. In the first section I explain why understanding care as a corporate virtue is justified. In the second section I explore the conceptual aspects of care as a corporate virtue and give some examples of caring corporate policies. Finally, I outline the scope of care as a corporate virtue, defend against the charge that this proposal is unjust to corporations, and explain how such a virtue might be motivationally implemented.

Grounding Care as a Corporate Virtue

It is estimated that in the United States over 65.7 million people identify as caregivers, and that most of these are working women who experience stress relating to the difficulties of balancing care and paid work (National Alliance for Care-Giving and AARP 2009). Here I configure care as a corporate virtue in order to reduce the difficulties of balancing the responsibilities of work and care, with special attention to the unequal and non-reciprocal balance of care work for women.

M. Sander-Staudt (✉)
Arizona State University, Phoenix, AZ, USA
e-mail: maureen.sander-staudt@asu.edu

M. Hamington, M. Sander-Staudt (eds.), *Applying Care Ethics to Business*,
Issues in Business Ethics 34, DOI 10.1007/978-90-481-9307-3_14,
© Springer Science+Business Media B.V. 2011

Although virtue ethics, feminist ethics, care ethics, and business ethics are distinct fields that are sometimes problematically aligned or conflated, their collaboration suggests that care could fruitfully be understood as a corporate virtue (Sander-Staudt 2006; Borgerson 2007). According to Aristotle, a virtue is an actively expressed trait of excellence, beneficial both to possessor and others, which habitually hits a mean between excess and deficiency. A care ethic informed by feminism offers two justifications for construing care as a corporate virtue in this sense, one derived from the gender neutral ideal of caring for the basic needs of all and one from a gender sensitive ideal of justice. As Gloria Albrecht puts it, two specific values must be held together: the health and well being of families, and the full social equality of women (Albrecht 2002). To develop the first justification I draw from Daniel Engster's principle of consistent dependency, and for the second I build on Lisa Tessman's description of burdened virtue (Engster 2007; Tessman 2005). Both accounts justify construing care as a corporate virtue that predisposes corporate leaders to support the caring responsibilities of employees, but are different in terms of favoring gender-neutral or gender-sensitive approaches to this goal.

The Principle of Consistent Dependency as Justification for Understanding Care as a Corporate Virtue

The first reason why care should be understood as a corporate virtue emerges from the principle of consistent dependency (PCD) articulated and defended by Daniel Engster. For Engster, individuals have an obligation to provide care and develop caring virtues, because we are (and have been and will be) dependent upon others. Engester's PCD stipulates that because all human beings depend and implicitly call upon the care of others for survival, development, and basic functioning, we should consistently recognize that others should receive care from us when they need it, and when we are able to provide it without significant sacrifice to ourselves. This is a logical principle in that one cannot consistently recognize one's own need for care without implicating oneself in providing care for others in need. As Sarah Clark Miller argues, electing a general policy whereby one avoids the burden of helping others in need by agreeing never to have one's own needs met is inconsistent and ruinous (Miller 2005). For Engster, this obligation is gradated, extending first to oneself, then to those closest in special relations, then to unknown others in close proximity, and finally to all others.

Engster primarily focuses on the obligation of governments to create caring economic conditions, but in many societies this responsibility also falls to businesses because they shape the structure of economic conditions (if not more so) than governments. Businesses depend upon workers to "care for" the corporation by contributing their labor and directing a good will toward the larger interests of their employer. They depend upon managers, employees and consumers to "care-about" the corporation in the form of being willing to engage in fair trade and not despoil the company.[1] Increasingly, financial institutions in the United States are sustained by tax breaks and government subsidies that draw from social resources. Firms are thereby obliged by the PCD to provide caring provisions for the basic needs of workers and worker's dependents, and to care about others they affect, such as stakeholders and consumers. As Mona Harrington states: "The reigning idea that the sole corporate responsibility is to create value for shareholders must be replaced by one that expands corporate obligation to include social health, and that means an obligation to support families and care" (Harrington 1999). Establishing care as a corporate virtue via the PCD is bolstered by the care ethical notion of reciprocity based on mutual interdependency. This notion of reciprocity does not construe moral obligations as existing only between those precise individuals who have cared for one another, but between the larger spatial and temporal networks of caring relations (Kittay 1998). As global markets decline with disastrous results for workers and their dependents, this concept is increasingly salient. As current economic failings render interdependence more visible, it is plausible to posit that both individuals and corporations benefit when corporations care, and suffer when they do not. Thus, to the extent that businesses depend upon care but refuse to acknowledge or support caring practices, they fail to exhibit moral character.

Although some business leaders might object that they benefit only from past care work that created its current workers, but not care work that produces future workers, this argument fails to appreciate how caring relations are intergenerational and nested, such that caring for past and current workers entails caring for future and developing others. It may appear that most individuals receive care from a discrete set of particular persons, but acts of care are in reality facilitated by networks of care. Parents are able to care for their children only because someone cared for them, under complex historical social conditions that provided at least some minimal standards for the continuation of life, which today typically includes the provision of income. The care of current workers is thus intertwined with the care of past and future workers, because most workers have caring obligations and ties to such persons (Social Security is one such example.) Corporations are implicated in caring reciprocity as providers of income and controllers of the conditions under which some of these caring needs are now met. Corporations likewise depend upon networks of care, and could not function without basic social provisions for the maintenance of life, and shared conceptions about what counts as money and fair trade. Corporations reap the benefits of social arrangements that provide care for free or little pay, simultaneously tapping the profit potential of caring services without recognizing or reciprocating care to those within the scope of their power who give this care.

As such, Engster's political philosophy of care supports understanding care as a corporate virtue for gender-neutral reasons relating to basic need. To the extent

[1] The distinction between caring-for and caring-about was first made by Nel Noddings, who posited it as the difference between hands-on applications of care which are face to face with a care recipient, and a state of feeling a concern about something, planning or providing something, or having an idea that supports direct care.

that the basic needs of employees and their embedded relations are linked to the current organizational structures of corporations, Engster's analysis supports the idea that care is a virtue that corporations should reciprocate. Such a virtue does not dictate that employers must always exhibit a caring disposition toward employees (although this is generally recommended), but it does endorse attentiveness and responsiveness to the various needs of employees, concern for employees' dependents, and the implementation of policies and benefit packages in support of care work. However, Engster's political philosophy is self-described as minimally feminist, concerned with meeting the basic needs of women and children as humans. While this approach grounds care as a corporate virtue instrumental to the ability of many individuals to meet the needs of themselves and others, it lacks contextual specificity. It does little to reconfigure unequal distributions of caring burdens beyond those that contribute to neglect, and requires no serious revision of gendered hierarchical power differentials that characterize current care delivery systems, providing that they meet the basic needs of all within the effective management scope of a corporation.

Feminist Justifications for Understanding Care as a Corporate Virtue

Alternatively, a care ethic that is more explicitly feminist broadens Engster's notion of basic need to include the goal of achieving justice and parity for women care-givers, such that might emerge from Lisa Tessman's analysis of burdened virtues. Tessman explains that oppression causes moral damage to subordinated peoples in the form of "burdened virtues" (Tessman 2001, 2005). Based on Aristotle's insight that individual virtue is compromised by social injustice, Tessman argues that the oppressed are prevented from living the best possible lives. She notes that although Aristotle recognized the need of external goods for flourishing, he was short-sighted in considering the inability to access these goods as the result of accidental and natural qualities, rather than of relations of oppression. Indeed, he endorsed a political system within which many humans, including women care-givers, were excluded from the opportunity to flourish. Tessman traces how oppression causes "moral damage" that justifies the continued maltreatment of the oppressed. She states that care qualifies as a burdened virtue for women in these ways, but her claim warrants further explication (Tessman 2005).

There are three ways in which care could be said to be a burdened virtue for employed women care-givers. First, the virtues associated with care and the corporate workplace conflict in ways that prejudicially reflect poorly on their characters. Elizabeth Anderson identifies two ideologies that impugn the virtue of this group—the andocentric model of work, and a work ethic that defines a "general reciprocity principle" only in terms of paid work (Anderson 2004). The andocentric model of work is based on the traits of an "autonomous man", and pressures employees not to have care-giving responsibilities. Coupled with a "general reciprocity principle" that requires able bodied citizens to assume their fair share of social burdens, but only counts work that commands a market price, the andocentric model of work turns dependency into a vice. Care-givers are encouraged to work for a wage in order to avoid the stigma of being perceived as lacking in personal responsibility and are given few other options. At the same time that employed women are expected to adopt the traits of "autonomous man" at their jobs, they are pressured to be devoted mothers, partners, and housekeepers at home.[2] Much of this first burden is due to scarce social concessions for the practice of care-giving, combined with the continued reality that women are held more responsible for direct forms of hands-on "caring-for" than most men, whose responsibilities more typically include indirect forms of "caring-about" (Meyers and Durfee 2006; Allard and Janes 2008).

Moreover, as Eva Feder Kittay notes, the demands of familial dependency work conflict with the demands of market based employment (Kittay 1998). Care-givers who work for an income struggle with competing schedules and intense demands on their time and attention, spurring some women care-givers to leave paid work if they are financially able (Waldfogel 1997; Rivers and Barnett 2000; Aloi 2005; Story 2005; Blades and Rowe-Finkbeiner 2006; Williams 2007). Those who stay in the paid work force may be faulted for being less competent as they strive to be good enough care-givers, while also being virtuous employees expected to behave as if they had no personal care responsibilities—a stressful condition that Judith Warner refers to as "this mess" (Warner 2005). When things predictably get neglected or go wrong at home, women care-givers may again be blamed. *Forbes* editor, Michael Noer, thus cautions men against marrying working women because "professional women are more likely to get divorced, more likely to cheat, less likely to have children and when they do have kids are more likely to be unhappy about it... You will be more likely to fall ill. Even your house will be dirtier" (Noer 2006). Rather than questioning these conflicting standards of virtue, or urging men and corporations to be more responsible for direct care, employed women care-givers are portrayed as vicious individuals with inherent character flaws.

The second way in which care is a burdened virtue for women in the U.S. is economically. A persistent motherhood related wage gap means that women care-givers suffer severe financial penalties within corporate America. Across a variety of fields, women with children are less likely to be promoted than men with children and childless women, even when they have comparable backgrounds and work hours (Crittenden 2001; Mason and Goulden 2004; Williams 2007). Motherhood is a key factor in pay differentials in that women without children make 90 cents to a man's

---

[2]Gender and sex plays out in workplace compensation in that there is more economic parity for women when they exhibit the masculine gender qualities of being (or appearing to be) unencumbered, or when they occupy "tough" male dominated fields. Women who gendered feminine in terms of hands-on "caring-for" dependent others are least likely to be financially compensated. At least one study shows this pattern to also be related to sex, however, holding for trans-gendered workers across sex-change transition. That is, men who change their sex to female, on average saw a pay decrease, while women who changed their sex to male, saw an average pay increase, on par with the larger wage gap. See Schilt and Wiswall (2008).

dollar, married mothers 73 cents, and single mothers 56–66 cents (Waldforgel 1997). Over the course of a lifetime, this gap costs the average full-time working mother between $700,000 and $2 million dollars (Rivers and Barnett 2000). Moreover, the U.S. is only one of six industrialized nations in the world that does not require a provision for paid maternity leave from employers and governments (Olson 1998). While the 1997 Family and Medical Leave Act (FMLA) requires larger corporations to offer 3 months of unpaid care-related leave to full-time employees at companies with over 50 employees, this provision offers no benefit to those who cannot afford unpaid leave, work part-time, or work at smaller businesses. Although child care benefits are provided for military and some federal workers, the bulk of child care-givers in the U.S. are expected to provide care themselves, or by self-arranged proxy. In 2006 only 7% of white collar occupations had access to on-site/off-site child care benefits, and only 2% of blue collar occupations did so (Sloan Work and Family Fact Sheet 2006). This policy suggests that for most workers, care-giving is thought compatible with the virtue of economic justice only if concessions are needed for a short time (3 months), and do not require financial support beyond the care-giver's sole means. Both expectations are unrealistic and unfair in today's world, given that the average period of care for care-givers is 4.6 years, and direct care-giving is correlated negatively with income.[3]

Finally, care is a burdened virtue because employed women care-givers risk becoming complicit in unjust care distributions when they depend upon others to meet their care responsibilities. As more workers pay others to provide care, the work of care is shifted down onto women more intersectionally disadvantaged, creating a caring economic distribution which Joan Tronto declares as frequently unjust (Tronto 2002). Those who provide care for pay face the same conflict of needing to meet their own care-giving responsibilities while earning a living, but are also typically further underprivileged in terms of race, class, age, and/or citizenship status (DiQuinzio 1993; Tronto 1994; Hondagneu-Sotelo and Avila 1997; Duffy 2005; Weir 2005; Mullin 2005). Dan Jacoby notes that keeping the cost of care-giving manageable for working class families divides the interests of women along race and class lines, as care workers are recruited from former welfare recipients, the lower class, and immigrant populations (Jacoby 2006). Factors such as age and kinship also figure into this distribution, as it is common for older women and/or female relatives to care *pro bono* so that other family members may earn a wage.

[3]Social Security is another work related policy in the U.S. that links care entitlements to paid work, implying that care-givers are deficient in the virtue of justice if they have not reciprocated the function of paid worker. It makes no provision for care-givers working outside of the paid work force, apart from reduced entitlements nested in marriage benefits, which single care-givers and homosexuals cannot obtain. Feminist economists Anne Crittenden and Nancy Folbre explain how the economic value of care is rendered invisible in the Social Security system, making motherhood related exclusion from paid work the leading cause of poverty for elderly women (Crittenden 2001, 77–78; Folbre 2001, 97–99).

A feminist care ethic posits the need for gender as well as sex equality in the corporate workplace that traces responsibility for "caring-for." The feminist call for men to share in the work of care has not eradicated these burdens, merely shifted them slightly. Both men and women responsible for caring-giving experience certain disadvantages associated with doing work perceived as more feminine, in comparison to men and women who adopt more masculine dispositions or professions. However, although men are not immune to discrimination as care-givers, women care-givers are often judged as less professionally competent than their male counter-parts because of the stronger negative connotations of care accruing to female sex and gender roles. One recent study found that actual employers are more likely to disfavor job applicants identified as mothers than fathers on a host of measures, including perceived competence and recommended starting salary, even when otherwise identical credentials are submitted (Correl et al. 2007). The study not only found that fathers suffered no equivalent hiring penalties, they sometimes benefited from their parental status. A caring corporation should thus implement policies capable of tracking care-related sex and gender disparities in the workplace. Corporate gender neutral policies such as the FMLA rightly construe care as the work of both men and women, but ignore social biases and physical differences that saddle women with heavier care-giving burdens. A more adequately feminist construal of care as a corporate virtue recommends policies with flexibility to respond to the contextual caring needs of employees. Having now established the justificatory grounds for understanding care as a corporate virtue, I turn to some conceptual aspects of this proposal.

Care as a *Corporate* Virtue

Identifying care as a corporate virtue begs the question of whether it makes sense to talk of the virtues of collectives. Aristotle's virtue ethic affirms the idea that virtues are both traits of individuals and collectives.

> one citizen differs from another, but the salvation of the community is the common business of them all . . . If . . . the happy life is the life according to excellence lived without impediment, and that excellence is a mean, then the life which is in a mean, and in a mean attainable by everyone, must be the best. And the same principles of excellence and badness are characteristic of cities and constitutions. (1254b25; 1276b30; 1295a35)

Here Aristotle attributes virtues and vices to civic collectives, but it is reasonable to suppose that they could also characterize other collectives such as corporations.

But what does it mean to suggest that care is a corporate virtue when most corporations are collectives comprised of individuals with diverse dispositions and powers? It is not clear that virtue and vices can be attributed as shared qualities, a point exemplified in the AIG scandal of 2009. In response to the public outrage that followed when corporate managers received millions of dollars in bonuses after having received a billion dollar subsidy from the U.S. federal government, many

AIG employees resisted accusations of corporate vice on grounds that these bonuses applied to only one division, and that the decision to award bonuses was beyond their control. Perhaps, then, corporations are the wrong sort of metaphysical entities to attribute virtue and vice because they lack certain necessary or reducible features, such as motives, rationality, appetite, happiness, or a need for moderation. If this critique is correct, a corporation cannot be virtuous or vicious because it is not a person, but a collection of persons with diverse dispositions and actions, with varying degrees of decisional power. It follows that we can only speak of the virtues and vices of corporations in a metaphorical or reductive sense.

While this critique indicates some of the difficulties with attributing virtues and vices to collectives, it does not succeed in rendering the idea of corporate virtue nonsensical. Some moral philosophers contend that a metaphorical use of vice and virtue terms is adequate for establishing corporate responsibilities (Moon, Crane, and Matten 2005). Others argue that collective virtues reduce to the idea that corporations are virtuous to the extent that at least some members are virtuous, especially those with governing powers. Yet others hold that corporations possess requisite features for having a distinct moral character in a more literal sense, such as motives and responsibilities (Wieland 2001). For example, Aditi Gowri argues that corporate virtues are derivable because firms have appetites for profit that are in need of moderation (Gowri 2006). Corporate virtues also can be derived from an implicit valuing of freedom or some other pervasive social good (like care). (Palmer 2007) Moreover, as Karl Schudt points out, corporations exhibit a rational calculation of means and ends, are treated as persons before the law, and in common speech are referred to as agents (Schudt 2000). They have vast stores of power, money and resources at their disposal to affect the lives of individuals, so to conclude that corporations lack moral agency, or have no moral obligations at all, as in "all's fair in business", is to put humans at the mercy of "corporate monsters" (Schudt 2000). As Robert Solomon concludes, "people in the corporation, individually and collectively, can and do care" (Solomon 1998).

Following from these arguments, corporate virtue ought to be understood as a habitual individual and collective property of excellence that refers to both disposition and practice. Jeanne Liedtka argues that in addition to being composed of individuals who are caring, a caring organization needs to actively support caring efforts through its goals, strategies, and values (Liedtka 1996). But in attributing care as a corporate collective virtue, it is important to track the varying degrees of power within businesses. A business might be characterized as caring, informally, if its low ranking employees care due to their own values and dispositions. But a feminist account of care as a corporate virtue suggests that a corporation is more formally or fully caring when those with governing power habitually exhibit the virtue of care through corporate policies and decisions in support of those with whom they relate. While a feminist ethic of care also recommends a reorganization of corporations away from power hierarchies toward more democratic and shared management styles, the stipulation that a corporation is caring to the extent that empowered executives care is needed to grapple with the reality that corporations are rarely configured as power sharing democracies. Having established that collective virtues and vices are feasible, the substance of care as a corporate virtue can be further delineated by appeal to the sub-virtues of care.

Sub-Virtues of Care as a Corporate Virtue

In addition to the more general description of care as a corporate virtue given above, a care ethic provides a more detailed account of this virtue via three sub-virtues of care: attention, responsibility, and respect. That is, a caring corporation is one that is attentive to the needs of those within its moral scope, responsive to these needs in competent ways, and respectful of the dignity and rationality of care recipients. I will describe each of these sub-virtues in turn and some their corresponding vices as they might apply in a corporate setting.

Attention—This is the first phase of caring, in which possible care-givers notice the needs that they are in the best position to meet. Care ethicists characterize this sub-virtue as a quality of moral perception that evokes sensitivity to situations that call for moral response (Ruddick 1989; Tronto 1994; Held 2006; Engster 2007). Engster states that attentiveness is a capacity for noticing and anticipating needs, and directs us to ask the question: "What do you need?"

An attentive corporation does not view persons as interchangeable, but notices the caring needs of the particular people whom it employees and affects, acknowledging both general and extenuating circumstances. It does not view employees as atomistic persons, but as persons embedded in chains of interdependency filled by individuals with varying needs and abilities. It is attentive to the different kinds of caring needs attributable to sex and gender, and attends to vulnerabilities created by other power differentials.

A corporation deficient in attention can be said to exhibit the vice of neglectful inattentiveness or selfish absorption, while one that is excessive may be said to exhibit the vice of smothering over-involvement. As an example of the former, Joan Tronto describes deficiencies of attention that take more particular and remote forms:

> when a boss orders all the employees to arrive a half hour earlier tomorrow, knowing that some of the women who work for him have children who require care, we might suggest that such inattentiveness is worse than if this same individual does not understand the moral dimensions of cutting Medicaid benefits to working single parents, [as this is an] inattentiveness that is more remote. (Tronto 1994)

Tronto counts both forms of inattention as vice, and finds that ignorance of caring need is built into social structures of capitalist economies. The role of corporations is linked to an increased insensitivity to caring need not only because in modern markets virtually all human needs can be met for a price, but also because "privileged irresponsibility" for care work is a reward and signifier of economic success, and caring needs typically are scrutinized by businesses only when profitable. On the flip side, the latter vice is one of excess, in that a corporation that is overly attentive to the needs of employees and others may be characterized as paternalistic. It may meddle in its employee's lives without good reason, at the wrong time, or with no purpose that serves the ones being scrutinized. The third virtue of respect thus serves as an important check on this vice.

Responsiveness—The second virtue of caring is responsiveness, or moving to meet a need, and monitoring our care so we may be certain that others are getting the care they actually need according to their own judgment. According to Engster, the virtue of responsiveness directs care-givers to ask the question "What do you need?" (Engster 2007).

This virtue governs the phase of care that involves taking care of, and requires concrete actions in recognition that care is a practice that must be done (Held 2006). Responsiveness emphasizes the importance of successfully meeting needs, beyond mere good intentions to do so, and encompasses what other care ethicists call "completion", or "competence." It requires that a corporation take positive action to meet caring needs, and be competent in doing so, as assessed by the intended recipients (Noddings 1984). As Daryl Koehn explains in this volume (Chapter 8), a virtuously responsive corporation shows competence in avoiding unintended consequences as it seeks to mitigate corporate imposed burdens on caring practice. Tronto notes that obligation for responsiveness may arise because of something we did or did not do that has contributed to the need for care, or because we simply recognize a need for caring and there is no other way that the need will be met except for by our meeting it (Tronto 1994). In most cases corporations are responsible for caring about employers and dependents in the latter sense, because businesses exclusively are able to meet some care needs for their employers, such as providing a stable income, or flexible work schedules. In some cases, however, corporations may also be responsible for care in the former sense, such as when an employee is injured on the job, an employee's family is rendered homeless because of a sudden layoff due to executive mismanagement, or a consumer is injured by a faulty product.

Again, the vices constituted by a deficiency of response in the corporate world are much more widely evident than the vices of excess. While some corporate leaders overtly ignore care-giving needs, many more recognize the value of *appearing* to be responsive, but secretly pursing their own selfish and narrow interests. Like the former CEO of General Motors, Roger Smith, as depicted in Michael Moore's documentary, *Roger & Me*, corporate leaders may strive to remain inattentive in order to dodge responsibility, even when giving lip service to the virtues of corporate care.[4] Others may have good intentions, but fail to be fully competent in their response to care-givers as assessed by intended recipients. As Albrecht explains, so called "family friendly" corporate policies, such as the FMLA, typically fail to respond to the *real* needs of families in terms of their effectiveness (original emphasis, Albrecht

[4]In one particularly poignant scene of *Roger & Me*, Smith, the former CEO of GM, quotes *The Christmas Carol* at a Christmas Eve pageant, espousing the virtue of care and love of humanity, paying no attention to the fact that many laid-off GM workers had been evicted from their homes just earlier that day.

2002). Likewise, Joanne Martin describes how even well intentioned companies seeking to help women with children often merely suppress gender conflict without alleviating gender inequalities (Martin 1990). Building from a virtue epistemology based on role models, corporations aspiring to care should turn to exemplars of corporate care on both the national *and* international level, and habituate themselves in ways of delivering just care locally and globally (Robinson 1999; Anderson 2003; Landsburg 2006; Weir 2005).

Although responsiveness is difficult to precisely delineate absent contextual knowledge of a corporation and its relations, a standard policy recommended by care ethicists is a paid and extended FMLA policy, which is transparent, easily accessible, and available to all workers. This leave could be funded by governments as well as corporations, but minimally requires corporate accommodation. It is also important to tailor the FMLA so it allows flexible response to the specific needs dictated by embodied and social particularities, such as those relating to sex and gender.

Fineman thus speaks against social policies that presume gender neutrality in order to create gender neutrality, because they ignore how caring-for is associated with responsible motherhood, and how pregnancy and lactation are biologically linked to women (Fineman 1995). A more flexible and attentive FMLA might offer pregnant women extended paid leaves, or reduced loads, out of recognition of the unique physical relationship between mothers and young children. Such leaves should extend beyond the first weeks of infancy, in recognition that caring needs evolve but persist as a child grows. However, in recognition that men are less likely to take or be granted leave for care responsibilities, a revised FMLA might offer men, and other secondary partners, a "use or lose" paid leave. This policy should likewise remain sensitive to other social factors that delineate caring benefits and burdens, including class, sexual orientation, ability, and race, in a way that seeks to mitigate dependency based workplace discrimination.

Caring corporate policies include a livable wage and health care provision, but also temporal and spatial organization of labor so that productive work does not unduly interfere with an individual's ability to care for self or dependents (Engster 2007). Care-giving employees require workplace and workday flexibility, as well as affordable, accessible, and just forms of delegated care (Bakst and Taubman 2008; Bakst 2010). Work weeks need to be reasonably limited to provide time for domestic work and leisure activity. Further suggestions might include work schedules compatible with school/social schedules, on-site care or referral services, paid sick leaves, elder care resources, and paid vacation time. Kittay recommends a social provision for *doulas*, or professionals who care for care-givers, and corporations should provide this service both by developing it as industry, but also by including it as an employee benefit (Kittay 1998). Finally, there should be strong reluctance to lay off workers, especially without notice or contingency plans. When unavoidable, lay-offs should include provisions for health care, housing, severance packages or pensions, with contingencies for dependents (Bragues 2006; Engster 2007).

Respect—The third sub-virtue of care is respect, which Engster describes as recognition that others deserve our attention and response, are "capable of understanding and expressing their needs", and are not inferior because they have needs that cannot be met on their own (Engster 2007).

Applying this sub-virtue to corporations suggests a need for management styles that open up communication with all employees. It recommends moving away from bureaucratic, "top-down" styles of communication in favor of shared interchanges, moving toward an overall reorganization of corporate hierarchies (Sevenhuijsen 1998; Wieland 2001; Hankivsky 2004; Folbre 2006). Although Engster seems correct that a caring corporation need not be owned by workers, there is strong consensus that it would create a hearty capacity for workers to influence corporate governance in terms of what Nancy Frasier calls "a politics of needs interpretation" (Engster 2007; Frasier 1989). A respectful caring corporation listens carefully to those with whom it relates without arrogance, welcomes diverse styles of communication, and takes in rather than quashes differences of opinion (Borgerson 2007). It develops a corporate culture of empathetic concern that moves beyond rational self-interest.

Again, the vices of deficiency in the matter of respect seem more common than vices of excess, although one can imagine a company that engages in so much respectful communication that it thwarts the ability to make quick and definitive decisions. But most often, the risk is one of deficiency. The fact that the needs of care-givers in America are so woefully unsupported in comparison to other industrialized nations can be explained in part to a lack of corporate respect, reflected in communication gaps, miscommunications and disjointed perceptions about corporate responsibility for care. At least one study has uncovered vast disparities of perception between top management and employees with regard to eldercare, childcare, and care for substance abusers, with employees viewing corporations as partially responsible for meeting and supporting these needs, and executives viewing corporations as not at all responsible (Miller, Stead, Pereira 1991). Respect speaks to the importance of including employees and their dependents in needs assessment and response. Albrecht thus urges businesses to recognize employees as their best resource for identifying work/family conflicts and for generating possible solutions (Albrecht 2002).

These sub-virtues of care help to fill out the content of care as a corporate virtue. In the final section I address remaining questions about the appropriate scope of care as a corporate virtue, the fairness of assigning care responsibility to corporations, and the best way to implement the virtue of care in business.

The Scope, Fairness, and Implementation of Care as a Virtue of Corporations

Like a person, a corporation cannot care for everyone. A feminist care ethics understands corporate responsibility as having broad, but graduated extension, which begins first with those who are most proximately and seriously affected by a company, and emanates out toward other relations. A corporate virtue of care tempered by an Aristotelian mean recommends a domain that is moderate, but more substantial than what currently exists in the United States. In recognition that most workers are employed in order to meet the needs of themselves and their families, a reasonable scope to the corporate virtue of care would have companies support workers' abilities to develop and maintain basic capabilities in the expanded feminist sense. Engster recommends that caring and commodity production be balanced, and that care theory remain flexible in defining the best means for delivering care, favoring experimentation and innovation. However, he concludes that contemporary societies would benefit from subordinating economic activity to the aims and virtues of caring. Liedtka further argues that corporate care is bounded by reach, self care, and the need to be competitive. Given these considerations, she posits that:

> ... the business organization, conceived of as a "community of mutual care," would have a responsibility to care for those in proximity to them who have needs that they are especially well-suited, by their capability base, to fulfill, where giving such care does not act against their own needs. (Liedtka 1996)

Within the circle of corporate care Liedtka includes employees, small town communities where corporations are located, and consumers who can be profitably served. She places competitors, larger cities, and potential customers who cannot pay within the realm of justice, although she makes an exception in cases where a company is uniquely suited to fill a need and can do so without harming itself.

Liedtka's account clarifies the scope of corporate care, but requires supplementation in at least three ways. First, this virtue should be understood as resisting corporate trade-offs between the needs of employees and paying consumers, evident in the practice of justifying low wages through the production and sale of cheap goods, recommending instead that there be certain livable minimal standards of care for all. Second, Liedtka's account is complicated by factors relating to the rise of big business on a global scale. Increasingly, multinational corporate conglomerates have numerous facilities around the world, blurring small and large town distinctions. What is today a competitor may tomorrow be a purchased subsidiary of a larger company, and potential customers who cannot pay may come from most needy populations.

In such cases we might turn to the principle recommended by Burton and Dunn, that corporations ought "care enough for the least advantaged stakeholders that they not be harmed; insofar as they are not harmed, privilege those stakeholders with whom you have a close relationship" (Burton and Dunn 1996). This principle moves in the right direction, but fails to track power, response-ability, and need as suggested by Tronto. A more positive and adequate version of this principle, then, demands special attention to the least advantaged members of the moral community, who are so disadvantaged because of corporate action or policy, or whose need is dire and are situated such that a corporation is proximately suited to meet their need.

Finally, Liedtka's account requires supplementation in that Fiona Robinson rightly points out that in the age of globalization, the corporate obligation to care for the "proximate" extends beyond national borders (Robinson 1999). As corporations expand, relocate, and seek cheap labor in foreign markets, populations are created that are vulnerable precisely because they reside outside of the spheres of influence in which corporate executives reside, and who may be doubly invisible not only because they are dependent on workers distant from corporate headquarters, but also because they reside outside of the market as agents altogether.

It may be objected that care as a corporate virtue as I have construed it places an ill-fitted or undue burden on business, a view that could be supported by appeal to Aristotle. In *Politics* Aristotle finds animals, women, and slaves to be naturally inferior to free men because "with their bodies [they] minister to the needs of life", a belief that persists in business today in the sense that care is viewed as the menial work of subordinates. Most company executives construe the caring obligations of their workers as private matters of personal responsibility, and care as a corporate virtue is rarely understood in this precise, expanded sense. As a disposition, care is sometimes viewed not as a virtue at all within corporate contexts, but as a vice and liability due to the perceived tough and competitive nature of business (Solomon 1992; Van Wensveen 1995).

Such an objection emerges from the "shareholder responsibility" argument, famously articulated by Milton Friedman, who held that the primary and sole obligation of corporations is profitability owed to shareholders (Friedman 1962, 1970). Applying this argument, it would follow that the obligation of corporations to care should at most be limited to caring provisions that do not interfere with the ability to maximize profit. Because in many cases there seem to be grave conflicts between the goal of maximizing profit and corporate care provision, such provisions are said to be unjust. Proposed mandates requiring businesses to provide health care or paid family leaves are often resisted on the grounds that they are too expensive and place undue burdens on corporations, especially small businesses.

An advocate of corporate care can begin to refute these charges by pointing out that, first, care functions as a corporate virtue even within shareholder theory to the extent that care (or at least its appearance) is conducive to profitability, and second, that corporations often underestimate the profit making potential of actual care. That care is acknowledged as a perceived corporate virtue is evident in ascriptions of care functioning in marketing and public relations strategies. Most companies strive to appear as caring in order to establish a reputation as a "better business." This goal recognizes that corporate care is esteemed by the larger public because it is a trait associated with honesty, trustworthiness, fairness, and compassion. Even businesses with aims running counter to the goal of "caring for" basic needs (such as tobacco companies or home foreclosure specialists), acknowledge the benefit of "caring about" clients, consumers, and fiscal profitability. Corporations that provide care services, such as hospitals, day care centers, or hospices, explicitly feature "caring-about" and "caring-for" as part of their mission, as well as caring about good business relations more generally.

An advocate of care as a corporate virtue can further stress, moreover, that care is an actual, and not just a seeming virtue in regard to profitability, because caring-about the basic needs of employees and proximate dependents is conducive to a company making money. In this manner, Julie A. Nelson contends that money, and even capitalist profit, are congruous with real caring motivations, because some activities done for money are motivated by the need to sustain life and its flourishing in material ways (Nelson 2006). Care provisions can yield profits by decreasing turnover, increasing productivity, and preventing unnecessary expenditures.

For example, although companies that allow workers to bring their babies to work report losses in short term productivity and focused work environments, they report long-term gains in employee loyalty, retention, and increased morale (Armour 2008). Paid family leave increases a chance of a woman returning to work after a child is born, decreasing the cost associated with employee replacement and retraining (Bakst and Taubman 2008). After implementing a back-up child care center, the company Bright Care reported that more than 68% of the 800 employees enrolled in the program would have missed work if not for it, saving 2,528 workdays, or the equivalent of 10 work years—a productivity savings of nearly $400,000 (Sloan Work and Family Fact Sheet 2006). Additionally, a caring disposition in business can facilitate better working relations, as reported by Ilene Philipson, a clinical psychologist who treats workplace induced anxiety. She describes how many of her clients feel betrayed by employers who "don't care", or who characterize work relations as familial and caring but in practice neglect, alienate, or antagonize workers (Philipson 2002). Many of these workers seek employment elsewhere although they have not been fired, and their contributions are often missed. In these ways caring corporate dispositions and policies are compatible with profit in the form of employee satisfaction.

But if care is so profitable, why is it not already standard corporate practice? No doubt reluctance to develop care as a corporate virtue is due in part to how care has been viewed as a demeaning trait, but also because it has not been necessary to do so, thanks to the un(der)compensated labor of women and other service workers. Traditional sex based divisions of labor have yielded persistent andocentric models of employment, which encourage corporations to underestimate the profitability of care today.

However, a certain cost of caring-for must be acknowledged by a feminist care ethic seeking to mitigate this cost for women. A stronger response to the above objection that corporations ought to care not just because it is conducive to profit, but because it contributes to social flourishing that moves beyond monetary value. Accordingly, profit ought to be viewed as an important, but not exclusive goal in business. Fineman thus contends that "in the case of accommodation for caregivers, employers should not be permitted to evade their responsibility for some costs of dependency, even if it means some reduction in profits" (Fineman 1995). Liedtka maintains that a caring organization should be focused on persons, not quality or profits, and should undertake care as an end in itself, not as a means for quality or profit (Liedtka 1996).

This premise gains support from Aristotle's own virtue ethic. Although Aristotle did not endorse an egalitarian system of economic distribution, his esteem of the temperate mean precluded an insatiable drive for profit that must be cultured: "the beginning of reform is not so much to equalize property as to train the nobler sorts of natures not to desire more" (1267b5). But how are such caring virtues to be cultured in corporate agents? Ideally, corporations would develop the virtue of care voluntarily. But whether corporations can be motivated to care simply because it is a virtue is questionable. They may need some coercive persuasion.

For this reason Engster sees governments as needing to regulate care responsibility in markets, meaning that care as a corporate virtue should be mandated to some extent, and also partially funded by governments. In addition to subsidizing care work, caring governments ought encourage care as a corporate virtue through incentives, and move away from a singular model of reactive litigation in compensation for corporate harm or neglect. As Roger King wryly observes, corporate powers may outstrip government powers (King 2001). But if state and global economic governing bodies regulate corporate care policies, making this virtue (like consumer safety) an expected formal standard for trade, there could be more assurance that corporations will care. However, taking Koehn's caution to heart, enforcing the corporate virtue of care through government sanction (such as penalizing companies for failing to conform to a FMLA policy) may have the unintended consequence of incentivizing businesses to avoid employing care-givers altogether. Thus, another tactic should be to educate and habituate business agents so that the virtue of care becomes part of their characters, and to increase the presence of care-givers in powerful corporate positions.

As Michael Slote notes, care is the motivational virtue that undergirds ethical concerns more generally (Slote 1998, 2007). Developing care as a basic motive in business agents, and empowering business agents already in possession of caring empathy can help move corporations beyond the basic goal of profit generation. That the shareholder responsibility argument is flawed in excusing corporations from any responsibility other than profit-making has already been well defended in business ethics, but not specifically with regards to the responsibility for just and adequate distributions of caring labor (Wieland 2001; Moore 2003; Corvino 2006). Similar contemporary arguments have been waged on behalf of other public goods, such as product safety and environmental health. Making such an argument on behalf of care requires showing that care provision is a supreme public good, and that corporations have unique and presiding functions in its delivery.

Conclusion

I have argued for understanding care as a corporate virtue defined as a habitual disposition and practice of individuals with corporate governing powers and reflected in corporate policies, characterized by the sub-virtues of care of attention, responsiveness, and respect. I have further argued that this virtue has a graduated scope, starting foremost with those most vulnerable to corporate policies, including employees, consumers, and community members, construed as particular others embedded in varying relations of dependency. Of course these basic suggestions are not meant to be a one-size-fits-all solution, but in accordance with care ethics and virtue ethics, must be applied contextually with practical wisdom. As corporations grow mightier in their global scope, with increasing power to determine the ability of individuals to care for themselves and others, corporations are becoming more immune to appeals of conscience. Yet, at the core of every corporation are individuals dependent upon collective efforts. It may be that through rising global market structures, inter-dependency will become more evident, and flourishing through mutual care can be facilitated by an expanded understanding of care as a corporate virtue.

References

Albrecht, Gloria. 2002. *Hitting home: Feminist ethics, women's work, and betrayal of family values*. New York, NY: Continuum.

Allard, Mary Dorinda , and Marianne Janes. 2008. Time use of working parents: A visual essay. *USA*: *Monthly Labor Review*: 3–14.

Aloi, Daniel. 2005. Mothers face disadvantages in getting hired, Cornell study says. *Cornell News Service*4 August.

Anderson, Gordon. 2003. Should America be France? CNNMoney.com, 6 October, www.money.conn.com/2003/10/06/pf/workless Aristotle. *The Politics*. J. Barnes (trans.) *The Complete Works of Aristotle*. Princeton, NJ: Princeton University Press, 1984.

Anderson, Elizabeth. 2004. Welfare, work requirements, and dependent care. *Journal of Applied Philosophy* 21 (3): 243–256.

Armour, Stephanie. 2008. Day-care's new frontier: Your baby at your desk. *USA Today*: 3–30.

Bakst, Dina. 2010. Testimony before the NYC council women's issues. June 16 2010. Accessed 3 June 2011. http://www.abetterbalance.org/web/images/stories/Documents/fairness/testimony/cc-testimony_dbakst.pdf

Bakst, Dina, and Phoebe Taubman. 2008. Testimony before the NYC council women's issues committee. *The Work and Family Legal Center* 7 April: 1–7.

Blades, Joan, and Kristin Rowe-Finkbeiner. 2006. *The motherhood manifesto: What America's moms want and what to do about it*. New York, NY: Nation Books.

Borgerson, Janet L. 2007. On the harmony of feminist ethics and business ethics. *Business and Society Review* 112 (4): 477–509.

Bragues, George. 2006. Seeking the good life: The Aristotelian approach to business ethics. *Journal of Business Ethics* 67: 341–357.

Burton, Brian, and Craig Dunn. 1996. Feminist ethics as a moral grounding for stakeholder theory. *Business Ethics Quarterly* 6 (April): 133–147.

Correl, S., S. Benard, and I. Paik. 2007. Getting a Job: Is there a motherhood penalty? *American Journal of Sociology* 112 (5): 1297–1338.

Corvino, John. 2006. Reframing the morality pays argument: Toward a better answer to 'Why be moral' in business. *Journal of Business Ethics* 67 (1): 1–14.

Crittenden, Ann. 2001. *The price of motherhood: Why the most important job in the world is still the least valued*. New York, NY: Owl Books.

DiQuinzio, Patrice. 1993. Exclusion and essentialism in feminist theory: The problem of mothering. *Hypatia* 8 (3): 1–20.

Duffy, Mignon 2005. Reproducing labor inequalities: Challenges for feminists conceptualizing care at the intersections of gender, race and class. *Gender and Society* 19 (1): 66–82.

Engster, Daniel. 2007. *The heart of justice*. New York, NY: Oxford University Press.

Fineman, Martha. 1995. *The neutered mother, the sexual family and other twentieth century tragedies*. New York, NY: Routledge.

Folbre, Nancy. 2001. *The invisible heart: Economics and family values*. New York, NY: The New Press.

Folbre, Nancy. 2006. Demanding quality: worker/consumer coalitions and high-road strategies in the care sector. *Politics and Society* 34 (1): 1–21.

Frasier, Nancy. 1989. *Unruly practices: Power, discourse and gender in contemporary social theory*. Minneapolis, MN: University of Minneapolis Press.

Friedman, Milton. 1962. *Capitalism and freedom*. Chicago, IL: University of Chicago Press.

Friedman, Milton. 1970. The social responsibility of business is to increase its profits. *New York Times Magazine*: 13 September.

Gates, Bill. 2008. Making capitalism more creative. Time.com. 31 July. http://www.time.com/time/business/article/0,8599,1828069-2,00.html. Retrieved 11 June 2009.

Gowri, Aditi. 2006. On corporate virtue. *Journal of Business Ethics* 70 (1): 399–400.

Hankivsky, Olena. 2004. *Social policy and the ethic of care*. Vancouver, BC, Canada: University of British Columbia Press.

Harrington, Mona. 1999. *Care and equality: Inventing a new family politics*. New York, NY: Routledge.

Held, Virginia. 2006. *The ethics of care: Personal, political, and global*. New York, NY: Oxford University Press.

Hondagneu-Sotelo, Pierette, and Ernestine Avila. October 1997. I'm here, but I'm there: The meanings of Latina transnational motherhood. *Gender and Society* 11 (5): 548–571.

Jacoby, Dan. 2006. Caring about caring labor: An introduction. *Politics and Society* 34 (1): 5–9.

King, Roger J.H. 2001. "Virtue and community in business ethics: A critical assessment of Solomon's Aristotelian approach to social responsibility. *Journal of Social Philosophy* 32 (4): 487–499.

Kittay, Eva Feder. 1998. *Love's labor: Essays on women, equality, and dependency*. New York, NY: Routledge.

Landsburg, Steven. 2006. Why Europeans work less than Americans. Forbes.com. www.forbes.com/2006/05/20_steven_landsburg_labor

Liedtka, Jeanne. 1996. Feminist morality and competitive reality: A place for an ethic of care. *Business Ethics Quarterly* 6 (April): 179–200.

Martin, Joanne. 1990. Deconstructing organizational taboos: The suppression of gender conflict in organizations. *Organization Science* 1 (4): 339–359.

Mason, Mary Ann, and Marc Goulden. 2004. Do babies matter (Part II): Closing the baby gap. *Acadame* November–December: 11–16.

Meyers, Marcia K., and Alesha Durfee. 2006. Who pays? The visible and invisible costs of childcare. *Politics and Society* 34 (1): 109–128.

Miller, Sarah Clark. 2005. A Kantian ethic of care? In *Feminist Interventions in Ethics and Politics*, ed. Barbara S. Andrew, Jean Keller, and Lisa H.Swartzman. New York, NY: Rowman and Littlefield.

Miller, J., B. Stead, and A. Pereira. 1991. Dependent care and the workplace: An analysis of management and employee perceptions. *Journal of Business Ethics* 10: 863–869.

Moon, Jeremy, Andrew Crane, and Dirk Matten. 2005. Can corporations be citizens?: Corporate citizenship as a metaphor for business participation in society. *Business Ethics Quarterly* 15 (3): 429–453.

Moore, Geoff. 2003. Hives and horseshoes: What future for corporate responsibility? *Business Ethics: A European Review* 12 (1): 41–52.

Mullin, Amy. 2005. *Reconceiving pregnancy and childcare: Ethics, experience and reproductive labor*. New York, NY: Cambridge University Press.

National Alliance for Care-Giving and AARP. 2009. "Care-Giving in the U.S., 2009", http://assets.aarp.org/rgcenter/il/caregiving_09_fr.pdf, retrieved 1-25-10

Nelson, Julie A. 2006. Can we talk? Feminist economists in dialogue with social theorists. *Signs: Journal of Women in Culture and Society* 31 (4): 1051–1074.

Noddings, Nel. 1984. *Caring: A feminine approach to ethics and moral education*. Berkeley, CA: University of CA Press.

Noer, Michael. 2006. Don't marry career women. Forbes.com. 22 August. http://www.forbes.com/2006/08/23/Marriage-Careers-Divorce_cx_mn_land.html

Olson, Elizabeth. 1998. U.N. surveys paid leave for mothers. *New York Times* February: 16.

Palmer, Eric. 2007. Corporate responsibility and freedom. In *Controversies in International Corporate Responsibility*, ed. John Hooker, John F. Hulpke, and Peter Madson. Charlottesville, VA: Philosophy Documentation Center.

Philipson, Ilene. 2002. *Married to the job: Why we live to work and what we can do about it*. New York, NY: The Free Press.

Rivers, Caryl and Barnett, Rosalind Chaitt. 2000. Wage gap for working mothers may cost billions. Women's enews. 7 July. www.womensnews.org/article.cfm/dyn/aid/161/context/archive

Robinson, Fiona. 1999. *Globalizing care: Ethics, feminist theory, and international relations*. Boulder, CO: Westview Press.

Ruddick, Sara. 1989. *Maternal thinking: Toward a politics of peace*. New York, NY: Ballantine Books.

Sander-Staudt, Maureen. 2006. The unhappy marriage of care ethics and virtue ethics. *Hypatia* 21 (4): 21–40.

Schilt, Kristen, and Mathew Wiswall. 2008. Before and after: Gender transitions, human capital, and workplace experiences. 9 November 2008. Accessed 27 January 2010. http://www.bepress.com/bejeap/vol8/iss1/art39

Schudt, Karl. 2000. Taming the corporate monster: An Aristotelian approach to corporate virtue. *Business Ethics Quarterly* 10 (3): 711–723.

Sevenhuijsen, Selma. 1998. *Citizenship and the ethics of care: Feminist considerations on justice, morality, and practice*. New York, NY: Routledge.

Sloan work and family research network fact sheet. 2006. Q & A about gender and use of workplace policies; Q & A about employer-supported childcare. www.bc.edu/wfnetwork.

Slote, Michael. 1998. Caring in the balance. In *Norms and values: Essays on the work of Virginia Held*, ed. Joram Haber and Mark S. Halfon. New York, NY: Rowman & Littlefield Publishers.

Slote, Michael. 2007. *The ethics of care and empathy*. New York, NY: Routledge.

Solomon, Robert. 1992. *Ethics and excellence: Cooperation and integrity in business*. : New York, NY: Oxford University Press.

Solomon, Robert. 1998. The Moral Psychology of Business: Care and compassion in the corporation. *Business Ethics Quarterly* 8 (3): 515–533.

Story, Louise. 2005. Many women at elite colleges set career path to motherhood. *The New York Times* September 20.

Tessman, Lisa. 2001. Critical virtue ethics: Understanding oppression as morally damaging. In *Feminists doing ethics, Rowman & Littlefield Publishers: Boulde*, ed. Peggy DesAutels, and Joanne Waugh Boulder, CO: Rowman & Littlefield Publishers.

Tessman, Lisa. 2005. *Burdened virtues: Virtue ethics for liberatory struggles*. New York, NY: Oxford University Press.

Tronto, Joan. 1994. *Moral boundaries: A political argument for the ethic of care*. New York, NY: Routledge.

Tronto, Joan. 2002. The nanny question in feminism. *Hypatia* 17 (2): 34–51.

Van Wensveen, Louke M. 1995. Is toughness a business virtue? *International Journal of Applied Philosophy* 9 (2): 15–25.

Waldfogel, Jane. 1997. The effects of children on women's wages. *American Sociological Review* 62 (2): 209–218.

Warner, Judith. 2005. *Perfect madness: Motherhood in the age of anxiety*. New York, NY: Riverhead Books.

Weir, Allison. 2005. The global universal care-giver: Imagining women's liberation in the new millennium. *Constellations* 12 (3): 308–330.

Wieland, Josef. 2001. The ethics of governance. *Business Ethics Quarterly* 11 (1): 73–87.

Williams, Joan. 2007. What is the hidden gender bias in academia? UC Hastings college of law: Worklife law. www.worklifelaw.org/genderbias_index.html

Bibliography

Aaltio-Marjosola, I., and J. Lehtinen. 1998. Male managers as fathers? contrasting management, fatherhood, and masculinity. *Human Relations* 51 (2): 121–136.
Abraham, Y. 20 March 2007. As immigration raids rise, human toll decried. *Boston Globe*, online edition. Accessed 31 January 2010. http://www.boston.com/news/nation/articles/2007/03/20/as_immigration_raids_rise_human_toll_decried/
Adams, E.S., and J.H. Matheson. 2000. A statutory model for corporate constituency concerns. *Emory Law Journal* 49: 1085–1135.
Albrecht, Gloria. 2002. *Hitting home: Feminist ethics, women's work, and betrayal of family values*. New York, NY: Continuum.
Aldana, R. 2008. Rights and remedies: Of Katz and "Aliens", privacy expectations and the immigration raids. *University of California-Davis Law Review* 41: 1081.
Allard, M.D., and M. Janes. 2008. Time use of working parents: A visual essay. *Monthly Labor Review* (June) 3–14.
Aloi, Daniel. 2005. Mothers face disadvantages in getting hired, Cornell study says. *Cornell University News Service* (August 4).
American Law Institute. 2006. Restatement (third) of agency. In the *Restatement of the law: Third records*, American Law Institute archives, ALI.04.003, Biddle Law Library, University of Pennsylvania Law School, Philadelphia, PA.
Anderson, Elizabeth. 2004. Welfare, work requirements, and dependent care. *Journal of Applied Philosophy* 21 (3): 243–256.
Anderson, Gordon. 2003. Should America be France? CNNMoney.com, Oct. 6, www.money.conn.com/2003/10/06/pf/workless
Argyris, C. 1960. *Understanding organizational behavior*. Homewood, IL: Dorsey.
Argyris, C. 1994. Good communication that blocks learning. *Harvard Business Review* 74: 77–86.
Argyris, C. 2003. A life full of learning. *Organization Studies* 24: 1178–1192.
Aristotle. 1984. *The Politics*. (Trans. J. Barnes) *The complete works of Aristotle*. Princeton, NJ: Princeton University Press.
Armour, Stephanie. 2008. Day-care's new frontier: Your baby at your desk. *USA Today*: 3–30.
Associated Press. 2009. Two Iowa Towns, 2 Perspectives on Immigration Raids (April 26).
Association to Advance Collegiate Schools of Business International (AACSB). 2004. Ethics Education in Business Schools. Accessed 23 January 2008. http://www.aacsb.edu/eerc/EETF-report-6-24-04.pdf
Baier, A. 1985. What do women want in a moral theory? *Nous* 19: 53–63.
Bakst, Dina, and Phoebe Taubman. 2008. Testimony before the NYC council women's issues committee. *The Work and Family Legal Center* 7, April: 1–7.
Bartky, Sandra Lee. 1991. *Femininity and domination: Studies in the phenomenology of opression*. New York, NY: Routledge, Basic Books.
Bartos, Otomar, and Paul Wehr. 2002. *Using conflict theory*. Cambridge: Cambridge University Press, 35, 44 ff.

M. Hamington, M. Sander-Staudt (eds.), *Applying Care Ethics to Business*, Issues in Business Ethics 34, DOI 10.1007/978-90-481-9307-3,
© Springer Science+Business Media B.V. 2011

Baruchello, Giorgio. 2008. Capitalism and freedom: The core of a contradiction—an essay on Cornelius Castoriadis and John McMurtry. *Nordicum-Mediterraneum: Icelandic E-Journal of Nordic and Mediterranean Studies*.

Bauman, Yoram, and Elaina Rose. 2009. Why are economics students more selfish than the rest? University of Washington, Department of Economics, Working Papers Series.

Bazar, E. 25 June 2008. Citizens sue after being detained in workplace. *USA Today*: 1A, Final Edition, News.

Bell, Linda. 1993. *Rethinking ethics in the midst of violence: A feminist approach to freedom*. Lanham, MD: Rowman and Littlefield.

Bem, S.L. 1981. Gender schema theory: A cognitive account of sex typing. *Psychological Review* 88 (4): 354–364.

Benhabib, S. 1987. The generalized and the concrete other: The Kohlberg-Gilligan controversy and moral theory. In *Women and moral theory*, ed. E.V. Kittay, and D.T. Meyers. Lanham, MD: Rowman & Littlefield.

Berry, Christopher J. 1997. *Social theory of the Scottish: Enlightenment*. Edinburgh: Edinburgh University Press, 45.

Bhide, A. 1999. The questions every entrepreneur must answer. In *Harvard Business Review on Entrepreneurship*, 1–28. Harvard Business School Press, Boston MA. (Original work published 1996).

Billing, Y.D., and M. Alvesson. 2000. Questioning the notion of feminine leadership: A critical perspective on the gender labelling of leadership. *Gender, Work and Organisations* 7 (3): 144–157.

Blades, Joan, and Kristin Rowe Finkbeiner. 2006. *The motherhood manifesto: What America's moms want and what to do about it*. New York, NY: Nation Books.

Blasi, A. 2005. Moral character: A psychological approach. In *Character psychology and character education*, ed. D.K. Lapsley, and F.C. Power, 67–100. Notre Dame: University of Notre Dame Press.

Boatright, J. 1994. Fiduciary duties and shareholder management relation: Or, what's so special about shareholders? *Business Ethics Quarterly* 4: 393–407.

Bok, S. 1983. Whistleblowing and professional responsibility. In *Contemporary issues in business ethics*, ed. J. DesJardins, and J. McCall, 295–300. Belmont, CA: Wadsworth.

Borgerson, J.L. 2001. Feminist ethical ontology: Contesting the "bare givenness of Intersubjectivity." *Feminist Theory* 2 (2): 173–189.

Borgerson, J.L. 2007. On the harmony of feminist ethics and business ethics. *Business and Society Review* 112 (4): 477–509.

Bourdieu, Pierre, and Jean-Claude Passeron. 1990. *Reproduction*. London: Sage.

Bowes-Sperry, L., and J. Tata. 1999. A multiperspective framework of sexual harassment: Reviewing two decades of research. In *Handbook of gender and work*, ed. Gary N. Powell, 263–281. London: Sage Publications.

Bowie, N. 1999. *Business ethics: A Kantian perspective*. Oxford: Blackwell.

Brady, F.N., and G.E. Wheeler. 1996. An empirical study of ethical predispositions. *Journal of Business Ethics* 16: 927–940.

Bragues, George. 2006. Seeking the good life: The Aristotelian approach to business ethics. *Journal of Business Ethics* 67: 341–357.

Brewis, J., and S. Linstead. 2004. Gender and management. In *Management and organisation*, ed. S. Linstead, L. Fulop, and S. Lilley. Suffolk: Palgrave Macmillan.

Brown, Vivienne. 1994. *Adam Smith's discourse: Canonicity commerce and conscience*. London: Routledge.

Bubeck, D. 1995. *Care, gender, and justice*. Oxford: Clarendon Press.

Bubeck, D. 2002. Justice and the labor of care. In *The subject of care: Feminist perspectives on dependency*, ed. Eva Kittay, and Ellen Feder. New York, NY: Rowman & Littlefield.

Buchholz, R.A., and S.B. Rosenthal. 2001. A philosophical framework for case studies. *Journal of Business Ethics* 29: 25–31.

Buff, R. 2008. The deportation terror. *American Quarterly* 60 (3): 523–551.

Bulger, B., and Gessner, C. 2001. Sign of the times: Implementing reductions in force. In *Business ethics*, ed. M., Snoeyenbos, R., Almeder, and J. Humber, 218–224, 3rd edn. Amherst, NY: Prometheus.

Burnier, D. 2003. Other voices/other rooms: Towards a care-centered public administration. *Administrative Theory & Praxis* 25 (4): 529–544.

Burton, Brian, and Craig Dunn. 1996. Feminist ethics as a moral grounding for stakeholder theory. *Business Ethics Quarterly* 6 (April): 133–147.

Butterfield, A., and J.P. Grinnell. 1999. Re-viewing "gender, leadership, and managerial behavior: Do three decades of research tell us anything". In *Handbook of gender and workgary*, ed. N. Powell, 223–238. London: Sage Publications.

Calás, M.B., and L. Smircich (Eds.). 1997. Predicando la moral en calzoncillos: Feminist inquiries into business ethics. In *Business ethics and women's studies*, ed. A. Larson, and R.E. Freeman. Oxford: Oxford University Press.

Campbell, T.D. 1971. *Adam Smith's science of morals*. London: Allen & Unwin, Ltd.

Capps, R. 2007. Paying the price: The impact of immigration raids on America's children. The Urban Institute. http://www.urban.org/UploadedPDF/411566

Carbone, J.H. 1997. Loyalty: subversive doctrine? *The Academy of Management Executive* 11 (3): 80–86.

Card, C. 1990. Caring and evil. *Hypatia* 5: 101–108.

Card, C. 1996. *The unnatural lottery: Character and moral luck*. Philadelphia, PA: Temple University Press.

Carli, L.L. 1999. Gender, interpersonal power, and social influence. *Journal of Social Issues* 55 (1): 81–89.

Carli, L.L., and A.H. Eagly. 1999. Gender effects on social influence and emergent leadership. In *Handbook of Gender and Work*, ed. Gary N. Powell, 203–222. London: Sage Publications.

Carli, L.L., and A.H. Eagly. 2001. Gender, hierarchy, and leadership: An introduction. *Journal of Social Issues* 57 (4): 629–636.

Castro, J. 2009. Second-class citizens: The Schism between immigration policy and children's health care. *Hastings Constitutional Law Quarterly* Fall 37: 199.

Cavanagh, G.F. 2010. *American business values: A global perspective*. Upper Saddle River, NJ: Pearson Prentice Hall.

Chen, Shu-Ching Jean. 2007. Mass layoffs? In booming china? Forbes.com. www.forbes.com/2007/11/13/china-mass-layoffs-markets-econ-cx_jc_1113markets02.html.

Cialdini, R. 2001. *Influence: Science and practice*. New York, NY: Allyn and Bacon.

Ciulla, J.B. 2009. Leadership and the ethics of care. *Journal of Business Ethics* 88: 3–4.

Clement, G. 1996. *Care, autonomy, and justice*. Boulder, CO: Westview Press.

Cobb, John B. Jr. 2007. Towards a Just and sustainable economic order. In *Environmental ethics: An anthology*, ed. Andrew Light, and Holmes Rolston III, 359–370. Oxford: Blackwell Publishing Ltd.

Coffey, E., C. Huffington, and P. Thomson. 1999. *The changing culture of leadership—women leaders Voices*. London: The Change Partnership Limited.

Collins, J.C., and J.I. Porras. 1994. *Built to last*. New York, NY: Harper Business.

Collins, J.C., and J.I. Porris. 2000. *Built to last: Successful habits of visionary companies*. 3rd edn. London: Random House Business Books.

Correl, S., S. Benard, and I. Paik. 2007. Getting a job: Is there a motherhood penalty? *American Journal of Sociology* 112 (5): 1297–1338.

Corvino, John. 2002. Loyalty in business? *Journal of Business Ethics* 41:179–185.

Corvino, John. 2006. Reframing the morality pays argument: Toward a better answer to "Why be moral" in business. *Journal of Business Ethics* 67 (1): 1–14.

Cotter, D.A., J.M. Hermsen, S. Ovadia, and R. Vanneman. 2001. The glass ceiling effect. *Social Forces* 80 (2): 655–681.

Cox, A., and C. Rodriguez. December 2009. The President and Immigration Law. *Yale Law Journal* 119: 458.

Crittenden, Ann 2001. The price of motherhood: Why the most important job in the world is still the least valued. New York, NY: Owl Books.

Daly, Herman E. 2005. Economics in a Full World. *Scientific American* 293 (3): 100–107.

Daly, Mary. 2002. Care as good for social policy. *Journal of Social Policy* 31 (2): 251–270.

Davidson, M.J., and S. Fieldn. 1999. Stress and the working woman. In *Handbook of Gender and Work*, ed. Gary N. Powell, 413–426. London:Sage Publications.

Davis, M.A., M.G. Andersen, and M.B. Curtis. 2001. Measuring ethical ideology in business ethics: A critical analysis of the ethics position questionnaire. *Journal of Business Ethics* 8: 855–862.

DeLeire, Thomas. 2000. The unintended consequences of the Americans with disabilities act. *Regulation* 23 (1): 21–24.

DeMoss, M., and G. McCann. 1997. Without a care in the world: The business ethics course and its exclusion of a care perspective. *Journal of Business Ethics* 16: 435–443.

Department of Homeland Security, http://www.dhs.gov/xabout/responsibilities.shtm,accessed 30 January 2010; Fact Sheet, Accessed 8 February 2010. http://www.ice.gov/doclib/pi/news/factsheets/worksite_strategy.pdf

Dewey, J. 1921. *Human nature and conduct*. New York, NY: Henry Holt and Company.

Dienhart, J. 2000. Just caring, caring justice. *Business and Society Review* 105 (2): 247–267.

Dinan, S. 2 February 2009. Raid on immigrants dismays Obama backers. *Washington Post*, Page One; A01.

Dinnen, S. 31 May 2009. How an immigration raid changed a town. *Christian Science Monitor*: 17, Cover Story.

DiQuinzio, Patrice. 1993. Exclusion and essentialism in feminist theory: The problem of mothering. *Hypatia* 8 (3): 1–20.

Donaldson, T., and L. Preston. 1995. The stakeholder theory of the corporation: Concepts, evidence, and implications. *Academy of Management Review* 20: 65–91.

Donaldson, T., and P.H. Werhane. 1996. *Ethical issues in business*, 5th edn. Upper Saddle River, NJ: Prentice-Hall.

Donaldson, T.J. 1997. Morally informed iconoclasm: A response to Ferguson's "postmodernism, feminism, and organizational ethics." In *Women's studies and business ethics*, ed. J. Larson, and R.E. Freeman. New York, NY: Oxford.

Dower, Nigel. 1998. *World ethics: The new agenda*. Edinburgh: Edinburgh University Press, 166.

Drew, S. 1999. Building knowledge management into strategy: Making sense of a new perspective. *Long Range Planning* 32: 130–136.

Drucker, P. 1992. The new society of organizations. *Harvard Business Review* 70: 95–105.

Drucker, P. 1995. Introduction: Mary Parker Follett: Prophet of management. In *Mary Parker Follett: Prophet of Management*, ed. P. Graham, 1–9. Boston, MA: Harvard Business School Press.

Dubinsky, A.J., and B. Loken. 1989. Analyzing ethical decision making in marketing. *Journal of Business Research* 19 (2): 83–107.

Duffy, Mignon. 2005. Reproducing labor inequalities: Challenges for feminists conceptualizing care at the intersections of gender, race and class. *Gender and Society* 19 (1): 66–82.

Duska, R.F. 1984. Whistleblowing and employee loyalty. In *Contemporary issues in business ethics*, ed. J. DesJardins, and J. McCall, 142–147. Belmont, CA: Wadsworth.

Duska, R.F. 1992. Why be a loyal agent? A systemic ethical analysis. In *Ethics and agency theory*, eds. E. Freeman, and N. Bowie, 143–168. New York, NY: Oxford University Press.

Duska, R.F. 2006. *Contemporary reflections on business ethics*. Springer.

Eagly, A.H., and L.L. Carli. 2003. Finding gender advantage and disadvantage: Systematic research integration is the solution. *The Leadership Quarterly* 14 (6): 851–859.

Easlea, B. 1980. *Witch hunting, magic and the new philosophy: An introduction to debates of the scientific revolution, 1450–1750*. Atlantic Highlands, NJ: Humanities Press.

Easterby-Smith, M., R. Thorpe, and P.R. Jackson. 2008. *Management research*.3rd edn. London: Sage Publications.

Education Forum. 2009. *The Three Faces of Power*. Education Forum. Accessed 8 February 2009. http://www.educationforum.co.uk/sociology_2/power2.htm

Eisler, Riana. 2007. *The real wealth of nations: Creating a caring economics*. San Francisco, CA: Berrett-Koehler Publishers.

Elkington, J. 1997. *Cannibals with forks: The triple bottom line of the 21st century business*. Stony Creek, CT: New Society Publishers.

England, P. 2003. Separative and soluble selves: Dichotomous thinking in economics. In *Feminist economics today: Beyond economic man*, ed. M.A. Ferber, and J.A. Nelson, 33–59. Chicago, IL: University of Chicago Press.

Engster, D. 2007. *The heart of justice: Care ethics and political theory*. Oxford: Oxford University Press.

European Commission. 2007. *Women and men in decision-making 2007- Analysis of the situation and trends*. European commission. Accessed 10 February 2009. http://ec.europa.eu/employment_social/publications/2008/ke8108186_en.pdf

Evan, W., and Freeman, R. 1988. A stakeholder theory of the modern corporation: Kantian Capitalism. In *Ethical theory and business*, ed. T. Beauchamp and N. Bowie, 101–105, 3rd edn. Englewood Cliffs, NJ: Prentice-Hall.

Ewin, R.E. 1993. Corporate loyalty: Its objects and its grounds. *Journal of Business Ethics* 12: 387–396.

Federal Interagency Forum on Child and Family Statistics. 2007. *America's Children: Key National Indicators of Well-Being* 8. http://www.childwelfare.gov/systemwide/statistics/wellbeing.cfm

Ferber, M.A., and J.A. Nelson. (Eds.). 1993. *Beyond economic man: Feminist theory and economics*. Chicago, IL: University of Chicago Press.

Ferguson, K.E. 1997. Postmodernism, feminism, and organizational ethics: Letting difference be. In *Women's studies and business ethics*, ed. J. Larson, and R.E. Freeman. New York, NY: Oxford University Press.

Ferrell, O.C., and L.G. Gresham. 1985. A contingency framework for understanding ethical decision making in marketing. *Journal of Market* 49 (3): 87–96.

Fine, M. 1988. Sexuality, schooling and adolescent females: The missing discourse of desire. *Harvard Educational Review* 58 (1): 29–53.

Fineman, Martha. 2004. *The autonomy myth: A theory of dependency*. New York: The New Press.

Fineman, Martha. 1995. *The neutered mother, the sexual family and other twentieth century tragedies*. New York, NY: Routledge.

Flanagan, O., and Adler, J. 1983. Impartiality and particularity. *Social Research* 50: 576–596.

Fleischacker, Samuel. 2004. On Adam Smith's "Wealth of Nations": A Philosophical Companion. Princeton University Press.

Fletcher, J.K. 1999. *Disappearing acts: Gender, power, and relational practice at work*. Cambridge MA: The MIT Press.

Flores-Figueroa v. United States, U.S. 129 S. Ct. 1886, 173 L. Ed. 2d 853, 2009 US Lexis 3305, WL 1174852 (4 May 2009).

Fogarty, M., A.J. Allen, I. Allen, and P. Walters. 1971. *Women in top jobs*. Oxford: Alden Press.

Folbre, N., and J.A. Nelson. 2000. For love or money—or both? *Journal of Economic Perspectives* 14 (4): 123–140.

Folbre, Nancy. 2001. *The invisible heart: Economics and family values*. The New Press: New York.

Folbre, Nancy. 2006. Demanding quality: worker/consumer coalitions and high-road strategies in the care sector. *Politics and Society* 34 (1): 1–21.

Follett, M.P. 1951. *Creative experience*. New York: Peter Smith. (Original work published 1924).

Franfurt, Harry. *On Bullshit*. Princeton, NJ: Princeton University Press.

Frappaolo, C. 2006. *Knowledge management*. West Sussex, England: Capstone Publishing.

Fraser, Nancy, and Linda Gordon. 2006. "Dependency" demystified: Inscriptions of power in a keyword of the welfare state. In *Contemporary political philosophy: An anthology*, ed. Robert E. Goodin and Philip Pettit, 591–606. Oxford Blackwell Publishing Ltd.

Frasier, Nancy. 1989. *Unruly practices: Power, discourse and gender in contemporary social theory*. Minneapolis, MN: University of Minneapolis Press.

Freeman, R. 1984. *Strategic management: A stakeholder approach*. Boston, MA: Pitman.
Freeman, R. 1994. The politics of stakeholder Theory: some future directions. *Business Ethics Quarterly* 4: 409–421.
Freeman, R. 2004. A stakeholder theory of the modern corporation. In *Ethical theory and business*, ed. T. Beauchamp, and N. Bowie, 7th edn. Upper Saddle River, NJ: Prentice Hall.
Freeman, R. Edward, and Daniel R. Gilbert, Jr. 1988. *Corporate strategy and the search for ethics*. Englewood Cliffs, NJ: Prentice Hall.
Freeman, R., and D. Reed. 1983. Stockholders and stakeholders: A new perspective on corporate governance. *California Management Review* 25: 88–106.
Freeman, R., and W. Evan. 1990. Corporate Governance: A Stakeholder Interpretation. *Journal of Behavioural Economics* 19: 337–359.
Freeman, R., and Jr. D. Gilbert. 1992. Business ethics and society: A critical agenda. *Business and Society* 31: 9–17.
Freeman, R., and Liedtka, J. 1991. Corporate social responsibility: A critical approach. *Business Horizons* 34: 92–98.
French, J. and B. W. Raven. 1959. The bases of social power. In *Studies in social power*, ed. D. Cartwright, 150–167. Ann Arbor, MI: University of Michigan Press.
French, W., and Weiss, A. 2000. An ethics of care or an ethics of justice. *Journal of Business Ethics* 27: 125–136.
Friedman, A., and Miles, S. 2006. *Stakeholders: Theory and practice*.Oxford: Oxford University Press.
Friedman, M. 13 September 1970. The social responsibility of business is to increase its profits. *New York Times Magazine* 32–33, 122, and 126.
Friedman, Marilyn. (September 2008). Care ethics and moral theory. *Philosophy and Phenomenological Research* 77 (2): 539–555.
Friedman, Marilyn. 1993. *What are friends for?* Ithaca, NY: Cornell University Press.
Friedman, Milton. 1962. *Capitalism and freedom*. Chicago, IL: University of Chicago Press.
Friesen, J. (24 May 2008). Hardening the line on illegal works. *The Globe and Mail* (Canada), International News; Weekend Special, A16.
Garvin, D.A., C.R. Christensen, and F. Gino. 2008. Is yours a learning organization? *Harvard Business Review* 86: 109–116.
Gatens, M. 1998. *Feminist ethics*. Brookfield, WI: Ashgate Dartmouth.
Gates, Bill. 2008. Making capitalism more creative. Time.com. 31 July. http://www.time.com/time/business/article/0,8599,1828069-2,00.html. Retrieved 11 June 2009.
Gilligan, Carol. 1977. In a different voice: Women's conceptions of self and morality. *Harvard Educational Review* 47 (4): 481–517.
Gilligan, Carol. 1995. Hearing the difference: Theorizing connection. *Hypatia* 10 (2): 120–127.
Gilligan, Carol. 2008. Moral orientation and moral development. The *Feminist Philosophy Reader*, ed. Alison Bailey and Chris Cuomo, 467–478. Boston, MA: McGraw Hill.
Gioia, D.A. 2002. Business education's role in the crisis of corporate confidence. *Academy of Management Executive* 16 (3): 142–145.
Goldberg, D.T. 1993. *Racist culture: philosophy and the politics of meaning*. Oxford: Blackwell.
Goodin, R. 1996. Structures of political order: The relational feminist Alternative. In *Nomos XXXVIII: Political order*, ed. Russell Hardin and Ian Shapiro, 498–521. New York: New York University Press.
Goodpaster, K. 1991. Business ethics and stakeholder analysis. *Business Ethics Quarterly* 1: 53–73.
Goodpaster, Kenneth. 1993. Business ethics and stakeholder analysis. In *Applied ethics: A reade*r, ed. Earl R. Winkler and Jerrold R. Coombs, 227–248. Oxford: Blackwell Publishers.
Gordon, L. 1997. *Her Majesty's other children: Sketches of racism from a neocolonial age*. Lanham, MD: Rowman and Littlefield.
Gorman, A. 26 July 2009 Obama sets the priorities on immigration. *Los Angeles Times*:13, Part A.
Gouldner, A.W. 1957. Cosmopolitans and locals: toward an analysis of latent social roles. I. *Administrative Science Quarterly* 2 (3): 281–306.

Gouldner, A.W. 1958. Cosmopolitans and locals: toward an analysis of latent social roles. II. *Administrative Science Quarterly* 2 (4): 444–480.

Gowri, Aditi. 2006. On corporate virtue. *Journal of Business Ethics* 70 (1): 399–400.

Greene, J.D., and Haidt, J. 2002. How (and where) does moral judgment work? *Trends in Cognitive Sciences* 6 (12): 517–523.

Greene, J.D., R.B. Sommerville, L.E. Nystrom, J.M. Darley, and J.D. Cohen. 2001. An FMRI investigation of emotional engagement in moral judgment. *Science* 293 (September 14): 2105–2108.

Greenhaus, J.H. And Parasuraman, S. 1999. Research on work, family, and gender: Current status and future directions. In *Handbook of gender and work* Gary N. Powell, 391–412. London: Sage Publications.

Greenlaw, U.S. 128 S. Ct. 2559, 171 L. Ed. 2d 399, 2009.

Grieve, Andrew, and Steve Dickinson. 2000. China's new labor contract law—clarifications a Comin. http://www.chinalawblog.com/2008/05/chinas_new_labor_contract_law_1.html

Groenhoul, Ruth E. 2004. *Connected lives: Human nature and an ethics of care*. Oxford: Rowman & Littlefield Publishers, Inc.

Gustafsson, C. 2005. Trust as an example of asymmetrical reciprocity: An ethics perspective on corporate brand management. *Business Ethics—A European Review* 14 (2): 143–150.

Habermas, Jürgen. 1990. *The philosophical discourse of modernity: Twelve lectures*. (Trans. Frederick G. Lawrence) Cambridge, MA: MIT Press.

Haidt, J. 2001. The emotional dog and its rational tail: A social intuitionist approach to moral judgment. *Psychological Review* 108 (4): 814–834.

Hajdin Mane. 2005. Employee loyalty: An examination. *Journal of Business Ethics* 59 (3): 259–280.

Hamington, M. 2004. *Embodied care: Jane Addams, Maurice Merleau-Ponty and feminist ethics*. Champaign, IL: University of Illinois Press.

Hamington, M. 2009. Business is not a game: The metaphoric fallacy. *Journal of Business Ethics* 86: 474–484.

Hamington, M., and Miller D. 2006. Socializing care: Feminist ethics and public issues. Langham, MD: Rowman & Littlefield.

Hamington, Maurice, and Dorothy Miller. 2006. Introduction: A modern moral imperative. In *Socializing care: Feminist ethics and public issues*, ed. Maurice Hamington and Dorothy Miller, xi–xxii. New York, NY: Rowan & Littlefield.

Hankivsky, Olena. 2004. *Social policy and the ethic of care*. Vancouver, BC, Canada: University of British Columbia Press.

Harding, S. 1986. *The science question in feminism*. Ithaca, NY: Cornell University Press.

Harrington, Mona. 1999. *Care and equality: Inventing a new family politics*. New York, NY: Routledge.

Hart, D.W. and Thompson, J.A. 2007. Untangling employee loyalty: a psychological contract perspective. *Business Ethics Quarterly* 17:297–323.

Hart, S.L. 2005. *Capitalism at the crossroads: The unlimited business opportunities in solving the world's most difficult problems*. Upper Saddle River, NJ: Wharton School Publishing.

Hart, S.L. and Christensen, C.M. 2002. The great leap: Driving innovation from the base of the pyramid. *Sloan Management Review* 44 (1): 51–56.

Hartman, E.M. 1994. The commons and the moral organization. *Business Ethics Quarterly* 4: 253–269.

Haslam, S.A., Reicher, S.D., and Platow, M.J. 2010. *The new psychology of leadership: Identity, influence and power*.

Haslam, S.A., and M.K. Ryan. 2008. The road to the glass cliff: Differences in the perceived suitability of men and women for leadership positions in succeeding and failing organisations. *The Leadership Quarterly* 19 (5): 530–546.

Hasnas, J. 1998. The normative theories of business ethics: A guide for the perplexed. *Business Ethics Quarterly* 8: 19–42.

Hegel, G.W.F. 1952 [1820]. *Hegel's philosophy of right*. (Trans. T.M. Knox). Oxford: Oxford University Press.

Held, Virginia. 1990. Feminist transformations of moral theory. *Philosophy and Phenomenological Research* 50: 321–344 (Supplement): 332.

Held, Virginia. 1993. *Feminist morality: Transforming culture, society, and politics*. Chicago, IL: University of Chicago Press.

Held, Virginia. 1995. The meshing of care and justice. *Hypatia* 10 (2): 128–132.

Held, Viriginia. 2004. Care and justice in the global context. *Ratio Juris* 17 (2): 141–155.

Held, Virginia. 2006. *The ethics of care: Personal, political, and global*. Oxford University Press: Oxford.

Held, Virginia. 2006. The ethics of care. In *The Oxford handbook of ethical theory*, ed. David Copp. Oxford: Oxford University Press.

Hendry, J. 2001. Economic contracts versus social relationships as a foundation for normative stakeholder theory. *Business Ethics: A European Review* 10: 223–232.

Henrik, E. 2008. Mad as hell or scared stiff? The effects of value conflict and emotions on potential whistle-blowers. *Journal of Business Ethics* 80: 111–119.

Herman, S.W. 1992. The modern business corporation and an ethics of trust. *Journal of Religious Ethics* 20: 111–148.

Herzberg, F. 1987. One more time: How do you motivate employees? *Harvard Business Review* (September–October): 109–120.

Hirschman, A.O. 1970. *Exit, voice, and loyalty: Responses to decline in firms, organizations, and states*. Cambridge, MA: Harvard University Press.

Hoagland, Sarah. 1991. Some thoughts about caring. In *Feminist Ethics*, ed. Claudia Card, 246–263. Lawrence, KS: University Press of Kansas.

Hochschild, Arlie R. 2002. Love and gold. In *Global women: Nannies, maids, and sex workers in the new economy*, ed. Barbara Ehrenreich and Arlie R. Hochschild, 15–30. New York: Henry Holt & Co.

Hoffman, M.L. 2000. *Empathy and moral development: Implications for caring and justice*. Cambridge: Cambridge University Press.

Hoffmann, E.A. 2006. Exit and voice: Organizational loyalty and dispute resolution strategies. *Social Forces* 84: 2313–2330.

Hondagneu-Sotelo, Pierette, and Ernestine Avila. 1997. I'm here, but I'm there : The meanings of Latina transnational motherhood. *Gender and Society* 11 (5), October: 548–571.

Hsu, S. 21 July 2008. In immigration cases, employers feel the pressure; But critics fault laws as ineffective. *Washington Post*: A01, Met 2 Edition, A-Section.

Hsu, S. 31 March 2009 Proposed immigration raids delayed. *The Boston Globe*: 5, National News.

Hubbard, Ruth. 1995. *Profitable promises: Essays on women, science, and health*. Monroe, ME: Common Courage Press.

Humber, J. 2001. Why I am not a normative stakeholder theorist. In *Business ethics*, ed. M. Snoeyenbos, R. Almeder, and J. Humber, 3rd edn. Amherst, NY: Prometheus.

Hunt, S.D., and Vitell, S. 1986. A general theory of marketing ethics. *Journal of Macromarketing* 6 (1): 5–16.

Injunctive Order at 7, Swift & Co. v. ICE, No 2:06CV-314-J (N.D. Tex. Dec. 7, 2006). http://www.aif.org/lac/clearinghouse122106ctorder.pdf

Jackall, Robert. 1988. *Moral mazes: The world of corporate managers*. New York, NY: Oxford University Press.

Jacoby, Dan. 2006. Caring about caring labor: An introduction. *Politics and Society* 34 (1): 5–9.

Jaffee, S., and J.S. Hyde. 2000. Gender differences in moral orientation: A meta-analysis. *Psychological Bulletin* 126 (5): 703–726.

Jaggar, A.M. 1989. Love and knowledge: Emotion in feminist epistemology. In *Gender/body/knowledge*, ed. A.M. Jaggar, and S.R. Bordo, 45–171. London: Rutgers University Press.

Jashapara, A. 2004. *Knowledge management: An integrated approach*. Essex, UK: Pearson Education.

Jensen, J.V. 1987. Ethical tension points in whistleblowing. *Journal of Business Ethics* 6: 321–328.

Jodalen, H., and A. Vetlesen (Eds.). 1997. *Closeness: An ethics*. Oslo: Scandinavian University Press.

Johnson-Cramer, Michael E. 2008. Stakeholder theory. In *Encyclopedia of business ethics and society*, Volume 4, ed. Robert W. Kolb, 1992–1999. Thousand Oaks, CA: Sage Publications.

Jones, T.M. 1991. Ethical decision making by individuals in organizations: An issue- contingent model. *Academy of Management Review* 16 (2): 366–395.

Kant, Immanuel. 1960. *Observations on the feeling of the beautiful and the sublime*. (Trans. J.T. Goldthwait). Berkeley, CA: University of California Press.

Kant, Immanuel. 1998. *Groundwork of the metaphysics of morals*. (Trans. Mary J. Gregor). Cambridge: Cambridge University Press, 32.

Kanter, R.M. 1995. Preface. In *Mary Parker Follett: Prophet of management*, ed. P. Graham, xiii–xix. Boston, MA: Harvard Business School Press.

Keller, E.F. 1985. *Reflections on gender and science*. New Haven, CT: Yale University Press.

Keller, S. 2007. *The limits of loyalty* New York, NY: Cambridge University Press.

Kennedy, Gavin. 2005. *Adam Smith's lost legacy*. New York: Palgrave Macmillan.

King, Roger J.H. 2001. Virtue and community in business ethics: A critical assessment of Solomon's Aristotelian approach to social responsibility. *Journal of Social Philosophy* 32 (4): 487–499.

Kirkland, R. 2006. The real ceo pay problem. *Fortune*.

Kittay, Eva Feder. 1998. *Love's labor: Essays on women, equality, and dependency*. New York, NY: Routledge.

Kittay, Eva Feder, 2008. The global heart transplant and caring across national boundaries. *The Southern Journal of Philosophy* XLVI: 138–165.

Knutson, K.M., L. Mah, C.F. Manly, and J. Grafman. 2007. Neural correlates of automatic beliefs about gender and race. *Human Brain Mapping* 28: 915–930.

Koehn, Daryl. 1998. *Rethinking feminist ethics: Care, trust and empathy*. New York, NY: Routledge.

Koehn, Daryl. 2009. *Living with the dragon: acting ethically in a world of unintended consequences*. New York: Routledge.

Kohlberg, L. 1969. *Stages in the development of moral thought and action*. New York, NY: Holt Rinehart & Winston.

Kohlberg, L. 1976. Moral stages and moralization: The cognitive-developmental approach. In *Moral development and behavior*, ed. T. Lickona, 31–53. New York, NY: Holt Rinehart & Winston.

Konrad, A.M., and Linnehan, F. 1999. Affirmative action: History, effects, and attitudes. In *Handbook of gender and work*, ed. Gary N. Powell, 429–452. , London: Sage Publications.

Kristie, James. 1999. A delicious irony in governance ideology. *Directors & Boards* Magazine.

Kroeger-Mappes, J. Summer 1994. An ethic of care vis-à-vis an ethics of rights. *Hypatia* 9 (3): 108–131.

Kuhse, H., Singer, P., and Rickard, M. 1998. Reconciling impartial morality and a feminist ethic of care. *The Journal of Value Inquiry* 32: 451–463.

Kusnet, D. 2008. *Love the work, hate the job: Why America's best workers are more unhappy than ever*. Hoboken, NJ: John Wiley & Sons.

Lakoff, G., and Johnson, M. 1980. *Metaphors we live by*. Chicago, IL: University of Chicago Press.

Landsburg, Steven. 2006. Why Europeans work less than Americans. Forbes.com. www.forbes.com/2006/05/20_steven_landsburg_labor

Lapsley, D.K., and Narvaez, D. 2004. A social-cognitive approach to moral personality. In *Moral development, self and identity*, ed. D.K. Lapsley, and D. Narvaez, 189–213. Mahwah, NJ: Lawrence Erlbaum.

Larmer, R.A. 1992. Whistleblowing and employee loyalty. *Journal of Business Ethics* 11: 125–128.

Larrabee, M.J. (Ed.) 1993. *An ethic of care: Feminist and interdisciplinary perspectives*. New York, NY: Routledge.

Laszlo, K.C., and Laszlo, A. 2002. Evolving knowledge for development: the role of knowledge management in a changing world. *Journal of Knowledge Management* 6: 400–412.

Lewis, N. 20 November 2009. In search for illegal workers, immigration officials will audit more companies. *The New York Times*: 14, Late Edition, Final, Section A, Column 0, National Desk.

Leys, T. 28 August 2009. Critics tie scant new charges to wariness after Iowa raid. *Des Moines Register*: 1A.

Liedtka, Jeanne. 1999. Linking competitive advantage with communities of practice. *Journal of Management Inquiry* 8 (1): 5–16.

Liedtka, Jeanne. 1996. Feminist morality and competitive reality: A place for an Ethic of Care? *Business Ethics Quarterly* 6:179–200.

Lindemann, Hilde. 2005. *An invitation to feminist ethics*. New York: McGraw-Hill.

Little, M.O. 1995. Seeing and caring: The role of affect in feminist moral epistemology. *Hypatia* 10 (3):117–137.

Loy, David R. 1997. The religion of the market. *Journal of the American Academy of Religion* 65 (2): 275–290.

Lozano v. City of Hazelton, 2007 U.S. Dist LEXIS 17118 (M.D. Pa., Mar 9, 2007), at P4.

Lurie, Y. 2004. Humanizing business through emotions: On the role of emotions in ethics. *Journal of Business Ethics* 49 (1): 1–11.

Machold, S., Ahmed, P., and Farquhar, S. 2008. Corporate governance and ethics: A feminist perspective. *Journal of Business Ethics* 81: 665–78.

Maguire, Daniel C. 2010. *Ethics: A compete method for moral choice*. Minneapolis, MN: Fortress Press.

Mahowald, M. 2006. Review: ethics of care: Personal, political, global. *International Journal of Feminist Approaches to Bioethics* 2: 1.

Mandel, R.B. 2003. A question about women and the leadership option. In *The difference "difference" makes*, ed. Deborah L. Rhode, 66–75., Stanford, CA: Stanford University Press.

Manning, Rita C. 1992. *Speaking from the heart: A feminist perspective on ethics*. Lanham, MD: Rowman & Littlefield.

Marcoux, A. 2003. A fidicuiary argument against stakeholder theory. *Business Ethics Quarterly* 13: 1–24.

Marens, R., and Wicks, A. 1999. Getting real: Stakeholder theory, managerial practice, and the general irrelevance of fiduciary duties owed to shareholders. *Business Ethics Quarterly* 9: 273–94.

Martin, Joanne. 1990. Deconstructing organizational taboos: The suppression of gender conflict in organizations. *Organization Science* 1 (4): 339–359.

Martin. J.R. 1994. *Changing the educational landscape: Philosophy, women, and curriculum*. New York, NY: Routledge.

Mason, Mary Ann, and Marc Goulden. 2004. Do babies matter? (Part II): Closing the baby gap. *Acadame* November–December: 11–16.

Mayeroff, M. 1971. *On caring*. New York, NY: Harper & Row.

McCluskey, M. 2002. Subsidized lives and the ideology of efficiency. In *The subject of care: Feminist perspectives on dependency*, ed. Eva Kittay and Ellen Feder, 115–137. New York, NY: Rowman & Littlefield.

McLaughlin, J. 1997. An ethic of care: A valuable political tool? *Politics* 17 (1): 17–23.

McNay, L. 2000. *Gender and agency: Reconfiguring the subject in feminist and social theory*. Cambridge: Polity.

Meadows, J. 2001. *Understanding information*. Munich: K.G. Saur.

Mele, D. 2001. Loyalty in business: subversive doctrine or real need? *Business Ethics Quarterly* 11: 11–26.

Merritt, N. Winter 2009. The conflicting interests of labor demands and employer based immigration laws. *The Scholar: St. Mary's Law Review on Minority Issues*, 11 Scholar, 281.

Meyers, Marcia K., and Durfee, Alesha. 2006. Who pays? The visible and invisible costs of childcare. *Politics and Society* 34 (1): 109–128.

Mill, J.S. 1836. On the definition of political economy; and on the method of philosophical investigation in that science. *London and Westminster Review*: 1–29.

Mill, J.S. 1981. *Utilitarianism*. Indianapolis, IN: Hackett Publishing.

Miller, J., Stead, B., and Pereira, A. 1991. Dependent care and the workplace: An analysis of management and employee perceptions. *Journal of Business Ethics* 10: 863–869.

Miller, Sarah Clark. 2005. A Kantian ethic of care? In *Feminist Interventions in Ethics and Politics*, ed. Keller Andrew, and Swartzman. New York, NY: Rowman and Littlefield.

Mishra, R., and B. Ballou. 9 March 2007. DSS to check on detainees sent to Texas: Some workers' children may lack care, officials fear. *Boston Globe*: A1.

Mitchell, R., B. Agle, and D. Wood. 1997. Toward a theory of stakeholder identification and salience: Defining the principle of who and what really counts. *Academy of Management Review* 22: 853–886.

Moon, J., A. Crane, and D. Matten. 2005. Can corporations be citizens?: Corporate citizenship as a metaphor for business participation in society. *Business Ethics Quarterly* 15 (3): 429–453.

Moore, Geoff. 2003. Hives and horseshoes: What future for corporate responsibility? *Business Ethics: A European Review* 12 (1): 41–52.

Mora, Mora et al. v. Maricopa County, US District Court for the State of Arizona, 29th U.S. District Lexis 101403, No. CV-09-1719-PHX-DGC, 28 October 2009.Morgan, G. 1986. Exploring power. In *Images of Organisation*, ed. Gareth Morgan, 158–185. London: Sage Publications.

Morton, N.O.'R., and S.A. Lindquist. 1997. Revealing the feminist in Mary Parker Follett. *Administration & Society* 29 (3): 348–371.

Mullin, Amy. 2005. *Reconceiving pregnancy and childcare: Ethics, experience and reproductive labor*. New York, NY: Cambridge University Press.

Myrdal, A., and V. Klein. 1956. *Women's two roles*. London: Routledge and Kegan Paul Ltd.

National Alliance for Care-Giving and AARP. 2009. Care-Giving in the U.S., 2009. http://assets.aarp.org/rgcenter/il/caregiving_09_fr.pdf, retrieved 25 January 2010.

National Highway Traffic Safety Administration (NHTSA). 2003. Automotive Fuel Economy Program: Annual Update Calendar Year 2003. Available at www.nhtsa.dot.gov/cars/rules/cafe/FuelEconUpdates/2003/index.htm.

Nelson, Julie A. 1992. Gender, metaphor, and the definition of economics. *Economics and Philosophy* 8: 103–125.

Nelson, Julie A. 1996. *Feminism, objectivity and economics*. London: Routledge.

Nelson, Julie A. 2003. Separative and soluble firms: Androcentric bias in business ethics. In *Feminist economics today: Beyond economic man*, ed. M.A. Ferber, and J.A. Nelson. Chicago, IL: University of Chicago Press.

Nelson, Julie A. 2006. *Economics for humans*. Chicago, IL: University of Chicago Press.

Nelson, Julie A. 2006. Can we talk? Feminist economists in dialogue with social Theorists. *Signs: Journal of Women in Culture and Society* 31 (4): 1051–1074.

Nelson, Richard R. (Ed.). 2005. *The limits of market organization*. New York, NY: Russell Sage Foundation.

Nietzsche, Friedrich. 1998. *On the genealogy of morality*. (Trans. M. Clark and A. Swensen). Indianapolis, IN: Hackett.

Noddings, Nel. 1984. *Caring: A feminine approach to ethics and moral education*. Berkeley, CA: University of California Press.

Noddings, Nel. 2002. *Starting at home: Caring and social policy*. Berkeley, CA: University of California Press.

Noer, Michael. 2006. Don't marry career women. Forbes.com. 22 August. http://www.forbes.com/2006/08/23/Marriage-Careers-Divorce_cx_mn_land.html

Nosek, B., M. Banaji, and Greenwald T. 2007. Gender-science IAT. http://implicit.harvard.edu/implicit/

Nozick, Robert. 1974. *Anarchy, state, and utopia*. Oxford: Basic Books, Inc.

Nunner-Winkler, G. 1993. Two moralities?: A critical discussion of an ethics of care and responsibility versus an ethic of rights and justice. In *An ethic of care*, ed. M. J. Larrabee. New York, NY: Routledge.

Nürnberger, Klaus. 1998. *Beyond marx and market: Outcomes of a century of economic experimentation*. New York, NY: Zed Books Ltd.

O'Fallon, M.J., and K.D. Butterfield. 2005. A review of the empirical ethical decision-making literature: 1996–2003. *Journal of Business Ethics* 59: 375–413.

O'Neill, Onora. 2004. Global justice: Whose obligations. In *The ethics of assistance: Morality and the distant needy*, ed. Deen K. Chatterjee, 242–259. Cambridge: Cambridge University Press.

Oakley, J.G. 2000. Gender-based barriers to senior management positions: Understanding the scarcity of female CEOs. *Journal of Business Ethics* 27 (4): 321–334.

Oliner, P.M., and S.P. Oliner. 1995. *Toward a caring society*. Westport, CT: Praeger Publishers.

Olson, Elizabeth. 16 February 1998. U.N. surveys paid leave for mothers. *New York Times*.

Paine, L.S. 2002. *Value shift*. New York, NY: McGraw-Hill.

Palmer, D. 1999. Upping the stakes: A response to John Hasnas on the normative viability of the stockholder and stakeholder theories. *Business Ethics Quarterly* 9: 699–706.

Palmer, Daniel E., Mary Lyn Stoll, and Abe J. Zakhem. 2008. Introduction. In *Stakeholder theory: Essential readings in ethical leadership and management*, ed. Daniel E. Palmer, Mary Lyn Stoll, and Abe J. Zakhem, 15–22. Amherst, NY: Prometheus Books.

Palmer, Eric. 2007. Corporate responsibility and freedom. In *Controversies in International Corporate Responsibility*, ed. J. Hooker, J. Hulpke, and P. Madson. Charlottesville, VA: Philosophy Documentation Center.

Pamental, G.L. 1991. The course in business ethics: Why don't the philosophers give business students what they need? *Business Ethics Quarterly* 1:385–393.

Pedler, M., J. Burgoyne, and T. Boydell. 2004. *A manager's guide to leadership*. London: McGraw-Hill Business.

Perrott, B.E. 2006. Knowledge management in health: An evolution? *Proceedings of Knowledge Management: The Key to Innovative Health Programs*. Sydney, Australia.

Petersen, C. November 2009. An Iowa immigration raid leads to unprecedented criminal consequences. *University of Iowa Law Review* 95: 323.

Pfeiffer, R.S. 1992. Owing loyalty to one's employer. *Journal of Business Ethics* 11: 535–543.

Pfeiffer, R.S., and R.P. Forsberg. 1993. Is the customer always right? In Ethics on the job, ed. R.S. Pfeiffer, and R.P. Forsberg, 144–145. Belmont, CA: Wadsworth Publishing.

Philipson, Ilene. 2002. *Married to the job: Why we live to work and what we can do about it*. New York, NY: The Free Press.

Phillips, R. 1997. Stakeholder theory and a principle of fairness. *Business Ethics Quarterly* 7: 55–66.

Phillips, R., Freeman, R., and Wicks, A. 2003. What stakeholder theory is not. *Business Ethics Quarterly* 13: 479–502.

Pickersgill, Gary M., and Pickersgill, Joyce E. 1974. *Contemporary economic systems: A comparative view*. Upper Saddle River, NJ: Prentice-Hall Inc.

Plumwood, Val. 1993. *Feminism and the mastery of nature*. New York, NY: Routledge.

Polanyi, M. 1966. *The tacit dimension*. New York, NY: Doubleday.

Porter, E. 1999. *Feminist perspectives on ethics*. New York, NY: Longman.

Postow, Betsy. 2008. Care ethics and impartial reasons. *Hypatia* 23: 1–8.

Powell, G.N. 1999. Reflections on the glass ceiling: Recent trends and future prospects. In *Handbook of Gender and Work*, ed. Gary N. Powell, 325–346. London: Sage Publications.

Powell, G.N., and Butterfield, D.A. 1994. Investigating the "glass ceiling" phenomenon: An empirical study of actual promotions to top management. *The Academy of Management Journal* 37 (1): 68–86.

Prahalad, C.K., and Hamel, G. 1990. The core competence of the corporation. *Harvard Business Review* 68: 79–91.

Prahalad, C.K., and S.L. Hart. 2002. The fortune at the bottom of the pyramid. *Harvard Business Review* 80 (9): 48–57.

Preston, J. 26 May 2009. Dismissal of guilty pleas is sought for immigrants. *New York Times*: 19, Late Edition, Final, Section A, Column 0, National Desk.

Quinn, J.B. 1992. *Intelligent enterprise: A knowledge and serve based paradigm for industry*. New York, NY: Free Press.

Ranciere, Jacques. 1999. *Disagreement: Politics and philosophy*. (Trans. Julie Rose). Minneapolis, MN: University of Minnesota Press.

Randels, G.D. Jr. 2001. Loyalty, corporations, and community. *Business Ethics Quarterly* 11: 27–39.

Rawls, John. 1971. *A theory of justice*. Cambridge, MA: Harvard University Press.

Reed, Darryl. 1999. Stakeholder management: A critical theory perspective. *Business Ethics Quarterly* 3: 453–483.

Reiter, S. 1996. The Kohlberg-Gilligan controversy: Lessons for accounting ethics education. *Critical Perspectives on Accounting* 7: 33–54.

Reskin, B. 2003. What's the difference? A comment on Deborah Rhode's "The Difference 'Difference' Makes." In *The Difference "Difference" Makes*, ed. Deborah L. Rhode, 59–65. Stanford, CA: Stanford University Press.

Rest, J.R. 1986. *Moral development: Advances in research and theory*. New York, NY: Praeger.

Rest, J.R. 1994. Background: Theory and research. In *Moral development in the professions: Psychology and applied ethics*, ed. J.R. Rest, and D. Narvaez, 1–26. Hillsdale, NJ: Lawrence Erlbaum Associates.

Reyes, R. 8 August 2008. What are ICE raids accomplishing? *USA Today*: 9A, Final Edition, News.

Rhode, D.L. 2003. The Difference "Difference" Makes. In *The difference "difference" makes*, ed. Deborah L. Rhode, 3–50. Stanford, CA: Stanford University Press, pp.

Rhor, M. 12 March 2007. Immigration raids split kids from moms. *Seattle Times*: A1.

Rivers, Caryl, and Rosalind Chaitt Barnett. 2000. Wage gap for working mothers may cost billions. Women's enews. 7 July. www.womensnews.org/article.cfm/dyn/aid/161/context/archive.

Robinson, Fiona. 1999. *Globalizing care: Ethics, feminist theory, and international relations*. Boulder, CO: Westview Press.

Rosanas, J.M., and M. Velilla. 2003. Loyalty and trust as the ethical bases of organizations. *Journal of Business Ethics* 44: 49–59.

Rousseau, Jean-Jacques. 1979. *Emile*. (Trans. Allan Bloom). New York, NY: Basic Books.

Rowley, J., and P. Gibbs. 2008. From learning organization to practically wise organization. *The Learning Organization* 15: 356–372.

Ruddick, S.A. 1984. Maternal thinking. In *Mothering: Essays in feminist theory*, ed. J. Trebilcot, 213–230. Totowa, NJ: Rowman and Allanheld.

Ruddick, Sara. 1989. *Maternal thinking: Toward a politics of peace*. New York, NY: Ballantine Books.

Ruiz, A. 31 January 2010. Immigration reform dies in 36 words. *Daily News (New York)*: 37.

Rutten, T. 3 October 2009. Stripped of jobs by Obama. *Los Angeles Times*: 29, Part A.

Ryan, M.K., and S.A. Haslam. 2005. The glass cliff: Evidence that women are over-represented in precarious leadership positions. *British Journal of Management,* 16 (2): 81–90.

Ryan, M.K., and Haslam, S.A. 2007. The glass cliff: Exploring the dynamics surrounding the appointment of women to precarious leadership positions. *Academy of Management Review* 32 (2): 549–572.

Ryan, M.K., S.A. Haslam, M.D. Hersby, C. Kulich, and C. Atkins. 2007. Opting out or pushed off the edge? The glass cliff and the precariousness of women's leadership positions. *Social and Personality Psychology Compass* 1 (1): 266–279.

Ryan, R.M., and E.L. Deci. 2000. Intrinsic and extrinsic motivations: Classic definitions and new directions. *Contemporary Educational Psychology* 25: 54–67.

Sacchetti, M., and B. Bailou. 11 March 2007. DSS teams arrive in Texas to interview detained immigrants. *Boston Globe*: B3.

Salvá-Ramirez, M.-A. 1995. The San Ysidro massacre—Ten years later. *Public Relations Quarterly* 40 (1): 38–43.
Sama, L.M., S.A. Welcomer, and V.W. Gerde. 2004. Who speaks for the trees? Invoking an ethic of care to give voice to the silent stakeholder. In *Stakeholders, the environment and society*, ed. S. Sharma, and M. Starik, 140–165. Northamton, MA: Edward Elgar.
Sander-Staudt, Maureen. 2006. The unhappy marriage of care ethics and virtue ethics. *Hypatia* 21 (4): 21–40.
Schilt, K., and M. Wiswall. 2008. Before and after: Gender transitions, human capital, and workplace experiences. *The B.E. Journal of Economic Analysis & Policy* 8: 1 Article 39. http://www.bepress.com/bejeap/vol8/iss1/art39, Accessed 27 January 2010.
Schmitt, John. 2009. Inequality as policy: The United States since 1979. *Real-World Economics Review* (51): Online journal.
Schrag, B. 2001. The moral significance of employee loyalty. *Business Ethics Quarterly* 11: 41–66.
Schudt, Karl. 2000. Taming the corporate monster: An Aristotelian approach to corporate virtue. *Business Ethics Quarterly* 10 (3): 711–723.
Schumacher-Matos, E. 1 August 2009. When law flies out the door. *Washington Post*: A15, Regional Edition, Editorial Copy.
Schutte, O. 2002. Dependency work, women, and the global economy. In *The subject of care: Feminist perspectives on dependency*, ed. Eva Kittay and Ellen Feder, 138–158. New York, NY: Rowman & Littlefield.
Schweickart, David. 1980. *Capitalism or worker control?: An ethical and economic appraisal*. New York, NY: Praeger Publishers.
Schweickart, David. 1992. Economic democracy: A worthy socialism that would really work. *Science and Society* 56 (1): 9–38.
Schweickart, David. 1996. *Against capitalism*. Boulder, CO: Westview Press.
Sen A. 1983. The profit motive. *Lloyds Bank Review* (147): 1–20.
Seper, J. 13 December 2006. Agents raid job sites for illegals; Identity theft prompts effort. *The Washington Times*: 3, Nation3.
Seper, J. 8 March 2007. ICE to query 500 workers in illegals probe. *The Washington Times*: A04, Nation.
Sevenhuijsen, Selma. 1998. *Citizenship and the ethics of care: Feminist considerations on justice, morality, and practice*. New York, NY: Routledge.
Shaw, William H. 2011. *Business ethics: A textbook with cases*. 7th Edition. Wadsworth Publishing.
Sherwin, S. 1996. Feminism and bioethics. In *Feminism and bioethics: Beyond reproduction*, ed. Susan Wolf, 49–54. New York, NY: Oxford University Press.
Shulman, R. 18 March 2007. Immigration raid rips families: Illegal workers in Massachusetts separated from children. *Washington Post*: A06.
Simola, Sheldene. 2003. Ethics of justice and care in corporate crisis management. *Journal of Business Ethics* 46: 351–361.
Simola, Sheldene. 2007. The pragmatics of care in sustainable global enterprise. *Journal of Business Ethics* 74: 131–147.
Singer, Peter. 1994. Rethinking life and death: The collapse of our traditional ethics. New York, NY: St. Martin's.
Singer, Peter. 1994. The famine relief argument. In *Social and Political Philosophy*, ed. Elizabeth Smith and H. Gene Blocker, 456–465. Englewood Cliffs, NJ: Prentice-Hall.
Sloan work and family research network fact sheet. 2006. Q & A about gender and use of workplace policies; Q & A about employer-supported childcare. www.bc.edu/wfnetwork.
Slote Michael. 2007. *The ethics of care and empathy*. New York, NY: Routledge:
Slote, Michael. 1998. Caring in the balance. In *Norms and values: Essays on the work of Virginia Held*, ed. Joram Haber and Mark S. Halfon. New York, NY: Rowman & Littlefield Publishers.
Slote, Michael. 2001. *Morals from motives*. Oxford: Oxford University Press.

Smeyers, P. 1999. "Care" and wider ethical issues. *Journal of Philosophy of Education* 33 (2): 231–255.

Smith G. 1998. The shareholder primacy norm. *The Journal of Corporate Law*, Winter.

Smith, Adam. 2009. *Inquiry into the nature and causes of the wealth of nations*. Indianapolis, IN: Liberty Fund.

Smith, Adam. 2009. *Lectures on jurisprudence*. Indianapolis, IN: Liberty Fund.

Smith, Adam. 2009. *The theory of moral sentiments*. Indianapolis, IN: Liberty Fund.

Smith, Susan J. 2005. States, markets, and an ethic of care. *Political Geography* 24: 1–20.

Snyder, Lois, and Richard L. Neubauer. 2006. Pay-for-performance principles that ensure the promotion of patient centered care— an ethics manifesto. http://www.acponline.org/running_practice/ethics/issues/policy/p4p_ba.pdf

Soles, D.E. 1993. Four concepts of loyalty. *International Journal of Applied Philosophy* 8: 1.

Sollenius. January 2000. *Humane economy*. Stockholm: Almqvist and Wiksell International.

Solomon, Robert. 1992. *Ethics and excellence: Cooperation and integrity in business*. New York, NY: Oxford University Press.

Spears v. United States, US 129 S. Ct 840, 172 L. Ed. 2d 596, 2009.

Spelman, E.V. 1989. Anger and insubordination. In Women, knowledge, and reality: Explorations in feminist philosophy, ed. A. Garry, and M. Pearsall, 263–273. Boston, MA: Unwin Hyman.

Spender, J.-C., and Scherer, A.G. 2007. The philosophical foundations of knowledge management: Editor's introduction. *Organization* 14: 5–28.

Stack, C.B. 1993. The culture of gender: Women and men of color. In *An ethic of care: Feminist and interdisciplinary perspectives*, ed. M.J. Larrabee, 108–111. New York, NY: Routledge.

Starrman, R.G. 1993. Tragedy at McDonald's. In *Crisis response*, ed. J.A. Gottschalk, 309–321. Detroit MI: Invisible Ink.

Steib, J.A. 2006. Clearing up the egoist difficulty with loyalty. *Journal of Business Ethics* 63: 75–87.

Story, Louise. 20 September 2005. Many women at elite colleges set career path to motherhood. *The New York Times*.

Sugden, Robert. 2002. Beyond Empathy and Sympathy: Adam Smith's Concept of Fellow-feeling. *Economics and Philosophy* 18: 63–87.

Swan, J., H. Scarborough, and J. Preston. 1999. Knowledge management: the next fad to forget people? *Proceedings of the 7th European Conference on Information Systems*, Copenhagen.

Tessman, Lisa. 2001. Critical virtue ethics: Understanding oppression as morally Damaging. In *Feminists doing ethics*, ed. Peggy DesAutels, and Joanne Waugh. Boulder, CO: Rowman & Littlefield Publishers.

Tessman, Lisa. 2005. *Burdened virtues: Virtue ethics for liberatory struggles*. New York, NY: Oxford University Press.

Thronson, D. Summer 2008. Creating crisis: Immigration raids and the destabilization of immigrant families. *Wake Forest Law Review* 43: 391.

Tolman, D.L. 1991. Adolescent girls, women and sexuality: Discerning dilemmas of desire. In *Women, girls & psychotherapy: Reframing resistance*, ed. C. Gilligan, A.G. Rogers, and D.L. Tolman, 55–69. New York, NY: Harrington Park Press.

Tong, Rosemarie. 2009. Feminist ethics. *Stanford Encyclopedia of Philosophy*. Available at http://plato.stanford.edu/entries/feminism-ethics/.

Training Reference., 2007. Revised code aims to promote more effective leadership. Accessed 1 March 2009. http://www.trainingreference.co.uk/news/ls070502.htm

Treviño, L.K. 1986. Ethical decision making in organizations: A person situation interactionist model. *Academy of Management Review* 11 (3): 601–617.

Treviño, L.K., and K. Nelson. 2006. *Managing business ethics: Straight talk about how to do it right*. 4th edn. New York, NY: John Wiley & Sons.

Treviño, L.K., and M.E. Brown. 2004. Managing to be ethical: Debunking five business ethics myths. *Academy of Management Executive* 18 (2): 69–81.

Treviño, L.K., G. Weaver, and S.J. Reynolds. 2006. Behavioral ethics in organizations: A review. *Journal of Management* 32 (6): 951–990.

Tronto, Joan. 1993. Beyond gender difference to a theory of care. In *An ethic of care*, ed. M.J. Larrabee. New York, NY: Routledge.

Tronto, Joan. 1993. *Moral boundaries: A political argument for an ethic of care*. New York, NY: Routledge.

Tronto, Joan. 1996. Care as a political concept. In *Revisioning the political: Feminist reconstructions of traditional concepts in western political theory*, ed. Nancy J. Hirschmann, and Christine Di Stefano, 139–155. Boulder, CO: Westview Press.

Tronto, Joan. 2002. The nanny question in feminism. *Hypatia* 17 (2): 34–51.

Tronto, Joan. 2006. Vicious circles in privatized caring. *Socializing care: Feminist ethics and public issues*, ed. Maurice Hamington, and Dorothy Miller, 3–25. New York, NY: Rowan & Littlefield.

United States v. Agriprocessors, Inc., Sholom Rubashkin, Brent Beebe, Hosam Amara and Zeev Levi, No. 08-CR-1324-LRR, U.S. District Court for the Northern District of Iowa, Eastern Division, 2009 U.S. Dist. LEXIS 65165, 28 July 2009.

United States v. Ingram, No. CR 07-4056-2-MWB, 613 F. Supp. 2d 1069; 2009 U.S. Dist. LEXIS 40075; 79 Fed. R. Evid. Serv. (Callaghan) 735, 11 May 2009.

United States v. Mendoza-Gonzalez, 520 F.3d912 (8th Cir) 2008.

United States v. Sholom Rubashkin, No. 08-CR-1324-LRR, US District Court for the Northern District of Iowa, Eastern Division, 2009 U.S. Dist. Lexis 109115, 20 November 2009.

US Immigration and Customs Enforcement. 2010. www.ice.gov., http://www.ice.gov/documentbenefit-fraud/, Criminal Alien Program, http://www.ice.gov/criminal-alien-program/, Postville Press Release: http://www.ice.gov/news/releases/0805/080520waterloo.htm, http://www.ice.gov/news/library/factsheets/cap.htm, Accessed 31 Jan 2010.

Van Wensveen, Louke M. 1995. Is toughness a business virtue? *International Journal of Applied Philosophy* 9 (2): 15–25.

Vandekerckhove, W., and M.S.R. Commers. 2004. Whistle blowing and rational loyalty. *Journal of Business Ethics* 53: 225–233.

Varelius, J. 2009. Is whistle-blowing compatible with employee loyalty? *Journal of Business Ethics* 85: 263–275.

Varian, Hal R. 2000. What use is economic theory? *Variants in economic theory: Selected works of Hal R. Varian*, 352–360. Nothhampton: Edward Elgar Publishing.

Veraz-Munoz, Sandra C. 2005. Corporate governance reforms: Redefined expectations of audit committee responsibilities and effectiveness. *Journal of Business Ethics* 62 (2): 115–127.

Wadhia, S. Summer 2008. Emerging issues in immigration law: Immigrants' rights and the rule of law. *University of Memphis Law Review* 38: 853.

Waldfogel, Jane. 1997. The effects of children on women's wages. *American Sociological Review* 62 (2): 209–218.

Waldron, Jeremy. 2006. Superseding historic injustice. *Contemporary political philosophy: An anthology*, ed. Robert E. Goodin, and Philip Pettit. Oxford: Blackwell Publishing Ltd.

Walker, M. 1998. *Moral understandings*. New York: Routledge.

Warner, Judith. 2005. *Perfect madness: Motherhood in the age of anxiety*. New York, NY: Riverhead Books.

Warren, K.J. 2000. *Ecofeminist philosophy: A western perspective on what it is and why it matters*. Lanham, MD: Rowman & Littlefield.

Weber, D. 11 March 2007. Delahunt says congress will investigate immigration raid. *Boston Globe*, online edition: http://www.boston.com/news/local/massachusetts/articles/2007/03/11/delahunt_says_congress_will_investigate_immigration_raid/

Weir, Allison. 2005. The global universal care-giver: Imagining women's liberation in the new millennium. *Constellations* 12 (3): 308–330.

Werhane, P.H. 1999. *Moral imagination and management decision-making*. New York, NY: Oxford University Press.

Werhane, P.H. 1994. Justice, impartiality, and reciprocity: a response to Edwin Hartman. *Business Ethics Quarterly* 4: 287–290.

Werhane, P.H. 1999. Justice and trust. *Journal of Business Ethics* 21: 237–249.

Whitbeck, C. 1983. A different reality: Feminist ontology. In *Beyond domination*, ed. C.C. Gould, 64–88. Totowa, NJ: Rowman and Allanheld.

White, J. 2000. *Democracy, justice, and the welfare state*. University Park, TX: Pennsylvania State University Press.

White, T. 1992. Business ethics and Carol Gilligan's "two voices". *Business Ethics Quarterly* 2: 51–61.

White, T. 1998. Sexual harassment: Trust and the ethics of care. *Business and Society Review* 100/101: 9–20.

Wicks, A.C., Jr. D. Gilbert, and R.E. Freeman. 1994. A Feminist Reinterpretation of the Stakeholder Concept. *Business Ethics Quarterly* 4: 475–497.

Wicks, A.C., R.E. Freeman, and P.H. Werhane et al. 2010. *Business ethics: A managerial approach*. Upper Saddle River, NJ: Prentice Hall.

Wieland, Josef. 2001. The ethics of governance. *Business Ethics Quarterly* 11 (1): 73–87.

Wilber, Charles K. 1998. Trust, moral hazards, and social economics: Incentives and the organization of work. In *Economics, ethics, and public policy*, ed. Charles K. Wilber, 93–105. Oxford: Rowman & Littlefield Publishers, Inc.

Wilde, O. 1915. The devoted friend. In *Novels and fairy tales of Oscar Wilde*, ed. Nichols H.S. New York, NY: Little & Ives.

Williams, Joan. 2007. What is the hidden gender bias in academia? UC Hastings college of law: Worklife law. www.worklifelaw.org/genderbias_index.html.

Wolff, Richard D., and Stephen A. Resnick. 1987. *Economics: Marxian versus neoclassical*. Baltimore, MD: John Hopkins University Press.

Wolin, Richard. 2003. *Heidegger's children*. Princeton, NJ: Princeton University Press, 117–118.

Wollstonecraft, M. 1985. *Vindication of the rights of woman*. Harmondsworth: Penguin.

Wotruba, T.R. 1993. A framework for teaching ethical decision making in marketing. *Market Educational Review* 3: 2–8.

Yack, Bernard. 1991. Injustice and the victim's voice. *Michigan Law Review* 89: 1334, 1342–1343.

Young, Iris Marion. 1990. *Throwing like a girl and other essays in feminist philosophy and social theory*. Bloomington, IN: Indiana University Press.

Young, Iris Marion. 1997. *Intersecting voices: Dilemmas of gender, political philosophy, and policy*. Princeton, NJ: Princeton University Press.

Young, Iris Marion. 2006. Responsibility and social justice: A social connection model. *Social Philosophy and Policy* 23: 102–130.

Zakhem, A., D. Palmer, and M. Stoll. 2008. *Stakeholder theory: Essential readings in ethical leadership and management*. Amherst, NY: Prometheus.

Zounes, S. Spring 2007. Current development: Children without parents: An unintended Consequence of ICE's worksite enforcement operations. *Georgetown Immigration Law Journal* 21: 511.

Contributor Biographies

Matthew Brophy teaches both graduate and undergraduate business ethics as an assistant professor at High Point University in North Carolina. His additional areas of concentration include ethical theory, and social and political philosophy. His current research programs deal with the application of Rawlsian methodology to the stockholder/stakeholder debate; virtue ethics and corporate cultures; and feminist critiques of business ethics. Some of his selected essays include, "The Villainy of the RDA Corporation: Maximizing Profits for Principals/Principles" in *Avatar and Philosophy* (forthcoming), (ed. George Dunn); "Sex for a College Education: Self-Exploitation for Empowerment" in *College Sex and Philosophy* (ed. Michael Bruce); and "Santa's Sweatshop: Elf Exploitation for Christmas," in *Christmas and Philosophy* (ed. Scott Lowe). Brophy holds degrees from the University of California, Santa Barbara, B.A., California State University, M.A., and the University of Minnesota, Ph.D.

Daniel Engster is an Associate Professor in the Political Science Department at the University of Texas at San Antonio. He is the author of *The Heart of Justice: Care Ethics and Political Theory* (Oxford University Press, 2007) as well as articles on care ethics, the family, and welfare state policy.

Dimitria Electra Gatzia is assistant professor at The University of Akron, Wayne College. She received her Bachelor's degree from the University of California, Los Angeles and her doctorate degree from Syracuse University. Her primary research focuses on colour and colour perception. Her research interests extend to economics, political theory, and feminism.

Maurice Hamington is Professor of Women's Studies and Philosophy and Director of the Institute for Women's Studies and Services at Metropolitan State College of Denver. His publications include *Feminist Interpretations of Jane* Addams (Penn State Press, 2010) an edited volume; *Feminism and Hospitality: Gender in the Host/Guest Relationship* (Lexington Books, 2010), an edited volume; *The Social Philosophy of Jane* Addams (University of Illinois Press, 2009); *Socializing Care: Feminist Ethics and Public Issues* (Rowman & Littlefield, 2006) co-edited with Dorothy C. Miller; *Embodied Care: Jane Addams, Maurice Merleau-Ponty and*

Feminist Ethics (University of Illinois Press, 2004); *Revealing Male Bodies* (Indiana University Press, 2002) co-edited with Nancy Tuana et al; and, *Hail Mary? The Struggle for Ultimate Womanhood in Catholicism* (Routledge, 1995). Hamington has earned Ph.D.'s in Philosophy and Religious Studies as well as an M.B.A. in Organizational Behavior.

Thomas Hawk is Professor of Management, Emeritus, Management Department, College of Business, Frostburg State University. He holds a Ph.D. in Business with a major in Strategic Planning and Policy and a minor in Organizational Change and Development from the University of Pittsburgh, an MBA from Harvard, and a BS from the United States Naval Academy. He taught at Frostburg State University from 1972 through 2009, where his primary teaching responsibilities were the integrative capstone strategy MBA course as well as graduate courses in consulting, strategic cost analysis, and financial management. His research interests emphasize the case method, learning styles, the role of feedback in the learning process, learning and teaching models, an ethic of care, philosophy of education, strategic change, and theory-building research methods. He has published articles in the *Journal of Management Education*, *Coastal Business Journal*, *Industrial and Commercial Training*, *Strategy and Leadership*, and the *Decision Sciences Journal of Innovative Education* where he received the 2007 Best Paper Award for his article on learning styles. He has memberships in OBTS—The Teaching Society for Management Educators, the Academy of Management, the Philosophy of Education Society, and the Decision Sciences Institute. He focuses his consulting on the education and health care sectors.

Jill Hernandez (Ph.D. Memphis, 2006), publishes primarily in the areas of ethics, early modern philosophy, and existentialism. She is Assistant Professor of Philosophy at the University of Texas at San Antonio and an affiliated faculty member with UTSA's Womens Studies Institute. She is the author of *Gabriel Marcel's Ethics of Hope* and the editor of *The New Intuitionism*, both forthcoming with Continuum.

Daryl Koehn is a Professor in Business Ethics at the University of St. Thomas in Minneapolis/St. Paul, Minnesota. She has a Ph.D. in ethics (University of Chicago), an MBA in finance (Northwestern University), and a BA in both philosophy (University of Chicago) and philosophy, politics and economics (Oxford University). She has written many articles and seven books on the subjects of ethics and corporate governance, including *Trust in Business*; *The Ground of Professional Ethics; Corporate Governance/Ethics Across the Board; Rethinking Feminist Ethics; Local Insights, Global Ethics for Business; The Nature of Evil; and Living with the Dragon: Thinking Ethically in a World of Unintended Consequences.* Her fellow business ethicists elected her President of the Society of Business Ethics and she served on the SBE board from 2000–2005.

Julie A. Nelson is on the faculty of the Department of Economics at the University of Massachusetts Boston, and was a founding member of the International Association for Feminist Economics (IAFFE). Her books include *Economics for Humans* (Univ. of Chicago Press, 2006) and *Feminism, Objectivity, and Economics* (Routledge, 1996), and her research has appeared in journals ranging from *Econometrica* and the *Journal of Political Economy* to *Signs: Journal of Women in Culture and Society* and *Hypatia: Journal of Feminist Philosophy.*

Julinna Oxley is Assistant Professor of Philosophy and Director of the Women's and Gender Studies Program at Coastal Carolina University. Her research focuses on issues in ethics and political philosophy, emotions, the family, feminism, moral psychology, and applied ethics. Her book *The Moral Dimensions of Empathy: Limits and Applications in Ethical Theory and Practice* (Palgrave Macmillan) examines empathy's epistemic contribution to moral thought as it is defined by a variety of ethical perspectives, including care ethics.

Daniel E. Palmer is an Associate Professor of Philosophy at Kent State University, Trumbull Campus. His primary areas of interest are ethical theory and applied ethics, with a special emphasis upon business and professional ethics. He has published numerous articles in these areas in such journals as *Business Ethics Quarterly*, *Journal of Business Ethics*, and *The Journal of Value Inquiry*. He is co-editor, with Mary Lyn Stoll and Abe Zakhem, of the book *Stakeholder Theory: Essential Readings in Ethical Leadership and Management* (Prometheus Books, 2008) and editor of the volume *Ethical Issues in E-Business* (IGI Global, 2010). Currently, he is in the process of co-authoring a volume on business ethics in management.

Bill Puka is a professor in the Cognitive Science Dept of Rensselaer (RPI) where he teaches ethics and political policy. He has consulted for various corporations and government agencies (including the US Senate Budget Committee and Small Business Committee), and at a prison in Connecticut. Among his 60 or so publications is a seven volume book series, *Moral Development: A Compendium*, which includes *Caring Voices and Women's Moral Frames*. Bill received a Ph.D. in philosophy, and in psychology, form Harvard University while a recording artist for Columbia Records.

Maureen Sander-Staudt is an assistant professor at Arizona State University where she teaches feminist ethics, bioethics, environmental ethics, and world literature. She specializes in feminist ethics of care, and has published on the topics such as care ethics and virtue ethics, artificial womb technology, the moral status of embryos, and the political agency of care-givers. Her ongoing interests are in the areas of reproductive technology, care as political practice, and family ethics. She is currently working on projects that explore the ethics of polygamy, and human genetic patents. She is co-editing a forthcoming anthology on motherhood and philosophy, and authoring a book on care ethics and reciprocity. She lives in El Mirage where she is creating a water efficient oasis in the desert with her family and animal companions.

Sheldene Simola completed her MBA at the School of Business and Economics, Wilfrid Laurier University and her Ph.D. at Queen's University. She is an Assistant Professor in the Business Administration Program at Trent University. Her research has been published in many scholarly journals including *The Leadership Quarterly*, *Journal of Business Ethics*, *Canadian Journal of Administrative Sciences*, *Consulting Psychology: Research and Practice*, *Education + Training*, *Journal of Personality Assessment*, *Professional Psychology: Research and Practice*, and *Society and Business Review*. Her research in the area of human resources management has been discussed through many popular media outlets and professional magazines in both Canada and the United States, including the Globe & Mail Report on Business, Canada A.M., CityTV, Exchange Morning Post, the Canadian Human Resources Reporter, and the prestigious U.S. Society for Human Resources Management. Sheldene has consulted to multiple private and public sector businesses and/or associations. This research was supported by a grant from the Social Sciences and Humanities Research Council of Canada.

Mary Lyn Stoll is currently a member of the Department of Philosophy at the University of Southern Indiana in Evansville, Indiana. She earned her Ph.D. in philosophy from Purdue University. She has published a number of articles devoted to questions concerning media ethics and the relationships between corporations and free speech rights. She has also co-edited a volume of essays on stakeholder theory. Her more recent research in business ethics concentrates upon issues concerning corporate accountability and environmental sustainability.

Andrew Terjesen received his Ph.D. from Duke University after completing a dissertation on Adam Smith's moral theory. He has been a visiting assistant professor at Austin College, Washington and Lee University and Rhodes College, where he taught classes in ethics, moral psychology and the philosophy of economics.

D.E. Wittkower is an Assistant Professor of Philosophy at Old Dominion University, where he teaches philosophy of technology and applied ethics and conducts research on business ethics, digital media, and online culture. Recent and forthcoming publications concern topics such as copyright in e-business, friendship online, and the phenomenology of audiobooks. He also writes philosophy for a general audience and is editor of several books, including *Facebook and Philosophy* and *Philip K. Dick and Philosophy*.

Index

MIX
Papier aus verantwortungsvollen Quellen
Paper from responsible sources
FSC® C105338

FSC
www.fsc.org

If you have any concerns about our products,
you can contact us on
ProductSafety@springernature.com

In case Publisher is established outside the EU,
the EU authorized representative is:
Springer Nature Customer Service Center GmbH
Europaplatz 3, 69115 Heidelberg, Germany

Printed by Libri Plureos GmbH
in Hamburg, Germany